About This Book

Why is this topic important?

An organization's success depends on the skills and knowledge of its employees. *Developing Talent for Organizational Results* brings together the work of many of the most renowned learning providers in the world—all of them members of ISA: the Association of Learning Providers—to develop the skills and knowledge of your employees. The book provides activities and surveys, insight, and ideas to develop the talent required to ensure your organization's success.

What can you achieve with this book?

This book offers you a broad selection of topics that are critical to your organization's progress and future. The members of ISA wanted to publish something that you can implement immediately, so the book offers a wonderful array of tools that you can use with confidence that they will achieve the results they promise. Each chapter is a stand-alone slice of content focused on one topic. In addition, most chapters are accompanied by workshop activities; assessments, surveys, or questionnaires; processes, models, and tools; or training, consulting, or coaching techniques. These tools can be downloaded from the website, saving you time and energy during your implementation step.

How is this book organized?

The book is divided into nine sections, forty-seven chapters, and six bonus activities. The sections address topics that are critical to attaining organizational results by developing talent: communication, management, executive skills, developing leaders, corporate culture, training process, training techniques, individual development, and customer service. Each chapter focuses on one topic within the section, and all will enrich your training design. In addition, you will find a reading list near the back of the book that the authors provided to accompany many of the chapters should you wish to delve deeper into the topic. The back of the book also contains a list and brief description of each of the electronic tools found on the website.

About Pfeiffer

Pfeiffer serves the professional development and hands-on resource needs of training and human resource practitioners and gives them products to do their jobs better. We deliver proven ideas and solutions from experts in HR development and HR management, and we offer effective and customizable tools to improve workplace performance. From novice to seasoned professional, Pfeiffer is the source you can trust to make yourself and your organization more successful.

Essential Knowledge Pfeiffer produces insightful, practical, and comprehensive materials on topics that matter the most to training and HR professionals. Our Essential Knowledge resources translate the expertise of seasoned professionals into practical, how-to guidance on critical workplace issues and problems. These resources are supported by case studies, worksheets, and job aids and are frequently supplemented with CD-ROMs, websites, and other means of making the content easier to read, understand, and use.

Essential Tools Pfeiffer's Essential Tools resources save time and expense by offering proven, ready-to-use materials—including exercises, activities, games, instruments, and assessments—for use during a training or-team-learning event. These resources are frequently offered in looseleaf or CD-ROM format to facilitate copying and customization of the material.

Pfeiffer also recognizes the remarkable power of new technologies in expanding the reach and effectiveness of training. While e-hype has often created whizbang solutions in search of a problem, we are dedicated to bringing convenience and enhancements to proven training solutions. All our e-tools comply with rigorous functionality standards. The most appropriate technology wrapped around essential content yields the perfect solution for today's on-the-go trainers and human resource professionals.

www.pfeiffer.com

Essential resources for training and HR professionals

Developing Talent for Organizational Results

TRAINING TOOLS FROM THE BEST IN THE FIELD

Elaine Biech

Editor

Pfeiffer

A Wiley Imprint
www.pfeiffer.com

The Association of Learning Providers

Published by Pfeiffer
An Imprint of Wiley
One Montgomery Street, Suite 1200, San Francisco, CA 94104-4594
www.pfeiffer.com

Library of Congress Cataloging-in-Publication Data

Developing talent for organizational results : training tools from the best in the field / Elaine Biech, editor.
    pages   cm
   Includes bibliographical references and index.
   ISBN 978-1-118-12375-1 (pbk.)
    1. Employees—Training of.   2. Organizational change.   3. Personnel management.   I. Biech, Elaine.
 HF5549.5.T7442   2012
 658.3′124—dc23

                          2011048576

Acquiring Editor:	Marisa Kelley
Director of Development:	Kathleen Dolan Davies
Production Editor:	Dawn Kilgore
Editor:	Rebecca Taff
Manufacturing Supervisor:	Becky Morgan

Printed in the United States of America

PB Printing   10 9 8 7 6 5 4 3 2 1

For Shane and Thad,
my first developing talent experience

Contents

Foreword

It was scheduled for Atlanta and everyone would be there: prospects, customers, and competitors alike. It was 1977. Every year the ASTD national conference was the event that drew them together. "Why not have Forum Corporation host a cocktail party during this convention?" thought Richard Whiteley. "But a different kind of gettogether . . . one that excludes customers and suppliers. One that is for competitors only."

That was the genesis of ISA (Instructional Systems Association). Invitations were sent to the CEOs and presidents of a number of prominent training companies of the day inviting them to a first-ever exclusive gathering of competitors. Wilson Learning, Psychological Associates, Xerox Learning Systems, Forum, and others were invited. In all there were about fifteen attendees.

> *"The atmosphere was electric and the sharing was candid and wide-spread. The desire to continue such dialogue was sown and ISA's norm of open sharing was cast."*

> Richard Whiteley

Between 1977 and 1978, three organizational meetings followed. Larry Wilson of Wilson Learning hosted the first in Eden Prairie, Minnesota; Chuck Cole the second at Tratec in Los Angeles; and John Humphrey the third in New York City. During these meetings, the association was named, its purpose was articulated, and the by-laws were drafted. Participants in these early start-up meetings included Mathew Juechter, Larry Wilson, Don Schrello, Chuck Cole, Tom Blodgett, Todd White, Bill Byham, Richard Whiteley, and John Humphrey.

By the end of 1978, the association received its formal IRS sanction as a 501(c)6 trade association. As a result, ISA's first annual meeting was held in February 1979 at the Hilton Riviera in Palm Springs, California, where John Humphrey was elected ISA's first president and Nancy Lague became the first administrator of ISA.

The first ISA membership roster consisted of nineteen firms—these were the forerunners in the practice of sharing competitive industry insights.

- Blessing & White
- Deltak
- DDI
- Forum
- Kepner-Tregoe
- Louis A. Allen
- McGraw-Hill (Edutronics)
- National Training Systems
- Organizational Dynamics, Inc.
- Practical Management Associates
- Psychological Associates
- Research Media
- Schrello Associates
- Systema Corporation
- Thomas BLODGETT Associates
- Tratec
- Training House
- Wilson Learning Corporation
- Xerox Learning Systems

This purposeful network of dedicated training industry architects changed the lives of the individuals leading these companies as well as those of their clients. Without realizing the long-term impact, these pioneers established a collaborative venue to test their thinking as they pursued the design, development, and delivery of solutions for their clients. Little did they know that their efforts and their support of each other would change the lives of corporate executives and enhance and accelerate the success of worldwide corporate enterprises.

In the early days of ISA, the issues focused on packaged, off-the-shelf products. The emphasis was on training for individual performance. Products were based on nearly 100 percent classroom instruction and were almost exclusively paper-based. ISA members had published a smattering of books, and content expertise was overwhelmingly focused in the soft skills interpersonal arena. ISA was on the budding edge of an emerging industry that didn't have much boardroom clout. Neither we nor Wall Street knew much about each other.

By 1998, ISA member firms offered not only quality training products but extensive research and consulting capabilities for improving workplace learning and performance. The emphasis was on organizational performance and teams of individuals rather than "the" individual. Some form of non-classroom study was incorporated into the delivery of product and services and content emerged in every format—paper, CD-ROM, satellite, internets, intranets. By this time more than three hundred books authored by ISA members were on best-selling lists, and thousands of articles were in circulation. Many ISA members were considered "gurus" in the industry. While soft skills continued to be a significant offering, technical knowledge and skills was becoming a more prominent topic. ISA members recognized the significant investment their clients were making in their most precious asset—their people. They found themselves in frequent consulting discussions in the boardrooms of their clients.

"I am often asked what the acronym ISA represents. The easy answer is instructional systems association, but the significance is rooted in ISA's foresight. Back in the founding days of the association, the founding members intuitively knew that inter-connectedness and inter-dependence were crucial in organizational learning—it would always require a system or systemic thinking and solutions to realize results."

Pam Schmidt, ISA Executive Director

In 2005, ISA "renamed" the association in an effort to reflect the expansive nature of the solutions ISA members provide worldwide. When the membership was asked about retiring the ISA acronym, there was a strong majority, including many newer members beyond the founders, who wanted the ISA acronym to remain. Today ISA is known as *ISA—The Association of Learning Providers*.

In the late 1990s, thanks to the leadership of Jerry Noack, ISA member, *Training* magazine interviewed several ISA CEOs to discuss lessons learned over more than fifteen years. So much of what was shared is taken for granted today. These lessons are worth repeating and their underpinnings are embedded in the chapters of this book.

"When we ask customers what's important, reliability is first and honesty—imagine that, honesty—is second."

Richard Whiteley

"Reengineering is being bastardized across this country to manipulate and dislocate people."

Steve Wall

"Boards are not holding CEOs accountable for dealing with some of those large change issues."

Mathew Juechter

"Training has to connect not as a program but in increasing communication within the entire culture."

Herb Cohen

"Once the company re-forms, training builds trust, it builds futures, it builds common dreams."

Kevin Daley

Today, ISA member firms serve more than 100,000 client companies around the world. Every learning medium is utilized and every venue is committed to organizational results. The fundamental belief is that improved individual performance at every level of the enterprise will exponentially improve and enhance the performance of the organization. Agility, creativity, and innovation are critical skills in today's organizations. Learning virtually and on mobile platforms is a necessity, not a convenience.

Despite the magnitude of global unrest and economic upheaval during the past decade, ISA continues to stand strong. The association enjoys an impressive retention rate greater than 90 percent and a promising trend in new member enrollments is gaining momentum. ISA membership is available to any firm whose business is dedicated to the transfer of learning and knowledge for work-related performance. The association is dedicated to helping training and performance firms build, enhance, and share their success with one objective in mind—the client. If you are interested in becoming a member of ISA, feel free to call me. I would welcome the conversation.

As for the industry, ASTD reports that business leaders continue to dedicate substantial resources to employee learning and development, estimating U.S. organizations spent $125 billion in 2009. In ASTD's 2010 *State of the Industry Report*, it was reported that 26.9 percent of overall spending was spent on outsourcing (utilization of external providers). For the first time since 2004, there was an increase in utilization of external providers. And there is every indication that this will continue.

I am humbled by what ISA member firms have accomplished over the last thirty years. If you read the short company summaries after each chapter, you will be amazed at what they have done and stand ready to do for the future.

Pamela J. Schmidt
ISA Executive Director
3735 Franklin Road SW, #281
Roanoke, VA 24014
(540) 890-3197
pschmidt@isaconnection.org
www.isaconnection.org

Introduction

Any time a group of talented, professional leaders join forces to pool the best that they have to offer, the result is astonishing. *Developing Talent for Organizational Results* is a perfect example. The book brings together the work of many of the most renowned learning providers in the world—all of them members of ISA: the Association of Learning Providers. Forty-six inspiring chapters and six bonus activities present the wisdom of these leaders in the field of training and development. You know their corporate names: The Ken Blanchard Companies, DDI, Forum, Herrmann International, Career Systems International, Zenger Folkman, and others. All have generously shared insights in their primary areas of expertise. This book is filled with a million dollars' worth of consulting advice to help your organization achieve desired results.

Why This Title?

The best companies win with highly talented, highly committed employees—hiring the talent when they can and developing it when they must. As the world turns faster, each organization recognizes the need to adapt to the future or face failure. Organizations are made up of people who lead, manage, create, produce, teach, learn, communicate, and engage. Developing an organization's talent is a basic requirement to achieve positive organizational results.

According to the American Society for Training and Development's (ASTD) 2010 *State of the Industry Report,* U.S. companies spend $126 billion annually on employee learning and development programs. This book brings together methodologies, practices, processes, and other key information that will help you make wise decisions about your organization's investment in developing its talent. For example, do you need ideas for improving communication? See Section I. Do your leaders need to be developed? Section IV will have answers. You will find answers to many of your most sought-after employee development concerns to improve leadership, management, and communication skills; to address training, learning, and engagement issues; and to shape the culture and care for your customers.

How Do You Find Answers?

With this book, you hold in your hands ideas from 52 of the top consulting and training firms in the United States. Each has provided you with complete information to address an issue that may be plaguing your organization, to launch an idea you may have considered, or to implement a process.

Several of the activities could fit into more than one category; for example, Chapter 12, "Leading with Integrity," appears in Section III, Executive Essentials. It could just as easily have appeared in Section V, Shaping a Vital Culture. I advise you to use the table of contents and the index liberally to ensure you identify all of the chapters that may be related to your need. A general description of each of the sections may give you a head start.

- *Section I, Communicating to Succeed,* delivers content about good communication skills such as using stories to communicate, being more candid, assessing your interpersonal skills, and communicating in a world economy. Two bonus activities address better use of email as a communication tool and provide a tool to use to build or repair a relationship.

- *Section II, Moving into Management,* addresses skills new managers need to develop such as project management, building engagement through decision-making, increasing influence, speaking to senior executives, developing business acumen, and overcoming emotions as a leader. The bonus activity is one I've used often. It is a favorite of mine. It is invaluable for addressing conflict between two groups.

- *Section III, Executive Essentials,* focuses on the high standards we have for our leaders who reside in the C-suite, presenting topics such as finding time to communicate, leading with integrity, communicating with stories from the top, building accountability, and improving employee engagement.

- *Section IV, Developing Leaders,* delivers on three different concerns when you design your leadership development programs. It also features a creative bonus activity you will want to build into your final leadership development training design.

- *Section V, Shaping a Vital Culture,* addresses the elusive topic of culture change. The research behind these topics is impressive. So what changes are required in your culture? Building a high-passion/high-performance work environment? Increasing engagement or respect and safety? Building the capacity to change? The bonus activity will assist you in any of these situations by helping you explore your organization's culture.

- *Section VI, Invigorating Your Training Process for Results,* incorporates ideas that will help you kick your training up a notch. Topics include evaluation tactics, measuring return on investment, designing from start to finish, and ideas for ensuring that learning occurs and behaviors change.

- *Section VII, Timely Training Techniques,* introduces ideas for refining training in your organization such as expanding facilitation skills, maximizing simulations, getting results from e-learning, and developing ways to teach wisdom. If you don't know what you need, a training triage process is also presented.

- *Section VIII, Focus on Individual Development,* is important because it all comes down to people. People make up your organization and developing talent is about the people in your organization. The chapters in this section address a variety of topics such as a process to communicate about individuals' development and the importance and development of business acumen and resiliency. Individuals need feedback, and three chapters are dedicated to obtaining feedback from peers and 360-degree assessments. The bonus activity brings it all together with a way for individuals to figure out what is important to them.

- *Section IX, Caring Customer Service and Sales,* reminds us that an organization is in business to serve customers. Each of the ISA organizations addresses the topic in its own unique way. All three provide you with creative ideas to consider.

Need More Assistance?

As we developed this book, we wanted to ensure that it is as useful as it is impressive. We wanted to ensure that the content is something that you could easily implement in your day-to-day work. And we wanted to ensure that you had a way to find all the support you required to apply the content to what you do. To address this, we have provided a resource list, downloadable tools, and contact information for each of the ISA member contributing companies.

Reading List. After reading the chapters, you may want additional resources to delve deeper into the chapter topics. Most of the chapters are accompanied by a reading list in the back of the book to make it easy for you to find additional resources.

Ready to Deliver Tools. Each chapter is also accompanied by a tool—a survey, process, questionnaire, assessment, tips, quick references, and the like—that is briefly described in the back of the book. You can download these tools directly from the website at **www.pfeiffer.com/go/isa [user name: training; password: biech]** for your immediate use. Here's the best part—as long as you maintain the copyright information and the "used with permission" designation on the tools, you may use all of them for your daily work. This is a generous gift from the ISA companies.

Contact the ISA Member Companies Directly. Do you need more specifics? Want to take the concept to the next level? Want to bring the company on-site? All contact information is located at the end of each chapter. These companies are interested in your success. Call them and schedule a meeting or a conversation. The ISA member companies either have the answers you need, or know how to help you find them.

ISA's *Developing Talent for Organizational Effectiveness* is the culmination of the efforts of many of the most influential and respected leaders in the learning and development field whose work continues to shape the industry.

And It Would Not Have Been Possible Without . . .

- Pam Schmidt, ISA's competent executive director, who created the vision and ensured that we stayed true to it throughout. Thank you.
- The expert authors, who skillfully synthesized some of the best learning techniques into single chapters and an exciting ISA project, a tool that will be used globally. Thank you.
- ISA board and member companies who envisioned a practical go-to resource to boost organizational success. Thank you for the opportunity to be a part of this worthwhile project.
- Lisa Shannon and Marisa Kelly, editors, who recognized the uniqueness of this book and broke a few rules to ensure we offered the readers the best of the best. Thank you both.
- Susan Rachmeler, Kathleen Dolan Davies, and Rebecca Taff editors, who are wise, wonderful, and oh so competent. What a delight to work with all of you.
- Dawn Kilgore, production editor, for a winning design. Great job!
- Lorraine Kohart, ebb associates' right hand, who juggled authors, submissions, permissions, and timelines. Thank you.
- Dan Greene, who turned my frets and rants into productive processes. Thanks . . . again.

Elaine Biech
ebb associates inc
Norfolk, VA
January 2012

SECTION I

COMMUNICATING TO SUCCEED

Introduction

You spend most of your working time communicating. We all need to write and speak no matter what our jobs happen to be, whether we are directing, collaborating, supervising, instructing, inspiring, persuading, leading, or selling. And you had better be darned good at it if you expect results—both personal and business. Your career advancement depends on your ability to communicate well. Your success in achieving organizational and department goals depends on your communication abilities as well.

The changing environment and increasing complexity of the 21st century workplace make communication even more important, and it is not getting easier. Technology has in fact made communication faster, more complex, and expanded the volume. There are more communication methods, and each generation has its own preference—and all are correct. In addition, the increased global presence of organizations and the expectation of 24/7 communication makes clear, complete, and concise communication more crucial than ever.

Good communication matters because business organizations are made up of people. In business, communication is everything. Although often termed a "soft" skill, communication in a business organization provides the critical link between functions, creates avenues to our customers, and ensures the goals of the organization are achieved.

Consider the alternative—poor communication, or even worse, not communicating at all. Oh, you have had that experience? Communication still reigns as the number one issue in almost every employee satisfaction survey.

Good communication is good business. We need to continue to work toward improving communication personally, interpersonally, and corporately. Communication is a broad topic that covers many aspects. It is fitting that the four chapters in this section are spread almost as far as the topic of communication itself.

- In Chapter 1, "Communicate with Stories" by The Ariel Group, you will receive tips for selecting your own stories to tell to make a point. Telling stories is an effective method of communicating, and most of us do not practice this skill often enough.

- Chapter 2, "Reclaiming Your Peer Power" by NetSpeed Learning Solutions, will challenge you to be a better communicator by examining your interpersonal strengths, weaknesses, and beliefs. You might be surprised at how a slight attitude adjustment might increase your communication abilities.

- Chapter 3, "The Candor Advantage" by Ridge Training, delivers a strong argument for why we need to be more candid in conversations. The chapter also identifies techniques for fostering candor in your organization.

- Chapter 4, "Opening Your Business to the World" by ECCO International, will open your eyes to ways to improve global communication. Naming a product is communication at its simplest level. Yet products have failed in other countries simply because a name has a different meaning in translation: the Olympic copier Roto in Chile (roto in Spanish means "broken"); the Chevy Nova in Puerto Rico (no va means "doesn't go"); or the successful European chocolate product introduced to the U.S. with the unfortunate name "Zit."

Accompanying the four chapters are two dynamite activities.

- Bonus activity 1 is "Turning e-Mail Drains into Productivity Gains," submitted by Better Communications. No one can argue that a good email requires a good communicator, and this activity shows that a few tips can make a huge difference.

- Bonus activity 2 is "Build or Repair," submitted by Global Novations. This activity is sure to have your team back on track with improved communication and a renewed attitude about working together.

Chapter 1

Communicate with Stories

THE ARIEL GROUP

In This Chapter

- How to identify effective stories.
- How to communicate using stories.
- How to integrate a story into a conversation or presentation.
- Tips for telling a good story.

Storytelling is a powerful communication tool.

An engineer I know makes a compelling case for telling stories in business. Now, of course, we don't often connect engineers, those whose livelihood depends on facts, empirical data, mathematical formulae, and structural accuracy, with the softer, creative, and somewhat vague notion of storytelling. But this particular engineer was the grandson of Choctaw Indians from Northwestern Oklahoma. As a young boy he'd listened to the history, tradition, and knowledge of his tribe passed down to the younger generations by the elders through stories told around the coffee shop on a Saturday evening. He remembered these stories because they made an emotional connection as well as an intellectual one. He retained the information in his brain because of a connection that was made with his heart. Of course, still being an engineer, he had reduced this concept to a formula that looks like this:

$$DATA + STORY = KNOWLEDGE$$

As Peter Guber, the well-known producer, once said, "Although the mind may be part of your target, the heart is the bull's-eye." Data, while the lifeblood of an engineer, does not amount to knowledge unless combined with the story of its application. The engineer knew that his calculations had to be exact if the bridge he was building was to bear the appropriate load without collapsing, and he appreciated the elegance of the technical designs he created. But he also knew that the stories about who would be crossing the bridge—the families that may be united, the businesses that would thrive, the relationships that could develop, the cultures that could collaborate, the goods and services that would be delivered, and the city that could grow—were what would ultimately get that bridge built.

As with the engineer, stories are an effective way for a leader to communicate information to an audience while also building a relationship with them. When you tell stories, especially personal stories, it helps people relate to your message and allows you to show your strengths, challenges, and vulnerability. Stories can be used to communicate your values, help to develop trust, inspire your employees, and move your audience to take action. Presidents from Ronald Reagan to Barack Obama, both brilliant storytellers, brought their legislative initiatives to light by telling the stories of real individuals during important speeches.

Here are some of the most effective ways to use stories to communicate.

- **Share Yourself:** Share moments that made you who you are or that clarified your values so that others understand your leadership perspective.

- **Share Your Organization:** Share values of your organization. What makes up the DNA of your organization?

- **Teach a Lesson:** How you learned something through failure or success, how you mastered an organizational capability, how you overcame resistance to change.

- **Provoke Change:** Create dissatisfaction with present, share dangerous mistakes in business, establish the case for change, create a vision for future state.

- **Change Perspective:** Allow your audience to see a problem through a different lens, change the emotional climate.

- **Build a Relationship**: Sharing personal or personal business stories with direct reports or clients can highlight the common ground between you.

With all of this evidence supporting the effectiveness of storytelling, why do we use them so infrequently to communicate? Why do so many of us leap into our PowerPoint presentations replete with data, research, facts, and figures and then watch the faces glaze over as this presentation blends with three others the audience sat through that day?

Many people have told us, "I'm just not good at telling stories" or "I just don't have any good stories to tell." Nonsense. Every human life is full of interesting stuff. As many of you read this, several interesting things have already happened on the drive to work, in a conversation with your partner, as you walked to the office. From the knock, knock joke your five-year-old told you over breakfast to the inspiring and life-changing efforts of your team to develop an entirely new and exciting product, stories from your everyday life can contain universal themes relevant to your organization's or clients' key issues. Why not leverage the archetypal nature of stories by creating a catalog of some of the significant moments in your personal and business life as a resource to draw on when planning any meeting, conversation, or presentation?

What follows is a process we use to coach our clients on how to identify, refine, and tell a good story in the context of business. We hope that by following these steps you'll discover stories from your life that you can use to further your business or organizational goals. At a minimum we hope that just taking the time to reflect on life will prove to be an enlightening exercise and prove that you've got some darned interesting stories to tell.

I'll start by sharing a story I've told in a business setting a number of times. Then we'll tackle the issue of how to identify and remember stories that can be valuable in a business context. Once you've started to collect your stories, we will share some ideas about how to categorize them into types of stories that make specific points. A minister we know, for instance, has a filing cabinet with a range of topics for future sermons. He will often drop a scrap of paper with a simple topic like "Leaving your turn signal on" into a folder for future sermons, which are always illustrated with wonderful stories.

Of course, just remembering stories and cataloging them isn't enough. Learning how to integrate a story into a business context can be tricky. Luckily, we have a simple framework that will help get you started. Finally, we come to the telling—the performance of your story that brings it to life for the listener. Drawing on our experience from theater, we encourage you to rehearse your story (and any presentation or critical conversation) so that you can add the appropriate emphasis, emotion, timing, and body language to have maximum impact. We don't expect you to become Shakespearian actors overnight, but you'll be surprised by the increased impact you will have by employing some theatrical tips.

Let's Start with a Story

Running a small company (that teaches leadership) and attending various conferences and meetings, I'm called upon to speak to groups large and small. Here is a story I told at a trade association meeting. It is drawn from personal experience many of us can relate to—when stress from work and family clash and how that can undermine our most precious relationships:

It has been a stressful eighteen months. The recession has hit business hard and I'm about to send a second child off to college. I'm working long days and I'm managing tight budgets at the office and at home.

One dark evening in mid-January, I'm standing in my kitchen transferring three days of dishes from the sink into the dishwasher. The children have used every cup and bowl we own, including a decorative Bavarian beer stein that is now encrusted with fossilized cereal! I'm muttering bad language under my breath.

"Hey pops, whassup? How was your day?"

Clare, my seventeen-year-old daughter enters. I tense, expecting this to be an expensive conversation.

"Sooooo, I wanted to ask you something. Julie's family is going to Vegas and then Miami for winter break and they've invited ME! Can I go?"

I explode.

"We've had this conversation! We have a lot of expenses right now and you still owe me money from last summer. You are supposed to be saving for college. I can't believe you're even asking!"

She explodes back.

"I can't believe you are yelling at me! You're not even listening to me. Julie's dad has free tickets. I just picked up more hours at the restaurant. Ugh! You never listen. And you're never around and you're always preoccupied and we never have any time alone together. You're just mean and grumpy all the time!"

She pauses, picks up a piece of paper, and throws it at me.

"Oh and by the way, here's my report card. I made honor roll. Again!"

She runs to her room in tears.

What did my daughter teach me here? Well, I learned that under stress I have much less patience, I don't listen, and I jump to conclusions. And that this behavior can cause a breach in a precious relationship.

The lesson for me is to be sure to take my own emotional temperature at home and at work, particularly in times of stress or extreme busyness. I also learned that it is important to stop, be fully present, and truly listen to what others are telling you before

Developing Talent for Organizational Results

answering. This is hard to do when stressed out and in a hurry, but not doing these things can cause great damage to relationships and, ultimately, to productivity.

Remembering and Using Stories

You, too, already have dozens of stories like the one above at your fingertips—actually remembering them when you need them is the hard part. Begin collecting stories from your life that might serve as powerful illustrations of your ideas. Next, write down impactful stories from other sources such as your friends, the news, or the movies. You don't need a full-blown filing system like our minister friend—a simple manila folder titled "story ideas" would be a useful place to collect ideas that strike you during the day. Even better, keep a journal specifically for stories and enter any interesting daily occurrences. A comedian we know who teaches stand-up keeps a small notebook in his pocket at all times and records anything that he thinks might be the foundation of a good joke. Eighty percent are tossed, but the 20 percent he keeps are gems. If paper isn't your thing, engage technology: one of our execs actually calls himself and leaves himself a voice mail with story ideas. Another—slightly more technically sophisticated—uses the note app on his iPhone to record ideas.

If you don't do it often, remembering and using stories can seem like an insurmountable task. We experience so much in the course of a day that is it hard to identify individual moments and turn them into stories. It can help to think in terms of categories or "types" of stories as a way to identify and store stories for future use. Below is a tool that can help you start. Start by thinking about small moments rather than complete stories and record them in the following categories. Don't try to be perfect right away. Simply start writing, like our comedian friend, and understand that for every ten moments you come up with, at least two or three will be perfect. So quiet the inner critic and take a few moments to jot down some thoughts below:

STORIES I COULD TELL AS A LEADER IN A BUSINESS SETTING

The following story planning tool can be downloaded at this chapter's online tools.

Personal Stories

Think of:

- Moments that made you who you are or that clarified your values
- Moments when you discovered your voice or leadership potential
- *"When I was seventeen . . ."*

I could tell a personal story about . . .

_____

_____

This would be a great story to tell at the following event/for the following purpose:

_____

_____

Personal Business Stories

Think of:

- Heroic moments—difficult but worthwhile struggles or extraordinary feats in business
- Times when you or a company overcame an obstacle such as resistance to change

- Moments of truth
- *"When I was working at . . ."*

I could tell a personal business story about . . .

_____

_____

This would be a great story to tell at the following event/for the following purpose:

_____

_____

General Business Stories

Think of:

- Dangerous mistakes in business
- Stories of how your company has handled these things in the past
- Stories of how the future could look: bright or dark
- *"The day Jack Welch started at GE . . .*

I could tell a general business story about . . .

_____

_____

This would be a great story to tell at the following event/for the following purpose:

_____

_____

Universal Myths or Fables

Think of:

- The Trojan Horse from Homer's "Odyssey" as a metaphor
- The "Three Little Pigs" fairy tale as an analogy

I could tell a universal myth or fable story about . . .

_____

_____

This would be a great story to tell at the following event/for the following purpose:

_____

_____

I Couldn't Possibly Tell That Story at Work!

HOW TO INTEGRATE A STORY INTO A CONVERSATION OR PRESENTATION

Now that you have a variety of stories at your fingertips, it's time to try incorporating one into a conversation or presentation. Here is a basic format to get you started:

1. Introduce the Subject Matter or Business Content

- Conversation example: "I think you've been doing a great job heading this initiative despite the hiccups you've encountered along the way and I want to make sure you don't beat yourself up over this too much. . . ."
- Presentation example: "Today I would like to speak to you about a new marketing strategy for our product. . . ."

2. Transition into the Story

- Conversation example: "In fact, back when I was a team leader, I had a similar experience . . ."
- Presentation example: "Let me share with you a story to illustrate a vision of how we can work together . . ."

3. Tell the Story

- Set the stage
- Describe the conflict
- Describe the resolution
- *"It's 1982. I'm out on the soccer field with my son when he turns to me and says. . . ."*

4. Connect the Story to a Teaching Point or Subject Matter

- Personal Learning: "What my son said to me reminded me so powerfully that there is always a fresh, new way to look at any challenging situation."
- Message for the Group: "Ladies and gentlemen, are we willing to shift our marketing strategy in a whole new direction, to take a risk in the way that my son did? I certainly am."

A Good Story Well Told: Tips from the World of Theater

"Once more into the breach dear friends!" Not every story should be delivered like the fiery, troop-rallying Saint Crispin's Day speech from Shakespeare's Henry V. Actors need to modulate their tone, expressiveness, body language, volume, and facial expression to suit the role and circumstance of their performance. Whether speaking one-on-one with a peer or simply trying to get focus from your team on a new project, picking the right story and then telling it in an appropriate manner for the situation is important to consider.

With practice, stories will come to you in the moment as you need them. You will even be able to use the same stories in multiple situations by changing the delivery and shortening or lengthening them on the fly. Until then, you will need to take time to walk through your story in advance, particularly if you are using it for a large presentation—after all, actors like to say it takes six weeks of rehearsal to sound spontaneous!

Below are some tips to prepare and rehearse your story before you use it:

BE SUCCINCT

Boil it down. It's possible to tell a powerful, complete story in under a minute. Practice alone and time your story. Consider recording and listening to yourself. Cut out anything that doesn't serve the main point of the story. You may end up with several good short stories from one long one!

Use "bullet phrases" instead of lengthy sentences. For example, the word "CRASH!" can be more powerful (when spoken expressively) than saying "Suddenly, the car I was driving collided with another vehicle." Take note: this method is particularly effective in a group presentation but could be jarring in a one-on-one situation.

Delineate a clear beginning, middle, and end—each can be as short as a sentence or two. Set up the context, describe the event and tie it up with a conclusion or learning point.

EMPHASIZE THE EMOTIONAL IMPACT

Slow down to accentuate and experience for yourself moments of real feeling: anger, fear, joy, a realization, etc. If you feel something, the audience will.

Many good stories have drama or conflict. For example, instead of saying "Company X's costs were higher than their profit," underscore the drama by saying "Company X was on the verge of collapse and hundreds of people's jobs were at stake."

Highlight the "emotional arc" of the story. How does the main character change? Is he or she different at the end of the story? What did he or she learn? If you are the main character, what was the emotional arc you went through? Some of the best stories involve a setback or failure and the personal learning we gain from going through something challenging.

CHANNEL YOUR FAVORITE ACTOR OR ACTRESS

Be careful not to overdo it and only do what is comfortable, but adding some theater and drama to your stories will allow them to hit home effectively.

Think about how actors use tone of voice and body language to bring a story to life. Be expressive.

If your story involves different characters, play those roles when appropriate, rather than just talking about them. Let your body and voice change in small ways to suggest how they looked and sounded. You could even speak as the characters; even a brief dialogue and you'll help capture your audience's imagination.

MAKE IT HAPPEN NOW

Bring your audience right into the action by employing what actors call the vertical take-off. Instead of leading up to the real story with a lot of runway time, for example, *"Before I describe what happened that day, let me give you a little background. . . ."* Begin in the middle of the action, e.g. *"From the tense look on Rob's face, I can see the meeting is a disaster. . . ."*

Re-experience your story as you tell it. Imagine that it's happening right now. Let it affect you emotionally. Speaking in the present tense, whenever possible, can bring the audience into the action, for example, *"It's the day of the big announcement. I'm nervous as heck."* You can also begin in the past tense and shift to present tense for the climax of the story.

Don't give away the ending. As much as possible, tell the story from a *"point of innocence"* as if you don't know how it will end. This will keep your listeners waiting for the outcome, and the impact will be more profound, particularly if the ending is a surprise.

EXCITE THEIR SENSES

Sensory details help people visualize the story. Try "marble conference table" instead of "conference table" or "ten-pound computer printout" instead of "computer printout." These examples evoke senses of vision and touch. You can also appeal to your audience's sense of smell, hearing, and taste.

In fact, a good way to remember a story is to think back on some of the sensory details of the event. How old were you? What were you wearing? What was the weather like? Who was there? How were you feeling? Be sure to be selective with your use of sensory details. One or two are sufficient at the beginning of a story to set the scene; then use them sparingly but effectively throughout.

Review

Let's recap here by going back to the story I told about losing my patience with my daughter. First, let me admit that I was reluctant to tell this story. It was quite personal and exposed things about me that I'm not proud of: my impatience and short temper. But I'm glad I did because sharing my vulnerability with that group of people really connected us. Some speakers, up on the platform, delivering pearls of wisdom from their extensive research, can seem distant and superior. As I told this story I saw nods of understanding and smiles as I seemed to hit a universal chord that many of us encounter. As leaders I encourage you to think about personal stories first as you explore the notion of storytelling in a business setting.

Take a look back at my story and notice where I may have used the tips and techniques we discussed here. Was the story personal? Did it have a lesson? Could you imagine using a similar story in a business setting?

Although you can't tell from reading it, I did my best to re-experience the moment as I told the story. I used short phrases, sensory detail, and, for the most part, present tense. I also kept it short—it was probably no more than ninety seconds. Preparing that story definitely took some rehearsing and practice to get it down to its essentials, but in the end, it was well worth the effort.

Let me end with another story:

It is 1958. John Kavanagh, my father and the eldest son of Annie Malone, a widowed Irish Catholic from Liverpool, England, is walking to Manchester to pawn his accordion. He is the young father of three children who has just lost his day job as a lab technician and he hopes the accordion will bring him rent money and bus fare home. Of course, selling the instrument also means he'll be stopping his evening job as a stand-up comedian, which he did several nights a week to make some extra cash.

On the bus home he determines that if he can make twelve pounds a week, he'll be fine. He recalls that the salesmen at his old company wear suits and drive cars and decides to apply for a position in chemical sales. Twenty years later he is the managing director of Phillips Petroleum, Europe, the $700 million European subsidiary of the American oil company.

So how did this uneducated son of immigrants make it so far? Well, he was certainly smart and ambitious, but I would argue that his storytelling skills, honed in the theaters and clubs of the north of England, played a significant part in his success. His ability to match his message and delivery to his audience made him an inspiring boss and a gregarious colleague—one who could just as easily have dinner with the prime minister as have a pint with a dockworker.

What kind of leader and colleague are you? What stories do you have that can engage an employee, connect with a co-worker, or inspire a crowd? These stories are inside you, lying dormant and ready to be discovered and brought to life. The process described here will help you discover and exploit this amazing natural resource to improve your communication.

About The Ariel Group

Using an unorthodox experiential approach, based in the performing arts, The Ariel Group helps individuals discover their authentic leadership talents and make enduring improvements in their ability to connect with clients and employees. Our powerful experiential executive training programs are led by facilitators with a unique combination of experience in theater, business, and education. Since 1992, The Ariel Group has provided transformational learning experiences to 30,000 people in over a dozen countries. We have coached executives and CEOs of the world's largest companies as well as teachers and non-profits.

Our leadership and communication skills training workshops have been integrated into leadership development programs at major corporations around the world. We also deliver our workshops as part of the executive education curriculum at leading graduate schools of business, including Harvard, Columbia, Darden, and Duke.

Submitted by Sean Kavanagh, CEO

The Ariel Group

1050 Waltham Street, STE 600

Lexington, MA 02142

(781) 761-9000

info@arielgroup.com

www.arielgroup.com

Chapter 2

Reclaiming Your Peer Power

NETSPEED LEARNING SOLUTIONS

In This Chapter

- An interpersonal strengths, weaknesses, and beliefs assessment.
- Explanations for why some seemingly appropriate communication beliefs may actually cause difficulty in the long haul.

The most challenging aspect of any job is working with other people. Difficult co-workers and bosses can test anyone's ability to get along and get things done.

In a survey about workplace conflict conducted by NetSpeed Learning Solutions, six hundred respondents felt that interpersonal difficulties had seriously damaged their productivity and job satisfaction. Sixty-two percent of the respondents said they left a job in part because of a difficult person. Thirty percent reported a challenging co-worker was currently frustrating them. When asked to write about the frustrating co-worker, some of the responses included:

- *"I dread going to work to be barraged by her negativity."*
- *"I often need to 'run interference' because other employees also find him difficult to work with."*

For many of the respondents, the person causing them the most trouble was their boss:

- *"He is a childish, overbearing micromanager, leaving me powerless to perform my job and therefore feeling demeaned and demoralized."*
- *"I frequently have to circumvent her to get projects from the department completed."*

How do these difficult co-workers and bosses make things hard for the people around them? Their dysfunctional behavior is expressed in different ways: the manipulators deceive people to get what they want; the whiners complain about people who bug them; the attackers verbally assault those who won't budge; the bullies intimidate in order to get their way.

As difficult as these relationship problems have been in the past, they are intensified by the demands of the new workplace. Today the need to collaborate with others to get work done has never been greater. But there are business trends that make dealing with others infinitely more challenging. Employees are burdened with increased responsibility but limited authority. They need to deal with people across the country or across the world, in different time zones, with different cultural expectations; yet they don't see people's facial expressions or body language. In work settings like these, a simple email might be misconstrued and create conflict.

With such escalating challenges, is there a way to change the outcome? Yes—by using the principles of open, honest communication, your workplace relationships can be transformed. Take a moment to complete the About You Questionnaire to understand your underlying beliefs about your workplace challenges.

ABOUT YOU QUESTIONNAIRE

This questionnaire asks you to think about your interpersonal strengths, weaknesses, and beliefs. Answer honestly—no one will see this but you. We will review your responses later in the chapter. As you answer the questions openly (and later review our responses) you'll begin to understand the communication philosophy that underpins all of the case studies in our book *Peer Power: Transforming Workplace Relationships*.

1. I can improve my communication skills.

   Yes   No

2. What happens to me at work is usually not related to my own behavior.

   Yes   No

3. I prefer to take responsibility for my own actions.

   Yes   No

4. Even if I change my behavior, the situation usually doesn't change.

   Yes   No

5. I am willing to make the first move to improve a challenging situation.

   Yes   No

6. When someone is behaving badly, it's hard for me to feel compassionate.

   Yes   No

7. It's easy for me to put myself in the shoes of other people to imagine their points of view.

   Yes   No

8. I try to be open about my thoughts and feelings.

   Yes   No

9. I find gossip to be a great stress reliever.

   Yes   No

10. I discourage complaining.

    Yes   No

11. I wish that the top leaders in my organization would just fix the messes at work and leave me out of it.

    Yes   No

12. I strive to listen before I speak.

    Yes   No

13. If I have an opinion, I always put it on the table first.

    Yes   No

14. I often feel impatient with others.

    Yes   No

15. I try to leave my emotions at the door when I arrive at work.

    Yes   No

16. I expect others to apologize when they offend me.

    Yes   No

17. I offer an apology even though I may not be 100 percent at fault.

    Yes   No

18. I make sure I know who's at fault when things go wrong.

    Yes   No

19. When it gets confrontational, I shut down.

    Yes   No

20. I reach out to someone I may have offended.

    Yes   No

21. If I'm not sure what someone is thinking or feeling, I ask for his or her thoughts.

    Yes   No

22. I take people at face value.

    Yes   No

23. I'm good at reading others, so I rarely need to ask their opinions.

    Yes   No

24. I thank others often.

    Yes   No

25. My communication skills are as good as my technical skills.

    Yes   No

Learn from Our Mistakes

Before we examine your responses, consider some of our lessons learned.

In writing *Peer Power*, we talked through our failures, embarrassing moments, and just downright humiliating attempts to get others to change their behavior or do what we wanted. It was humbling to revisit the dumb mistakes we made with challenging peers. We attempted to get their support or manage their difficult behaviors by manipulating, whining, attacking, and bullying. We still aren't perfect, but we have learned from these common mistakes and we can speak from painful experience: these behaviors may work in the short run, but they rarely work in the long run.

We're going to take them one by one and tell you exactly why they don't work. (The names in these case studies are fictitious.)

MANIPULATING

Cynthia has a confession to make. In the past she has resorted to subtle manipulation to try to get her own way. Once she was responsible for recruiting volunteers to work on the board of a non-profit organization. Her approach to volunteers sometimes involved telling them that her highly intuitive nature gave her a strong feeling that they were "perfect" for the role.

In truth, Cynthia was more worried about filling a vacancy on the board than whether a volunteer was well-suited for the job. Often her target would feel special and pleased to be seen as someone who was just right for a spot on the board. Cynthia didn't like the way she felt after these encounters, and in time she realized that this form of manipulation preyed on people with lower self-esteem. The result was often mistrust, blame, and board members who quit.

We define "manipulating" as attempting to influence someone's attitude or behavior through deception or secrecy. If you tell someone you don't have adequate resources, even though you do, so he won't ask for your help, you're manipulating the situation. If you pretend you don't want something from somebody when you do him a favor (but you're really expecting that now he'll "owe you one"), you are manipulating him. If you intentionally make ambiguous statements in an email hoping to buy additional time, you are manipulating the situation. If you pretend to agree with someone to get her to like you, you are engaging in manipulation. If you withhold critical information that might influence a decision, you are manipulating the outcome. If you flatter someone so she will support you or give you what you want, you are manipulating.

Whether your manipulation becomes blatantly obvious or people simply feel uneasy around you, manipulating is usually discovered. Manipulators often find that it is very hard to keep track of all of the little deceptions they engage in. Ultimately, manipulators damage trust, which can be difficult, if not impossible, to regain. In the long run, manipulators find that they are no longer able to influence others because people begin to go out of their way to avoid being manipulated.

WHINING

When Ray worked at an aerospace company, he was unhappy with his colleague Bill (again, all names are fictitious). He frequently noticed Bill using a computer for personal business, even though Bill insisted he did not have time to share the workload when Ray was stretched thin. Each time Ray saw Bill slacking off, he became more frustrated and whined to Bill and another peer, Mary. Ray attempted to make Bill feel guilty—after all, look how overworked Ray was! And look how unfairly Bill was treating him! In private conversations with Mary, Ray whined about how unfair Bill was being. Ray winces even now remembering this situation.

As you can imagine, neither Bill nor Mary appreciated Ray's approach. It only made the situation worse. Bill began to defend himself by complaining about Ray to other co-workers. Mary pointed out to Ray how he had sometimes been unreliable and finally told Ray to knock it off. Ray realized that he needed to find more constructive ways of working with people who disappointed him.

Whining is complaining without seeking to improve the situation. We might whine directly to the co-worker who is frustrating us with an "Oh, poor me" tone of voice: "Shannon, I can't get my work done. This job is just impossible. You're making it so hard for me. I can't even sleep at night." Or we might gossip and whine about Shannon to someone else: "Shannon is driving me nuts. She never gives me what I need."

Whether you whine to your co-worker directly, whine to others behind her back, or send whiny emails to your peers, you are assuming the role of the victim in a workplace drama. Playing the victim can result in satisfying, self-righteous feelings. But people find whiners to be annoying and rarely respect them. Whiners lose credibility because their complaints often seem exaggerated. When your co-workers listen to you whine about your peers, they probably wonder what you're saying about them behind their backs. And when they learn that you have been whining about them, they may attack you with anger. They may even forward your negative emails to the person you're complaining about. You may have experienced the escalating cycle of whining, attacking, whining, and attacking that can be set into motion. Sad to say, whiny victims bring out aggressive attacks from others.

Does this mean you should never discuss your frustrations about someone at work with your friends? Of course not! Talking a problem through with someone you trust can be helpful. Listening to advice can help you prepare to handle a situation. But if you find that you are constantly complaining about the same person or situation to many different people, you've fallen into the trap of whining. If you vent your frustrations about someone without seeking a resolution, you're whining. Instead of tackling an issue head on, you're reinforcing your negative view of a person or situation, intensifying your own anger, damaging someone's reputation, losing your own credibility, and probably annoying everyone around you.

Avoiding whining does not mean you remain silent about workplace problems. Organizations need employees who speak up. Share your concerns with the appropriate people. As long as you do your homework, avoid blaming and embarrassing, and focus on solutions, you are not whining.

ATTACKING

Cynthia (again, a fictitious name) has been known to attack when under stress. (Please note that she has always felt bad when she has resorted to this coping technique.) On one occasion, she prepared to lead an important meeting despite feeling under the weather. She wrote the agenda, created materials for the people who would be attending, and organized binders that were carefully placed on the table for the meeting attendees.

Cynthia was expecting to hear appreciative comments for her efforts. Instead, as the meeting began, one of the participants stated that she didn't think the agenda was on target, didn't agree with the decisions made at the last meeting, and wanted to take this meeting in a different direction. Cynthia lost her composure (imagine a volcano erupting), began to rant about what it had taken her to get ready for the meeting, and verbally attacked the woman who dared to oppose her. After quashing all dissenting opinions, Cynthia led a very quiet meeting to a rapid conclusion.

Attacking is the repeated expression of anger and frustration in the form of inappropriate personal criticism. It often may include name-calling and blaming statements. It rarely gets people to cooperate. Most victims of an attack give in, comply, and bow down to end the aggressive attack.

If you attack as your method of gaining compliance, you may have experienced verbal abuse or flaming email attacks yourself and believe that it toughens people up. You may think that creating fear will motivate them to change. You're right; fear *is* a motivator. People will do what you want as long as they believe you can harm their careers, their reputations, or their work lives. If you attack your colleagues, you may feel better momentarily and even see immediate results.

In the end, however, those who attack others fail to gain loyalty, trust, enduring relationships, or commitment from others. Instead, people go around them, quit their jobs to escape the attacks, and may eventually respond by attacking the attacker.

BULLYING

Ray (a fictitious name) worked with Brit at a data processing company. The two of them were assigned to create a class jointly. Ray worked very hard to prepare his portions of the class. Usually, when he met with Brit to review their progress, she indicated she had not been able to complete her segments.

After a while Ray began to bully Brit to deliver on her promises. When these demands were ignored, Ray told Brit that he would just prepare the class by himself, but would let others know of her lack of cooperation. As a result of that threat, Brit contributed a bare minimum of work. In the end, Ray was forced to share credit with Brit for a successful class, which he resented, just as Brit resented Ray's attempts to bully her. Tension between the two of them continued for several months. In looking back, Ray realized that Brit lost all desire to collaborate with him because of his bullying.

Bullying occurs when someone makes unreasonable demands or uses inappropriate threats that exceed natural and appropriate consequences. The bully stamps his feet, raises his voice, and insists that others do what he wants. If they don't, the bully will make sure there are negative consequences. You've probably run across a bully before, whether on the school playground, in your neighborhood, or in the next cubicle at work.

Be honest now: Have you ever prematurely told someone you'll go over her head if she doesn't do what you want? You've engaged in bullying. Have you ever copied someone's boss on every little issue or problem? That's a form of virtual bullying. Have you ever pushed hard to get someone to do something with a tone that implies she has little choice? That's bullying. Have you ever threatened to drag your heels on a decision or undermine someone else's initiative? That's actually a form of bullying as well.

The problem with bullying is that it often produces long-lasting resentment and retaliation. Bullies have few allies at work (except those people who align themselves with the bully as a way to protect themselves or gain power from the association).

Four Key Principles

We hope you felt a little better reading about some of our embarrassingly human moments. We have given up these ineffective coping tactics, practiced healthier techniques, and have developed four key principles that are your springboard for effective, satisfying interactions. We invite you to leave behind powerless coping techniques and replace them with these principles:

- *Be Real:* Be open and authentic rather than manipulative.
- *Take Responsibility:* Choose to be accountable instead of whining.
- *Extend Respect:* Treat people with kindness instead of resorting to personal attacks.
- *Build Relationships:* Partner with others instead of bullying them.

Interpreting Your Responses to the About You Questionnaire

By now you've probably figured out what we think about responses to these questions. Compare our responses to yours.

1. I can improve my communication skills.

   If you answered "yes" to this statement, your head is in the right place. Everyone can improve his or her communication skills; it's within your control.

2. What happens to me at work is usually not related to my own behavior.

   If you agree with this statement, you may often feel victimized by others' actions. We invite you to consider the many ways your behavior may be helping or hindering the situation.

3. I prefer to take responsibility for my own actions.

   This is a powerful statement. If you said "yes," you are indicating your readiness to act in new ways that will benefit your difficult relationships.

4. Even if I change my behavior, the situation usually doesn't change.

   If you answered "yes" to this statement, you may want to try out some new behaviors, including respecting your own needs when necessary.

5. I am willing to make the first move to improve a challenging situation.

   Answering "yes" to this statement puts you in the driver's seat. If you're at an impasse with a colleague, someone must make the first move. We're glad it will be you.

6. When someone is behaving badly, it's hard for me to feel compassionate.

   If you find it difficult to feel compassion when someone's behavior is a problem, you're not alone. As you develop your peer power, you may be able to answer "no" to this statement.

7. It's easy for me to put myself in the shoes of other people to imagine their points of view.

   If you responded with a "yes," this is a great gift. Being able to view the world through another's eyes will allow you to respond with less defensiveness in difficult conversations.

8. I try to be open about my thoughts and feelings.

   We encourage openness in most work relationships. If you answered "yes" to this statement, there are probably no hidden agendas in your relationships with others.

9. I find gossip to be a great stress reliever.

   Let's face it—most people would answer "yes" to this statement. However, we'd like to suggest that when gossip is used in this way, the price you pay (in mistrust and conflict) is too steep.

10. I discourage complaining.

    "Yes" is a great answer. Since complaining often seems like a national pastime, learning to discourage it can take time. We guarantee that you will be happier, if not more productive, when you give it up.

11. I wish that the top leaders in my organization would just fix the messes at work and leave me out of it.

    We bet the top leaders wish they had the power to fix the messes at work, too! If you answered "yes" to this statement, look for opportunities to reclaim some personal power.

12. I strive to listen before I speak.

    This is a critical practice that takes discipline. If you answered "no" to this practice, you may wish to experiment by letting others speak while you listen with all ears.

13. If I have an opinion, I always put it on the table first.

   While this statement sounds reasonable on the surface, if you answered "yes," you may be dominating others in work situations. Let others speak first and see what happens.

14. I often feel impatient with others.

   When you have a to-do list a mile long, having to slow down to deal with others may seem like a trial. If you answered "yes" to this statement, your brusqueness may be blocking your success.

15. I try to leave my emotions at the door when I arrive at work.

   If this were possible and we could teach everyone how to do it, we'd be rich. If you said "no," you know you're human—your emotions are part of the package. Don't try to check them at the door.

16. I expect others to apologize when they offend me.

   Many a relationship has ended because that apology never came. If you answered "yes" to this question, you may find that you must move on in search of new people who will never offend you.

17. I offer an apology even though I may not be 100 percent at fault.

   Answering "yes" to this question demonstrates a willingness to accept partial responsibility for problems that arise in relationships. You've probably learned it "takes two to tango."

18. I make sure I know who's at fault when things go wrong.

   The impulse to assign blame is a strong one. If you answered "yes" to this question, you have the opportunity to consider just how damaging this impulse can be.

19. When it gets confrontational, I shut down.

   For many of us, shutting down is the way to maintain peace of mind. If you answered "yes" to this statement, you may be missing opportunities to influence others.

20. I reach out to someone I may have offended.

   We hope that you were able to say "yes" to this statement. Reaching out, even when it may not have been your intention to offend, demonstrates your concern for the other person.

21. If I'm not sure what someone is thinking or feeling, I ask for his or her thoughts.

   Yes! Checking in to see what is happening for someone is the only way to know for sure what he or she is experiencing. We recommend it.

22. I take people at face value.

   While this sounds positive, if you said "yes," it may mean that you are relying more on the words people say and less on the unspoken messages sent by body language and tone of voice.

23. I'm good at reading others, so I rarely need to ask their opinions.

   If you answered "yes" to this statement, your confidence in your intuition may lead you astray. Unless you're a mind reader, you must ask others' opinions.

24. I thank others often.

   Yes, yes, yes! This simple practice makes a big difference at work. We can't remember the last time we met someone who thanked people too much.

25. My communication skills are as good as my technical skills.

   Productive contributors are able to answer this question with a resounding "yes!"

You can find a copy of the About You Questionnaire in this chapter's online tools. We also invite you to explore more constructive principles, practices, and strategies in *Peer Power: Transforming Workplace Relationships.* If you begin implementing some of these concepts, you'll be well on the way to becoming a powerful peer.

About NetSpeed Learning Solutions

NetSpeed Learning Solutions develops better leaders and more engaged employees through face-to-face and virtual learning. We help clients rapidly launch programs, develop skills, reinforce learning, and measure the impact. Our programs include:

- *NetSpeed Leadership*® for managers and supervisors
- *Blazing Service*™ to improve the delivery of customer service
- *Peer Power*™ to develop collaborative workplace relationships
- The NetSpeed Learning Center™, online, post-class reinforcement tools to reinforce learning transfer
- NetSpeed Fast Tracks™, an integrated learning system to blend social media with instructor-led training
- Virtual facilitation courses to help trainers and instructional designers transition to the virtual classroom environment

Submitted by Cynthia Clay, President, CEO; Ray Olitt, Consultant

NetSpeed Learning Solutions

3016 NE Blakeley Street, Suite 100

Seattle, WA 98105

(206) 517-5271

cclay@netspeedlearning.com

www.netspeedlearning.com

Chapter 3

The Candor Advantage

In This Chapter

- A working definition for the practice of candor.
- Three ways individuals can become more candid in their communication.
- Techniques for fostering candor in your organization.

Business literature (particularly in the United States) is filled with calls for workforce candor. Jack Welch devoted an entire chapter to it in his best seller, *Winning*. Jim Collins encourages business leaders to "confront the brutal facts" to get from *Good to Great*. Larry Bossidy and Ram Charan talk about the importance of "robust dialogue" in *Execution*. Warren Bennis, Daniel Goleman, and James O'Toole call on leaders to create more organizational openness in *Transparency: How Leaders Create a Culture of Candor*.

Why is candor such a pressing issue? Because candor (or the lack of it) is a key variable in three major organizational and human capital arenas: employee engagement, change management, and corporate performance. Welch succinctly articulates three advantages of organizational candor. First, by getting more people in the conversation the organization becomes idea-rich: "More ideas get surfaced, discussed, pulled apart, and improved. Instead of everyone shutting down, everyone opens up and learns. Any organization—or unit or team—that brings more people and their minds into the conversation has an immediate advantage" (Welch & Welch, 2005, p. 27). A second plus is that candor generates speed by surfacing more issues and driving higher quality decisions more quickly. Finally, candor cuts costs by eliminating unnecessary meetings and other corporate rituals designed to sidestep the awkwardness candor can create.

So if candor holds such promise, why does it remain so rare in organizational life? More importantly, what can managers and human resource professionals do to promote it? Let's explore these questions.

A Working Definition of Organizational Candor

By itself, candor is an abstract principle that can be used to mean many things. People often criticize others in the name of candor, thinking of it as "brutal honesty." (Note that Jim Collins talks about confronting the brutal facts, not confronting others brutally.) We also defend ourselves in the name of candor; remember Jack Nicholson's famous speech in *A Few Good Men*? "You can't handle the truth!"

Often people use "candor" and "honesty" interchangeably. But in meaning and in practice, candor is closer to "authenticity" and "openness" than it is to "honesty." *The American Heritage Dictionary* includes two definitions of candor as it relates to organizational communication:

- "Frankness or sincerity of expression" (that's the authenticity part) and
- "Freedom from prejudice; impartiality" (or openness).

It's a willingness to openly and skillfully express your thoughts and feelings while being open to hear the thoughts and feelings of others in return. Communicating this way moves people beyond their comfort zones to what I call the "candor zone." In the candor zone your assumptions and ideas are challenged. You may give or receive unexpected feedback. It's a state of rigorous curiosity and exploration. Remaining open and engaged in the candor zone is uncomfortable and can be difficult. It should also be exhilarating; it's here that insight, innovation, and growth occur.

There's one more aspect of candor that is implied but not stated in the dictionary: candor occurs in the here and now. Candor is what happens during the meeting, not in the meeting after the meeting.

Putting these pieces together, our working definition of organizational candor is:

Listening and speaking openly in real time about the things that matter

Putting Candor to Work

When it comes to enhancing candor in organizations, we can learn a lot from Kurt Lewin, a leading behavioral scientist of the last century. An organization development pioneer, Lewin created a simple, useful formula for understanding human behavior: $b = f(P,E)$: <u>B</u>ehavior is a <u>f</u>unction of the <u>P</u>erson in his/her <u>E</u>nvironment (Lewin, 1952). In essence, this "Field Theory" asserts that an individual's behavior is influenced by the social context in which it occurs and vice versa. It provides a model for understanding ways of improving candor at the personal and organizational levels.

BENEFITS OF CANDOR

To You

- Your good ideas are heard and inform the decisions your team/colleagues make.
- Because you have actually said them, you stop worrying about the things you wish you had said.
- You learn by being open to others' ideas.
- Open communication fosters productive, high-trust work relationships.
- Candor minimizes "cognitive dissonance" and contributes to higher levels of job satisfaction.

To the Teams You're On

- Everyone's best thinking is included in the discussion and decisions your team makes.
- Full and candid participation in the team's process results in full commitment during implementation.
- Candor promotes inclusion and openness, two criteria of high-performing teams.
- Candor prevents false consensus and potentially bad decisions that might result from conflict avoidance.
- Meetings are more effective because teams are not afraid of dissent or conflict. Open and authentic discussions in these meetings accelerate problem resolution and improve the quality of decision making.

To Your Organization

Candor drives organizational goals and core values in the following ways:

- It helps you model accountability, honesty, and risk taking by speaking up when it counts.
- It enhances respect by creating an environment in which people listen to and learn from diverse points of view.

Developing Talent for Organizational Results

- It promotes fast decisions by getting to the root cause of business problems so you solve them the first time.

- It helps teams be flexible by being open to multiple points of view and adapting as necessary.

- It promotes quality decisions by surfacing and improving ideas that result in better outcomes.

- It improves trust and teamwork by fostering collaboration and turning meetings into high-value interactions whereby meaningful work is accomplished.

IMPROVING THE P: THE PERSONAL PRACTICE OF CANDOR

Looking at the "P" first, there are typically three challenges individuals confront when it comes to candor:

- The decision to speak up in the first place.
- Saying what you want to say professionally and respectfully.
- Listening openly to others (instead of reacting) when they have a strong need to talk.

Deciding to Speak Up

If you're nervous that what you have to say won't be well received, your challenge is to stop stopping yourself from speaking. Here are some tips to help do that:

- *Disconnect "feeling comfortable" with speaking up.* People unconsciously connect feelings and actions in their minds. People who are significantly overweight are often coached to disconnect the feeling of hunger from the act of eating; they learn to be hungry and not eat. Similarly, individuals can train themselves to speak up even if they're uncomfortable when they do so.

- *Consider the best-case or likely scenarios to balance the worst-case scenario.* We automatically think of the bad things that might happen to us if we speak up. But what about the good? Maybe your idea will take the team in a new direction. Then there's the likely scenario: maybe your idea isn't the best or worst but one of many that will be considered along the way to a team's decision. Creating this balance can defuse some of the stress you feel before you speak.

- *Ask someone you trust on your team to give you feedback.* Let that person know that you are trying to find ways of contributing constructively and that you'd like to know how your efforts are impacting the group.

- *Don't take responsibility for other people's reactions.* We often stop ourselves from speaking because we're worried about how others will react. This actually does a great disservice to others as well as to ourselves. We don't say hard things that may help others improve because we don't want to hurt their feelings. And so they don't get better. Manage your half of the relationship and let others manage theirs.

- *It's not making a mess but cleaning it up that counts.* People often think that once they say what's on their minds, the consequences will be lasting. But by our definition candor is a process that unfolds over multiple interactions. If you say something that didn't come out as you intended or if it is misunderstood, you can clarify what you meant, apologize, or try stating your message a different way. Your speaking isn't the end of your candor. It's the beginning.

How to Say What You Want to Say Professionally and Respectfully

Some people have no problem with the choice to speak up; their issue is how to speak in ways that are respectful as well as authentic. It is possible to disagree without being disagreeable. Here are some ways to do that:

- *Be curious about the reasoning.* When we disagree with someone or don't like what that person has said, we automatically become judgmental. As an alternative, inquire into others' thinking first. Inquiring *before* you react gives you insight into their thinking and it requires them to justify their position(s). You may find common ground in this discussion, and you will have more clarity that can inform your response.

- *Disclose versus criticize.* "That idea is doomed to fail." "I'm concerned with the potential consequences of that option." While the meaning of these two statements is similar, the impact will likely be very different. The second is a disclosure, a statement about you. Disclosures promote openness because you're making your internal reactions public to the other person or the group. By talking about yourself, there isn't the same edge that can trigger defensiveness in others. Emotions will be lower and easier to manage.

- *Invite other reactions and perspectives.* If you have a reaction to what's been said, others may as well. If you're in a team setting, a broader conversation about others' reactions can help the group surface the range of reactions on the team. For example, "It would help me to hear what others think about this proposal before moving on. Can we do a quick check-in to see where we are as a group?"

Listening Openly When Others Have a Strong Need to Talk

Listening is the forgotten skill of candor. When we find ourselves in a candor moment, we are far more concerned about our ability to express ourselves than we are about our ability to listen. We worry that we won't be heard; rarely if ever do we worry that we won't hear others' concerns.

Listening when emotions and stakes are high is especially difficult. It's also when listening is most important. In these circumstances listening can help:

- Clarify differing points of view.
- De-escalate non-constructive emotions people are experiencing.

- Help others speak with candor.
- Maintain/restore constructive interpersonal dynamics.

Listening is defined as demonstrating that you understand the thoughts and feelings a speaker is communicating from his or her frame of reference. In the candor zone, listening requires discipline, curiosity, and skill.

- You need to be **disciplined** so you can remain engaged in the conversation rather than reactive. When we become hijacked by our emotions, we listen to our own self-talk (usually critical comments about the other person or our own rightness) instead of the speaker.
- You need to be **curious** about the other person's goals and feelings about what's at stake when he or she decides to speak up. Ask yourself, "What's the real issue and why does it matter?" to that person.
- You need **skill** to be disciplined, curious, and able to restate or reflect the speaker's issue in a mature and respectful way.

Here are a few examples of what listening sounds like when emotions are high:

- "You're frustrated with our decision-making process. From your point of view, the window of opportunity is closing while we try to figure out what to do."
- "You're irritated because the project specs keep changing but our deadline doesn't change with them."
- "You're angry because you think I'm opposing your idea for personal reasons."

Once the other person has confirmed that this represents his or her point of view, you can respond with your own point of view—with candor. The Personal Candor Checklist is a reminder of what you can do.

PERSONAL CANDOR CHECKLIST

Say What You Mean

❑ Speak clearly and neutrally about the issues.

❑ Give specific examples that support your point of view.

❑ Be concise.

Be Professional and Respectful

❑ Control the emotionality of your words, gestures, and tone of voice.

❑ When responding, refrain from criticizing or telling the other person that he or she is wrong.

❑ Search for others' real needs and issues that are underneath their emotional statements.

Be Open to Others' Points of View

❑ Build trust by listening to the other's point of view, even when you disagree with it or it upsets you.

❑ Ask clarifying questions to understand different perspectives.

❑ Work to understand feedback you're given, even when it's poorly delivered or, in your eyes, inaccurate.

❑ Seek constructive conflict; actively seek reactions to what you've said.

Speak Up in Real Time

❑ Challenge proposals and offer dissenting perspectives before decisions are made.

❑ If you feel internal conflict, speak up so that the group can grapple with the issue at a deeper level.

❑ Preface your comments to prepare others for what's to come (e.g., "I have a different point of view . . . ").

IMPROVING THE E: FOSTERING TEAM CANDOR

At its essence, candor is an individual, situational choice. Yet the culture, systems, and processes of an organization have a strong influence on individuals' decisions to practice or withhold their candor. As Chris Argyris observes in his early writings, the relationship between the individual and the organization isn't always an easy one (Argyris, 1957). Argyris notes that individuals strive toward self-actualization—a state of psychological maturity and wholeness. Organizations, on the other hand, strive toward efficiency; in that pursuit they've instituted processes and controls that constrain an individual's development pursuits. As it relates to candor, organizations try to counterbalance these processes with values, norms, and competencies that extol open communication and risk taking, but these are rare enough to overcome the operational and managerial mechanisms that squelch candor. Thus when a candor moment presents itself, people choose to be safe rather than sorry.

How, then, do organizations foster candor and enjoy the benefits Jack Welch describes? By aiming lower. Articulating values, norms, and competencies is important, yet insufficient to create a culture of candor. The same is true for the personal practice of candor. What's missing is the connective tissue to link organizational initiatives and individual behavior. That's where teams come in: they have a culture of their own, they're small enough that personal candor can make a difference, and they can put the organization's values into practice.

For those interested in whole systems change, this trickle-up approach may seem slow and difficult to scale. But as OD theorist Peter Block has stated, the unit of authentic organizational change is the small group. Teams are the cells of the organization. To change the whole, change must begin and take root at the cellular level.

This approach to team change can take place concurrently, so it can scale, and improvements can be made quickly. By focusing on two areas of team interaction—participation and constructive dissent—teams can rapidly improve their dynamics and results. Rich participation maximizes the intelligence and resources of the team that are often left untapped; isn't this why teams come together in the first place? So effective participation is job one. As for dissent, some teams don't have enough—members don't challenge others' ideas because it's not safe or permissible to do so. Other teams have plenty of dissent, but that dissent is antagonistic. Their discussions sound and feel like arguments. While these two types of dissent are very different, the result is often the same: diminished participation and ultimately lower commitment to the decisions that the team makes.

To generate rich participation and constructive dissent, teams need three things in addition to the personal practice of candor:

1. Clear guidelines for membership, participation, and preparation that are championed by the team.

2. Facilitative tools to enhance participation when needed.

3. Facilitative tools to foster constructive dissent when needed.

These factors aren't new to talent management professionals. The problem is that team leaders and members don't know about these guidelines and tools, don't value them, are too busy to learn or apply them, or don't have the skills to implement them in the moment, when it most counts.

To help close these candor gaps, we've created a candor playbook for teams to improve in each of these areas. The Candor Checklist for Teams addresses many of the structural elements of team readiness that are fundamental to team effectiveness. The playbook also includes a simple assessment to raise members' awareness of team dynamics, as well as tools to help teams address their specific needs in real time.

CANDOR CHECKLIST FOR TEAMS

Preparation

- ❏ Publish agendas in advance so members know what to prepare and how to participate.

- ❏ To make best use of the group's time and talent, assure that everyone comes prepared to participate fully.

- ❏ Announce how decisions will be made (e.g., by the leader with input from the group, by the group, or other ways) so members know how their contributions will be used.

Norms

- ❏ Create and publish team norms so members understand how to participate in the group and the team knows what to do to improve.

- ❏ Include guidelines that encourage candor.

Participation

- ❏ Everyone gets a say. Invite quiet members to offer their ideas and reactions to what others have said.

- ❏ Include time to build on and critique each other's ideas.

- ❏ Test ideas with a "devil's advocate" brainstorming session before making decisions.

- ❏ Acknowledge members who demonstrate candor in high-stakes conversations.

- ❏ Test for commitment to decisions and implementation before closing the discussion. If the commitment isn't sufficient, more candor is required to uncover the reasons why.

- ❏ Close meetings with an instant survey: "How did we do in challenging and listening to all points of view?"

Accountability

❑ Hold each other accountable to the decisions made during the meeting.

❑ Check in immediately with members who aren't meeting their commitments. Seek to understand why.

❑ If new information or problems threaten implementation, raise the issues proactively so the team can respond with urgency.

Participation tools include:

- A simple check-in exercise that can be used to generate or balance discussion and make sure all voices are heard.

- Guidelines for brainstorming to quickly draw out the creativity of team members and encourage them to build on each other's ideas.

- Directions for using the nominal group technique, a way to quickly assure that (1) the two phases of problem solving—fact finding and evaluation—are treated separately and (2) no member(s) monopolize the discussion during group problem solving.

- Straw voting, to have a sense of where group members stand on a given issue.

Tools to promote constructive dissent include:

- Assigning a devil's advocate whose explicit role it is to find the weaknesses in an idea or argument (alternately, time can be set aside for the entire team to engage in devil's advocate thinking).

- The "five whys," which helps unpack team members' thinking to learn how they frame a solution, what the solution is trying to solve, and why they may be passionate about it.

- A criteria matrix activity that makes public the implicit and personal goals team members use when evaluating ideas/decisions.

- After-action reviews to openly debrief a team failure so the team can learn from what happened, how it happened, and why it happened.

If these tools look familiar, they should. They're time-tested, they're basic, and they're easy to use. They're effective! The goal of the playbook isn't to give teams new things to learn or do; teams don't have time for that. Our purpose is to help members be resourceful in the moment when candor counts most.

You will find a Personal Candor Assessment and a Team Candor Assessment in this chapter's online tools.

Conclusion

In *The Knowing-Doing Gap*, Jeffrey Pfeffer and Bob Sutton devote an entire chapter to the ways organizations confuse talk and action and another to how fear prevents them from acting on what they know. This is especially true when initiatives like candor remain undefined and abstract.

The goal of this chapter has been to bridge those gaps by providing managers, team leaders, and HR professionals with a working definition of candor and outlining strategies and tools that can move candor from talk to action. Doing so will help address the paradox Chris Argyris wrote of over fifty years ago: when individuals withhold less of themselves and become more open to others, every candor-zone interaction becomes an opportunity for stretching, for learning about themselves and from life. They're engaged in the process of self-actualization. Organizations win, too, as they tap into the well of actionable wisdom that resides within their talent and their teams.

Consider this challenge. It's easy to see the candor-based faults in others. As you've been reading, you may have been thinking about people and teams where candor is a problem. That's great! But most people leave themselves off this list. My encouragement is that you start the change process by elevating your own candor. What's your candor edge? Where can you improve? If you're not sure, let others know that you want to listen and speak more authentically and openly and ask them for their feedback. When they offer it, listen to them and thank them for their candor. You'll quickly see that you have the power to change the quality of any conversation you're in, for your benefit and for others.

Let candor start with you.

REFERENCES

The *American Heritage Dictionary of the English Language* (4th ed.). (2000). Boston: Houghton Mifflin, 2000.

Argyris, C. (1957). The individual and the organization: Some problems of mutual adjustment. *Administrative Science Quarterly, 2*(1).

Bennis, W., Goleman, D., & O'Toole, J. (2008). *Transparency: How leaders create a culture of candor.* San Francisco: Jossey-Bass.

Bossidy, L., & Charan, R. (2002). *Execution: The discipline of getting things done.* New York: Crown Business.

Collins, J. (2001). *Good to great: Why some companies make the leap . . . and others don't.* New York: HarperCollins.

Lewin, K. (1951). *Field theory in social science.* New York: Harper & Row.

Pfeffer, J., & Sutton, R. (2000). *The knowing-doing gap: How smart companies turn knowledge into action.* Cambridge, MA: Harvard Business School Press.

Welch, J., & Welch, S. (2005). *Winning.* New York: HarperBusiness.

About Ridge Training

Ridge Training helps employees at all levels of client organizations improve their people skills so they save more time, get more done, and have more fun. Thanks to our unique practice-driven training methodology, including real-play practice scenarios and personalized stretch coaching by master trainers, participants leave ready and able to perform at higher levels. When our training is linked to clients' strategy, we can reduce the cost, time, and pain associated with implementing their key initiatives.

The word "ridge" refers to a way of relating to people. It is taken from the writings of philosopher Martin Buber, who advocated living life "on the narrow ridge." The narrow ridge is a state of mind and heart that blends integrity, acceptance, and interpersonal skill, even when dealing with contradictory opinions and values. Some of the most creative thinking and living is done on this narrow ridge, where people meet person-to-person, not facade-to-facade. Some of the finest relationships are forged on the narrow ridge, and some of the most productive work is accomplished there. Believing in Buber's concept, we named our organization Ridge Training.

Submitted by Jim Bolton, President

Ridge Training

5628 Emerson Avenue South

Minneapolis, MN 55419

(800) 466.3393

jwbolton@ridge.com

www.ridge.com

Chapter 4

Open Your Business to the World

Improving Global Communications

ECCO INTERNATIONAL

In This Chapter

- The elements that make up a global mindset and ensure or detract from clear communication.

- Communication and behavioral strategies for effective multicultural interactions.

In *The Work of Nations*, University of California at Berkeley professor and former Secretary of Labor Robert Reich sums up the essence of "globalization," stating:

"We are living through a transformation that will rearrange the politics and economics of the coming century. There will be no national products or technologies, no national corporations, no national industries. There will no longer be national economies . . . all that will remain rooted within national boundaries are the people who comprise a nation."

—Reich, 1991, pp. 3, 8

Simply stated—the global marketplace is changing. Today we live in a business climate that is characterized by overwhelming ambiguity, paradox, shifting definitions of value, and the need for rapid, transformative change in a multicultural context. This affects business conduct as well as how we interact with different cultures on a personal and professional level.

Snapshot in Time

We live in a time of exciting—and challenging—marketplace transformation. The concept of doing business on a national level is no longer the norm; our corporate landscape extends beyond confined borders, reaching into a global pool of colleagues and competitors. While opportunities are available to all businesses, sustainable success comes to companies that are prepared to conquer the ever-evolving challenges of both technical ability and interpersonal acumen. This expertise demands more from employees than to simply speak and understand languages.

In the global marketplace, an organization's success at achieving its strategic goals, operating at peak performance, and creating competitive advantage all rely on one source: its ability to effectively appreciate, understand, value, trust, engage, and employ the multiple perspectives and learning abilities of the world's cultures. Indeed, how effectively an organization can harness its collective global thinking abilities, global learning capacities, and global creativity is literally all that separates it from every other organization.

Communication in a Global Marketplace

There's no disputing we live and work in a global age where advances in technology bring people of different cultures together—both in our personal lives and in the workplace. While this is an interesting and intriguing dynamic, the experience can be frustrating when communicating with those from another culture.

How do you start a conversation or discussion? What cultural "offenses" might be inadvertently committed? How can you motivate the global workforce, structure a project, or communicate a business strategy? Are we destined to only learn from our mistakes to understand cultural differences?

The answer is a resounding "no."

How Culture Impacts Business: The Research

Culture has long been studied by anthropologists and sociologists, and much of what we know comes from these academic disciplines. Some of the most important of these studies have been the work of Mildred and Edward T. Hall, who focused specifically on identifying how different cultures understand and manage time as well as the degree to which context contributes to meaning in communications. In addition, social psychologist Harry Triandis has extensively studied individualism and collectivism and their impacts on productivity and relationships.

In terms of studies about the direct impacts of culture in business, from 1967 to 1973, Dr. Geert Hofstede, an IBM psychologist, conducted what is considered the most comprehensive study of how values in the workplace are influenced by culture. Hofstede collected and analyzed data gathered from more than one hundred thousand people in forty countries. His results generated the basis for developing a model that identifies five primary dimensions to differentiate cultures and has since become an internationally recognized standard. Hofstede's dimensions analysis assists individuals and businesses alike in understanding the intercultural differences within regions and between countries, paving the way for heightened understanding, enhanced performance, and improved productivity.

Language vs. Understanding

Language ability is not the same as cross-cultural or business/management competence, and "common vision" does not always mean shared understanding. Miscommunications can significantly reduce productivity and increase organizational costs by creating unnecessary delays and obstacles in meeting business objectives. Consider the following:

- How much time passes between the time you send an email to an international colleague and the time you receive a response?

- Do you ask a question and get an answer to a different question—or don't receive an answer at all?

- How many clarifying emails do you send before receiving the correct or complete information you need to do your job?

- You hear your international colleague say "yes," but you find out it doesn't mean "yes, I'll do it," it means "yes, I heard you."

- How much time is lost—potentially delaying a project—while waiting for information from international colleagues?

- How many sales are lost in the international market due to misinterpreted client needs?

- How many misunderstandings happen because you don't know what your customer actually values?

From the executive level and planning stages to day-to-day operations, clear communications are a non-negotiable requirement for moving a company forward through the global marketplace.

GLOBAL LITERACIES: LESSONS ON BUSINESS LEADERSHIP AND NATIONAL CULTURES

A 2000 survey by Patricia Digh and Dr. Robert Rosen asked CEOs of the world's fifteen hundred largest companies what the one key skill they felt leaders needed to be successful in the global economy. In response, more than 70 percent of those surveyed said that the ability to work effectively across cultures was the single most important attribute leaders need in today's global marketplace. Indeed, contrary to conventional wisdom, this study made quite clear that in a borderless economy, culture matters more—not less.

Establishing a Global Mindset

A foundation of basic cultural concepts and the development of a global mindset contribute to effectively engaging in intercultural interactions in a global marketplace/workplace. But just how does one go about establishing such a mindset? It begins with culture.

Culture reflects a way of life for a group of people: the arts, beliefs, laws, morals, customs, habits, symbols, institutions, and transmitted behavior patterns—including styles of communication—of a community or population. Culture is determined by history, geography, and climate and influences how people feel, look, think, and act. Culture helps determine our beliefs, and thus affects our behavior. Embedded in our culture are specific cultural values.

Cultural values often determine how we each think about and approach our own behaviors and interactions with others. Cultural groups tend to hold beliefs and display behaviors that coincide with their values. Understanding what these values are, and how they operate and drive behavior, can help you interact with different cultural groups more effectively. When we attempt to understand other cultures, we are broadening our mindsets as well.

Mindset is a mental attitude or disposition that predetermines a person's responses to and interpretations of situations. Our mindsets open the more we are exposed to cultures different from our own. A global mindset is based on global knowledge and understanding of cultures and appropriate ways of interacting with members from varying cultures. We further develop a global mindset through personal experiences with other cultures and interaction with global markets and businesses. Acquiring a global mindset at a foundational level has broad application.

Stereotypes vs. Generalizations

Establishing a global mindset does not happen quickly. At times, our experiences, knowledge and understanding limit us. As a result, we fall back on stereotyping. Table 4.1 displays the differences between stereotypes and generalizations.

A stereotype is a standardized mental picture that is commonly held by members of a group and represents an oversimplified opinion, prejudiced attitude, or judgment about other groups. People tend to use stereotypes when they have limited knowledge about or lack first-hand experience with other cultures. While intent may be positive, stereotypes are not the best shorthand way to understand other cultural groups.

Generalizations are an acceptable shorthand method for understanding others. They are based on research about global cultures and values. Knowledge and

Table 4.1 Differences Between Stereotypes and Generalizations

	Stereotypes	Generalizations
How shorthand understanding is created	Based on incorrect and/or unproven assumptions	Based on correct and proven assumptions
Who creates and promotes shorthand understanding	Persons who wish to emphasize insider/outsider distinctions	Persons who wish to minimize insider/outsider distinctions
The result of using shorthand understanding	Exclusion and abuse of other groups	Better understanding and harmony regarding other groups
How shorthand understanding is regarded	Incorrectly regarded as fact	Based on research about cultural tendencies

understanding can be gained from multicultural interactions and from a variety of media outlets. Generalizations can be a helpful starting point in getting to know your co-workers and customers so you can recognize their preferences.

Foundation for Improved Multicultural Communications

UNDERSTANDING AND RECOGNIZING CULTURAL CONTINUUMS

Intercultural research shows us that there are behavioral tendencies within cultures and regions of the globe based on the common values people share. These values tend to fall somewhere between two opposite ends of the cultural continuums and impact both individual and team abilities to solve problems and make decisions. Figure 4.1 presents the five continuums.

It should be noted that, although these dimensions are presented separately to enhance their understanding, in practice they are intended to be considered together in order to "paint a picture." While the continuums are certainly valid individually, their power in terms of application is recognizing how each continuum directly

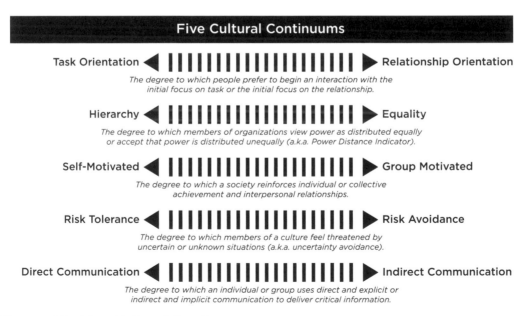

Figure 4.1 Five Cultural Continuums

Table 4.2 Continuum > Business Application

Continuum		Business Application
Task/Relationship Orientation	▶	Time Management/Interperosnal Relationship Strategies/Assertiveness/Conflict Resolution/Disclosure
Power Distance Indicator	▶	Management Styles/Assertiveness/Conflict Resolution
Individualism/Collectivism	▶	Team Orientation/Rewards and Recognition/Motivation/Feedback
Uncertainty Avoidance	▶	Decision-Making Practices/Conflict Resolution
Context Communication	▶	Communication Style/Nonverbal/Saying "No"

impacts the larger picture. Each of these five cultural continuums has a direct business application as shown in Table 4.2.

IMPROVED MULTICULTURAL COMMUNICATIONS IN ACTION!

Consider this situation: A large U.S.–based division of a multinational corporation was unable to obtain payment from a subsidiary in China. Everyone involved was highly educated and experienced in global markets. In an effort to communicate clearly, the U.S. team became increasingly direct and stern in email communication and referenced documentation, legalities, and late fees. In response, they received communication from their Chinese counterpart stressing the message was understood and that it would be discussed with their team. After months of unresponsiveness, the U.S. team resorted to legal taking over the communications.

What went wrong? First, direct and threatening communication was eroding trust. Second, the key decision-maker in China was not appropriately involved; the more direct the communication became, the worse the situation. What was needed was a personal trip, extended time in meetings to build relationships, and acknowledgement of appropriate decision channels.

The rest of the story: After working with a global communications consultant, the U.S. team did make a personal trip, toured the facility, and spent time with the team. They met the key decision-maker and did not discuss money. In the end, the U.S. team was rewarded with a payment of the full amount as they boarded the plane. Indeed, a happy ending to a real story.

Global Business Is Not a Choice, It Is a Reality

It is imperative for organizations to bridge cultural and language barriers to be able to achieve more effective cross-cultural business relationships and improve global performance. Today's workforce requires knowledge of the ways in which culture impacts and influences work-related outcomes on a day-to-day basis, and organizational leaders at any level must become more globally productive using a cross-cultural mindset.

By gaining an understanding of and appreciation for the value that can be created or captured through effective cross-cultural interactions, organizations enhance their reputations as globally competitive businesses, communicate with customers and colleagues in a culturally sensitive manner, expand effectiveness in the global marketplace, and demonstrate flexibility and agility as an organization through effective cultural interactions.

Use the information in Table 4.3 to help you and your employees improve global communication and interaction. This Quick Reference Guide can also be downloaded from the online tools for this chapter.

The bottom line: When you open your mind, you open your world.

Table 4.3 Quick Reference Guide

Communication and Behavioral Strategies for Effective Global Interactions	
Characteristics	**Strategies**
A task-oriented person *has to see that you're serious about the business at hand*	• Begin with the business at hand, so he or she knows you are serious and credible • Be clear about the contract (cost, timelines, roles) and the work; details (product, services) • Meet or beat schedules and timelines

(continued)

Characteristics	Strategies
A relatioship-oriented person *has to know, like, and trust you before doing business with you*	• Plan your business trip, meeting, phone call with time for more than "just" business; allow time for visiting cultural sites, business sites and to participate in business socializing • Start to build relationships—and trust—before jumping straight into business • Don't assume informality; earn the right to be invited into their business/social circle
A person who prefers direct communication *respects you for saying what you mean*	• Be precise, to the point, and focused on the business issue • Provide details as needed; don't assume the person has much background on the topic being discussed • Say what you mean (respectfully, of course); it's okay to disagree
A person who prefers indirect communication *respects you for saving face and understanding nonverbal communication*	• Look for nonverbal cues • Be patient; expect talk on tangent subjects before getting to the point • Don't agree to anything that might not be followed up with a contact; the person will accept your word and consider it a breach of trust if you cannot keep your word
A person who values hierarchy *expects to be treated with the respect his or her position/status is due*	• Defer to the person who is the leader, even if that person isn't the expert • Expect to meet with a person at your equivalent status level; it could be a sign of disrespect if a supervisor meets with a department head or VP • Avoid open confrontation
A person who values equality *expects to be treated as an equal human being in most situations*	• Treat everyone as an equal partner, with everyone's ideas taken into account • Be informal in the use of titles, greeting, and dress • Expect this person to be open to confrontation and admitting problems

(continued)

Table 4.3 (Continued)

Characteristics	Strategies
A person who focuses more on the individual than the group *expects to hear how his or her needs are being met and does not mind being singled out for praise*	• Recognize and acknowledge the person's individual attributes and achievements • Refer to benefits for the individual • Respect the person's privacy
A person who focuses more on the group than the individual *expects to hear how the group's needs are being met and does not want to be singled out for praise*	• Recognize and acknowledge the group's attributes and achievements • Refer to benefits for the group as a whole • Be sure teamwork is a valuable part of your proposal/activity
A person who fears uncertainty or has a low tolerance for risk *is uncomfortable with "gray areas," ambiguity, deviant ideas, and change; wants and likes rules*	• Provide very specific details—regardless of the topic • Provide contingency plans • Outline agendas with as much content and timing as possible • Expect vague responses or protracted silences • Expect "ready, aim, aim, aim, aim, aim . . . " behavior • Recognize that what's new is potentially dangerous and adoption will be slow • Avoid matrix teaming structures
A person who has little fear of uncertainty or has a higher tolerance for risk *is comfortable in un- or ill-defined circumstances, appreciates novel or innovative ideas and behavior; prefers few rules*	• Expect gaps in information • Expect "ready, fire, aim" behavior • Expect to take the initiative • Set your own milestones—don't wait for risk-oriented colleagues to do so • Expect quick responses followed by adjustments or corrections • Recognize that what's new is interesting and exciting

REFERENCE

Reich, R. (1991). *The work of nations: Preparing ourselves for twenty-first century capitalism.* New York: Vintage Books.

About ECCO International

ECCO International (Effecting Creative Change in Organizations) specializes in developing global competence in multicultural organizations around the world. ECCO International earned the 2010 Best of St. Paul Award in the Human Resource Consulting Services category from the U.S. Commerce Association for its service to customers and community. ECCO International, in partnership with VisionPoint, launched Open Mind, Open World, a training program that helps multinational organizations overcome intercultural communication conflicts. ECCO consults and trains across the globe in the areas of multicultural competency development, increasing influence in organizations and managing a diverse workforce. Dr. Tolbert, principal, is the author of *Reversing the Ostrich Approach to Diversity: Pulling Your Head Out of the Sand*, a timely answer to the renewed urgency for actionable diversity information. Contact ECCO to strengthen your global competitiveness with enhanced communication strategies and cross-cultural skills.

Submitted by Amy S. Tolbert, Ph.D., CSP, Principal

ECCO International

1519 McClung Drive

St. Paul, MN 55112

(651) 636-0838

AmyTolbert@ECCOInternational.com

www.ECCOInternational.com

Turning e-Mail Drains into Productivity Gains: Which e-Mail Would You Rather Read?

BETTER COMMUNICATIONS

Many people have a hard time recognizing exactly what is wrong with a bad e-mail, much less how to fix it. To set standards and create a culture for good writing companywide, everyone needs to understand and agree on the attributes of a clear, action-driving document, whether an e-mail, report, or proposal. This exercise consists of editing followed by a side-by-side deconstruction of a poor document and an analysis of a good document. The objective is to learn to recognize at least five major mistakes and learn how to improve them.

AUDIENCE

Anyone who writes on the job! From new hires to leaders managing remote teams, clear writing is a strategic business essential. The group session can accommodate up to fourteen learners.

OBJECTIVE

- To practice identifying and correcting the attributes of a clearly written document.

TIME REQUIRED

It works best to allow at least 24 hours for the pre-work editing exercise. The group session should take 45 minutes at most.

MATERIALS AND EQUIPMENT

- Electronic copies of the *before* (un-annotated) document to send out for the pre-work editing exercise to each participant.

- Paper or electronic copies of the annotated *before* and *after* documents for each participant at the session. If you conduct the session on an online meeting platform, you will need to load electronic copies to share. ***Note:*** All three documents can be downloaded from this book's online tools.

- Training room with projection if you do the exercise in person.

AREA SETUP

The activity may be conducted live or online. Any space comfortable for a small group around a table.

PROCESS

Pre-Work

1. Introduce the editing activity with an e-mail including the following questions:

   - Have you ever received an e-mail and had no idea:

     - What the reader wanted you to do?

     - Why you received the message?

     - If there were next steps or deadlines?

   - How about the alternative? Have you ever received a message in which:

     - Headlines guide you to the most important points?

     - Next steps and deadlines are highlighted?

     - It's clear what the purpose and key message are?

2. Ask learners to critique the *before* document, paying particular attention to the attributes above. Tell them to bring the document to the group session. Extra points for rewriting it! Attach a copy of the annotated *before* document and send the e-mail.

At the Session

1. At the group session, invite all to share their document critiques and suggestions for improvement.

2. After everyone has shared, show the annotated *before* and *after* and discuss which they prefer and why. What did they miss?

3. The clear, easy-to-read *after* messages are reader-centered—and they drive action—reducing both writing time *and* reading time.

4. Summarize by asking participants both online and in person what they will implement as a result of this exercise.

INSIDER TIPS

- It is ideal to have a seasoned writer or editor lead this exercise.

- For even greater impact and buy-in, produce *before* and *after* documents from your department for the group portion. It's always better when learners see writing from their own organization; that's when the learning moment emerges.

About Better Communications

We enable companies globally to use written communications as a strategic advantage. Our expert team trains and coaches professionals and executives to write clearly and persuasively. Essential to success, great business writing delivers game-changing improvements in ROI and productivity. Clear writing—whether in documents or decks—provides a well-lit path that drives profitability across any enterprise.

Our easy-to-learn writing process means more business "wins":

- Improve and reflect the value of your brand.

- Double writing quality—as measured by our innovative assessment tools.

- Improve productivity: learners show a 30 to 50 percent gain in writing speed.

- Get your messages across fast—speeding decisions and action.

Our customers are loyal fans because of payoffs to the top and bottom line, vastly improved teamwork, and newfound agility.

Submitted by Deborah Dumaine

Better Communications

200 Fifth Avenue, 4th Floor

Waltham, MA 02451

(781) 895-9555

info@bettercom.com

www.bettercom.com

BEFORE

ROURKE, JED

From: Jed Rourke

Sent: November 13, 2020 1:04 PM

To: Tim Robinson, Amir Tardif, Juliana Rodriguez

Cc: Emilio Reinhardt, Jennie Martin

Subject: AquaNose batches

After reviewing the most recent QA report, I did some investigating into the capability of the carton checkweigher of detecting obvious low fills. We have had the checkweigher set at a minimum of 40.6 grams. However, we are averaging around 45.5 grams. I watched the checkweigher on a few different occasions for 5 minutes straight and never saw anything less than 44.7 grams go by.

If we were to set up the checkweigher at 95 percent of the average for each batch, which would be approximately 43.2 grams (this is very conservative since the only significant variation for any component is the coated bottle), I think we could detect some obvious low fills without running the risks of rejecting any good units or creating much more work for the operators. My proposal is that if a carton is rejected, the operators should check to be sure that everything is in the carton. If everything is indeed in there, run it through again. If it rejects again, we are going to have to assume it is a low fill since the checkweigher will be set based on lower-than-expected weights for each individual component. To see if we are actually detecting low fills, we should save and evaluate the rejected cartons for a while.

The reason for doing all this is to address the complaint problem for low filled units of New Zealand's product, which has been significant enough to be included on the Monthly QA Compliance

(continued)

Report, which is sent to Drucilla Sherman (VP of QA). I realize this is New Zealand's problem, not technically ours, and I assume they are addressing it, but if we have a chance to minimize the amount of defects going out of here I think we should probably do it. Talk to your operators to review my suggestion; then send me the rejects. This will enable me to determine if we're detecting low fills. Plus, as we fill more and more AquaNose here, it will provide a safety net for us to detect the obvious low fills that could prompt complaints in the field.

Jed

BEFORE (ANNOTATED)

ROURKE, JED

From: Jed Rourke

Sent: November 13 2020 1:04 PM

To: Tim Robinson, Amir Tardif, Juliana Rodriguez

Cc: Emilio Reinhardt, Jennie Martin

Subject: AquaNose batches

> *This subject line is vague.*

After reviewing the most recent QA report, I did some investigating into the capability of the carton checkweigher of detecting obvious low fills. We have had the checkweigher set at a minimum of 40.6 grams. However, we are averaging around 45.5 grams. I watched the checkweigher on a few different occasions for 5 minutes straight and never saw anything less than 44.7 grams go by.

> *This level of detail is unnecessary and confuses the reader.*

If we were to set up the checkweigher at 95 percent of the average for each batch, which would be approximately 43.2 grams (this is very conservative since the only significant variation for any component is the coated bottle), I think we could detect some obvious low fills without running the risks of rejecting any good units or creating much more work for the operators. My proposal is that if a carton is rejected, the operators should check to be sure that everything is in the carton. If everything is indeed in there, run it through again. If it rejects again, we are going to have to assume it is a low fill since the checkweigher will be set based on lower-than-expected weights for each individual component. To see if we are actually detecting low fills, we should save and evaluate the rejected cartons for awhile.

> *This sentence is 64 words long.*

> *The proposal is buried in the middle of a paragraph.*

The reason for doing all this is to address the complaint problem for low filled units of New Zealand's product, which has been significant enough to be included on the Monthly QA Compliance Report which is sent to Drucilla Sherman (VP of QA). I realize this is New Zealand's

> *He introduces the reason for this e-mail at the end.*

(continued)

problem, not technically ours, and I assume they are addressing it, but if we have a chance to minimize the amount of defects going out of here I think we should probably do it. Talk to your operators to review my suggestion, then send me the rejects. This will enable me to determine if we're detecting low fills. Plus, as we fill more and more AquaNose here, it will provide a safety net for us to detect the obvious low fills that could prompt complaints in the field.

Jed

AFTER

ROURKE, JED

From: Jed Rourke

Sent: November 13 2020 1:04 PM

To: Tim Robinson, Amir Tardif, Juliana Rodriguez

Cc: Emilio Reinhardt, Jennie Martin

Subject: Using the checkweigher to detect AquaNose low fills

Problem: complaints of low-filled AquaNose

We have received several complaints about low-filled units of AquaNose packaged in New Zealand. These complaints have shown up on the Monthly QA Compliance Report. I investigated the capability of the carton checkweigher and learned we can better use this tool to detect under-filled units.

Current setting of 40.6 grams is too low to detect most low fills

We currently have the checkweigher set at a minimum of 40.6 grams, but the average for each batch is 45.5 grams. When I observed the checkweigher, I did not see any weight less than 44.7 grams.

Suggested way to detect low fills: set checkweigher to 43.2 grams

By setting the checkweigher at 95 percent of the average weight for each batch (43.2 grams), we can detect obvious low fills without rejecting good units or creating more work for the operators. The setting of 43.2 grams is conservative—the coated bottle is the only component that varies.

(continued)

Bonus Activity I.1

Let's try this procedure for a future batch

1. If a carton is rejected, make sure everything is in the carton.

2. If everything is there, run the carton again.

3. If the checkweigher rejects the carton again, assume it is a low fill.

4. To see whether we are accurately detecting low fills, save and evaluate the rejects.

Next Steps

1. Please meet with your operators to review the new procedure.

2. Send me the rejects at the end of the batch—I will determine whether we are detecting low fills. If so, we can make this a permanent procedure.

Help us prevent future complaints

I realize this is New Zealand's issue, but we should take any opportunity to minimize the number of defects. Plus, as we fill more and more AquaNose here, we'll have a safety net to detect the low fills. This could save us from receiving the same complaints.

Please let me know if you have any questions.

Thanks,

Jed

Build or Repair: A Tool for Difficult Communication

GLOBAL NOVATIONS

Build or Repair is an engaging and practical tool that will equip and empower participants to have necessary conversations, even when the dialogue may be difficult. It enables participants to explore with whom they may need to build or repair relationships—especially the critical ones, such as leader, manager, peer, direct report, mentor, advocate—within the workplace via a structured process.

This tool challenges participants to think and prepare strategically for courageous conversations focused on building or repairing relationships, to ensure that they get what they need from the dialogue while maintaining the relationship. It is designed to enhance participants' communication, collaboration, and conflict-resolution skills. Build or Repair often complements the following workplace conversations: performance (individual and team), development, new reporting relationships, and networking (visibility).

OBJECTIVES

- To gain skill and comfort in having necessary conversations, even when it may be difficult.
- To prepare to think strategically for potentially challenging conversations.
- To move beyond awareness to the application of the Build or Repair tool.

AUDIENCE

Conducted with members of an intact team. An even number of participants to engage in the paired conversations is required.

TIME REQUIRED

60 to 75 minutes (allows for one to two rounds of conversation per participant pair).

MATERIALS AND EQUIPMENT

- One Build or Repair Worksheet for each participant. *Note:* This worksheet can be downloaded from this book's online tools.

AREA SETUP

A large space set up with chairs and tables with sufficient room for private, paired conversations.

PROCESS

1. Open by saying, "Research shows that high trust companies outperform low trust companies by nearly 300 percent and are three times more profitable. This fact clearly articulates and reinforces why organizations are focused on creating high trust environments in which everyone can effectively communicate and collaborate as well as fully contribute. Building and repairing relationships via courageous conversations will enable and empower organizations to create an inclusive, trusting environment where everyone is engaged and their differences are embraced to accelerate growth, drive innovation, and optimize talent. Today we will focus on engaging in courageous conversations to build and repair relationships." (The source for the opening statistic is Stephen M.R. Covey's *The Speed of Trust*.)

2. Review the objectives and explain that this will be an individual, introspective exercise.

3. Distribute one Build or Repair Worksheet to each participant. Say that you would like them to reflect on two relationships with people in the room: one that they need to build because the relationship is new or where they need to take trust to the next level to achieve optimal performance and one in which trust has been broken for some reason (e.g., lack of accountability, clarity, collaboration, commitment, or confidence) and is in need of repair. Repairing relationships is all about having challenging and courageous conversations to elevate performance and enhance collaboration, communication, and most importantly, contribution.

4. Say that with these two relationships in mind, they should spend the next 20 minutes completing the Build or Repair Worksheet that outlines courageous conversations for these relationships. Tell them to challenge themselves to complete the entire worksheet. Say, "While the work to repair a relationship is tough and may test you, it will also allow you to reap rewards beyond belief if it is done appropriately and authentically."

5. After 20 minutes say, "I'd like you to get up and find one of the people for whom you completed part of the worksheet." Allow a few minutes for pairs to form, then say, "If you were able to connect with a person for whom you completed a Build or Repair worksheet—GREAT! If you were selected by someone before you were able to reach a person for whom you completed the worksheet, stay with your current partner (the person who selected you) and try to reach your person next time." *Note:* Unselected people can come to the front of the room and review their worksheets in pairs to obtain ideas.

6. Next, say, "With your partner, engage in a real-time and real-life courageous conversation focused on the information captured on your worksheet. Don't be taken aback if you are selected by a person you didn't anticipate would select you. This is one of the reasons that this exercise is so powerful. It allows you to discover discretely relationship-related challenges that you may have not known otherwise. In addition, remember that no one knows whether you and your partner are "building" or "repairing" your relationship."

7. State that one person within the pair will lead the conversation by going first. While a member of the pair is speaking, it is important for the other person to actively listen and ask clarifying questions as appropriate. Once the first person is finished, switch roles and the second person will share. Tell them that if they are not paired with the person for whom they intended the message, they can use it as a practice opportunity to obtain feedback.

8. Say that they have 20 minutes for both to share. Give a 5-minute warning and have them form new pairs and repeat the process.

9. After two or three rounds state, "I know that there are people who did not have an opportunity to engage in a courageous conversation with the person of his or her choice. I encourage you to continue this exercise after today's session or over coffee or lunch."

10. Summarize the activity by saying, "Let's come back together. After engaging in such a powerful and thought-provoking exercise, I'd love to hear your insights

and learning from the paired conversations. Remember that the specifics of your paired conversations are confidential. Therefore, I'd like for you to share your insights and how you will apply this new knowledge upon your return to work." After three to five comments, encourage them to use the tool to engage in courageous conversations with others.

11. Lead a debriefing with some of these questions:

- What was it like to have this type of conversation?

- What were you thinking and feeling?

- What worked well?

- What challenges did you encounter? How do you recommend productively and proactively addressing these challenges?

- What suggestions can you share with the rest of the group to have these conversations successfully?

- How could you use this tool in your career or personal life?

- When is it easiest to build or repair a relationship? When is it the hardest?

- What strategies can you leverage to prepare for a courageous conversation?

FACILITATOR NOTES

- This is a tool that allows potentially emotional issues to be explored in a non-judgmental way.

- It provides a safe environment that encourages transparency and truthfulness.

- It takes defensiveness and debate out of the conversation because participants are engaging in productive dialogue that is collaborative and solution-focused.

- In order to receive maximum benefit from this tool, participants should:

  - Lean into their discomfort or the uncomfortable zone that this exercise may cause.

  - Practice active listening.

  - Be respectfully curious by showing up as interested in the other person's perspective and point of view.

  - Have open minds.

  - Ask questions to confirm understanding.

- Be present and fully engaged in the conversation.
- Have a willingness to be vulnerable.

INSIDER'S TIPS

1. Facilitating this exercise requires everyone being non-judgmental.

2. Make sure the environment is safe for all participants by modeling calmness and objectivity.

3. The exercise requires the facilitator to listen more than talk; let participants take the lead.

4. During the debriefing, focus on the process versus the content in order to maintain confidentiality.

About Global Novations

Global Novations helps organizations unleash the capacity of their employees. Formed by the 2010 merger of industry leaders Global Lead Management Consulting and Novations Group, the new firm provides an enhanced suite of services around diversity and inclusion, talent optimization, and market optimization. Global Novations is based in Boston, with an office in Cincinnati, and maintains operations in Europe, Asia, and Latin America.

Submitted by Janet Reid, Ph.D., Managing Partner; Paul Terry, Vice President; LaToya Everett, Business Sector Director

Global Novations

10 Guest Street, Suite 300

Boston, MA 022127

(888) 652-9975

info@globalnovations.com

www.globalnovations.com

◼◼◀ GLOBALNOVATIONS

BUILD OR REPAIR EXERCISE WORKSHEET

The following worksheet can be downloaded at this book's online tools.

To begin: Ask yourself with whom you need to have a crucial conversation and about what. Do you want to build or repair a relationship? When you are clear, prepare for your dialogue by completing the build and/or repair section of the worksheet provided.

Date: _____

Name: _____

I would like to build my relationship with

_____

The key reason(s) I want to build the relationship is/are:

_____

_____

_____

_____

I would like to repair my relationship with

_____

The key reason(s) I want to repair the relationship is/are:

_____

_____

_____

_____

Build Section

Directions: Complete the following questions if you would like to build a new relationship with someone you don't know very well or if you'd like to build upon an existing relationship by taking it to the next level.

It is important that you know . . . (Jot down anything that you think is critical for the person to know as it relates to building your relationship.)

_____

_____

_____

_____

_____

_____

_____

_____

I will commit to building our relationship by . . . (List specific actions you will take to help build the relationship.)

_____

_____

_____

_____

_____

_____

_____

I would like for you to take the following actions to ensure that we build our relationship . . . (List specific actions that you would like the other person to take.)

_____

_____

_____

_____

_____

_____

_____

_____

What are your thoughts on what I have said so far?

_____

_____

_____

_____

_____

_____

Would you like to build our relationship?

_____

_____

_____

_____

_____

_____

Bonus Activity I.2

If you would like to build our relationship, from your perspective, how will you know that it has been built? (Ask the person this question and capture his/her thoughts.)

_____

_____

_____

_____

_____

_____

_____

We will commit to the following actions and next steps to build our relationship . . . (Complete after you both have discussed the commitment and next steps.)

_____

_____

_____

_____

_____

_____

_____

_____

Additional thoughts:

_____

_____

_____

_____

_____

_____

_____

Repair Section

Directions: Complete the following questions if you would like to repair an existing relationship

I feel our relationship is broken and in need of repairing because we don't have . . . (Be specific as it relates to what the relationship is missing, e.g., trust, communication, accountability, commitment.)

_____

_____

_____

_____

_____

_____

I feel that our relationship is broken because of the following events, actions, conversations, etc. (Be specific on what caused the issue(s) cited above.)

_____

_____

_____

_____

_____

_____

_____

I would like to hear your thoughts on what I have said so far . . . (Ask the other person for input. The objective is to gain the other person's perspective. Therefore, listen carefully and don't interrupt. Capture his/her thoughts.)

_____

_____

_____

_____

_____

_____

_____

I will commit to repairing our relationship by . . . (List specific actions you are willing to take.)

_____

_____

_____

_____

_____

_____

_____

I would like for you to take the following actions to ensure that we repair our relationship . . . (List specific actions that you would like the other person to take.)

_____

_____

_____

_____

_____

_____

_____

_____

I will know that we have repaired our relationship when . . .

_____

_____

_____

_____

_____

_____

_____

How will you know when we have repaired our relationship? (Ask the person this question and capture his/her thoughts below.)

_____

_____

_____

_____

_____

_____

_____

We commit to the following actions and next steps to repair our relationship . . .
(Complete after you both have discussed the commitment and next steps.)

_____

_____

_____

_____

_____

_____

_____

Additional thoughts:

_____

_____

_____

_____

_____

_____

_____

_____

SECTION II

MOVING INTO MANAGEMENT

Introduction

In many organizations, once you have proven your abilities, the next logical step is to move into management. Although this might appear logical, many organizations do not take the time to ensure that those who are moving into management positions have the skills, abilities, knowledge, and even attitude that will ensure they will be successful in a managerial position. In most cases, managers manage people and manage projects—two very different tasks.

Managing is very different than doing. There is a whole set of skills, knowledge, and attitudes you need to succeed. How good are the individuals your organization is moving into management at these skills: influencing, directing, collaborating, managing change, accepting responsibility and accountability, motivating, delegating problem solving, project management, decision making, presenting to executives, understanding financial reports, or working in teams, just to name a few.

Unfortunately, new managers who have not been developed for their roles emulate their previous managers, whether they were effective or not. The managers of almost every organization could be better prepared and developed for their roles as they move in management.

Whether you are a moving into a new managerial job or are responsible for developing employees in your organizations to be prepared for their new roles, I think you will appreciate the professionalism and content that went into each of the six chapters in this section.

- Chapter 5, "Are You Prepared for Your Next Project?" by Systemation, explains the process and activities of project management, defining the roles held by various individuals.

- Chapter 6, "Using Involvement in Decision Making to Increase Engagement" by Interaction Associates, Inc., will prove to be helpful to any new (or seasoned) manager. The model and definitions for five decision-making methods demonstrate the need for the level of involvement to increase as the need for ownership increases.

- In Chapter 7, "How to 10X Your Influence," VitalSmarts offers an easy to remember matrix that demonstrates how a manager can be more persuasive by simply tapping into more than one source of influence.

- Chapter 8, "Speaking Up" by PowerSpeaking, Inc., is fun to read and so filled with practical advice about presenting to the C-suite, you will wonder why you haven't learned this common-sense approach before.

- Chapter 9, "Raising the Talent Bar" by Paradigm Learning, Inc., delivers a definition of business acumen and why it is a critical business skill. Suggestions are provided for how an organization can improve managers' business acumen. You will love the sample list of questions.

- Chapter 10, "Eliminate Us vs. Them Dynamics" by Learning as Leadership, tackles the very difficult emotional situation when someone has argued too long and too hard for a certain position. Learning to reverse the spiral is a skill all of us could use—even if we are not managers or even future managers.

- The bonus activity, "3D Perception Sharing," submitted by The Dede Henley Group, happens to be one of my all-time favorite activities. It is designed for building communication and improving relationships between two teams that need to work together. A skilled facilitator is required for success.

Chapter 5

Are You Prepared for Your Next Project?

SYSTEMATION

In This Chapter

- Explanation of projects and the four disciplines involved.
- Explanation of what occurs in the four phases of a project.
- Definition of the roles required for a successful project.

What Is a Project?

Big projects are easy to spot. Building a bridge. Merging a company. Organizing a major sports event. Creating new software. Other projects are simpler and smaller scale. Small projects tend to be less than three months in duration and have one to three people working on them who also have other work responsibilities. All projects share this definition:

- Projects are temporary endeavors undertaken to create a unique product.
- "Temporary" means every project has a definite beginning and a definite end.

- "Unique" means the product is different in some distinguishing way from other similar products.
- The product can be tangible or intangible.

Projects have three different types of people involved in them:

- Team members do the actual work required to complete the project.
- One or more sponsors authorize the project, commit organizational resources, and make crucial decisions.
- Stakeholders have a vested interest in the outcome of the project and can influence it positively or negatively.

Even though most work in today's world is done through projects, not all people label their work as projects. As a result, they may not take advantage of the well-developed project disciplines available to them. Failure to use these disciplines can lead to:

- Poor quality products.
- Disorganized and wasted efforts.
- Chronic delays.
- Frustrated project stakeholders.

It's time to recognize projects (big and small) for what they are and embrace the disciplines associated with them. It's time to prepare.

The Four Vital Project Disciplines

Successful projects involve four distinct disciplines:

- Project management
- Business analysis
- Product development
- Change management

Each of these disciplines has standardized roles and responsibilities, terminology, skills, and processes. Some even have trade associations and professional certifications. Medium- to large-sized projects generally need one or more professionals from each discipline on the project team. On smaller or budget-strapped projects, one person may be responsible for all four areas.

The Four Distinct Project Phases

All projects involve four phases:

- Planning
- Specifying
- Building
- Implementing

Certain industries have subdivided these phases into additional categories to fit their specific project needs. Some industries use different jargon. But whatever terminology you use, these four phases are essential for successful projects. During each project phase, the professionals from each project discipline have varying responsibilities—from none at all to full-time engagement.

Too often, the leaders for small projects have the responsibility for a successful outcome but lack project training. People are not born with an understanding of project dynamics, the project lifecycle or the four vital project disciplines listed above. They need training or coaching from an experienced peer, manager, or outside expert. The following sections will look at the four vital project disciplines in detail and the role of each discipline at each project phase.

Project Management

Definition: Project management is predicting, with as much certainty as is possible or required, the project's scope, time, and cost at completion and then embracing reality and influencing activities to meet those predictions.

The role of a project manager is broad. Project managers:

- Provide leadership and motivation.
- Maintain focus and commitment.
- Coordinate team member activities.
- Use resources efficiently and effectively.

Project managers are involved in five activities (shown in Figure 5.1) over the life of a project, all with the goal of moving the project to a negotiated end point:

- *Initiate:* recognize that a project or phase should begin and commit to do so.
- *Plan:* devise and maintain a workable scheme to accomplish the objectives of a project.

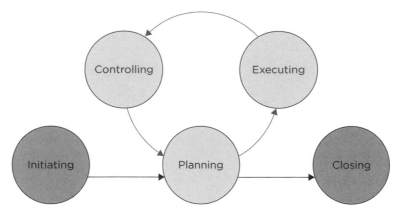

Figure 5.1 Project Manager Roles

- *Execute:* coordinate people and other resources to carry out the plan.
- *Control:* ensure the project objectives are met by monitoring and measuring progress and taking necessary corrective actions.
- *Close:* formalize the acceptance of the project or phase and bring it to an orderly end.

The initiating and closing phases of a project happen only once during the life of the project. Planning, executing, and controlling are cycles that happen throughout the life of the project, usually on a weekly basis.

The benefits of project management include:

- Products delivered closer to the predicted scope, time, and cost.
- More trust in client relationships.
- Better ability to make strategic decisions at the organizational level.
- Cleaner management of stakeholder expectations.
- Less unnecessary chaos for team members.
- Increased productivity.

Business Analysis

Definition: Business analysis is acquiring knowledge of an organization's structure, policies, and operations; identifying areas needing improvement; and recommending solutions that enable the organization to achieve its goals.

Business analysts must understand the business goals and objectives, as well as the background, of the organization. Their role is to:

- Find cost saving opportunities.
- Increase efficiencies.
- Decrease errors and issues.
- Identify the impact of a solution inside and outside the organization.

Business analysts engage in the four activities shown in Figure 5.2:

- *Elicit:* Gather requirements from stakeholders.
- *Analyze:* Organize and prioritize requirements so they can be communicated and approved.
- *Validate:* Assess proposed solutions and validate the stated requirements have been met.
- *Implement:* Prepare the organization to accept the solution.

These activities require interfacing effectively with people at all levels of the organization. Business analysis enables a more precise description of what is needed, which leads to on-target deliverables and more efficient work during product development. It also ensures greater communication between the business unit and the product development team.

Product Development

Definition: *Product development is creating products, tangible or intangible, with new or different characteristics that offer new or additional benefits to internal or external customers.*

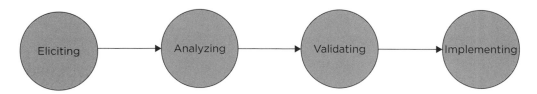

Figure 5.2   Business Analyst Activities

Domain experts are the individuals who fulfill the role of the product developers. The unique nature of the product determines which domain experts are needed. These experts:

- Advise the project manager when needed.
- "Build" their portion of the product as specified.
- Integrate their work with the work of the other domain experts.

Product developers are responsible for the three activities shown in Figure 5.3:

- *Design:* Create a conceptual detailed specification of what is going to be developed.
- *Develop:* Take the conceptual specification and make it a reality.
- *Verify:* Ensure the end product meets the stated requirements.

The benefits of product development are short and sweet. Products are developed in a much more efficient way and at a higher level of quality. This results in a shorter development cycle.

Change Management

Definition: *Change management supports the implementation of a change within an organization to minimize stress and ensure its sustainability.*

Change managers:

- Identify the behaviors required for the product or service to have the desired impact on the organization.
- Determine how to encourage the behavioral shift.
- Ensure the overall change goal is clear to stakeholders.
- Obtain buy-in from stakeholders.

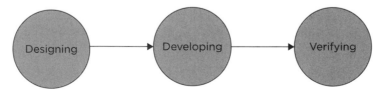

Figure 5.3 Product Developer Activities

- Inspire adoption of the required behaviors.
- Create "stickiness" so the required behaviors become habits and not a here-today-gone-tomorrow endeavor.

Often, change managers have communication, learning, and reward specialists available on an as-needed basis throughout the change. Change managers engage in the three activities displayed in Figure 5.4:

- *Prepare:* Define the change management strategy and develop the sponsorship model.
- *Manage:* Develop and implement the change management plan.
- *Reinforce:* Collect and analyze feedback, diagnose gaps, and manage resistance.

Change management shortens and diminishes the dip in performance that results from a change. It also sustains the change, making it less likely that things will revert back to the status quo.

Roadmap to Project Success

Now, let's go through the different phases of a project and describe how each discipline contributes during each phase. As mentioned earlier, larger project teams may have one or more representatives from each discipline. On smaller projects, one individual may be responsible for all four disciplines. Before assigning project responsibilities, a project lead needs to weigh each team member's strengths and weaknesses. Sometimes, it is necessary to assign a task for which a person is not prepared, but that is not an ideal arrangement.

Table 5.1 shows three different assignment scenarios. There are many more options, depending on the size and complexity of your project, as well as your budget and timetable.

Figure 5.4   Change Manager Activities

Are You Prepared for Your Next Project?

Table 5.1 Assignment Scenarios

Functional Roles Assigned

Team Member	Project Manager	Business Analyst	Domain Expert	Change Manager
Project Lead	X	X	X	X

Functional Roles Assigned

Team Member	Project Manager	Business Analyst	Domain Expert	Change Manager
Project Lead	X	X	X	X
Member 2			X	

Functional Roles Assigned

Team Member	Project Manager	Business Analyst	Domain Expert	Change Manager
Project Lead	X		X	
Member 2		X	X	X
Member 3			X	

Planning the Project

Definition: During the planning phase of a project, an initial plan is developed that describes what is going to be delivered by the project, how long it is going to take, and what resources will be needed to complete the work.

Putting together the plan is the responsibility of the *project manager*, with input from others.

It is a scary thing for project managers to predict where a project will end up because it holds them accountable. But the planning phase is imperative. If there isn't an end point for the project manager to drive toward, there won't be any management or direction for the project. The project will drift.

Scope, time, and cost make up the three sides of what is known as "the project triangle," as shown in Figure 5.5:

- Scope is the sum of all products to be delivered. It includes all the incremental work required to deliver the product at the negotiated grade of quality.

Developing Talent for Organizational Results

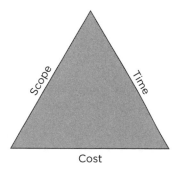

Figure 5.5 Project Triangle

- Time is the duration needed to complete all the associated project work and is measured in calendar days, months, and years.

- Cost is the monetary value of the labor expended and all other direct charges that will be incurred during the project.

When the value of one side of the project triangle is changed, one or both of the other sides are almost always affected. Successfully managing projects requires an understanding of the dynamics of these relationships. When one side of the triangle is an accurate reflection of the demands of the other two sides, the project triangle is "harmonized."

Example: Can you build a 5,000-square-foot home in two months at a cost of $40,000? No. The time does not accurately represent the demands of scope and cost. To harmonize the triangle for this project, the cost of the home would have to be increased or its scope decreased, or both.

The project manager assembles the initial plan, which needs to include several elements. Some of the elements come from other team members:

- Description and purpose of the project.

- High-level objectives to be accomplished.

- Description of the end product.

- The approach to developing the product.

- Identification of the sponsor(s) and stakeholders.

- A milestone schedule.

- A list of required resources.

Once approved, the initial plan becomes a baseline for gauging progress and actual results.

Business analysts articulate the project objectives and provide a detailed description of the end product. They have insight into the customer's organization, know what needs to change or be created, and why it is important. The product may already exist and simply need modification. Or the customer's situation may call for something entirely new. An end product can be tangible (consumable, document, widget), intangible (service, process, experience), or a combination of both.

When it comes to the project approach, it is the *domain experts* who take this on. They must ask themselves, "Does the end product need to be delivered in one fell swoop (that is, putting on a conference, changing a benefit system, or selecting a vendor) or can it be developed through multiple 'less than perfect' versions?" For example, some software can be developed in phases—with Version 1 having certain basic features and Version 2 have more bells and whistles, etc.

Domain experts need to ask themselves whether the project has special circumstances such as a severe time constraint or extreme development risks. If the project is under a time constraint, the domain expert may have to modify the standard approach and conduct development phases in parallel instead of sequentially.

If there are big development risks, then domain experts may choose an iterative development approach, where the project is completed in small pieces and each small piece is checked for functionality and quality before moving to the next step. Iterative development allows the team to find and correct problems as they happen, instead of finding a show-stopping problem after months of hard work. Iterative development yields a more certain finish and also allows quick project shut down if a course correction or Plan B is needed.

Specifying the Product

Definition: *Defining the deliverable in detail.*

Here, the *business analyst* plays a prominent role in eliciting requirements from stakeholders and creating a requirements roadmap for the domain experts.

A business analyst's primary tool for eliciting requirements is interviews. These interviews are not casual. The analyst prepares carefully for them by developing a list of stakeholders to be interviewed and tailoring interview questions for each one.

To obtain high-quality information, the business analyst needs to:

- Pose open-ended questions.
- Elicit both facts and emotions.

- Watch for resistance and hostility.
- Listen to and observe what is said and not being said.
- Ask questions to fill in the gaps.

After the interviews are complete, the business analyst writes a requirements document. Requirements need to be stated in a way so they contain the characteristics of SMART:

- **S**pecific: wording is clear, concise, and unambiguous.
- **M**easurable: contains criteria that can be tested.
- **A**chievable: can be successfully attained, given the project environment.
- **R**ealistic: is appropriate to the project scope and available resources.
- **T**raceable: can be associated with a stakeholder request.

After documenting all the requirements, the business analyst will notice natural groupings. The requirements should be sorted into these groups, and each group should have a title and description. This will aid the project sponsor and stakeholders in reviewing and approving them.

Project managers need to make sure the requirements fit the objectives and product description in the project plan. If they do not, the project triangle will need to be harmonized again by adjusting the time and resources needed to complete the project.

Issues

1. Need final approval on the brochure copy.
2. Need to add a "brochure mailed" milestone for brochure distribution. Awaiting mail house input.
3. Do we want to offer a vegetarian meal in addition to the meat and fish meals?
4. Do we need to add a temp between September 10 and October 20 to help with registration?
5. Should conference follow-up be a separate project or added here?

At the start of this project phase and until the project ends, the project manager will begin a weekly cycle of orchestrating the week's activities, monitoring progress to identify gaps between what was planned and what actually happened, and adjusting the next week's activities to close the gap.

Table 5.2 Sample Status Report

Milestone	Baseline	Scheduled	Variance	Complete	Notes
Start	1-Jun	1-Jun	0 d	Yes	
Venue selected	5-Jul	8-Jul	3 d	Yes	
Speakers under contract	25-Jul	22-Jul	-3 d	Yes	
Brochure printed	6-Aug	15-Aug	9 d	No	
Caterer selected	2-Sep	2-Sep	0 d	No	
Event night	26-Oct	26-Oct	0 d	No	
Payments made	28-Oct	28-Oct	0 d	No	
Finish	29-Oct	29-Oct	0 d	No	

A status report, like the one shown in Table 5.2, is sent out weekly to keep all stakeholders abreast of the project status. The report includes a "project milestones schedule" that shows the baseline dates from the project plan and the actual or planned dates. In addition, the report should list any open issues that are being worked on.

Building the Product

Definition: The build phase is when the "wants" become realities.

This phase is often the busiest part of the project and takes the majority of the project's duration to complete.

Depending on the product being built, one or more *domain experts* will carve out the set of requirements they are responsible for and begin fulfilling them as planned by the project manager. Each of the domain experts will build portions of the product. They all will verify their work meets their set of requirements and is at the desired level of quality.

It is the *business analyst's* responsibility to make sure all individual portions of the end product integrate as planned and meet the total set of requirements that came out of the planning phase of the project. If all requirements are not met, then the domain experts need to resolve the discrepancies. The business analyst also needs to look at the totality of the end product and validate that it meets the objectives stated in the project plan. It is not uncommon to find small portions of objectives that are not totally satisfied. When this happens, additional requirements need to be developed and additional product portions built.

The *project manager* will continue the cycle of orchestrating the week's activities as planned, monitoring progress to identify gaps between what was planned and what actually happened, and adjusting the next week's activities to close the gap. However, there is a good chance that sometime during the life of the project, a gap—either in scope, time, or cost—will be so large there is no chance of meeting the initial baseline defined in the project plan. During these times, project managers often become overly optimistic and think they can overcome the situation by working harder or relying on a miracle. These are bad ideas.

The best way to handle a gap is to meet with the project sponsor(s) and key stakeholders and present the situation to them. At any time in a project's lifecycle, there is an implied priority scheme for the project triangle. This priority scheme establishes which side of the project triangle is most flexible (lowest priority) and which is least flexible (highest priority). Based on which side of the project triangle is out of whack with the baseline and which sides of the project triangle are most flexible, a best-case compromise can be put together by the project manager and approved by the sponsor(s) and key stakeholders. No project manager wants to do this, but it is a common occurrence. Project sponsor(s) and key stakeholders are much more amenable when they are told of the situation as early as possible. Sponsors and stakeholders can become very angry and frustrated if a project manager surprises them with a problem at the eleventh hour.

This phase in the project is also when the *change manager* begins preparation for the implementation phase. All projects bring about change. Either they are changing something that already exists or creating something new. Change requires getting people on board, setting new expectations, and more. The first thing a change manager must do is get a handle on the level of change taking place. To do this, they need to define the *current* state from the perspective of:

- Structure (organization, job responsibilities, infrastructure).
- People (skills, job description, capabilities).
- Process (work flow, responsibilities, enablers).
- Culture (attitudes, beliefs, rules).

Then, the change manager must do the same for the *future* state. From this information, it is possible for the change manager to identify the potential concerns and stress levels individuals will have during the transition from current to future state. Concerns and stress can lead to resistance, and change managers need a strategy for overcoming resistance.

A change strategy is developed by the change manager with input from the project sponsor(s) and key stakeholders. It takes into consideration the current and future states and uses communication, training, and rewards to create and sustain a successful change.

Implementing the Product

Definition: In this exciting phase, the product meets the real world.

The *business analyst* makes sure the desired impact is taking place by conducting review meetings to get feedback from stakeholders.

Often, the transition from current state to future state is not proceeding exactly as hoped for. Unforeseen resistance occurs, and the *change manager* needs to find a way to overcome that resistance.

The *project manager* continues the familiar weekly routine of orchestrating activities, identifying gaps, and taking corrective action until the project is complete. The project manager's last activity is to get final approval for the end product and close the project out.

Where Do You Go from Here?

Now that you have a high-level view of the four project disciplines, you may want to explore more. The following links will take you to the formal trade associations for each discipline:

- Project Management Institute: www.pmi.org
- International Institute for Business Analysis: www.theiiba.org
- Product Development and Management Association: www.pdma.org
- Association of Change Management Professionals: www.acpm.info

Next time you are assigned the lead on a project, you can impress your project sponsor and stakeholders with these deliverables:

- Project plan
- Status reports
- Stakeholders' interview questions
- Requirements document
- Change strategy

- A product that is exactly what everyone was anticipating, delivered on time and within budget
- It's sure to get you noticed.

KEY DEFINITIONS

Projects are temporary endeavors undertaken to create a unique product.

Project Disciplines

Project management is predicting, with as much certainty as is possible or required, the project's scope, time, and cost at completion, and then embracing reality and influencing activities to meet those predictions.

Business analysis is acquiring knowledge of an organization's structure, policies, and operations; identifying areas needing improvement; and recommending solutions that enable the organization to achieve its goals.

Product development is creating products, tangible or intangible, with new or different characteristics that offer new or additional benefits to internal or external customers.

Change management supports the implementation of a change within an organization to minimize stress and ensure its sustainability

Project Phases

During the *planning phase* of a project, an initial plan is developed that describes what is going to be delivered by the project, how long it is going to take, and what resources will be needed to complete the work.

Specifying the product means defining the deliverable in detail.

The *build phase* is when the "wants" become realities.

Implementing the product is the phase in which the product meets the real world.

About Systemation

Systemation is a results-driven training and consulting company that optimizes the performance of individuals and organizations by instilling practical, project-related processes and techniques across the enterprise. With unparalleled expertise in project management, business analysis, and agile development, we help transform the way people perform to maximize overall businesses success.

Our best-in-class services portfolio includes a broad range of measurable, observable, and reliable performance improvement learning solutions, including individual assessments, workshops, certificate programs, coaching, and post-training support. And unlike most other training companies that provide highly theoretical advice, Systemation provides only practical, immediately usable learning solutions that obtain desired business results!

Submitted by Ben Snyder, CEO

Systemation

12503 E. Euclid Drive, Suite 55

Centennial, CO 80111

(303) 756-1600

systemation@systemation.com

www.systemation.com

Sys·tem·a·tion

Chapter 6

Using Involvement in Decision Making to Increase Engagement

INTERACTION ASSOCIATES, INC.

In This Chapter

- A model and definitions for five decision-making methods.
- Clarification of the best situations in which to use each decision-making method.
- A case study that illustrates how the model may be used.

A tough challenge for managers and leaders today comes down to a central question: How do you involve stakeholders in critical business decisions—at the right time and at the right level—to achieve success? The challenge is compounded for leaders working in complex or matrix systems.

Regardless of the type or size of company, leadership experts usually agree about the value of leaders involving people who will be affected by decisions in the decisions themselves. It's critically important, and it can be mastered using simple and flexible frameworks. The example of Interaction Associate's client, Bon Secours St. Francis Health System, offers a powerful illustration of stakeholder involvement strategies in action.

Recently, Bon Secours St. Francis Health System in Greenville, South Carolina, sought to innovate a fundamentally new approach to patient care, while implementing a new electronic records system called Bon Secours ConnectCare. The complicated change initiative affected many stakeholders in a complex environment. The effort, led by Chief Medical Officer Mary Jo Cagle, required a savvy stakeholder strategy to engage physicians, nurses, patients, staff, and others in creating successful outcomes.

Dr. Cagle reports: "Our challenge was simple and ambitious at the same time: We wanted to deliver the right care, at the right time to the right patient . . . while minimizing the disruption that conversion to electronic records might cause. To succeed at this dramatic change, we needed to engage everyone across the spectrum—from our leaders to the people at the bedside delivering care."

Results

The results are nothing short of dramatic. "We've seen drops in mortality, complications, length of stay—all with no increases in costs," according to Dr. Cagle. "Physician satisfaction rates have also risen, according to our Gallup survey," she added.

St. Francis saw impressive results in just six months, much faster than the average of two years it takes most hospital systems to achieve similar goals from implementing electronic records.

The results included:

1. A 33 percent reduction in hospital-acquired infections (eighty-four patients annually).

2. The true engagement of a wide range of stakeholders—including housekeeping, pharmacists, chaplains, and palliative care nurses—to improve ICU care and reduce stay times.

3. A 50 percent reduction in readmissions of chronic obstructive pulmonary disease and acute renal care patients.

4. Successful negotiations with stakeholders to improve the patient environment at the diagnostics and therapeutics unit.

5. Improved physician satisfaction.

6. Increased bed availability.

7. Shortened average patient stay.

Maximum Appropriate Involvement

Dr. Cagle credits these results to strategies and tactics taken from Interaction Associates' powerful Facilitative Leadership® practices—especially a key practice of engaging stakeholders and vetting all points of view in order to solve problems. We call this practice, "Maximum Appropriate Involvement™." Dr Cagle says, "We needed to engage our leaders and those at the bedside, and we needed buy-in to make it work."

How does Maximum Appropriate Involvement work? It involves two steps to form a dynamic strategy for change leaders. The first is to assess exactly who needs to be involved and their level of support for the effort. The second is a model for decision-making called Levels of Involvement. This model helps leaders clarify the rationale behind a decision, drive to agreement, and get everyone on board for the change.

Without a decision-making model, change is fraught with pitfalls. Here's one: It begins with a leader soliciting input from key stakeholders. "Do it this way," the IT director, a key stakeholder, advises—thinking she is making the decision. When the change leader makes a different decision based on a variety of stakeholder inputs, the IT director is alienated and upset.

To the change leader, clear and transparent decision-making is a best friend. When a leader is clear at the outset, stakeholders know when and how their input will be used. At the same time, no time and energy are wasted on unnecessary rounds of agreement-building or, worse yet, backtracking to patch up hard feelings. The leader can make some up-front, conscious choices about how much collaboration is appropriate for each decision—and then move ahead. After all, there are many degrees of collaboration between making a decision unilaterally and delegating it to others.

As the level of involvement in decision making increases, so does the level of ownership or buy-in to the process and the outcome. Most leaders believe there are two modes of decision making: "decide and announce" or "consensus" (the scary one we all avoid). Because our model provides five modes of decision making, a change leader's ability to manage efficient and effective collaborative work increases exponentially. Examine the model in Figure 6.1 to consider these possibilities.

Notice that the horizontal axis represents "level of involvement" and the vertical axis represents "level of ownership." As you move up the circles from left to right, the decision-making methods require more stakeholder involvement—and so inspire in stakeholders a greater sense of ownership of the decision. Increased ownership inspires people to bring more of themselves and their talents to an initiative or project. This increased discretionary effort is directly linked to increased performance.

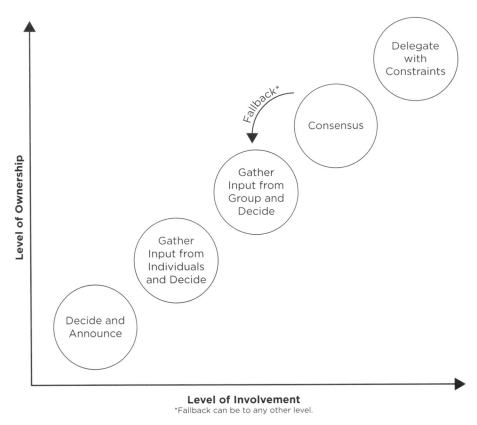

Figure 6.1 Levels of Involvement in Decision Making

Each of the decision-making methods is described in more detail below:

Decision Method	Definition
Decide and Announce	The change leader makes a decision with little or no input and announces the decision to those who will be affected by, or must carry out, the decision.
Gather Input from Individuals and Decide	The change leader asks selected individuals for ideas, suggestions, or information, then makes a decision.

Gather Input from Team and Decide	The change leader asks team members or a group of stakeholders to share their ideas in a meeting. The leader decides after hearing from everyone.
Consensus	A consensus decision is one that each and every member of the group or team is willing to support and help *implement* (even if they don't agree 100 percent with the decision). All key stakeholders have had an opportunity to give their opinions and to understand the implications of various options. Everyone, including the change leader, has the same formal power to support or block proposals. If consensus cannot be reached, the change leader has the ability to use a fallback decision-making option.
Delegate Decision with Constraints	The change leader defines the decision that needs to made in the form of a question(s), clarifies the constraints on the decision (e.g., budget, timeframe, quality requirements), and delegates the decision to others. The leader does not alter the decision as long as it adheres to the constraints/criteria set forth to the group.

Deploying the Model

How do you know when to use which decision-making option? It depends on the specifics of the decision you are making. Consider these factors as you make your choice:

- *Stakeholder Buy-In*. How much do key stakeholders need to be involved so that they can confidently support implementation of the decision?

- *Time Available*. How much time can be spent on making the decision? If you need an instant decision to respond to an emergency situation, *Decide and Announce* is your best bet.

- *Importance of the Decision*. How important is the issue to the people in your organization or community? The more important it is, the more the people who will be affected will want to be involved.

- *Information Needed*. Who has information or expertise that can contribute to making a quality decision? Involve those experts early.

- *Capability*. How capable and experienced are people in operating as decision-makers or as a decision-making team? If people are perfectly capable of making good decisions, why not trust them to make them? On the other hand, it may be helpful to let less seasoned employees test their decision-making "muscles" by giving them restraints and then seeing what they come up with.

- *Building Teamwork*. What is the potential value of using this opportunity to create a stronger team? A group working together on a tough decision will develop a lot over this process.

Applying clear decision-making processes and an appropriate level of involvement required for each decision inspires trust. The people on whom the leader must depend to support and implement business decisions will feel included and supported. As the level of trust grows in a group or organization, employees and teams become more willing to trust the leader to make decisions on their behalf. And in turn, leaders will feel more trust in delegating decisions to them.

As Dr. Cagle reports, "We have vital parties, nurses, board members, patients, and so on, who are not physicians, and you really need their cooperation. We, as doctors, only have one perspective; we cannot see the entire solution. Our perspective is one way. Someone has to smack us upside the head and say there's a bigger worldview we need to consider.

"This way of working together generates lots of solutions. The solution is faulty without the right people in the room. 'Ready–fire–aim' creates so much rework. I believe in the concept: 'Go slow to go fast.' Without it, we might otherwise spend days and weeks redoing what we could have done right the first time. A results-only focus and an action-oriented approach are appropriate for an emergency, but we can actually think and plan our actions with these long-term goals."

As decisions, structures and problems become more complicated, the numbers of vital stakeholders grow. Facilitative managers and leaders use Levels of Involvement as a core part of their toolkit to mange complex change and ensure measurable results.

About Interaction Associates, Inc.

Interaction Associates (IA) is a forty-year innovator of leadership development through consulting, training, and coaching services. IA's advanced methods empower leaders to build trust, engage employees, and foster collaboration to drive strong business results. IA's proprietary research shows that the "Return on Involvement" of employees yields measurable business results. In 2011, IA was named to Training Industry's Leadership Companies Watchlist of top innovators in the leadership field.

IA has global delivery capability and has consulted to more than one-third of the Fortune 500. It has corporate offices in Boston and San Francisco. More information is available at www.interactionassociates.com.

Submitted by Andrew Atkins, Director, Research and Development

Interaction Associates, Inc.

70 Fargo Street, Suite 908

Boston, MA 02210

(617) 535-7000

88 Kearny Street, Suite 1200

San Francisco, CA 94108

(415) 343-2600

info@interactionassociates.com

www.interactionassociates.com

Chapter 7

How to 10X Your Influence

VITALSMARTS

In This Chapter

- Six sources of influence managers/leaders use to drive organizational change.
- Rationale for the value of using multiple influences to effect change.
- Six cases describing how organizations have used the six influences.

Leaders who successfully drive organizational change rely on six different sources of influence at the same time. We have documented the success of this multi-pronged approach across organizational levels and across different problem domains. Those who succeed predictably and repeatedly don't differ from others by degrees. They differ exponentially. Managers and leaders who understand how to combine four to six sources of influence are up to ten times more successful at producing substantial and sustainable change in their organizations.

Our Serious Problems Are Rooted in Human Behavior

The U.S. financial sector has some of the most sophisticated risk assessment technologies and most sound regulatory policies in the world. Yet from 2003 to 2007, the world watched some of this country's most mature financial institutions fling themselves off a fiscal cliff. And this in spite of the fact that the capital markets had experienced a catastrophic "bubble" just seven years earlier. Just how could our behavior diverge so profoundly from painfully recent knowledge?

Unfortunately, the trend doesn't stop in the financial sector. In fact, the knowing/doing gap pervades every facet of our lives. For example, this year, U.S. healthcare organizations will harm hundreds of thousands of patients by making the same mistakes they've made for decades. More than three-fourths of management initiatives like six sigma, process reengineering, mergers and acquisitions, and major IT investments will fall far short of their potential for improving results. And despite our vast knowledge of human health, the leading causes of death are, at some level, *consensual*. It is not a failure of knowledge that increases our risks of suffering from heart disease or cancer—it is a failure of human behavior.

Planetary problems like terrorism, global warming, and the AIDS epidemic further confirm that the most important problems facing the human race escalate through human behavior.

Because We Lack Influence

In a world filled with never-ending streams of new technology and improvements in leadership methods, problems that can be solved with an invention, a well-delivered speech, or an influx of capital and equipment have already been solved. If articulating an argument or writing a check will eliminate a challenge, you can bet that challenge has already been put to rest.

However, chronic, persistent problems can't be solved so easily. That's because they're rooted in human behavior, and behavioral-based challenges typically won't go away with a single potent intervention. Unless and until we develop far more effective ways of thinking about and exerting influence on human behavior, we will never solve the most profound and persistent problems in our organizations, our personal lives, and our world.

Why Quick Fix Solutions Fall Short

Unfortunately, we live in a quick-fix world full of people who are gimmicked into believing simple solutions exist for their monumentally complex behavior problems—both personal and professional. We want one trick to get employees to improve quality and one trick to help us shed thirty pounds.

Unfortunately, most quick fixes don't work because the problem isn't fed by a single cause—it's fed by a conspiracy of causes.

Exponentially Increasing Your Success

If you want to confront persistent problem behavior, you need to combine multiple influences into an overwhelming strategy. Successful changers succeed where others fail because they "over-determine" success (Freud, 2010). Instead of focusing on a single root cause, they address all the root causes by combining a critical mass of influence strategies.

Patrice Putman, former director of employee development at MaineGeneral Health, understood this principle. When she wanted to improve patient safety and employee satisfaction by radically changing employees' confidence and ability to speak up candidly at critical times, she over-determined success with a multi-pronged influence effort.

Identifying the high-leverage behaviors that needed to change in her organization was only the first step for Putman. Training the target behaviors was also insufficient. Getting her employees to routinely act in new ways called for several additional influence strategies.

For instance, to help employees candidly speak up, she linked the new behavior to existing values. She instituted training to teach people how to voice concerns with ease. She garnered the support of key opinion leaders and aligned the performance-review systems with the target behaviors. She even made several changes to policies, work layout, and organizational structure. By targeting individual, social, and structural influence sources, Putman and her team completely transformed the corporate culture. Forty-one of the forty-two questions improved on the annual employee satisfaction survey, and employees are now 53 percent more likely to confront dangerous shortcuts and address mistakes in providing patient care.

The Study

Our research of the complexities of changing human behavior included three studies.

C-LEVEL CHALLENGES

In our first study, we interviewed twenty-five C-level leaders about their foremost challenges, including bureaucratic infighting, silo thinking, and lack of accountability. We constructed a survey to measure the scope of these issues and, more importantly, see what organizations did to deal with them. Fully 90 percent of the nine hundred managers and supervisors who took the survey said their organizations struggled with at least one entrenched habit; most said the problem negatively impacted areas including employee satisfaction, productivity, quality, and customer satisfaction. A high percentage of those surveyed employed only one influence strategy—for example, they offered training, redesigned the organization, or held a high-visibility retreat. A handful—fewer than 5 percent—used four or more sources of influence in combination. The differences in outcomes between these two groups were astounding. Those who used four or more sources of influence in combination were ten times more likely to succeed than those who relied on a single source of influence (the success rate jumped from 4 to 40 percent).

CORPORATE CHANGE INITIATIVES

Our second study involved a larger sample of C-level leaders and explored how they approached change initiatives. We focused on one hundred mission-critical initiatives—efforts such as internal restructurings, quality and productivity improvements, and new product launches. We wanted to see which sources of influence companies used to support their initiatives—and how many sources they employed. Here, too, we found that a high percentage of executives used only one approach, and that those who used four or more had the greatest likelihood of success.

PERSONAL CHALLENGES

In our third study, we focused on personal challenges such as overeating, smoking, overspending, or binge drinking. We randomly surveyed more than one thousand individuals, asking them to describe their attempts. Many attempted to alter their own behavior using a single approach (for example, join a gym, follow prescriptions in a book, or attend AA meetings)—and nearly all of them failed. Only 14 percent approached their problem using four or more strategies; for them, the success rate was four times higher, moving from 10 to 40 percent.

The Six Sources of Influence

Six sources of influence drive our behavior, and anyone with the ability to make change successful is adept at employing these sources in combination.

Motivation and ability are the foundation of our six-source model. We then subdivide these domains into three distinct categories: personal, social, and structural, which in turn reflect separate and highly developed bodies of literature: psychology, sociology, and organizational theory.

The first two domains, Personal Motivation and Ability, relate to sources of influence within an individual (motives and abilities) that determine that person's behavioral choices.

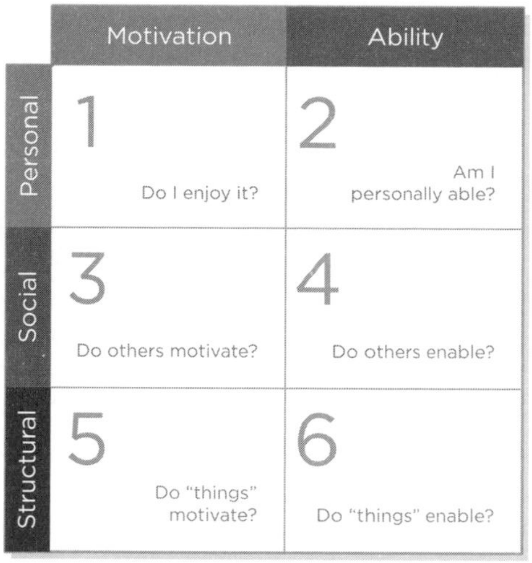

Figure 7.1   The Six Sources of Influence

The next two, Social Motivation and Ability, relate to how other people affect an individual's choices.

The final two, Structural Motivation and Ability, encompass the role of nonhuman factors, such as compensation systems, space, and technology. These are shown in Figure 7.1.

Using the Six Sources of Influence

Successful influencers increased their chances of success tenfold by combining strategies from at least four of the six sources of influence. In the following pages, we'll develop the six sources to see how leaders capitalize on the power found in each.

SOURCE 1: DO I ENJOY IT? PERSONAL MOTIVATION LINK TO MISSION AND VALUES

Change is hard because new behaviors are often difficult, uncomfortable, or even painful, whereas old behaviors are familiar and routine. For example, when a leader asks employees to undertake dramatic quality improvement efforts, there is enormous discomfort, conflict, and uncertainty. People are pushed to rethink processes, uncover problems, and reapportion power in the organization. Most people aren't motivated to do things that are uncomfortable or stressful, which is why most of these efforts fail (Black & Gregersen, 2008).

So how do you motivate someone who isn't motivated? The short answer is, "You don't." And that's because it's nearly impossible to get people to do something they aren't motivated to do. However, ineffective influencers compensate by putting pressure on people (Social Motivation) or bribing or threatening them with carrots and sticks (Structural Motivation). These strategies often backfire when used on someone who doesn't care.

Skilled influencers know how to build personal motivation to get people to care. They link new behaviors to values people already have. They find ways to invest new behaviors with meaning and drive home human consequences. In short, they put a human face on the new behaviors.

The key to personal motivation is to help people see the true implications of their actions and choices by connecting the new behaviors to deeply held values.

Although personal motivation is necessary, it's rarely enough. Successful influencers engage personal motivation, but then combine it with several additional sources of influence.

Source 1 Case Study: Connecting to Values at Spectrum Health

Who: Matt VanVranken, President, Spectrum Health

Influence Challenge: Influence 10,000 weary, overworked, and stressed health-care professionals to go beyond their basic job descriptions to create exceptional patient experiences.

Action: Make patient care personal. Connect employees' responsibilities to individual patients.

VanVranken periodically brings together several hundred managers and directors. At the start of a recent meeting, VanVranken asked a man in his early sixties to speak about his motorcycle accident.

The man described to the hospital staff his treatment experience at Spectrum Hospital following the accident. He introduced the physicians and nurses who attended him and also singled out countless others—for example, the employees who provided warm blankets before his surgeries and the people who ordered him popsicles when he wasn't allowed solid foods. He expressed his sincere thanks for the excellent care and for those who went out of their way to make his recovery possible. In a very poignant moment he described how a surgeon called his son the night before a crucial operation to remove his leg. In this conversation, the surgeon received key

Developing Talent for Organizational Results

information about his personality and work ethic that changed the course of the surgery. Ultimately, his leg was saved because a doctor took an extra moment to understand his unique circumstances.

Results: Through this touching experience, employees were poignantly reminded of how their actions affected the health and well-being of individual patients.

SOURCE 2: AM I PERSONALLY ABLE?
OVER-INVEST IN SKILL BUILDING

Far too many leaders unknowingly equate influence with motivation. We envision the iconic image of a leader at the podium revving up his or her troops and then sending them off to conquer. To these leaders, the name of the game is motivation. But true influencers don't make this mistake.

Successful leaders understand new behaviors can be far more intellectually, physically, and emotionally challenging than they appear. In truth, many problems stem from a lack of ability. Individuals often simply don't know how to do what's required.

A whole new body of literature reveals that most forms of expertise or talents that we thought were genetically determined are actually a function of careful practice. Elite performers aren't smarter or faster; they are, however, better trained. So before you leap on the motivation wagon, check for ability.

The key to personal ability is to over-invest in skill building—to build in extensive practice in the toughest, most realistic settings. Results show that a robust training initiative is at the heart of almost all successful influence strategies. Seventy-seven percent of the successful initiatives in our sample included training as one of their influence strategies.

Source 2 Case Study: Training at AT&T

Who: Mike Miller, Vice President of Business Customer Billing, AT&T

Influence Challenge: Turn around a three-thousand-person IT function by creating a culture in which everyone speaks up early and honestly about the risks they see affecting project goals.

Action: Train employees in how to step up to crucial conversations.

Early in his change initiative, Miller saw that people needed more than the motivation to speak up. He realized people also needed the ability to step up to crucial conversations. In the heat of the moment, speaking up about emotionally risky issues requires as much skill as motivation. So Miller made sure people were well trained in these difficult interpersonal skills.

Research shows that training is markedly more successful when spaced over time. So Miller trained slowly, in one- to two-hour segments over several months. His goal was to keep people focused on the training long enough to adopt new behaviors. He also trained realistically, using real business problems and extensive practice. For example, participants role played how to challenge bosses on unrealistic deadlines, how to report project risks, and how to hold peers accountable to missed deadlines.

Results: Within six months, internal surveys showed behavior was changing markedly, and within nine months, virtually every software release in Miller's group came in on time, on budget, and with no serious errors.

SOURCE 3: DO OTHERS MOTIVATE? HARNESS PEER PRESSURE

No matter how motivated and able individuals are, they'll still encounter enormous social influences that usually support the status quo and discourage behavior reform.

Whether people acknowledge it or not, there are few motivators as potent as the approval or disapproval of friends and coworkers. A few examples on the power of social influence:

> "After a senior engineer tells a junior engineer that 'production work is for dropouts,' the junior engineer proceeds to make career choices that he now believes will bring honor and prestige.
>
> "After a new hire challenges an idea in a meeting only to be ostracized by her colleagues, she decides to never again speak candidly and freely in her meetings.
>
> "When senior physicians don't wash their hands before treating patients, less than 10 percent of their residents wash up." (Lankford, 2003)

Effective influencers understand that many small interactions shape and sustain the behavioral norms of an organization. The key to effective social motivation is to get peer pressure working for you instead of against you.

Source 3 Case Study: Social Support at Lockheed Martin

Who: Ralph Heath, Lockheed Martin

Influence Challenge: Get the F-22 Raptor off the drawing boards and into production in eighteen months while garnering the support of five thousand employees, many of whom consider the move to production as a threat to their jobs.

Action: Invest in the most influential people—both the formal leaders and the opinion leaders.

Heath met monthly with 350 supervisors, managers, and directors. He brought in customers from various military agencies and encouraged them to explain their frustrations and concerns with the program. In these sessions, Heath described the kinds of behaviors that were slowing the transition and which behaviors needed to change. He spoke candidly about the problems he saw and demonstrated a willingness to be challenged when his own actions conflicted with the behavior he asked of this group. As Heath won the trust of supervisors, they began to influence others.

Heath also worked closely with opinion leaders, visiting informally with them every week. After only four months of working with opinion leaders, marked changes began to occur.

Results: In the end, the performance of Heath's group exceeded expectations. The group met production deadlines, and the resulting product was a success. The F-22's reliability is better than the F-15, which has been in use for decades; its operating costs are lower, its repair times are shorter, and its mission capabilities are far superior.

SOURCE 4: DO OTHERS ENABLE?
CREATE SOCIAL SUPPORT

Many leaders fail to appreciate how much help people need when attempting new behaviors. For example, someone working to overcome an addiction often requires enormous amounts of coaching and feedback from trusted friends. The same is true in organizations. If you want employees to improve quality, they will need a great deal of support from line leaders to enable and empower them to improve processes, implement new tools, and change policies.

Given that leaders don't have time to become coaches for everyone in the organization, how can they leverage their "social ability" to give them the greatest influence? The most influential leaders invest their time and energy with two groups that can magnify their influence:

- Formal leaders (managers at every level)
- Informal leaders (opinion leaders)

The key to building the social capital that will extend your influence into every corner of your organization is to spend time building trust with formal and informal opinion leaders.

Start every intervention by first identifying opinion leaders and then involving these opinion leaders in the change process. Involvement can range from enrolling the opinion leaders in training to inviting them to sit on committees to taking on a coaching role, etc. Let opinion leaders lead the way.

Source 4 Case Study: Leader-Led Training at Sprint

Who: Tom O'Dea, VP of Customer Relationship Management, Sprint

Influence Challenge: Improve the track record of a 1,700-person IT department to meet quality, schedule, and cost targets.

Action: Train internal leaders and have them facilitate the skill-based training initiative to the rest of the employees.

O'Dea found that an essential behavior for employees to adopt in order to reach his goals was the ability to discuss mission-critical issues rapidly and honestly with co-workers. While leaders encouraged this behavior, they didn't always enable it, and they weren't always accessible to employees who needed help.

So O'Dea turned the leaders into teachers. Each week, he taught new skills to the leaders and then tasked them to teach them to their direct reports. After six weeks, the skills cascaded down through the organization and were implanted in the culture. Two powerful things happened:

- The process of teaching influenced the teachers. Leaders fully embraced the concepts and encouraged others to do likewise. The real teaching moments didn't occur during the training, but rather when employees approached their leader for help on how to solve problems. Leaders became enablers of change. These teaching sessions also became "access opportunities" as employees candidly raised issues and concerns about work problems.

- The process also influenced the learners. In addition to receiving real-time coaching, employees had real-time access to bosses. A respected person (often the boss) helped them by offering advice and time exactly when they needed it to enable first-time attempts to raise tough issues.

Results: The combination of social motivation and social ability became a powerful force for change at Sprint. Soon after, other divisions solicited O'Dea's help to influence change in their areas.

SOURCE 5: DO THINGS MOTIVATE? ALIGN REWARDS AND ENSURE ACCOUNTABILITY

There's a famous saying: "If you want to know what's going on, follow the money." If a leader talks about quality but rewards productivity, employees will notice and quality will suffer. Chronic problems such as lack of accountability, poor productivity, and slipshod quality are often traced to poorly designed incentives that reward the wrong behaviors.

It is difficult to change behavior without changing the incentives. In fact, creating incentives is often the only real way senior leaders can separate serious priorities from pipedreams. The CEO might stick his neck out and say, "Starting now, at least 25 percent of our incentive pay should be contingent on achieving these new measures." This statement will instantly redirect the focus of senior managers.

But it's not just the top people who need to have a stake in changing entrenched behaviors. Employees at all levels won't support change if the behavior management wants to encourage doesn't make their lives better (in the form of opportunities, money, promotions, etc.).

The key to rewarding change in behavior is to make the external rewards both real and valuable—they need to send a supportive message. However, our advice is to use incentives as motivation third, not first. Otherwise, you might actually undermine people's intrinsic motivation (Deci, 1975). Begin with personal and social sources of motivation, and then reinforce them with well-designed incentive systems.

Source 5 Case Study: Leaders Taking Stake at Lockheed Martin

Who: Executives at Lockheed Martin

Influence Challenge: Change behaviors to secure desired results.

Action: Leaders put their own pay incentives on the line.

At Lockheed Martin, leaders tracked both results and behaviors. Improvement targets were set, and progress was reviewed three times a year. However, tracking progress wasn't enough to secure permanent change.

The president, vice presidents, and directors put their own skin in the game by risking their own pay incentives. The top two levels of management based 25 percent of their incentive pay on whether they met their targets for behavior change.

Results: This kind of extrinsic motivation ensured that the organization did everything it could to change behavior and secure results.

SOURCE 6: DO THINGS ENABLE?
CHANGE THE ENVIRONMENT

Three times more people die from lung cancer as from traffic accidents. Twice as many people die from tuberculosis as from fires. However, most people would guess otherwise. The reason: the daily information people see—the data stream—is at odds with reality. For example, a typical newspaper has forty-two articles about traffic accidents for every article about lung cancer (Tversky & Kahneman, 1974).

The key to changing an organization's mental agenda is to change the data that routinely crosses people's desks. Often, the crucial data stream doesn't exist, so it's management's job to create it (see Source 6 Case Study). In other settings, data streams may exist but are not used effectively. Consider the case of an international logistics company. Although the firm met all of its internal customer metrics, an alarming number of customers were defecting to competitors. Puzzled, the vice president of quality explored how the customer metrics were calculated. He found that customers requested to receive their deliveries within two days, at which point the salesperson responded, "Sorry, we can't do that—how about four?" Frequently, the customer would say that was okay.

When the company tracked whether packages were indeed delivered within four days, their record was nearly perfect. However, many customers still wanted two-day deliveries. Rather than measure the actual delivery date against the promised delivery time, the VP began tracking the delivery time against the customers' preferred delivery time. Using this metric, performance fell to below 50 percent—explaining their high customer-defection rate. While this performance metric was discouraging, it reset the mental agenda and motivated the organization to revamp the fulfillment system.

Sometimes changing the data stream isn't enough. Changing behavior may require structural changes. Spectrum Health Grand Rapids recently went so far as to create a separate physical space where people can work on new ideas without normal distractions. In the first year, Kris White, vice president of patient affairs, said employees set an unprecedented record in generating innovative ideas. In just one year, they identified thirty-five commercial ideas and received three provisional patents.

Source 6 Case Study: Improved Reporting at OGE Energy

Who: Pat Ryan, Vice Chairman, OGE Energy

Influence Challenge: Turn around the utility's reputation for being insufficiently customer-driven.

Action: Create a new weekly reporting mechanism to help managers monitor and repair broken streetlights within five days.

Ryan discovered the biggest contributing factor to the company's negative reputation was not the quality of service in many of their standard utilities and offerings. Rather, the public's poor perception came down to OGE's past unresponsiveness to fixing burned-out streetlights.

Developing Talent for Organizational Results

So Ryan established a company-wide target to repair streetlights within five days. To make this happen, he created a new weekly reporting mechanism that helped managers monitor problems. The report listed streetlights by area that had been dark for more than five days.

Results: Within a short period of time, all but two areas had fixed the problem. What's more, as citizens and police began to see OGE's responsiveness to burned-out lights, they improved their reporting of the problem and changed their perception of the company.

The Conclusion

Novice investors make the mistake of betting on a single stock instead of creating a diversified portfolio of investments. Despite their poor judgment, they sometimes win. It's what we call "dumb luck."

However, dumb luck never works against entrenched organizational and personal problems. And yet, our research shows nearly all of us make the mistake of betting our success on a single source of influence. In fact, only 5 percent of the leaders we studied combined four or more sources of influence, and these 5 percent were ten times more likely to succeed.

Clearly, the main variable in success or failure was not which source of influence leaders choose. By far the more important factor was how many.

Next Steps

Here's what you can do to multiply your arsenal of influence strategies and exponentially increase your influence.

1. PICK A PROBLEM TO SOLVE

Start by identifying the chronic challenges in your organization—issues that negatively affect key metrics and bottom-line results and that have resisted prior attempts at change. Or identify some strategically important result you must achieve that will require substantial changes in behavior to succeed. You will find a matrix for the six influences that includes thought-provoking questions and strategies in this chapter's online tools to assist you with this process.

Next, ask yourself whether a crucial key to solving this problem will be influencing new behavior. If the answer is yes, then don't make the mistake of implementing policy, process, or technology solutions without carefully developing a six-source strategy for driving and supporting the behavior you'll need to succeed.

2. BE TRAINED IN CHANGING BEHAVIOR

Involve the core of managers and leaders who must influence new behavior in studying the Influencer Model—the step-by-step approach to diagnosing and resolving chronic problems outlined in this chapter. Your leaders may consider attending Influencer Training to learn how to discover and counteract the complex web of forces underlying resistant organizational problems.

The process includes identifying results, finding and targeting vital behaviors, and applying the six sources of influence. This model was named the 2009 Change Management Approach of the Year by *MIT Sloan Management Review*. Additionally, Influencer Training was named a 2009 Top Training Product of the Year by *Human Resource Executive* magazine. Your leaders will learn to:

- Diagnose the causes behind any team or organizational problem.

- Rely less on formal authority to effectively motivate and enable others.

- Identify high-leverage behaviors that, if changed, will lead to desired results.

- Use six sources of influence to make profound organizational change inevitable.

3. TRAIN YOUR EMPLOYEES TO BECOME FLUENT IN CHANGE

Managers and leaders who can drive organizational change will reap large organizational results. However, our research shows that employees who are fluent in a model for changing their own behavior can return similar results to the bottom line. We've found that employees skilled in improving their performance, overcoming career-limiting behaviors, and achieving career-oriented goals save their organizations anywhere from $10,000 to $50,000 for each behavior they affect. That's because employees stuck in poor performance create inefficient workarounds, shoddy output, poor working relationships, and drag corporate performance by as much as 40 percent.

REFERENCES

Black, J.S., & Gregersen, H.B. (2008). *Start with one: Changing individuals changes organizations.* Philadelphia: Wharton School Publishing.

Deci, E.L. (1975). *Intrinsic motivation.* New York: Plenum Press.

Freud, S. (2010). *Interpretation of dreams.* (J. Strachey, Trans.). New York: Basic Books.

Developing Talent for Organizational Results

Lankford, M.G., Zembower, T.R., Trick, W.E., Hacek, D.M., Noskin, G.A., & Person, L.R. (2003, February). Influence of role models and hospital design on hand hygiene of health care workers. *Emerging Infectious Diseases, 9*(2).

Tversky, A., & Kahneman, D. (1974, September 27). Judgment under uncertainty: Heuristics and biases. *Science, New Series, 185*(4157), 1124–1131.

About VitalSmarts

VitalSmarts is an innovator in corporate training and organizational performance. The firm helps teams and organizations achieve the results they care about most. With award-winning training products based on more than thirty years of ongoing research, VitalSmarts has helped more than three hundred of the Fortune 500 realize significant results using a proven method for driving rapid, sustainable, and measurable change in behaviors. VitalSmarts has been ranked six times by *Inc*. magazine as one of the fastest-growing companies in America and has trained more than 650,000 people worldwide.

VitalSmarts' newest one-day training program, Change Anything Training, is designed to give the individual employee tools to solve any individual behavior challenge—at work or at home. Building the capacity to adapt one's own habits to interpersonal, team, and organizational change leads to improved productivity, a more engaged workforce, and the ability to solve complex problems. Influencer two-day workshops and Change Anything one-day workshops are held around the country.

Submitted by Brittney Maxfield; Joseph Grenny, Co-Founder; Andrew Shimberg, CEO

VitalSmarts

282 River Bend Lane, Suite 100

Provo, UT 84604

(800) 449-5989

info@vitalsmarts.com

www.vitalsmarts.com

Chapter 8

Speaking Up
Presenting to Executives®
POWERSPEAKING, INC.

In This Chapter

- The critical importance of an appropriately crafted C-level presentation.
- Clarification of presentation rules at the executive level.
- Tips for a successful executive level presentation.

This chapter is based on the work the PowerSpeaking, Inc., team has done over the past ten years to understand what makes top-level speaking so different. We have interviewed more than forty C-level executives to find answers to these questions. They told us very clearly what works and what is career-limiting in their meetings. This chapter is a summary of what we've learned from them. If you are a manager whose project, budget, and future depend on approval from people at the top, this chapter will help.

In Fortune 500 presentation rooms around the world, management careers are careening off the tracks. Why? Poor delivery? No. Bad content? No. It's because people don't understand the C-level environment. They don't understand who these people are, the world they live in, and what they demand from subordinates who are on their meeting agendas. The carnage of these presentation train wrecks can be avoided by knowing more about these people and giving them what they want.

Who Are They and What Is Their World Like?

The people who rise to the top have traits that set them apart. They are extremely bright, aggressive, successful "Type A" personalities. Most are males, often Ivy League–educated. They are under heavy pressure to produce in a highly competitive market. Your goals must be in line with their goals: to move the company forward. They don't have time for pleasantries, diversions, or people who can't respond quickly and efficiently to what *they* think is important. Let's take a look at their world.

WHAT JOB SECURITY?

Why is it a bare-knuckles world at the top level? For starters, there isn't much job security. If you plan to work with C-levels to get things done, be advised they may not be there for long. According to *CLO* magazine ("In Conclusion," 2006) the average tenure for someone in the "C-suite" is only 23 months.

Additionally, the *Harvard Business Review* ("Surviving Your New CEO," 2007) reports that, if after becoming a new CEO, the company's stock price goes up, there is a 75 percent chance that one year later that new CEO will still be in his or her job. But if the stock price goes down, there is an 83 percent chance he or she will be fired. The demand to obtain immediate results is unrelenting. Few of us live under such daily, weekly, or monthly performance pressure.

But even success is no guarantee. According to Chuck House and Ray Price in their book, *The HP Phenomenon*, boards ask CEOs: "What have you done for me lately?" Shortly after generating record-breaking profits for their companies, boards fired John Akers, IBM; John Young and Lou Platt, HP; Ken Olson, DEC; Ed McCraken, Silicon Graphics; and Rod Canion, Compaq.

Those looking up to the CEO may see an imposing figure to be admired or feared. However, from the vantage point of the CEO, it's very different. Ginger Graham, former CEO of Amylin Pharmaceuticals and now a consultant to new CEOs, observed that CEOs often feel like "hired help." With a board that demands quarterly profits and understands little about the day-to-day problems of running the company, the CEO may feel like a puppet on a string with little job security.

THE POWER CULTURE

According to researcher Adrian Savage, what gets you ahead at the lower levels is competence, but at the top it is all about raw power. In his breakthrough paper, "The

Real Glass Ceiling" (Savage, 2002), Savage describes the shift that must happen as a manager moves up into the senior levels:

> "As he or she crosses the invisible barrier, the rules change. To advance further, s/he must play by the new rules, even though they've probably never been explained or even acknowledged openly: succeed in getting and keeping a position of influence and power, from which to secure resources for his or her division or function. Do this amongst a highly competitive group of people who are all outstanding individuals, all working hard to secure their own positions and resources, and all committed to winning first and worrying about any casualties later, if at all." (p. 5)

Welcome to the power culture. Savage goes on to explain that some people are better at adjusting to this change than others. Shortly after reading the Savage paper, one of the executives I'd been coaching told this powerful story:

> "I was giving my quarterly finance report to our top leadership. As had happened on three previous occasions, Bob, a peer from product development, began challenging my numbers in a derisive manner.
> "I walked over to him, paused, and said, 'Look, Bob, you do this to me every time I present. I am goddamned sick of it. This is my presentation and I plan to finish it. If you have something to say to me, you can do it after this meeting is over. But for now, I want you to shut up!'" (private conversation)

This executive had played college football and presented an imposing figure. He said the room grew deathly silent and Bob sank in his chair. "As I scanned the room, I could see looks of approval on the executives' faces. Six months later, I was promoted to CFO. Two years after that, I was president of the company." Today he is CEO of an up-and-coming Silicon Valley technology company.

YOU'RE ON YOUR OWN

> *"The perception of your work by senior people is what makes you stand out."*
> —Brenda Rhodes, CEO, In-Touch

When you're working with the top level, you're being watched for your leadership capabilities and potential. How savvy you are? How well do you pick up the cues? Can you be political without looking political? But, there is no handbook. For example, in a January 2005 *Harvard Business Review* article Dan Ciampa noted:

> "Would-be CEOs can't expect much help in moving to the top spot. Boards and chief executives will give only the slightest indications of the behavior they expect. They want to see whether a candidate is sensitive to subtle cues and can adjust his or her behavior accordingly. CEOs and chairmen are more likely to test than to counsel."

A recently promoted sales executive I worked with in a high-tech company felt he needed help in his new position. After a particularly contentious senior meeting, he approached the CEO complaining that he couldn't get things done without the CEO's support. The CEO said bluntly, "I don't have time for this. Okay, yes you have my support. Now get on with it." The end.

Another example: Bill was extremely talented and had moved quickly up the management ladder. He was on the verge of being promoted to the C-level. He complained to a VP I'd been working with that he'd presented an idea to the CEO and had been rebuffed. The VP said to Bill, "Well, you know what, the CEO doesn't give a shit about your problems. He worries about things like shareholder value, what the analysts are going to say in their next report, some employee lawsuit, or the fact that there's a quality problem in the manufacturing facility in Taiwan."

The VP went on to add, "Now, Bill, you may not like that, but it's not going to change. You may not be cut out to work at the C-level, and that's OK. There are lots of other places you can work. But if you are going to play at this level, that's the name of the game. So take care of *yourself*. The CEO isn't there to take care of you."

From the *Harvard Business Review*, to high-tech companies, to the Adrian Savage research, a clear picture emerges: the higher up you go, the more self-reliant you must become. We might also add to the old nostrum "It's lonely at the top"—"and, there's no help for you up there either."

No wonder executive life coaching has become a $1B+ industry.

VALUE OF THEIR TIME: WHAT COSTS $30K/HOUR AND HAS A 67 PERCENT FAILURE RATE?

When middle managers make requests to senior leadership for money, resources, and project support, they may not see the bigger picture. Focused only on their own wants and needs, they may fail to appreciate the cost of poor meeting performance. If we consider the top five leaders of a mid-sized company (CEO, CFO, COO, CTO, CMO)

Developing Talent for Organizational Results

with, let's say, $4 billion in revenue, and calculate what it costs to put them into an hour-long meeting, the numbers are shocking.

Their salaries, bonuses, stock options, and other perks can be determined from SEC public records. Our calculations indicate that the cost of having those five people in a decision meeting costs the shareholders around $30,000 per hour. $30,000 for one hour!!! To make matters worse, CEOs we've interviewed report that 67 percent of the meetings they sit through are *total failures*. The cost to the shareholders of bad meetings is staggering. No wonder the pressure is so high.

According to Mike Lyons, chairman, Future Point Systems, corporate boards operate under a tenet called "duty of care." That is, a board is charged with watching out for the shareholders' interests. We could assume that if a board knew the huge cost of poor presentations in front of the C-level, they would be expected to take action. Such losses could make the cost of your run-of-the-mill sexual harassment lawsuit pale in comparison.

THE ALPHA PERSONALITY

There is a wide variety of successful personality styles among people at the top. Consider the huge differences between well-known CEOs: Bill Hewlett and Dave Packard at HP; Andy Grove at Intel; Larry Ellison at Oracle; Bill Gates at Microsoft; Steve Jobs at Apple. While they are very different people, they have certain attributes in common. They all wield enormous power and can be intimidating to people who work for them.

According to Andrew Park, writing in *Fast Company* magazine (2006), "Convinced of their greatness, these alpha males lapse into arrogance, defensiveness, manipulation, and malevolence, leaving a tangle of confusion and unhappiness."

Psychologist Kate Ludeman noted in the *Harvard Business Review* (2004), "Possessing both intimidating personalities and genuine power, alphas expect the world to show them appropriate deference."

Writing on the death of George Steinbrenner in *The New York Times*, Benedict Carey (2010) commented that, "Recent research on status and power suggests that brashness, entitlement, and ego are essential components for any competent leader."

Life at the top levels of corporate America is a competitive, power-driven, dog-eat-dog world, Darwin's "survival of the fittest." For example, Chuck Tyler, physics Ph.D., was head of a major Hewlett-Packard research lab back in the early 1980s. He had one hundred engineers and scientists under him. He proudly quipped to me one day, "I'm the intellectually dominant primate in the room."

In our research on the personalities of top-level executives, we did a survey of middle management to see how they perceived people at the top. For a period of six months, in our training workshops, we had people describe the personalities and business values of their C-level executives. The top five adjectives used to describe senior leaders were *data-driven, impatient, aggressive, time pressured, and intimidating*, just the qualities boards prize in CEOs.

According to recent CEO research by Adam Bryant (2011) in his new book, *The Corner Office*, "To get to the corner office it takes a lot of ambition, impatience, and fierce determination." This Type A personality gets someone to the top, but can be hard for subordinates to work with. In order to continue to be successful, the new CEO must now ratchet back his or her style, and become a Type B personality, for example, listen more, acknowledge the hard work of others, and appreciate that not everyone wants to work 24/7.

"I'M BECOMING A REAL BITCH"

Susan was a forty-two-year-old senior director at a Bay-Area biotech firm. In one of our trainings, she had just heard the adjectives people use to describe their top leadership. She got a faraway look in her eye, as though she had just had a blinding insight about something very important.

After the workshop, she confided, "Look, I am moving rapidly up the management chain. I am headed for the C-suite, and I know I'm becoming a *real bitch*." She went on, "I am more time pressured than ever. I don't have patience to listen to people's problems. I have decisions to make, and quickly. This is just where I want to be in my career, but sometimes it's not a pretty picture." The good news here is that Susan is clear about where she is going and the sacrifices she is willing to make to get there.

Nine Tips for Success at the C-Level

Due to a "perfect storm" of personality variables, performance pressure, and environmental factors, top-level people can be a very tough audience. Additionally, to put them in a room together costs the shareholders a lot of money. This is made even worse by the fact that more than half of the presentations they receive are total failures. All this paints a dismal and scary picture for the aspiring presenter. But wait! There's hope.

First of all, let's remember that the executives want you to do well. It is in the best interest of the company to have successful, informative presentations. Secondly, in our interviews, they told us what they want. It is not rocket science. Follow these nine guidelines and you'll get in and out of that top-level meeting with your career intact and perhaps funding for your project.

USE YOUR SPONSOR

Presenting to top-level decision makers is "by invitation only." You'll have a sponsor who is higher up in your own functional area. That person has a lot riding on your success and wants you to hit the ball out of the park. He or she can enlighten you about the political realities before the meeting, keep things on track during the meeting, and help with the follow-up summaries after the meeting. Bring him or her on board early in the process.

PREPARE, PREPARE, PREPARE

"What happens *before* the meeting is more important than what happens *at* the meeting," says NetApp Executive Chairman Dan Warmenhoven. With your career hanging in the balance, plan carefully for that top-level presentation. Analyze the audience. Determine whether they demand qualitative or quantitative information. Find out who supports you and who opposes you.

Be strategic. Corinne Nevinny, general partner, LMN Venture Capital, advises, "Send your slides out before the meeting. That prevents it from being a 'free for all.' Most people won't bother to read what you send them. Being unprepared, they are less likely to attack your ideas."

Finally, check and recheck your numbers. At the top level, you are in front of a very numerate group. They can do math on the fly. If your numbers don't "tie," you're dead in the water. For example, one CEO we worked with recalled a hapless presenter who had gone through a number of slides about market share. The CEO noticed that the numbers didn't tie. He stopped the presenter and asked why. The presenter said, "Oh those numbers come from different sources. I blended them and rounded them off." The CEO exploded, "What the hell are you doing? I can't believe anything else you tell me. Why are you wasting my time?" Not the outcome you want.

GET TO THE POINT!

"You have thirty seconds to get to the point," says Steve Blank, co-founder and former CEO of Epiphany. "In the past five years, PDAs have gotten so good that I now have a telephone, a TV, the Internet, a computer, and my email at my fingertips. Trust me, all of that is more interesting than you are. If you don't get right to the point, I'm gone."

Executives live with unrelenting time pressure. Get to the point immediately. We heard time and again, "Make your first line your bottom line." Propel CEO Steve Kirsch put it succinctly: "Start with your punch line at the beginning."

DUMP THE SLIDES

"Senior executives are not a bunch of PowerPoint receptor machines," notes Felicia Marcus, former regional director, USEPA. Slash the number of slides to, perhaps, zero . . . but have back-up slides in case they want to do a "deep dive." Executives want a discussion, not a slide-driven lecture. Paradoxically, a detailed slide show does *not* convince them you know your stuff. In fact, it may cause them to doubt you have the expertise to talk without slides. Ned Barnholt, chairman of KLA-Tencor and former CEO of Agilent, says that when a presenter can't talk "off the slides," he loses Barnholt's trust. It requires a free form discussion to create that trust.

LIVE BY THE "10/30 RULE"

The "10/30 rule" says that if you are scheduled for thirty minutes on the agenda, prepare just ten minutes of material. The executives will hijack the other twenty minutes for discussion. Dan Warmenhoven warned, "If you have a half hour on the agenda, you're not going to get through a half-hour presentation. We're not going to let you. Remember, it's our meeting."

SKIP STORYTELLING

Rule 1: Research shows that stories are far more effective than data for getting attention and increasing retention.

Rule 2: Not at the C-level.

Because of the pressure of time, most executives do not find stories helpful in senior meetings. Robert Drolet, Brigadier General (Retired) and former defense industry executive, is very clear on this:

> "Decision briefings are serious. Decisions must be made that involve money, involve people, and involve resources. Time is a critical asset that has to be managed. These executives didn't come into that room to listen to a five-minute story from you. They came in to make a decision and leave because they have an agenda for that day they can't possibly meet."

Tolerance for stories will vary between companies and between executives, but generally you'll be more effective staying with data. As Jane Shaw, chairman of Intel, observed, "In God we trust. Everybody else bring data." If you do use stories, make sure they are short and get right to the point. Steve Blank cautions: "The amount of storytelling and emotion diminishes the higher in the organization you're presenting to."

DELIVERY STYLE

At the top level, it is all about your content and the strategy you are presenting. As Robert Drolet says, "Style is like icing on the cake. You can have lousy style, but if you have good content, you will be successful."

While executives are most interested in your content, if you have poor delivery, it will make it harder for them to buy into what you are saying. A speaker who mumbles, paces, fidgets, talks in a monotone, talks too fast without pauses, and won't make eye contact is seen as nervous and just not believable. Such poor delivery habits can completely ruin good content. The question is: "Are you conscious of what you are doing with your body as you deliver your message?" Many speakers are completely clueless about the physical part of their delivery. They are just too nervous to think about it. When we are nervous, the fidgeting starts up, and boom! there goes the value of the message.

The good news is, fixing this is not rocket science. If your style needs a tune-up, take a class. Make sure the class includes video feedback and private coaching. Your skills will improve in no time. Keep in mind, though, it is your content that matters, not your delivery. The only reason you should polish up your delivery is so people can hear your message more clearly. You don't want them looking at your hand-wringing and wondering why you are so nervous. They'll begin to doubt you are telling the truth.

DON'T EXPECT A PAT ON THE BACK

"The CEO ain't your dad," one executive told us. You may be thinking, "Of course not. I know who my father is. I'm not confused about that one." But wait. In fact, there are a lot of people in corporate America who ARE confused about that. Psychologists tell us that our attitudes toward established authority figures are often determined by our childhood experiences with the first and most powerful authority figure in our lives, our fathers. Several executives expressed frustration over how this authority problem shows up in meetings and takes up valuable time. Whether the presenter is angry and rebellious or pleading for approval, it absolutely is not what these meetings are about.

Ralph Patterson, former lab director at Hewlett-Packard in San Diego, described his frustration when junior-level engineers came to his meetings and spent a lot of time explaining how they did the experiment or the study and all the problems they had solved. He said he'd hammer on these presenters, "Don't tell me *how* you got the data. Tell me *what the data means*. We have to make decisions and move on." From Patterson's view, people were asking for approval—rather than coming in with a recommendation based on their expertise, which is what he really needed.

Fortunately, many people are able to balance the psychological dynamics of childhood authority issues and corporate top-level decision making. They don't become confused. They don't feel either anger in the face of authority or a pleading need for reassurance. Their locus of control is within themselves, not projected onto the external power structure around them. An excellent example of this comes from Cindy Skrivanek of LSI Corporation. Cindy speaks to her senior team all the time. She is clear about her role as a resource for decision making at the highest level:

> "I'm a *tool of management*. My job is to give senior executives information, lay out a set of options, or maybe ask for a decision . . . *and then leave!* I'm not there to be their buddy or to get pats on the back. A presentation isn't a personal development opportunity or a chance for increased visibility. I'm there to do a job. And that job is to help prepare the executives to make the best possible decisions for the company."

No confusion here about the purpose of the meeting.

Remember, you are asked to present at the meeting because you have something they need in the decision-making process. Do not be hurt if you don't receive the approval you'd hoped for. Former Johnson & Johnson EVP Harold Fethe notes, "You may crave reassurance in the meeting, but you will almost certainly get higher marks if you can acknowledge their goodbyes, whether friendly or terse, and allow them to move on to their other work." In other words, this is a serious decision meeting. It's not a place where you can expect to receive longed-for parental approval that may have been missing in childhood.

IMPROVISE

Successful C-level presenters perform like jazz musicians. When things go off the track, they improvise. In its May 2009 issue, *Harvard Business Review* ("Why Teams Don't Work") observed, "The best team leaders are like jazz players, improvising constantly as they go along."

The downfall of the over-prepared, nervous, mid-level presenter is the dogged determination to stay on script. Robert Drolet observes, "They come into the room with their slides stapled to the front of their suits, with the attitude, 'I'm going to get through these slides no matter what: earthquake, fire, building falls down, whatever.'" Guaranteed failure. Similarly, Steve Kirsch, CEO of Propel, observes that "Your success is 80 percent in your ability to facilitate the meeting and only 20 percent in the content per se." Being prepared, but flexible, is the winning strategy.

Conclusion

Presentations at the top levels of corporate America are done in rarified air. The people are unique and demanding. Failure can mean loss of a project, damage to a career, and even a new job search. In addition, success or failure affects the careers of people under the presenter. The stakes could not be higher. According to the C-level executives, 67 percent of the presentations they receive are total failures. In summary:

- Speaking at the top level of any organization, whether private sector or public sector can be a high-stakes event in anyone's career. A lot is riding on how well the presentation is done, and the rules at the top are very different from day-to-day presentations.

- To have a successful meeting with top-level executives, do what they love: get to the point and improvise. Your career and project will stay on track, and you will become a hero to the people in your organization.

REFERENCES

Bryant, A. (2011). *The corner office: Indispensable and unexpected lessons from CEOs on how to lead and succeed.* New York: Times Books, Henry Holt and Company.

Ciampa, D. (2005, January). How leaders move up. *Harvard Business Review.*

House, C., & Price, R. (2009). *The HP phenomenon: Innovation and business transformation.* Stanford, CA: Stanford Business Books.

Meister, J. (2006, January). Learning trends to watch in 2006. *Chief Learning Officer.*

Savage, A. (2002). The real glass ceiling. PNA, Inc.

About PowerSpeaking, Inc.

Launched in 1985, PowerSpeaking, Inc. (PSI) has grown from two people to twenty-five, offering more than 350 programs per year, worldwide. We specialize in speech communication training.

Our signature program is PowerSpeaking®, a two-day, trainer-led, video-based workshop for anyone who needs the basic skills. We offer HighTechSpeaking® for scientists and engineers, FastTrackSpeaking® for management, and Speaking Up® for people who address top-level executives. We also offer our programs as webinars. Speaking Up is an on-demand streaming program that can be accessed 24/7.

Submitted by Frederick Gilbert, Ph.D., Founder

PowerSpeaking, Inc.

200 B Twin Dolphin Drive

Redwood City, CA 94065

(800) 828-1909

(650) 631-8459

rick@powerspeaking.com

www.powerspeaking.com

Developing Talent for Organizational Results

Chapter 9

Raising the Talent Bar
Business Acumen As a Key Leadership Competency

PARADIGM LEARNING, INC.

In This Chapter

- Definition of business acumen.
- Why business acumen is a critical managerial skill.
- How an organization can improve managers' business acumen.
- Sample financial questions managers should be able to answer.

Too many managers today—at all leadership levels—lack a solid foundation of business acumen. Without it, they can't accurately assess the competitive landscape and connect their day-to-day decisions and actions with key financial and strategic performance goals. As a result, business acumen training is becoming a vital component of workforce learning and development and is finding its way into management curricula at leading organizations and universities.

The Business Challenge

The growing complexity and uncertainty of our rapidly changing global business environment is raising the stakes for managers at all levels. They are operating in an increasingly fast-moving and competitive environment, and the demands on them for stronger, faster, and more focused leadership has never been higher.

Managers are challenged to make the connection between what's happening in the world at large with the finer points of how the business functions internally. As their role in executing strategy continues to expand, they are accountable for making crucial, real-time decisions that directly affect financial outcomes at the unit and at the corporate level. To succeed, they need to have the insight and perception to balance the big picture with the day-to-day fundamentals of doing business.

For today's managers, these fundamentals include everything from leading change initiatives to talent management. On top of everything else, managers are increasingly in charge of retaining and developing high-performing teams and engaging employees with the organization's goals and objectives.

Pulled in so many directions, it's easy for managers to miss the forest for the trees. Without a clear understanding of both the external and internal landscape, they are more likely to develop the wrong capabilities, set the wrong goals, hire the wrong people, and enter the wrong markets. Worst of all, without a clear vision of financial objectives and metrics, they may fail to recognize the challenges the business is facing, the concerns of their people, and the impact their decisions have on the bottom line.

The good news is that business acumen can be learned. As more organizations and government agencies identify business acumen as a core leadership competency, business acumen training is quickly becoming one of the most sought-after and strategically important learning initiatives.

Business Acumen Defined

The dictionary defines acumen as "quickness, accuracy, and keenness of judgment or insight," especially in practical matters. The word comes from the Latin acuere—the root of acute—and it means "to sharpen."

Business acumen is an acute understanding of how a business works and what it takes for the enterprise to make money. It combines financial literacy—the ability to understand numbers on financial statements—with business literacy—recognizing how strategies, behaviors, actions, and decisions not only affect the numbers but also drive profitable and sustainable growth.

Consider this example: In team sports, players need to know how the game is scored. To affect the score, they need to know how to play the game. *In business, financial literacy is understanding the score and business acumen is knowing how to impact it.*

On any business team, managers with basic financial literacy can read a company's income statement by relying on a fundamental understanding of financial terms, ratios, and what the numbers represent. But that's about it.

Managers with business acumen, however, can interpret that income statement—what the numbers really mean—and act accordingly. With a solid understanding of industry, market, and financial information, they have a clear view of the company's current realities and potential opportunities. They are able to analyze and apply diverse financial data to the development of strategy. Most important, they can make decisions that lead to increases in profit or cash flow because they know how their actions affect the numbers and vice versa.

Some business analysts define business acumen as the ability to engage in "big picture thinking" and understand the organization's financial and strategic issues—the relationships between actions and consequences—within a holistic context. The managers who understand all the business drivers and key financial levers, as well as the relationships between them, are able to assess the total financial health of the business.

They not only have a clear understanding of how the business works but also how it sustains profitability, so they can figure out how their contributions can positively impact the bottom line. They make more profitable decisions, influence top-line revenue generation, establish priorities, and take actions that align with organizational and customer strategy.

As leaders, managers with business acumen are able to break down organizational silos, bridge communication gaps, and engage the employees they manage, so the entire workforce can understand how the company operates and what each person can do to contribute to its success.

Business Acumen As a Leadership Competency

In a recent SmartMoney.com interview, Gary Kelly, CEO of Southwest Airlines, was asked about the economic downturn. He said:

> "The speed at which we need to identify issues, study them, and make decisions is unlike anything I have experienced before. Any time you have that many points changing that rapidly, there are bound to be some rough spots. A couple of years ago, we had record earnings, so we were making plans with a lot of comfort. But we've lost our cushion now, so we have to manage our risk much more carefully."

Southwest Airlines is a highly successful business. But the company recognizes the need to be on high alert to changes and knows that decisions and actions made every day must align with marketplace conditions and customer preferences.

For organizations today, no matter how successful, it's critical for leaders to be able to accurately assess the competitive landscape and connect day-to-day decisions and activities with key financial, functional, and business performance metrics and goals.

Every key player must have a comfort level with the building blocks of making money—cash, profitability, assets, revenue growth, and process efficiency—and every enterprise must depend on the ability of these key players to connect and manage human, financial, and information resources strategically.

The best managers know that having a strong, comprehensive understanding of their business is critical for identifying which opportunities to grab and which to ignore. They recognize the importance of having a holistic understanding of their organization's financial and strategic realities. In other words, they are business savvy—no matter what department they are in—and know how to use that knowledge to align their departmental and personal objectives to the company's overall strategy.

BIG PICTURE THINKING

While a holistic view of the company is a byproduct of business acumen, it is not the norm. The common reality is that managers' main goals are to master business processes within their departments or functions, not to think about how the pieces fit together and how they affect the company as a whole. But leaders in today's complex world need to take a broader view and make decisions within that context.

In his critically acclaimed bestselling book, *A Whole New Mind*, Daniel Pink (2005) explains that we have moved into a "conceptual" age from the "information" age, and that requires a different kind of thinking—bigger picture, more holistic, more creative, and more empathetic.

He writes about the six "high-concept, high-touch" senses that are critical for managers to develop in our new conceptual world. One he calls "symphony."

"Symphony is the ability to put together the pieces . . . the capacity to synthesize rather than to analyze; to see relationships between seemingly unrelated fields; to detect broad patterns rather than deliver specific answers; and to invent something new" (p 126). He also says, "Seeing the big picture is fast becoming a killer app in business" (p 137).

Increasing the business acumen of leaders helps them develop this important sense of "symphony" and leads to a holistic appreciation of business drivers and goal alignment.

Too often, however, managers don't understand enough about the business of the business to make solid strategic decisions. In fact, at many companies if you asked non-financial managers the following questions, you might get more blank stares than answers:

- What are the most important ways that our business makes (or loses) money?
- What's the difference between profit and cash—and why is it important to closely monitor both?
- How do initiatives like quality/process improvements, capital investments, accounts payable strategies, and inventory management specifically affect financial metrics?
- In what ways do the goals of your department align with the organization's strategic and financial objectives?
- If we discount our products by 10 percent, how much will that impact our profitability?
- What is the difference between our company's income statements, cash flow statements, and balance sheets? What do each of them tell us about the business?
- What is involved in investing for the future (technology, new product development, or others) while balancing short-term profitability and shareholder return?

Without adequate business acumen, managers can't align their priorities with those of the company or help employees engage with the company's vision and goals. This narrow focus on their own departments and job functions prevents them from understanding how what they do rolls up into a financial statement or affects their customers, so there is no sense of urgency. And when income statements, balance sheets, cash flow statements, asset management initiatives, and other financial concepts are misunderstood or misused—and when managers don't grasp the connection between these financial concepts and corporate vision, goals, and strategies—they can't be effective leaders for the organization, themselves, or their teams.

Multiplied by hundreds or even thousands of employees, this gap in understanding the basics of the business, operating goals, and competitive comparisons means that too many decisions are being made and too many actions are being taken that don't align with business objectives. And this widespread lack of business acumen represents a critical need at an especially critical time.

Business Acumen Training

Until recently, business acumen has been a missing link in leadership and management curricula. Following standard operating procedure, many fundamentals of business such as accounting, economics, and business law are taught in business schools. These disciplines, however, are often specialized and segmented from the whole of running a business.

Finance for non-financial manager courses have become more available (and often avoided!) as awareness of the need for financial literacy has grown. However, a basic financial course that focuses on terminology, ratios, and financial statements isn't enough to arm managers for the current challenges of doing business. Instead, the key to producing real results is the development of higher levels of business acumen: going beyond basic financial literacy to a true understanding of what it takes for a business to make money.

Workforce development leaders are rapidly recognizing that business acumen training puts all of the organization's other development efforts into the context of executing corporate strategy. It not only teaches managers how to make faster and better business decisions, but it aligns everyone around a common language, provides clarity of purpose, and shows them how to leverage all their skills to strengthen the company's financial position.

Business acumen training also gives managers the tools to engage their teams in ways that build loyalty, increase their ownership in the process of building the company, and boost employee retention.

Determining what a foundational business acumen training program should look like depends to some degree on the education, experience, and competence level of participants and the business realities facing the organization. Senior managers, middle managers, first-line managers, team leaders, sales managers, and high-potential individual contributors are all possible audiences for business acumen training, and all may need specialized training or customized adaptations to meet specific needs. But the basic rules of effective adult learning delivery still apply.

First, business acumen training has to be engaging and energizing enough to overcome the "oh no" factor typically associated with any training that is "financial." Making it palatable to possibly reluctant learners and maximizing participant engagement is key.

Second, it can't overwhelm and frustrate learners by going beyond the needs of the audience. Three days of training around financial terms and statements, for example, is generally not necessary for those who aren't in finance jobs.

Third, since the focus of business acumen training for managers is, of necessity, at a higher level than most skills-based development, relevance is also essential. It's not just about learning specific skills—it's about driving insight and understanding of the enterprise as a whole. Can the learners take the experience and apply it directly and immediately to their roles in strengthening the financial performance of the company?

Finally, it needs to be memorable. Conventional wisdom shows a huge gap between knowledge retained from traditional instructor-dependent classroom training and knowledge gained from more interactive learning experiences. According to some estimates, most people retain just about 5 percent of learning from a lecture, compared to about 75 percent when they are actively involved in their learning experience.

Given the considerable spike in learning retention from hands-on experience, it stands to reason that experiential or "discovery learning" is rapidly gaining popularity for teaching business acumen—especially to manager-level audiences.

Simulations based on real business dynamics and learning experiences that use games, stories, and role playing provide multiple opportunities for these learners to practice and improve decision making. By allowing participants to act out and affect real outcomes—without real-life risks—they provide the context and consequences managers need to clearly visualize the impact of their actions on the organization as a whole. This kind of "learning by doing" enables them to not only absorb essential concepts but also transfer their knowledge directly to the workplace as changed behaviors.

Paradigm Learning's business simulation, for example, places small teams of learners into the simulated experience of running a company for three business years. Along the way, they deal with the decisions, actions, and events that impact the company's financial metrics and shareholder satisfaction. Customized exercises following the simulation tie knowledge and skills from the simulation to the learners' own organizations and departments.

Simulations that are fun, fast, and focused and that tie directly to an organization's financial and strategic issues can be a powerful way to develop the knowledge and skills of managers at multiple levels.

Summary

Business acumen is a missing leadership competency in too many organizations today. A quick look at these enterprises reveals an unsettling reality. Managers without business acumen don't understand key financial levers and critical financial concepts. They are unable to interpret financial statements as well as they should and don't know how profits and losses interact with the company's balance sheet. They lack an in-depth understanding about the interrelatedness of their decisions and the profitability of the company and they struggle to articulate the company's strategy or how their actions—and those of their teams—contribute to its execution.

Yet all of these things link directly to business success and sustainable growth in today's highly competitive and volatile business environment.

As a result, business acumen training has leapt to the forefront of workforce learning and development. More business acumen and financial literacy courses are finding their way into leadership and management curricula at top companies and universities. And more learning providers are developing robust, interactive, and hands-on learning experiences geared specifically to help managers acquire and sharpen their business acumen.

For managers undergoing this kind of training, the knowledge, insights, and skills that they develop can pay big dividends for the company and for themselves. The basic principles of sound business practice are demystified. With a deeper understanding of the financial workings of the organization, they can articulate the strategy behind the organization's numbers and explain how critical enterprise-wide initiatives affect financial success. Most important, they understand how the goals of their departments and teams align with the organization's strategic and financial objectives and how their own personal actions and decisions affect the bottom line.

REFERENCE

Pink, D. (2005). *A whole new mind.* New York: Riverhead.

About Paradigm Learning, Inc.

Paradigm Learning is a leader in learning innovation, offering unique education and communication programs to organizations around the world. Its award-winning, classroom-based business games, simulations and Discovery Maps®, enhanced with online options, customizing and consulting services, have been used by leading companies since 1994. Paradigm Learning's core methodology is discovery learning, a powerful educational approach that engages employees, accelerates learning, and increases retention.

As a leader in learning innovation, Paradigm Learning has created highly acclaimed business games and simulations in the areas of business acumen, project management, talent leadership, team building, change management, and leadership accountability. The company's flagship business acumen training program, Zodiak®: The Game of Business Finance and Strategy, has been conducted with over one million managers and employees worldwide.

Submitted by Catherine J Rezak, Co-Founder, Chairman

Paradigm Learning, Inc.

100 2nd Avenue South

St. Petersburg, FL 33701

(727) 471-3170

info@ParadigmLearning.com

www.ParadigmLearning.com

Chapter 10

Eliminate the Us vs. Them Dynamics
LEARNING AS LEADERSHIP

In This Chapter

- Introduction to the "unconscious demonization" concept, focusing on how we may villianize other people when their beliefs and intentions oppose our own.

- Five steps of the downward spiral of an "us vs. them" situation.

- How individuals' emotional investment keeps them in an "us vs. them" mode.

- Five steps to reverse the negative spiral to conscious humanization.

"We're facing a tempest of uncertainty in the coming years," the CEO of a publicly traded financial services company said ruefully, "and if we don't stop this in-fighting, we're not going to make it."

Human resources was exasperated with how operations pushed back on every initiative they launched; sales scorned HR for its disregard of their business needs; strategic initiatives despaired at how ineffectively operations followed through on their new business ideas, while operations belittled SI's plans as naively disconnected from reality; the middle of the organization despised senior management for their double talk and lack of clear direction; and, of course, everyone hated IT. In this charged climate of mistrust, performance issues weren't being addressed, senior leaders rarely agreed on decisions that impacted multiple departments, and several large clients walked away in disgust at the lack of integrated service they received.

I wish this organization were an anomaly, but it isn't. Whether in a government agency, multinational Fortune 500 corporation, privately owned brick-and-mortar company, or the finest academic institution of our land, individuals and teams expend tremendous amounts of time and energy focusing on how intolerable others' behaviors and intentions are. These dysfunctional inter-departmental dynamics often hijack an organization, overshadowing its most pressing business goals. Reorganizations are a popular, but ineffective, technique to address these issues, because *structural* solutions will always fail to curb the *interpersonal behaviors* at the root of these organizational clashes. More distressing, *possessing the best intentions of avoiding these dynamics is insufficient to prevent them.*

Here's why they happen and how to transform them.

An Illustration

The commissioner of social services of an eastern seaboard state strode into the highly charged atmosphere of a monthly meeting he chaired with the presidents of the state's psychiatric hospitals. He saw this group as self-serving and stridently resisted their constant drumbeat for more funding—which increased their profits—as long as they refused to question the inefficient way they managed the troubled children in their care. His schism with them had recently exploded in the local newspapers, as several youths had psychotic breakdowns while this committee argued over how the hospitals could maximize insurance payments. As the commissioner sat down, the leader of the largest private hospital handed him an agenda—for *his* meeting. This blatant power grab was the final straw in a long string of obstructionist affronts. As the commissioner glanced at the agenda, he resolved that he would never allow this group to force their profitable solutions down his throat at the expense of the state's poorest children. No stranger to conflict, his moral outrage triggered a verbal dogfight that both sides promised to continue in the press.

Although the commissioner knew that his outburst had left the problem of the neglected children completely unresolved, he was at a loss for how to work around the egos, selfish intentions, and longstanding inefficiency of his interlocutors. The feelings were mutual, and in my almost two decades of consulting with senior leaders from government and private industry, I have found this stance of exasperated contempt to be ubiquitous. My colleagues and I call this "unconscious demonization."

Phase I: The Five Steps of Initial Demonization (Downward Spiral)

What the commissioner—like most leaders I encounter—failed to realize was how he had been complicit in the deteriorating situation. In the eighteen months he had been in office prior to the above-cited crisis, he had observed innumerable examples whereby the psychiatric hospital heads lobbied aggressively for their interests. Despite being confident, highly successful, and undaunted by interpersonal conflict, he let many of these interactions become (1) unchecked misinterpretations regarding what their true intentions were. As they resisted his efforts to reform their inefficient hospital practices, his (2) certainty about their ruthless profiteering reinforced itself over time. Bitterly frustrated at his lack of progress on this intractable, high-profile problem, he vented on numerous occasions to his staff and anyone else who would listen, unconsciously (3) seeking reinforcements for his point of view. As he grew more outraged at the hospital presidents' intransigence, he became less trusting, more verbally aggressive in his interactions with them, and more entrenched in his own position—all the while remaining (4) blind to how his own behavior was threatening and frustrating to them. Throughout this time, the commissioner's sense of righteous victimization prevented him from realizing that he and his adversaries were locked in a destructive dance of (5) symmetrical escalation, as the hospital presidents misinterpreted *his* intentions, vented among themselves, and felt victimized by his aggressive personality.

In the end, the parties had "demonized" each other, only able to see what was wrong and untrustworthy in the other. Predictably, the staffs on both sides of the conflict were passionately loyal to their leaders, buying into their resentments and beliefs about the other organizations. "Systemic failure" was the result.

These *Five Steps of Initial Demonization* aim to shed light on how *the downward spiral starts.* But if reversing this cycle were simply a matter of assuming positive intent in others—a frequently expressed intention when the issue is recognized—Us vs. Them conflicts would not be raging out of control all across America's public and private sectors. If senior leaders of multinational corporations lose clients because their respective organizations are fighting with each other instead of taking care of business; if the programmatic and competency departments of matrix organizations around the country waste precious time and money blaming each other; if Democrats and Republicans in Congress are so hopelessly bi-partisan that they'll fight the other party's initiatives just to see them fail; when, in summary, we as humans are compelled to behave in ways that we intellectually know are destructive, *then something other than our professed sense of purpose must be driving us.*

Phase II: The Five Steps of Institutionalized Demonization (Emotional Investment)

The vast majority of leaders—like the Commissioner—fail to consistently implement common-sense tenets of how to collaborate because they have become *emotionally invested* in their demonization cycle. Interpersonal and inter-organizational conflicts can become so embedded in leaders' psyches that they deeply believe that they have no other option than to fight back or work around. Unfortunately, naming and challenging this emotional investment doesn't typically fill us with feelings of self-importance and success. To the contrary, it can feel raw, unnerving and vulnerable—in fact, any leader protective of his or her reputation would never admit to most of the feelings outlined below in the *Five Steps of Institutionalized Demonization*. So they don't—and our dysfunctional organizations continue unabated, costing us dearly in work stress, productivity, and money.

When the social services commissioner and I debriefed his explosive meeting, it was uncomfortable and unsettling for him to begin to acknowledge just how ashamed he had been feeling for months about his very public failure to improve this particular situation. He was sensitive and defensive, (1) unable to effectively manage the anxiety and criticism ricocheting through these meetings. Some people shut down when faced with blame, others lash out; the commissioner's angry rebukes of the hospital presidents' complaints fueled their (2) outrage at feeling misunderstood, unheard, and dismissed, which the commissioner felt himself when they vigorously denied his frustrated claims of their inefficiency. Each side unconsciously cherished (3) the addictive superiority of being right, certain that they were on the side of goodness and intelligence.

The intensity of these feelings built over time into a deeply defensive, morally righteous standoff, like what we might hear when a colleague privately vents his or her frustrations to us in about a colleague we both can't stand, or members of Congress disparage each other's misguided ideology. It gives us an *indomitable sense of power* when we unleash these pent-up feelings. The commissioner furthermore realized that demonizing the hospital presidents as arrogant and selfish had allowed him to (4) completely discredit all claims and issues they raised about his organization; he could justifiably ignore anything he didn't want to admit or that threatened his interests.

When confronted with these emotionally charged booby traps *within himself,* the commissioner copped to a "moral hangover," realizing that he had played a far more dysfunctional role in the previous eighteen months than he had believed. When he considered trying to redress the situation with council members in the next meeting, the prospect of (5) authentically communicating about how he had been feeling and behaving—as opposed to defensively repeating they were doing wrong—was viscerally uncomfortable. At a primal level, he realized with shock, he would rather let these neglected children—*his life's work*—suffer their fate than risk the disclosure of weaknesses that he was sure would be used by the for-profit presidents to counterattack him.

Phase III: Reversing the Spiral (Conscious Humanization)

No significant change in these costly dynamics will occur as long as people's unconscious emotional investment is left intact. No structural reorganization; no amount of incentive, punishment, or cajoling; no reiteration of a mission/vision statement will more than incrementally soften the powerful force of humans locked in this downward spiral.

When the commissioner recognized that the true source of his ire was in fact his own shame at publicly failing to fix this problem—leading him to scapegoat his council colleagues—he took his first step in (1) dispersing the charge of his emotional investment. Although he wanted nothing more than to continue to blame the presidents, he knew instinctively that the cost of doing so would be paid for by the very children he was committed to helping—an unacceptable outcome for him. Fighting through his fear and the resistance of his ego, he resolved to (2) be guided by his highest sense of purpose during these moments of threat and conflict. He accepted that *his* ideology about the problem might lose, as long as the suffering children were more effectively protected.

Terrified of appearing weak or being attacked by his opponents, he nonetheless realized that the most constructive course of action was to (3) create trust through an act of radical vulnerability. When he began the next council meeting with a transparent analysis of why he had reacted so intensely in the previous meeting, as well as how he had contributed to the deterioration of their collaboration since the beginning, it felt like an unthinkably suicidal act. And yet, it was the very person he had most demonized as selfish and close-minded—the leader of the largest for-profit hospital—who was the first to respond to his plea for a different relationship.

The president had long ago retreated into a deeply defensive state, often marked by aggressive counterattacks, in order to ward off the commissioner's war-like stance. When the commissioner offered instead authentic vulnerability, the president was able to (4) "re-humanize" his adversary, responding with a gracious and revealing statement of apology that similarly allowed the commissioner to see beyond the president's previously impenetrable interpersonal armor. These emotionally uncomfortable acts began to exorcise the sense of "danger" and suspicion from the room, and in the space of trust and aligned purpose that progressively emerged, both sides were able to (5) recognize the equal value of each side's perspectives, needs, and goals. The crisis and subsequent healing of these two meetings launched an intensive collaboration over the next eighteen months that saw this intractable, decade-old problem of lengthy wait time for psychiatric services decrease by an unimaginable 40 percent.

Table 10.1 summarizes the three phases of the Us vs. Them cycle. This summary tool is also available at this chapter's online tools.

Table 10.1 The Phases of the Us vs. Them Cycle

Phase I: The Five Steps of Initial Demonization (Downward Spiral)

Step	Explanation	Guiding Practices/Questions
1. Unchecked misinterpretations	We constantly make sense of others' behavior through assigning explanations, typically linked to their (lack of) competency and (ulterior and threatening) motives. The vast majority of leaders lack effective clarification skills, either avoiding the confrontation all together or reacting aggressively, which aggravates the misinterpretation instead of clarifying it.	Be vigilant when you think you know what someone means. Ask clarifying questions, especially if you believe you disagree, rather than debating/ responding. If you want to react aggressively or "shut down," ask yourself when the feeling started and clarify that comment.
2. Reinforcing certainty over time	These unchecked misinterpretations accumulate with each negative interaction, putting us in a biased state of heightened wariness. We progressively become absolutely certain about why we are right to dislike and distrust our adversary.	Pay attention to negative conclusions regarding colleagues' intentions and competency. Test conclusions directly with colleagues with *an exploratory mindset:* "When you say/ do, I conclude . . . " "Help me understand your perspective."

(continued)

3. Seeking reinforcements	Our anger and frustration in these situations can become acute that so we need to vent about it to someone. Invariably, we choose people who agree with us about the other person or group.	If you choose to discuss the issue with a third party, do so only with someone who is not invested in the situation or gaining your approval. Set a clear framework that, although you may need to vent for a few minutes, you want them *to challenge your thinking and views of the other.*
4. Blind to our own behavior	We cannot see ourselves (our tone and/or body language) and are typically unaware of how we might be interpreted by others. We tend to assume that the style and content of our communication is a transparent reflection of our good intentions. Nothing could be further from the truth.	If there is a difficult interaction, ask for feedback on how you communicated (vs. confirmation on how your colleague is at fault). Seek out people who maintain good relations with the colleague (or department), and draw out how your adversary might be experiencing/viewing you.
5. Symmetrical escalation	Everything occurring for us during this demonization cycle is also at play for our adversaries. They are interpreting our behavior, forming a strongly held opinion over time, venting within their own trusted circles, and seeing the entire problem as us, not themselves.	Ask yourself: What might they be feeling behind that behavior? (Beware of the easy answers where you write them off as egomaniacs!) If I were behaving that way, what might be going on for me?

N.B.: If you are reading these practices, and thinking about a difficult relationship—and have a strong negative reaction (e.g., "There's no way I'm going to do that with him/her"), take that as a sign that you are "emotionally invested" in demonizing that person. The Phase II outline below applies specifically to you!

(continued)

Phase II: The Five Steps of Institutionalized Demonization (Emotional Investment)

Step	Explanation	Guiding Practices/Questions
1. Ineffectively manage anxiety and (public) criticism	Our deeply engrained desire to appear competent, intelligent, and right in others' and our own eyes makes us very quick to react negatively to any comments that might imply the contrary. These automatic defensive postures shut down constructive dialogue (and limit our learning).	How are my defense mechanisms (tied to my own ego) triggered? Am I afraid of appearing incompetent? Being judged as stupid or weak? Of failing? (Phase II, Steps 1 and 2 are the true—and primary—sources of your anger at the other person. We call these your HOT BUTTONS.) What am I refusing to acknowledge about my shortcomings in this situation?
2. Outrage at feeling misunderstood, unheard, dismissed	This outrage is rarely experienced or expressed as a sense of being hurt, because "strong" leaders have thick skin. Current U.S. organizational culture makes it awkward and uncomfortable to discuss these feelings, so we ignore or rationalize them to our detriment. Instead, we act them out through criticizing, undermining, or withdrawing.	You need to be willing to be deeply honest and simple about these raw feelings. Express them as inarticulate bullet points vs. eloquent and rational paragraphs. How were my feelings hurt? Look in the places that feel "yucky"—where you feel petty, needy, insecure. Admit them (perhaps already just to yourself). Then offer empathy to yourself that you are a human being with feelings. If you are able, aim to recenter yourself on a guiding principle such as "I neither want to feel this way, nor cause others to feel this way."

(continued)

3. Addicted to the superiority of being right	There is a powerful high of holding the "right" position in a conflict, surpassed only by the discomfort of being wrong. Being right (i.e., my position and opinions are vindicated) often becomes the predominant concern in a leader's mind, overshadowing the end goal.	What am I sure—certain!—that I'm right about in this situation? Seek, with others, to challenge that your view is the entire view of reality. What can you acknowledge that contradicts your position? What are your colleagues sure they are right about? What is true about their point of view?
4. Discredit our adversary's claims and issues	If our adversary's skills and intentions lack value and integrity, it conveniently renders illegitimate the positions and issues he or she may have. This allows us to justify avoiding questioning or addressing our beliefs, views of reality, weaknesses or contributions to the conflict. Righteously preserving our status quo is one significant benefit of demonizing others.	What are their priorities and incentives? What would I be worried about were I in their shoes? How is what my organization or I are doing a threat to their priorities? How can I relate to their concerns? How do their concerns illuminate opportunities for improvement in my organization? How can I grow my understanding of the system to incorporate *both* perspectives? If I can rise above my silo and see a broader vision, then I am ready to *lead* at that next level.
5. Authentic communication is viscerally uncomfortable	Anger is a far more powerful and comfortable feeling than that of hurt, weakness, or vulnerability. Having and expressing these latter emotions can expose us to judgment, criticism, or being taken advantage of. Both avoidance and aggression are rooted in these fears. Emotional courage, very different than taking business risks, is a rare commodity.	What could I share that would feel uncomfortable to disclose but could help my colleagues see beyond my defensive armor? How do I feel judged or hurt by them? What am I struggling to do well in my organization? How do I need their help? Clarify and share my highest intentions in this situation (see Phase III, Reversing the Spiral).

(continued)

Phase III: Reversing the Spiral (Conscious Humanization)

Step	Explanation	Guiding Practices/Questions
1. Disperse the charge of emotional investment	People are not able to genuinely challenge their biases or begin to process and express their past pains if they are, consciously or unconsciously, captivated by the above types of emotional investment. Conversely—and this is the very hopeful part—I have repeatedly witnessed the dramatic diffusion of an otherwise intractable conflict when parties have been able to acknowledge their emotional investment.	The questions of Phase II aim to create the self-awareness necessary to uproot my blame of the other person and reclaim my responsibility in the situation. Do I "get" the other person's point of view? Can I articulate why I have been emotionally invested in demonizing the other group? Do I have distance from those feelings or I still talk about them in disparaging terms?
2. Be guided by our highest sense of purpose during moments of threat and conflict	Humans suffer from "confused" goals. On the one hand, we want to learn, contribute, collaborate (my ecosystem goals); on the other hand, we want to be right, respected, and perceived as highly competent (my ego system goals). When these two goals conflict, the latter type of goals (which protects our self-image and sense of self-worth) hijack our more noble intentions. Bob Kegan and Lisa Lahey refer to this as "competing commitments" in their book, *Immunity to Change*. We need to learn as a culture to not only prioritize our "true" goals, but to elicit that same ability in others.	What do I care about more than protecting my sense of self-worth? (Yes, there are *many* things, we just don't know how to be guided by them), such as my growth as a leader, what's at stake in our business, the quality of relationship I create, who I want to be as a human being. How is transforming this relationship an opportunity to grow to my next level as a leader? What leadership skills can I develop in leading from above the fray of this Us vs. Them dynamic? Test my clarity: even if I appear and/or feel in ways that trigger my hot buttons (incompetent, disrespected, weak, vulnerable), are these

(continued)

Developing Talent for Organizational Results

| 3. Create trust through radical vulnerability | Since this Us vs. Them mechanism is symmetrical, the other side of a conflict has as much *legitimate* mistrust and pain as we do. They are as convinced as we are that if they reveal anything truthful, we will use it against them. If each side waits for the other to become trustworthy, progress will be incremental at best. As uncomfortable as it may feel, only when a mistrusted colleague (you!) has acknowledged his or her suspect behaviors, explained the fears driving them, and undertaken to make change can others feel safe enough to tentatively trust. | other goals more important? Enough to keep me centered if the other person falls into threatening behaviors? See Phase II, Step 5. How am I threatening to these other colleagues? How do I create mistrust? Am I willing to search for the courage to take the first step in creating trust? If I don't, who will? What will be the consequences if no one does? |
| 4. Re-humanize our adversary | We must learn to actively challenge our demonized view of others. This does not mean throwing out what I believe and naively assuming the opposite, but using my awareness of the Initial Demonization cycle to galvanize a commitment to develop a complete view. It is important to highlight that this re-humanizing process must be a very deliberate, | See Phase II, Step 4. Don't allow myself or others to vent about these colleagues, even for a minute. Challenge yourself and others to see their points of view. Schedule regular meetings with a counterpart with whom you believe you can build rapport. Become a bridge between silos by proactively addressing issues that come up instead of letting hallway churn reinforce |

(continued)

Phase III: Reversing the Spiral (Conscious Humanization)

Step	Explanation	Guiding Practices/Questions
	proactive act, and will feel dissonant. No one deliberately believes in something false or wrong; thus, dismantling our certainties is cognitively and emotionally difficult.	each sides' negative beliefs about the other.
5. Recognize the equal value of each side's perspectives, needs, and goals	This piece of the puzzle seems like straightforward common sense. In the dialogue movement, Phase III Steps 4 and 5 are commonly practiced in aiming to resolve conflicts. Without significant progress on the first three points, however, resolution is limited and temporary.	See Phase II, Step 4. You have a lot to learn, especially from people you despise. Do they think, lead, communicate differently than you do? What could you emulate in them? What are their core priorities, and how could you help them achieve them? How could they do the same for you?

Soft Skills Are Hardest to Learn

What is generally known—people have egos, fight-flight behaviors don't make for effective leadership, turf wars undermine collaboration—doesn't necessarily translate into *personal self-awareness*. Most of us are not effective at analyzing the semi-conscious motivations of our behaviors, tending to mistake sophisticated rationalization for thoughtful reflection. While the top leaders in our corporations and government may be smart, well-educated, and hard-working, they are not typically aware of the massive blind spots that undermine their leadership. Furthermore, dismissing the uncomfortable work of acknowledging and dispersing our emotional investment in counterproductive behaviors as "touchy feely" simply allows these pervasive dysfunctions to proliferate—to the detriment of our personal productivity, work life stress, and organizational performance.

Several years after a financial services CEO lead his thriving organization to record profits, double-digit employee engagement gains, and an industry-unprecedented joint venture in India, he surveyed a multi-leveled leadership cadre emotionally invested in supporting each other to achieve their collective goals versus belittling their respective weaknesses. He summed it up: "When a lot of smart colleagues all stopped vying to be the smartest person in the room, we began learning from each other and leveraging our different perspectives to the company's benefit."

You, too, can learn to learn from each other and leverage your various perspectives for the benefit of your organization.

About Learning as Leadership

For more than twenty-five years, Learning as Leadership (LaL) has made a positive and lasting impact on some of the world's largest organizations. Through a combination of leadership retreats, individual and team coaching, and in-depth interview-based 360 assessments, LaL has supported such clients as M&T Bank, Shell Oil, LexisNexis, Capital One, Encore Capital, Fairchild Semiconductor, NASA, and the U.S. Navy to achieve powerful individual and organizational change. Ultimately LaL's aim is to free people/teams and organizations from the limitations of their "ego-systems." LaL's methodology is taught at the Harvard Business School, Stanford University, the University of California, Berkeley, the University of Michigan Ross School of Business, and the Darden School of Business.

Submitted by Shayne Hughes, CEO

Learning as Leadership

1000 4th Street, Suite 300

San Rafael, CA 94901

(415) 453-5050

shayneh@learnaslead.com

www.learnaslead.com

Learning as Leadership
A revolution in your evolution

3D Perception Sharing*

THE DEDE HENLEY GROUP

We are being called to work together more effectively, to collaborate, in many areas at work. The problems we are facing today are far greater than our current individual skill and ability to solve them. We must expand our skill to collaborate effectively together. In part, working together better means that we must increase the levels of trust and respect we have for one another. The exercise that follows is designed to increase trust, respect, and mutual understanding between two disparate groups at work.

This exercise can be used any time two groups are ready to listen and learn from one another: when two groups know that finding ways to work together better is the only reasonable answer. It is best done as a facilitated exercise using a skilled facilitator, especially if there are tensions between the two groups. Ideally, there are two facilitators, one to help facilitate each group on opposite sides of a room.

---

*Adapted from "Intergroup Image Exchange: Exploring the Relationship Between Two Teams," *A Handbook of Structured Experiences for Human Relations Training* (Vol. III, rev.), edited by J.W. Pfeiffer and J.E. Jones, 1974, San Francisco, CA: Pfeiffer.

OBJECTIVES

- To explore how two different groups perceive themselves and the other group.
- To assist the members of two groups to improve the relationship between the members of the two groups.
- To increase communication, understanding, and compassion across two disparate groups.

THE INTENDED AUDIENCE

Two groups of five or more people (up to a total of twenty-five participants) who must work together effectively and struggle to do so. This exercise is not for groups that are in union negotiations or in need of other remediation. It is for groups that are relatively healthy and need to increase trust, understanding, and respect.

TIME REQUIRED

75 to 90 minutes.

MATERIALS AND EQUIPMENT

- Two to four flip-chart stands with paper and markers.
- Markers.
- Bar chime or other means of getting the group's attention.

AREA SETUP

A room large enough to seat the members of both teams on opposite sides of the room so that each group can work without disturbing the other group. Participants may stand or can pull up chairs around their flip charts while they are working in two separate groups. Tables are not necessary. Be sure that there are no tables or chairs between the two groups in the middle of the room.

PROCESS

1. Before breaking the groups in two, explain that they are going to explore and respond to four questions.

   - How do we see ourselves?
   - How do we see them?

- How do we think they see us?
- How would we like to be seen by them?

   Explain that the groups will have about 10 minutes for each question.

2. Invite the two groups to move to opposite sides of the room either standing or sitting on chairs around their assigned flip charts. Face the flip charts away from the opposite group.

3. Ask them to write the first question at the top of their flip charts: "How do we see ourselves?"

4. Have them select a recorder from each group to record the group responses to each question. Allow for participants to respond in a "popcorn" style—no need to go around person by person. Whoever has a response just pops it out. The scribe does his or her best to succinctly capture what was said. Observe the groups, providing clarity or a summary when necessary.

5. You may need to push the groups to deepen honesty in each group's responses by asking questions such as: What don't you want to admit? What haven't you been acknowledged for?

6. When the energy starts to wane for the question, "How do we see ourselves?" move to the next question by starting a fresh piece of flip-chart paper. Have them write the next question at the top of the flip-chart pad: How do we see them?

7. Repeat with the last two questions:
- How do we think they see us?
- How would we like to be seen by them?

8. When both groups are finished, have participants gather together in seats formed in a circle. A representative from each group takes a turn reading the lists for the first three questions: How we see ourselves, How we see them, and How we think they see us. As the lists are being shared, invite participants to make eye contact with those from the other group.

9. After both sets of the first three lists are read, pause. Debrief and deepen the conversation, stating, "These thoughts, judgments, and stories we have about our group and the 'other' group are subverted when they aren't openly shared. In order to increase trust, we must become more responsible about our judgments and assessments of each other." Ask for their thoughts.

10. Ask each participant to find a new person of the opposite group to connect with, meeting his or her eyes and holding them while you read one of the group's list of how they want to be seen.

11. Invite the participants to make eye contact with someone new from the other group as they listen to you read the second group's response to the fourth question.

12. Invite participants to choose partners from the opposite group. Tell them to sit knee to knee with these partners (or form mixed groups of four) and share what they do or don't do that gets in the way of being seen how they want to be seen. For example, if one of the groups said that they want to be seen as trusted partners, have a member of that group in the knee to knee say what they do or don't do that limits them from being seen as trusted partners. Another way of asking this question is "How do you contribute to how you are seen?" Encourage participants to focus on the negative side, without shame or judgment. Challenge the participants to not make excuses. Say: "Do not get into a discussion. Be accountable for what you've done or not done. This is about being responsible for creating things to be the way they are, not blame. Becoming responsible increases trust." Give pairs about 5 minutes to share how they are responsible, what they have done that gets in the way of them being seen the way they want to be seen.

13. Next invite the participants to consider what they each might have to give up to be seen in this way. Ask: "What old pattern or habit are you holding onto? When are you not representing this list? In some form, we are creating these lists of how we are seen." Have them share with their partners from the other group.

14. Have each participant choose two ways that he or she would like to be seen from the written lists. Ask each of them to share these two with partners. Challenge them to choose areas that are a stretch. Suggest that they also share what they might have to give up or take on that would allow them to be seen this way and how to make it a reality. Ask them to tell their partners how, specifically, they will take this on and be committed to it. They could add who will they will practice this with and when they will do it.

15. Close the exercise by inviting the participants to thank their partners and to return to the large group. If time allows, you can ask for comments in the large group:

    - "What have you learned about yourself today?"
    - "What have you learned about the other group?"
    - "What will you take away from this exercise?"

16. To close the activity, invite each participant to state one word about what this exercise has been like for him or her.

INSIDER'S TIPS

- Keep the energy of the group moving as you are working with each group on opposite sides of the room in answering the four questions. Move on to the next question if you feel the energy starting to wane.

- Facilitate with care, knowing that sometimes antagonism can build between two groups. Do not allow personal attacks—no names on the flip charts.

- Keep pushing for personal responsibility. This is not about getting "them" to change. It is about how each individual can take personal responsibility for the way things are and make changes to make it better.

About the Dede Henley Group

The Dede Henley Group, a Seattle-based consulting firm, focuses on organization and leadership development. We are small enough to tailor our work to our clients' very specific needs and large enough to deliver whole system organization development. The diversity of our expertise allows us to partner with clients from many industries, bringing depth and breadth to each of our client engagements. We have deep expertise in leadership, team, and organization development.

We are skilled in transformational development. Traditional team and leadership development focuses on skill-building and incremental change, improvement bit-by-bit. Transformational team and leadership development is inquiry-based, meaning that there is no prescribed learning, but rather an inquiry into what matters most, where an individual is stopped or stuck and how to move. Skill-building still takes place, but it is done against a backdrop of transformational questions and inquiry. Transformational learning involves becoming more reflective and critical, being more open to the perspectives of others, and being less defensive and more accepting of new ideas.

Submitted by Dede Henley, MSOD

The Dede Henley Group

17837 First Avenue, South, PMB 302

Seattle, WA 98148

(206) 686-4400

dede@dedehenley.com

www.dedehenley.com

the DEDE HENLEY GROUP
the inspiration to lead

EXECUTIVE ESSENTIALS

Introduction

As an employee moves through the various roles of doer, supervisor, manager, and executive, it is clear that skill sets must both expand and deepen. What does it take to be an executive in a company? Clearly there is no single or simple answer, but recent interviews with individuals in executive positions yielded two broad categories of skills.

First is a set of characteristics describing the individual, or attributes. Second is a list of skills executives employ to get results, or competencies. These are, of course, blended in different combinations and extents in different people. Companies face different challenges at different points in time, and executives need the agility to draw upon the attributes and competencies depending on the challenges.

The following lists are not exhaustive but prove illustrative.

Individual attributes include integrity/ethics, trustworthiness, analytic intelligence, sense of urgency, willingness to ask for help, appropriate decision making, ability to simplify, candor, creative questioning approach, leadership, openness, empathy, potential problem identification, vision/perspective, ego drive, endurance, willingness to assume unqualified accountability, organized, and a willingness to take the lead.

Results-oriented competencies include things such as the ability to market, articulate, and champion a vision; communicate well; identify, grow, and deploy core competencies; take initiative; establish strategy; focus on profitability; build a team; define and deliver clear objectives; monitor self; remove obstacles for others; establish and enforce a culture; ask the right questions; innovate; focus on both short- and long-term future; identify problems early; solve problems; encourage continuous learning; and act with decisiveness and agility.

We have high expectations and standards for our executives. The chapters in this section are particularly exciting because they are generally outside the norm. They are, indeed, executive in nature.

- Chapter 11, "Brilliance in Brief" by Zenger Folkman, observes that interaction time between leaders and others is becoming shorter with no change in the foreseeable future. Since short discussions are the reality, the chapter suggests ways to maximize brief interactions.

- In Chapter 12, "Leading with Integrity" by Strategic Leadership Collaborative, Inc., leaders are challenged to align their values with those of their organization. A four-step process delivers an opportunity for leaders to determine what they represent and value.

- In Chapter 13, "How to Tell a Story . . . and Why," Kevin Daley Communications delivers a compelling rationale for why leaders should use the technique more often. The author, Mr. Storyteller himself, uses storytelling (what else) to make his points—five steps to tell a story the right way.

- Chapter 14, "Your Invitation to Greatness" by Impression Management Professionals, tells us how executives build accountability with consequences and how executives build strategic leaders. The chapter is filled with take-away snippets.

- Chapter 15, "How Does a CEO *Do* Engagement?" by Fierce, Inc., presents both the importance of engagement to executives and a method executives can use to gain involvement from employees. The introduction of beach ball meetings increases engagement during and following the meeting.

Chapter 11

Brilliance in Brief

ZENGER FOLKMAN

In This Chapter

- Introduction of the importance of brief interactions.
- Observations of leaders' effective time use.
- Suggestions for maximizing brief interactions.

In 1973 Henry Mintzberg published a landmark book entitled *The Nature of Managerial Work*. In it he described how managers whom he had observed engaged in extremely brief interactions. The average CEO interaction lasted nine minutes or less, with the average one-on-one meeting being only twelve minutes long. Their phone calls averaged six minutes.

The foremen that he observed had interactions that lasted on average forty-eight seconds. "Management," he concluded, "was simply one damn thing after another." Mintzberg then noted that the big dangers in this pattern of behavior centered around the tendency for all these interactions to become superficial and minimally productive.

In the nearly forty years since the book was published, the world has become even more hectic. Hours that managers spend on the job are longer. The pace is faster. Spans of control are wider. Many important interactions are invariably given short shrift or never occur at all. People development, including any kind of managerial coaching, is one of the activities being sacrificed. When asked about this choice, we have found that the reason that is given by more than 85 percent of the leaders is lack of time. In their jam-packed days, they feel they cannot take time to coach subordinates.

It is not likely that this pattern will change dramatically in the next few years. If we accept that reality, how can brief interactions be made more effective? What techniques can be given to leaders in any organization to help them cope with this unrelenting pace and yet utilize the leverage that their position gives them? How can this endless torrent of brief interactions be made more productive to free up time for the really important leadership acts?

The leadership techniques being proposed in this chapter are appropriate for any and all leaders; and they are equally helpful for the professional individual contributors in the firm. Our belief is that, while these key professionals don't have traditional managerial titles, they often provide a great deal of leadership inside most organizations.

The Main Message

Here are some conclusions for you to consider:

1. *The answer is not to cut back on the number of interactions.* Nor is the objective to try to make them shorter. Make them full of more substance and don't let them become superficial. Utilize the time spent in fruitful communication. One of the key functions of leadership is to inspire and motivate the people who report to you. This happens through meaningful interactions. Minimizing the frequency of such encounters is not in the best interest of the organization because it only minimizes your impact on people.

2. *There is not a direct correlation between the time spent interacting with someone and the amount of information that is exchanged or the influence exerted.* Many people labor under the assumption that there is a direct correlation between time and influence, or time spent and the amount of real communication that occurs. They believe that the longer the meeting, the more valuable it will be. They mistakenly think that the more extensive the conversation, the more likely it is that a message will get across.

   Malcolm Gladwell, in his book *Blink,* offers several intriguing examples that show how much communication occurs in extremely short snippets of time. Students can get a quite accurate view of how effective a professor will be by simply watching a twenty-second video clip. But experimenters then turned the audio off and had students watch a few-seconds-long, silent video clip. Students were still able to make an accurate prediction of how effective the professor would be. What's the point? We communicate a great deal in a very short time.

3. *Words make up only a tiny fraction of what is communicated.* Facial expressions, body language, tone of voice, sincerity, genuine interest—all these things convey far more than words. Our primary vehicle of communication is not merely words; it is our presence and persona. The great bulk of communication comes through the non-verbal signals that we send that obviously can be reinforced and supported by the words that we speak.

4. *Recognize that you are extremely contagious—emotionally contagious, that is.* We all know from experience that emotions are contagious. We can be in a meeting and soon come to realize that one sour, prickly person is sending the meeting into a downward spiral. Remove that person and replace him or her with an upbeat, positive individual and the meeting is transformed. People laugh. They are more creative. Honesty replaces caution and game playing.

   Now, if any one person's emotions spill over onto others, consider the influence of the leader who possesses role power in addition to whatever personal characteristics he or she might have. Leaders are exponentially contagious. The leader's emotions immediately permeate the entire work group.

5. *Others will hesitate less to connect with you if they know it won't be lengthy.* My wife has a short list of people whom she greatly resists calling because she knows it will inevitably be a lengthy conversation and she often feels she simply doesn't have the time. I suspect many of us can identify with that.

   I worked for several years for a person who inevitably launched into a forty-five-minute monologue on any topic that was introduced. He was a personable and extremely intelligent individual. But everyone thought twice about going to see him, hesitant about the amount of time it would take to get to the point.

6. *One way to convey respect for others is to use their time well.* One of the foundation principles of many courses on leadership is the one that describes the importance of treating people with respect. Obviously, there are many ways a leader does that. Tone of voice is one. Asking serious questions and listening for the answer is another. One that people often overlook is simply how leaders use the time of the people with whom they work.

   Respecting someone else's time is clearly a mark of respect. Avoiding a lengthy conversation when someone is busy is a mark of respect. Not holding lengthy, unproductive meetings is a mark of respect.

7. *Making frequent interactions highly productive frees blocks of time for planning, problem solving, and all those activities requiring more extended periods.* There clearly

are some activities that require blocks of time, ranging from thirty minutes to two hours. The evidence is that the great bulk of managers simply cannot find such chunks of time and that days, and sometimes weeks, pass without having that luxury.

The only way that such time blocks can be created on a regular basis is for the operating leader to efficiently handle the day-to-day interactions in a brisk way.

Maximizing Brief Interactions

SIX WAYS TO MANAGE BRIEF INTERACTIONS

1. When you are in the driver's seat, pick up the pace.
2. When others initiate the conversation, gently move it forward.
3. Train colleagues on what to expect from you.
4. Organize items to discuss with colleagues, a manager, or subordinates.
5. Schedule shorter meetings.
6. Move staff meetings at a brisk pace.

So are there some specific suggestions for better managing daily interactions? Try these:

1. *When you are in the driver's seat, pick up the pace.* There is great value in getting out of your office and visiting people. Make the rounds. Use a major part of the time to give people positive reinforcement. Ask questions that provide you with valuable information. Practice good listening skills. But at the same time, you can also pick up the pace. These interactions need not be lengthy.

2. *When others initiate the conversation, gently move it forward.* After appropriate pleasantries, ask what people want or need and how you can help them. "I sense you came in because you needed something—what would that be?"

3. *Train colleagues on what to expect from you.* Be slow to give directives or answer questions before finding out the other person's opinion. Ask, "What do you think?" or "What have you been considering?" If they seem unclear about what

they need, help them to get clear about what they need from you. In time, your colleagues will come to you with solutions to discuss, rather than merely asking questions or seeking decisions.

4. *Collect topics that need to be discussed with colleagues, your manager, and your subordinates.* Memories are treacherous. Using software programs such as Outlook or Notes, or a more traditional paper-based planner, provides a way to collect and organize items that have to be discussed so that meetings can be efficient and cover all necessary topics. How often have you had a meeting with someone, only to receive a call, or to make the call yourself, that says, "Oh, by the way, I forgot to discuss another important item with you. . . ." That is very inefficient.

5. *Schedule shorter meetings.* Not every meeting needs to last one hour—or even a half-hour. Meetings inevitably expand to fill the time allotted for them, so experiment with shorter times. Ask for everyone's help in adhering to the time and to avoid unnecessary tangents.

I worked in an organization in which the head of research also served as a professor at a local university. People would call his office asking for an appointment and his assistant would say, "He has three minutes tomorrow morning at 9:21." Yes, some were taken aback, and I suspect some were offended. But they came prepared, and he gave them his full attention for that time.

6. *Make staff and team meetings highly efficient.* Carefully prepared agendas, materials sent out in advance, clear objectives for each topic item, a person identified as responsible for that item, and action minutes of the meeting—these are the ingredients of effective meetings. But along with that, the person chairing the meeting needs to keep up the pace and monitor the process of the meeting, ensuring that people are included and that people are given a chance to be heard and understood.

Conclusion

We will not change the fundamental way in which organizations function. The hectic pace of leaders that is characterized by brief interactions will not go away. The opportunity is for us to manage that in a better way. Brief interactions can be very effective if we simply work at making them work.

There is a need for leaders to have more extended conversations. There is a need for longer discussions of planning and strategy. The only way most of us will ever create time for such meaningful discussions is for us to learn how to make the rest of the time maximally productive through better management of that steady stream of brief interactions.

About Zenger Folkman

Zenger Folkman improves organizations by developing the leadership strength required for them to grow and thrive. It increases leaders' and leadership teams' effectiveness by creating cultures in which productivity and engagement soar; where "silos" are replaced with collaboration; where behaviors are aligned with strategy; and where innovation blossoms.

Zenger Folkman is noted for pioneering, empirical research utilizing large databases. These currently include one million multi-rater (or 360-degree) feedback instruments that provide detailed data on over 100,000 leaders. This empirical research is then combined with decades of practical experience to create development programs that actually build leadership strengths.

The firm emphasizes sustainability through involvement of line managers. By combining implementation tools, personalized coaching, and programs with advanced instructional design, Zenger Folkman creates award-winning development programs for clients worldwide.

Submitted by Jack Zenger, CEO

Zenger Folkman

1550 N. Technology Way, Bldg. D

Orem, UT 84097

(801) 705-9375

info@zfco.com

www.zfco.com

 ZENGER | FOLKMAN

Chapter 12

Leading with Integrity
Walking Your Talk
STRATEGIC LEADERSHIP COLLABORATIVE, INC.

In This Chapter

- Increase self-awareness of what drives leaders.
- Helps leaders align their values with those of their organization and guard against ethical violations.
- Four-step process to help leaders clarify what they stand for.

Lofty goal or expected behavior? In either case, values-based leaders are becoming more and more accountable for what they say, how they act, and what they believe. Given the too-frequent recent accounts of outright unethical and often questionable behavior outside commonly accepted social norms, businesses expect their leaders to toe the line and to stay within the bounds of productive and morally acceptable behavior. The costs of not doing so are legion, as we have all seen on personal, professional, and organizational levels. What can organizations do to ensure these questionable behaviors don't occur? How can they be assured their leaders do, in fact, toe the line while taking the necessary calculated risks to help their organizations grow by continually meeting the needs of all their stakeholders?

Certainly, effectively identifying and assessing leaders before selecting them is one solution, but as is well known, this is anything but a science, and many cases exist where the so-called right person turned out to be a big disappointment. Sure, some leaders can be trained in how to be more honest, true to their company's and their own values, and clear about what they stand for. But what if the training doesn't work? Even excellent training finds it difficult to turn a sow's ear into a silk purse, especially when temptations and acquired power interfere with sound judgment. Nonetheless, helping leaders get in touch with who they are, what they believe, and how they need to act to be ethically and morally effective is paramount to leading with integrity.

An Example

Charlie was a young upstart in his organization, bright, good-looking, personable, and rapidly moving up the corporate ladder. He had graduated from the right schools, had the right job experiences, and was taken under the wing of several senior executives. He was, in fact, the perfect model for success, at least on the surface. The problem with Charlie, however, was that he tended to lead from the seat of his pants rather than from his heart. So, when recently asked to take on a major initiative for bringing to market a new product, he faced considerable consternation. With no true value system to anchor his beliefs, he wandered aimlessly, frequently changing his approach and showing inconsistency in his opinions and leadership style. You see, Charlie had moved up in the company by catering to the whims of whichever senior executive last spoke with him. He was fabulous at rolling with the punches but awful at either stating or showing his convictions. And when it came to taking a risk, even a calculated one, you could bet he'd take the safest route. It was no wonder this project suffered from delays, cost overruns, and in the end an unsuccessful product launch. Nothing Charlie did was unethical; Charlie simply possessed no values compass that guided him to make decisions and lead based on what he believed. You can imagine how frustrated his direct reports were during this process. One thing Charlie did very well, of course, was cover his backside. At the end of the day, he was perfectly comfortable with throwing everyone around him under the proverbial bus to save his own butt.

But then there was Sarah, who also worked for Charlie's company. Sarah was Charlie's peer in another division and grew up through the school of hard knocks. She worked her way up the ladder, wasn't handed anything on a silver platter, and pretty much purposely kept under the radar screen. She, too, was asked to take on a major initiative as a developmental experience, namely, to work on re-engineering the product manufacturing quality improvement process. Sarah was also a bright young future star of the company, although not with Charlie's so-called pedigree. In fact, Sarah didn't fit the corporate mold at all. She might even be one of the last people thought to be in the high-potential category. But what Sarah possessed was a clear sense of who she was, what she believed in, and just what was important to her both personally and professionally. Because of this it was easy for her to lead her team, and they loved working for her because, right or wrong, she stood up for her beliefs and they knew what to expect from her, whether they agreed or not. It didn't matter to her that she pleased anyone, but rather that she stayed true to her values in how she thought, acted, and interacted. When time came to complete her project, she did so on time, under budget, and with great success.

Now, we can't assume that Charlie and Sarah's paths to effectiveness were strictly a function of their disparate approaches to work. There may have been a number of other factors entering into their equations. But one thing we probably can conclude is that, all things being equal, Sarah had a better chance of success than Charlie, if for no other reason than that she was clear on what she stood for and acted accordingly. By the way, neither of them faced ethical or moral decisions, per se, which is to say that values-driven behavior isn't simply about staying out of trouble. It's more about being an effective leader.

Walking Your Talk

One thing is for certain: these days, all eyes are on leaders all the time, even though they might not expect it. Therefore, it is critical that leaders establish credibility in the eyes of their followers and lead with personal integrity by "walking their talk." Walking the talk directly relates to how others perceive someone, as perceptions are built from what one says and does and the degree to which these behaviors support what is espoused and valued. As a leader, one's reputation for leading by example directly influences one's ability to engage and influence others when communicating one's personal vision and being able to sustain momentum over time. Leaders may judge themselves by their principles and values, but others judge them simply by their actions.

The results of effectively walking the talk are that leaders will be able to:

1. Define, create, and communicate their unique leadership personas.

2. Align actions and behaviors with their personal values.

3. Enhance their understanding or the impact of their actions and interactions on others.

4. Communicate with others in an authentic and inspiring way.

The road to *walking your talk* involves four steps and the answers to their respective questions:

1. *Clarifying Your Leadership Brand:* Why is it so important to clarify your leadership brand? As we could see from Charlie and Sarah's stories, if for no other reason than to help guide you in your daily decision making so that you think, act, and interact consistent with your beliefs. This speeds up decision making because you don't have to constantly think about what it means. It just flows and comes naturally. There's no second-guessing. It doesn't mean you will always be right and make the so-called "right" decision, but it does mean that you will have followed your heart and won't have to wonder whether you did the right thing based on your beliefs.

   In clarifying you leadership brand you need to be able to comfortably and consistently answer these questions:

   - What do you value?

   - What is your leadership promise?

   - What do you value about leading and why?

2. *Articulating Your Leadership Story:* Storytelling is an ancient way to communicate. Indeed, before our ancestors learned to document their experiences through writing, they passed on their experiences and lessons learned by elders in the form of stories of their past. Many cultures even today, such as Native Americans, still rely on this format to teach new generations the customs of the past. Stories are a great way to put a stake in the ground around what you believe because they reflect examples of how you have previously acted and the results of those actions. They make it easier for not only you but the people around you to more fully understand where you are coming from. From real stories about your experiences, you are able to share what your values actually look like when they occur in the real world. They serve as anchors you can use to lean on in tough times and project yourself as you'd like to those around you. But, most importantly, being able to clearly articulate your leadership story helps you more fully recognize what you stand for and demonstrates ways you've actually manifested that in the past.

   To better articulate your leadership story you'll want to answer these questions:

   - What do you want others to know about you?

   - What is your talk?

3. *Leading by Example:* What does leading by example have to do with walking your talk? Very simply, it is the only way to actually validate what you say you believe. Stories are great, but they represent the past, can be embellished to make any point desired, and are often difficult to verify. But leading by example is where the rubber meets the road. It is "doing what you say you will do" (DWYSYWD). If you can't lead by doing what you believe in, how can you expect your followers to not only understand and accept your approach but to begin to more closely align themselves with you? This isn't to say you need to create lemmings who follow your every move and look and act like you. That's not the goal of leading by example. Rather, it is to provide people with an up-close and personal observation of what you actually stand for. Leading by example is the behavioral manifestation of your leadership story, in real and present time.

In order to be clear about how you lead by example, you will want to answer these questions:

- What will you say and do to ensure your leadership story is alive and demonstrated?
- What is your walk?

4. *Receiving Feedback and Evaluation:* Finally, why is obtaining feedback about what and how you are demonstrating your values so important? Well, how else are you going to know whether you are really acting the way you think you are? What better way to check in with yourself than to ask for and receive feedback from those observing you leading by example . . . or not? And what makes feedback so valuable is that you can obtain it from varied sources under different circumstance, from distinct people allowing you to better understand how you are "showing up" as opposed to guessing. Certainly, part of the feedback process involves your own self-reflection to see whether you feel you are aligned with the feedback from others you are receiving. So, whether is it via a 360-degree process or just from one source, it is invaluable information to have to check yourself on the extent to which you are indeed walking your talk.

As you engage in a feedback process, be sure to ask yourself these questions:

- Are your actions aligned with your beliefs?
- Do your behaviors reflect your values?

The online tool for this chapter will walk you through these same four steps in great detail. The exercise is valuable for leaders at every level in the organization. It's also an excellent exercise for coaches to use with leaders.

Conclusion

James Kouzes and Barry Posner have found in their extensive leadership research that "leaders who aren't clear about what they believe are likely to change their position with every fad and opinion poll" (2006, p. 97). By defining your values, you will better understand your actions, including:

- Moral judgments.
- Response to others.
- Commitments to personal and organizational goals.

When there is harmony between your personal values and those of your organization, there are significant payoffs for you, the people you lead, and the organization to which you belong. Consider the following benefits of shared values:

- Foster strong feelings of personal effectiveness.
- Create high levels of loyalty.
- Facilitate consensus about key organizational goals and stakeholders.
- Encourage ethical behavior.
- Promote strong norms about working hard and caring.
- Reduce levels of job stress and tensions.
- Foster pride in the company.
- Facilitate an understanding of job expectations.
- Stimulate teamwork and esprit de corps.

While shared values are important, an individual's understanding of and clarity about his or her personal values is more important. Ultimately, it's people in the organization who make decisions, not the organization itself. Therefore, the first and most critical step is to clarify your own personal values. In order to do this, you need to be able to clearly answer these three questions:

1. What is your persona?
2. What is your promise?
3. What do you want to be known for?

Remember Charlie's and Sarah's stories? Which one do you think was more likely to succeed? Which one was more likely to be comfortable in his or her own skin? Which one possessed an inner compass that would guide him or her in how he or she showed up? In fact, the story ends as might be expected. Charlie never moved up from his current position because it became clear he didn't possess that inner compass that illustrated to others just what he stood for. Thus, it was hard to get people to follow him and harder for him to influence those around him, even though they knew he was smart, hard-working, and generally a good guy. Sarah, on the other hand, was promoted after she completed her quality improvement project. It's pretty obvious it's not hard to *walk your talk* if you are committed to doing so. And the rewards are legion on many levels. Sarah's true colors were on display, and because of that everyone knew what she stood for and what they could expect from her, like it or not.

So, while Woody Allen's oft-quoted comment states that "80 percent of success is just showing up," it really doesn't do justice to what the real truth is. In reality, *80 percent of success is about HOW you show up.*

REFERENCE

Kouzes, J.M., & Posner, B.Z. (2006). *A leader's legacy.* San Francisco: Jossey-Bass.

About Strategic Leadership Collaborative, Inc.

Strategic Leadership Collaborative is a private consulting practice focused on helping organizations craft their leadership strategy, develop their leadership learning agenda, and assess their leaders' effectiveness. Founder and principal Dr. Stephen L. Cohen has spent nearly forty years committed to the talent management and leadership development industry, resulting in more than one hundred published articles, chapters, and research reports, as well as many accolades and awards for his thought leadership and contributions.

Strategic Leadership Collaborative designs, creates, and delivers custom leadership development experiences, primarily for senior management; conducts strategic growth planning sessions, largely for education and training firms; and researches and develops business plans for those interested in creating new talent management related enterprises.

Submitted by Stephen L. Cohen, Ph.D., C.P.T., Founder, Principal

Strategic Leadership Collaborative, Inc.

6264 Chasewood Drive

Eden Prairie, MN 55344

(952) 942-7291

steve@strategicleadershipcollaborative.com

www.strategicleadershipcollaborative.com

Chapter 13

How to Tell a Story . . . and Why

KEVIN DALEY COMMUNICATIONS

In This Chapter

- Rationale for storytelling and its importance to leaders.
- Five steps to tell a story the right way.

At some point we are all tapped on the shoulder and asked to be a speaker at some event. It could be a business luncheon or dinner, perhaps a wedding, maybe you are the head honcho and are being asked to inspire the people who work for you, or maybe it's a congratulatory talk when someone is being promoted.

Obviously, you are being asked to speak because you have credentials. You are an important person. You probably are stuffed with information they are not privy to. So what do you do? Lay out all that info? Bury them with facts and statistics? Show them your expertise? Paint them with it? . . . Is the answer "Yes"?

Sorry! The answer is "No." No speaker was ever serenaded because he or she broke a world record for providing facts. What we are serenaded for is being interesting.

Facts and statistics are forms of evidence we naturally use to support a viewpoint or a recommendation. We use them in business because that's the way business is run. And the listeners in that audience are looking for those forms of evidence to assure themselves that the basis for the recommendation is solid.

Not true for just about any other audience we might face. What they want is for the speaker to be interesting. And facts and statistics are not inherently interesting. Matter of fact, they are often boring. Of course, audiences are used to being bored. But we can dream, can't we? We can hope that every now and then a speaker will be interesting. And we want that speaker to be you.

As a speaker, you should have that as your goal. So how do you get there? How do you assure, or at least increase the odds, that you will be interesting? I'll tell you how. You can tell a story. Not just any old story, but a story that is right for the occasion and also makes whatever point you want to make.

Don't think of a story as a plaything. Whenever we try to persuade people to our point of view, we make sure we have evidence to back up what we say. There are five forms of evidence. A story is one of them . . . and may be the best. Here are the five.

1. *Facts and statistics*—Standard fare for business. Most recommendations have this form of evidence as its basis.

2. *Example*—A specific situation with various key factors similar to those of your premise.

3. *Expert opinion*—A statement by a recognized expert that appears to be supportive.

4. *Analogy*—A point of similarity between two unlike things.

5. *Story*—First-person testimony. A story out of your life that supports the point you are making. Or an incident you are familiar with, through study or experience, that allows you to tell the story in a captivating way.

Now that I've listed the five forms of evidence, put the other four aside and be ready to concentrate on only one . . . how to tell a story. Why do I say that? Because audiences tend to get lost with numbers. They can't follow a numerical argument well. Too many distractions. They are much more moved by a story. That's what piques their attention and sways their thinking. If you want an audience to love you, tell a story.

Here is a much loved truism:

Tell me a fact and I'll learn.
Tell me a truth and I'll believe.
Tell me a story and it will live in my heart forever.

—Indian Proverb

How Do You Find a Story?

Search your memory. What stories have you told your spouse or your kids? What experiences of yours have stuck in your mind? What experiences with your kids have stuck in your mind? Don't think it has to be earth-shattering. It just has to be interesting. If you've told it more than once, it probably fits the criteria.

Just make sure the story supports your viewpoint. Make sure it is a moving (not a boring) story. If it moved you and you tell it well, it will move an audience. All the world loves a story. And they go bananas over a good story. If it involves your kids, you can't miss. Why? Because kids are universal. Everyone relates to them and what they do.

Some caution, though. It must be a story. There must be tension. There must be drama, a chance of failure. And there should be a "moment of truth" or a point when someone's decision causes success or failure.

How to Tell a Story

There is a right way and a wrong way to tell a story. What stories do you remember from childhood? Chances are they all begin with, "Once upon a time. . . ." And why is that? It's because we are people and everything in our experience begins at a point of time. Everything also begins in a certain place. That lets us, as listeners, put ourselves into that time and that place. Once we do, the story has begun. In short, we start the telling of a story by answering two questions:

- When did it happen?
- Where did it happen?

Then let it flow.

Don't explain the story (wrong way). Re-create it the way it happened (right way). Use dialogue. Add rich detail so the audience will see what you saw, hear what you heard, and feel what you felt. Then make your point, tying it back to your overall message.

Below is an example of the same story told both ways so you can see the difference It is the story of a father and his daughter. To make it easier, it is told in the first person, as though you, the reader, are the father telling the story.

THE STORY—THE WRONG WAY

I want to tell you a story that happened to me. It is about my daughter not coming home when she was supposed to, and I decided that you can't always resolve problems right when they happen. I always set a curfew, and my kids know that I stick by it. The curfew is 11 o'clock on weekends. My daughter had a date on a Friday night and missed the curfew by one hour and fifteen minutes. She came in knowing she'd be in big trouble and told me a cockamamie story about getting two flat tires. That was her excuse. I didn't buy it for a minute, and I think she knew it. But I let her get away with it because I thought it was too late to confront her with the obvious. And actually it worked out pretty well, because I showed her I trusted her, and she was pretty good living up to that reputation in the future. We do the same thing in our company now, and it works.

THE STORY—THE RIGHT WAY

The occasion was a luncheon meeting of one hundred and fifty new employees of IBM. The story is adapted from my book, *Talk Your Way to the Top*. The featured speaker was an executive vice president (EVP) of the company. The purpose of the talk was to welcome the new people and give them an insight into the history and culture of the company. The EVP accomplished most of that in the first twenty minutes of his talk. Then he segued into a story to dramatize what he felt was one of the guiding principles of the company.

1. The Segue

Now that you are a member of our company, you are one of us and we value you as we would a family member. Let me share a story with you about my own family that shows you what I mean.

2. Set the Place and Time

It was 8 o'clock on a Friday night and my daughter, Liz, was sixteen years old. She had a date with Mark, her boyfriend. While she was waiting in the family room for her date to arrive, I asked, "What time will you be home, Liz?"

3. Launch into Action and Dialogue

"Twelve o'clock," she replied.

I said, "You know the rules. Eleven o'clock is your curfew."

Reluctantly, she said, "OK, Daddy, but sometimes problems come up and I can't make it at exactly eleven."

"Problems? What kind of problems?" I asked.

Liz looked up at me and said, "Like a flat tire."

I said, "OK, if you have a flat tire, you can get home at 11:30. Otherwise it is 11:00 o'clock." Mark came to the door. I told him, "Take good care of my daughter. Make sure she is home by 11." I kissed Liz goodbye and out she went into the night.

At eleven o'clock , I was sitting in the family room in my pajamas and bathrobe, watching TV. No Liz. At 11:15 I thought, maybe she had a flat tire. By 11:45, I was angry.

Liz came through the door at 12:15. I could hear the car tires screech as Mark backed out of the driveway as fast as he could. That was smart on his part. He escaped feeling my hands around his neck. With hands on hips, I said to Liz. "Well, where have you been?"

"Daddy. You probably won't believe this but we had a flat. We put on the spare and then had another flat. We had no second spare so we had to get help before we could get home. That's why I'm so late."

I stared down at my beautiful sixteen-year old daughter. I didn't buy the story of the two flats, and I think she knew I didn't buy it. She knew she was wrong. I knew she was wrong. But we were going to have to live together in this house, as father and daughter, for a lot more years yet.

4. Moment of Truth

I wasn't sure an argument would get either of us anyplace. It was after midnight, and we were both tired. It was no time to start the Father-Daughter War of the Century. I would talk to her in the morning. I put my arms around her and said, "Next time, no flats, OK?"

Liz pulled her head back, looked up at me with her beautiful green eyes, and said, "OK, Daddy, I love you." She ran off to bed.

The next morning we had a talk. I didn't accuse her of lying—nothing to be gained there. I didn't say the flats were a made-up story, or that she was being irresponsible, or that she was thoughtless. Nothing gained there either.

I didn't say I was worried about her as I waited there. I told her that I had complete confidence in her, that I knew she would always do what was right. I said that was why I was so worried. I knew she would call if she were detained for any reason. I knew she wouldn't be that late knowing her father was sitting up waiting for her.

Liz looked at me and said, "Daddy, I'm sorry. It won't happen again."

5. Conclusion

And, you know what, I felt good about what I had done, and I think Liz did, too. She also taught me a lesson. There's no question that giving her a fine reputation to live up to was much more effective than catching her doing something wrong and berating her for it.

. . . And the Point

We try to do the same thing in our company. We consider it one of our guiding principles to trust our people and give them a fine reputation to live up to. And we have discovered over the years that almost all of us will reach higher when expectations are higher. We go out of our way to demonstrate that we are all equals as people, regardless of our titles. So if you ever wondered what differentiates our company from other companies, what makes our company great, it's that fundamental principle that will never change . . . respect for the individual.

Compare the two stories. The wrong-way version is not as powerful, is it? The setting (time and place) is not established in the first sentence. This makes it hard for the audience to draw a mental picture of the situation.

There is no dialogue, so it is devoid of personality. The audience doesn't really get any impression, good or bad, of the daughter, the boyfriend, or the father who is giving the speech. There are no details that would allow you to experience the story. Even though the moral of the story is the same, we don't feel the same impact. This means that the audience is less likely to remember the point. The story is forgettable—and so is the speaker.

Make It Memorable

People will remember a good story. If you were to tell that father/daughter story as a part of a luncheon talk you were giving, and let's say the whole talk lasted thirty minutes and that story lasted five, what do you think people would remember about your talk? Probably the story, right?

Members of the audience would probably come up to you afterward and say things like: "I loved the story about your daughter." "I think you handled your daughter just right." "Your daughter is lucky to have a father like you." "I wish our company respected the individual the way your company does." The reason they would say those things is that you would have gotten inside their heads and their hearts. You moved the audience, because you made your point come alive for then in the form of a story. You expanded their life experience. Audiences love that. It makes the talk special.

Want your next story to be memorable? Use the tool in the online section for this chapter.

About Kevin Daley Communications

Kevin Daley Communications delivers results for delivering presentations, enhancing executive presence, handling analyst meetings, and addressing media. Founder Kevin Daley pioneered the communications skills industry as we know it today. He was the founder and CEO of Communispond, which, under his tenure, became the largest company of its kind in the field, having trained some 480,000 executives.
Kevin has personally trained sixty-two board chairmen, 320 company presidents, and 3,100 business managers. Ultimately, Kevin sold Communispond and now devotes his time to working on a consulting basis with senior executives. Kevin Daley Communications provides one-on-one coaching and delivers keynote presentations.

Submitted by Kevin Daley, Founder of Communispond

Kevin Daley Communications

197 Sheephill Road, Suite A

Riverside, CT 06878

(203) 637-4707

Kdaley@kdspeak.com

www.kdspeak.com

Kevin Daley Communications
Executive Coaching

Chapter 14

Your Invitation to Greatness

A Three-Step System for Building Strategic Leaders

IMPRESSION MANAGEMENT
PROFESSIONALS

In This Chapter

- Ten traits of strategic leaders.
- How executives build accountability with consequences.
- How executives build strategic leaders.

Are Great Leaders Born or Made?

That is a question that has been plaguing people from the beginning of time. It is the issue discussed in books such as *From Good to Great* and *Winning*.

The answer is a little of both. Some people seem to naturally develop at a younger age some key leadership skills, while others need the proverbial coconut to hit them on the head before they develop these traits, and some people never do learn. Consider this your invitation to greatness and use this three-step system to be a top leader!

Step 1: Practice the Top Ten Traits of Strategic Leaders

YOU MUST ENFORCE ACCOUNTABILITY WITH CONSEQUENCES

I can't tell you how many corporations I work with in which there are no consequences for people who don't follow a procedure or who undermine the system. In one corporation I was working with, our program with an executive team was to start at 8 a.m. When the team leader looked around and saw that some members of the team were not there, he said, "*Well they're all grownups. They know the time.*" Essentially, he was saying he wasn't going to hold them accountable for time but instead was going to have them self-monitor.

The reality is that your company can NOT have consequences at the lowest level if there are no consequences at the highest level. You have to have some principles that you adhere to strongly and make sure others do as well.

It is much like parenting. You need to know which items are worth going to war for and which are merely skirmishes. Watch how we expand on this idea later in this chapter.

Ask yourself, "How good am I at holding people's feet to the fire?"

YOU MUST BE CANDID AND CARING

You can't have an innovative, creative, and enriched organization if you can't have candid and direct conversations. You must be able to talk about the proverbial elephant in the room without being judgmental.

Organizations are a lot like a person. Each one takes on a corporate culture or personality that allows it to run. This means that past hurts, judgments, history, and frustrations keep resurfacing unless they are dealt with effectively.

Most corporations deal with these by "allowing" different departments and different people to operate under different rules. Remember that candid doesn't mean saying whatever you want whenever you want and assuming others ought to be able to "take it." Instead, it means you must be able to talk about issues in a safe and open way that allows people to be vulnerable and honest without being ashamed.

Ask yourself, "Are my meetings ones where all players speak up and people leave energized?"

Developing Talent for Organizational Results

YOU MUST BE CONGRUENT

This means all aspects of your life, style, and communication must tie in to each other. I know of one organization in which members had little trust and respect for one another. It came out that the CEO was having an affair with his assistant.

Now even though you may say that is his business and no one else's, it did put others in a sticky spot. What were they to say to his wife at the parties? Were they supposed to cover up for him when he was gone? And if he would treat his wife this way, what would he do behind their backs?

As the leader, the view others have of your company or your department is based on the view they have of you. Does it match what you want?

Ask yourself, "Does the view people have of me match how I want my company perceived?"

YOU MUST HAVE CLARITY IN ALL YOU SAY AND DO

You need to be able to communicate clearly so that people understand what they need to do, what you want them to do, and how it impacts the company or department.

If people can't clearly understand what you are saying, they cannot accurately execute. If they can't execute, that means you essentially have a lot of ideas floating around with no action or sporadic action happening. This means you become a "sit and spin" organization filled with useless meetings.

Ask yourself, "Are we a company of lots of meetings with no action?"

YOU MUST BE ABLE TO COACH OTHERS

Now this one is a fine line. I don't mean being able to demonstrate what you need others to do and I don't mean you need to be able to tell others what to do. You need to be able to show others how to THINK so they can do it for themselves.

Too many leaders TELL others what they need to do. If you do this, then the accountability and the results are always your problem, not theirs. This also allows people to participate in turf wars with you as the head litigator.

Instead, you must help them to reflect on their behavior, attitude, or choices and show them how to think at an executive level so they create their own solutions. This will bring greater accountability and ownership at all levels.

Ask yourself, "How good am I at building confidence and skill in others so they become stronger leaders in the company?"

STOP TRYING TO HAVE THE RIGHT ANSWERS AND START ASKING THE RIGHT QUESTIONS

As the leader, your role is to set up the guidelines so that people know what to do and how to do it. Your job is to be up in the trees so you can see how to clear the path for those who are in the trenches.

This means you have to be able to synchronize what you see up in the trees with what they see down on the ground. If you don't do this, you may give direction and guidance that can't be followed. This will lead to people feeling that you are out of touch with the reality of the front lines.

Remember clarity? This is where it is imperative that you can clearly communicate what you see from the trees in relationship to what they have happening on the ground. You must unite the two.

Ask yourself, "How can I ask better questions and align all areas in the company?"

BE PASSIONATE ABOUT WHAT YOU DO

How can you expect others to be passionate about your product or services when you yourself don't exhibit that passion? Your energy, creativity, and belief in all you do have to be felt by all in the organization. You are essentially the head cheerleader.

Ask yourself, "What am I passionate about?"

BE A STEWARD OF PHILANTHROPY

Part of the core of a company is the belief that you do things because they are the right things to do. That means employees need to see that you have beliefs and causes that you follow because they fit you. This generosity of spirit lets them know that you believe in giving back as well as receiving.

Now this doesn't mean that you push others to support your concerns or that you throw the company's weight behind your beliefs. It does mean that you show you have enough passion and interest in something outside the company and that you feel accountable as a person to honor those beliefs.

Ask yourself, "What does giving back mean to me?"

DARE TO BE DIFFERENT

Let your creativity fly and be willing to search out the blue oceans for your company. Encourage others around you to explore all sides of a problem or challenge. Look for innovative ways to spark the creativity and uniqueness of your office.

I have one client that has the Banana Award for creativity. Another one has a pool table so employees can take a quick break and shoot a game of pool to spark their juices.

Ask yourself, "When was the last time I did something for the first time?"

BE AUTHENTIC IN YOUR INTEGRITY AND CHARACTER

Employees can spot a phony leader a mile away. These are the people that put "good job" stickers on your work, yet they also stand at your cubicle and yell at you in front of others. Or they say "great idea" in a meeting and then roll their eyes behind your back.

In order to make sure each person in your company brings his or her full character and integrity into the office, you need to bring yours. Employees will "show up" at the office and maintain loyalty as long as they believe in the company and what they are doing there.

If you bring yourself fully to the role as a leader, then there is no reason why you can't expect that of all players in your company.

Ask yourself, "How authentic do others see me being?"

Step 2: Build Accountability with Consequences

Remember in Step 1 where it was mentioned that you need to know which items are worth going to war over? *Ask yourself, "How good am I at holding people's feet to the fire?"*

Let's expand on this idea here.

I've been asked, "What should I do if the leaders in the company whom I need to make the decision come in late to the meeting?"

My question back to this was, "Does this happen often or only with one person?" The entire group yelled out, "Our whole company is run like that. Everyone comes late to meetings." That comment alone lets me know the corporate culture is one that talks about accountability but doesn't enforce it.

You cannot have high accountability without having consequences. I don't believe in juvenile consequences like if you are late you have to sing, or if you are late you put money in a jar. Both of those consequences make people feel like kids and, worse yet, if the late person can tolerate them, there is no need to change their behavior.

Your consequences need to align with your corporate vision and goals. They need to be reinforced from the top on down. There are far better ways to deal with this. The first thing I would look at is the blatant message people are sending: "We have too many meetings that are not important so I can come late."

Here are some things you can do:

- *Review which meetings are relevant.* When a meeting is scheduled, make people *define clearly the goal of the meeting* and who needs to be a part of it. If people just schedule meetings on your calendar, ask them why you are relevant to the meeting. You will be surprised how many times the wrong players are at a meeting.

- *Keep your meetings tight and to the point.* Thirty minutes to one hour is best.

- *Avoid "book report" meetings* where people just recite what they are working on. Instead make people phrase things so others can learn from them, collaborate with them, and gain insight. Answer the "What's in it for me?"

- *Start meetings right on time and end on time.*

- *Record the meeting.* If a person misses the meeting or arrives late, then have the person stay after and listen to the recording. People will soon get the idea that they will spend the thirty minutes regardless, so being late is not an option.

- *Address chronically late people* privately and immediately. Then be consistent with marking down the times he or she is late and have it be a part of the person's review. Let him or her know it is unacceptable to be late.

- If you are just starting a new project or leading a new team, *set up the meeting guidelines right up-front,* along with consequences that the group agrees to, so people can start off on the right foot. Ask them what needs to be done to make the meeting relevant for all. Remember there are times that people will legitimately be late. The goal is not to eliminate lateness completely but instead to make meetings engaging and effective so all want to participate. Look at what you can eliminate from your meetings to shorten them up and keep them on point.

Step 3: Build Strategic Leaders on Your Team

IQ is your intelligence—your ability to capture information and store it in your brain and then extract it when needed. All of us have run into people who are highly intelligent but lack common sense. If you are looking for a great leader, what makes one stand out? Why do some people do great at one level of a job but struggle when you promote them?

In order to grow great leaders, you need to understand the difference knowledge and critical thinking play in HOW a leader makes decisions. Knowledge is based on learning or experiences that you then anchor in your mind and can extract when you need to apply it. This is great and can really get you promoted in a company fast. *The problem comes when you are faced with situations you have never experienced before*. How do you make good decisions then? What do you base them on when you can't anchor them to any experience you have ever had?

This is where things fall apart in many companies. All of a sudden Joe, who was a great foreman, is struggling as an operations manager. In unknown situations, it becomes far more important that you make decisions based on critical thinking skills, not knowledge. Critical thinking skills help you determine what the correct assumptions are and what the root of the problem is, and creates a more strategic way of looking at things. Outcome Thinking® is all about how you think critically about situations so you can be more strategic and transformational versus tactical and transactional. Too many leaders are tactical in how they approach problems or situations and they base the rationale of their thinking on the knowledge they have today. This limits their ability to really LISTEN so they can uncover what is not being thought or talked about.

Let's explore the differences between *tactical* and *strategic* leaders. When asked to put together a presentation on an expansion, a tactical leader will pull together the cost of the expansion, why the expansion is necessary, and the steps for the expansion. A strategic leader will pull together a presentation that shares the problem the expansion will solve, how the expansion will help solve this problem, the pros and cons of the expansion, what the cost will be, and how it will fit in to the overall company mission. A tactical leader will try to make the expansion fit the budget. A strategic leader will ask how the expansion will solve the problem and then figure out what it will cost to work long term. A tactical leader approaches thinking as a constrained, step-by-step process. A strategic leader is not afraid to say we are thinking too small.

If your organization is weighted down with people delivering "book report" presentations, people looking for strategy to come from the senior management, people missing executing on corporate initiatives (which means they didn't understand the message at a strategic level), then you are most likely creating more tactical versus strategic leaders.

In today's world, where you need to move at a fast pace, you need to have leaders who can be critical thinkers at multiple levels in your organization. Without that you will end up creating more and more rules for people to make decisions by, rather than systems that allow people to achieve excellence.

Take Action

To be a great leader, you must continually strive to learn, grow, and stretch yourself. Use the accompanying online self-assessment tool to evaluate your effectiveness as a leader. Ask yourself, *"How can I expect my team to continually strive to grow if they don't see me constantly moving my performance up to the next level?"*

About Impression Management Professionals

Influence outcomes by expanding the way you think, listen, and speak! Impression Management Professionals goes beyond other training companies by expanding how you think so you influence outcomes, see opportunities others miss, communicate the complex clearly, and do it all in less time with greater ease. We help clients develop leaders and sales professionals to build trusted relationships, transform cultures, and speak candidly, clearly, and with great authenticity at all times.

Outcome Thinking® will help you with lasting results that will allow you to maximize all high-stress situations without stressing you out. You will be able to remove 70 percent of what hits the negotiation table; use conflict as a building block, not a stumbling block; present complex ideas clearly so people can take action on what you say; excavate in client discussions so you can better cross-sell or close the deal; and to be able to exude authority, authenticity, and integrity each time you communicate. With the option of training programs, customization, train-the-trainer, and online programs, you are sure to find a match to your needs and time to deliver outstanding and long-lasting results.

Submitted by Anne Warfield, CSP, CEO

Impression Management Professionals

15768 Venture Lane

Minneapolis, MN 55344

(952) 921-9421

(888) IMP-9421

contact@imp.us.com

www.impressionmanagement.com

Chapter **15**

How Does a CEO
Do Engagement?

FIERCE, INC.

In This Chapter

- The importance of engagement to executives.
- One method executives can use to get involvement from employees.

In early February of 2011, Engadget published an internal memo written by Nokia's CEO, Stephen Elop, in which he likens the once-dominant Finnish phone manufacturer to the oil worker trapped by a fire in the dead of night on the burning platform of a rig in the North Sea. He had seconds to consider the 150-foot drop into the ocean, the knowledge that there was floating debris and burning oil on the surface of the water, and that if the fall didn't kill him, he would die of exposure in fifteen minutes. His only option for survival was to ignore what he had been told never to do and jump into the icy waters of the North Sea, a situation in which Nokia now finds itself after having made a series of poor decisions. But while the oil worker survived, Nokia may not be so fortunate. In what may prove to be a final strategic blunder, Elop, a former Microsoft executive, announced later that week that the key to Nokia's viability and success is to use Windows Phone 7 for its smart phone. At their joint announcement, Steve Ballmer, Microsoft CEO, said, "I am excited about this partnership with Nokia. Ecosystems thrive when fueled by speed, innovation, and scale."

Unfortunately, with apologies to my friends in both companies, apart from Xbox Kinect, neither Microsoft nor Nokia has demonstrated speed, innovation, and scale for at least a decade, so it's no surprise that Nokia's employees, customers, and shareholders expressed dismay at this decision; in fact, many employees took the next day off, as PTO, in protest.

With so many shocked employees, partners—*think Intel*—and shareholders, Nokia provides a current example of a company that has arrived, gradually, then suddenly, at the edge of disaster with a workforce of emphatically unengaged employees, one failed, one missing conversation at a time. It's unlikely that things will go smoothly in the execution department.

Elop may be brilliant and his decision may be the right one. I sincerely hope it is. But if he fails to re-engage his unengaged workforce, he is in no danger of a smooth implementation because he cannot mandate accountability, innovation, or collaboration. No one can. These are private, non-negotiable choices individuals make about how to live their lives, about how much of themselves to bring in the door each day.

We all know that if employees aren't engaged, companies will suffer. Good people will quit, defect, disappear; or, worse, they'll show up every day—in body—but only bringing a tiny piece of themselves in spirit. They'll become disgruntled, disenchanted, and disillusioned, which profoundly affects the bottom line. Yet, despite all the hype about what companies are doing to promote employee inclusion and engagement (these go hand-in-hand), many still see this as a soft topic, nice to do, something that makes people feel good. Of course, employee inclusion and engagement makes people feel good AND increases productivity and builds revenue.

I think of it this way: **Inclusion + Engagement = Execution Muscle**

. . . plus happy people; but as far as I'm concerned, without execution muscle, you might as well hang it up. Let's define terms.

Employee inclusion suggests that people of every stripe—gender, age, sexual orientation, ethnicity, religion, aspiration, disability, position or title, and whatever other differences are possible in the human population—feel that they have a place at the table, that they are seen, heard, and valued, and that, given stellar performance, they have an opportunity to advance. That they do not feel marginalized, "less than," left out, overlooked, invisible, made wrong, taken advantage of, disrespected, ignored, or mistreated. At its heart, inclusion is about membership, belonging to a community.

The overriding theme of employee engagement is a heightened emotional connection that an employee feels for his or her organization that influences him or her to exert greater discretionary effort. And the direct relationship with one's manager is the strongest driver of employee engagement.

Employee engagement and inclusion isn't a cognitive issue. It's an emotional issue. The problem isn't out there. It's in here. We want employees to be engaged and feel included, while we ourselves are detached, distracted, disengaged, and focused on our to-do lists and the stock price. We want others to bring that elusive, coveted "discretionary effort" in the door with them every day, but we don't have time to engage in the kind of conversations that could enrich our relationships with them.

The fact is, *not* having those conversations will take longer and cost more in the long term. When you disengage from the world, the world disengages, too, in equal measure. It's a two-step, you and the world, you and your organization. Your employees lost interest in you because you lost interest in them. Calling them *associates* or *partners* is often window dressing. If you want high levels of employee engagement, you must gain the capacity to connect with your employees—at a deep level—or lower your aim. And that connection occurs or fails to occur one conversation at a time. If you're a fan of Angry Birds, the eagle is to Angry Birds what human connectivity is to the relationships central to your success. It gets the job done!

What is talked about in your company, how it is talked about, and who is invited to the conversation determines what will happen. Or won't happen. Your conversations must be fierce: conversations in which you and others come out from behind yourselves, into your conversations, and make them real. Once an organization crosses the line into "fierce" territory, very little else is required to create a culture of highly engaged, kick-ass employees. Without such conversations, your platform may be smoldering.

This is where it becomes personal. In a very real sense, the progress of your organization depends on *your* progress as an individual *now*. Want high levels of engagement, cooperation, and collaboration throughout your organization? Innovation? Agility? Execution muscle? Look to the conversations *you* are having. Are they confined to the C-suite? What is your level of candor and that of your direct reports? Are you seeking agreement or do you want the truth? Are *you* different when your conversations are over?

And what if your company is doing fine? I recently gave a keynote to a company poised to distribute millions in profit sharing, a cause for celebration. Meanwhile, one of the divisions is troubled, unhappy. How much of the CEO's attention does this require, given that his board just gave him an A on his report card?

Let's revisit the oil rig, Piper Alpha.

Investigators traced the cause to a missing component on a condensate pump. The pressure safety valve on pump A was removed for maintenance. Paperwork prohibiting the pump from being used was lost or misplaced. When pump B broke down,

How Does a CEO Do Engagement?

pump A was switched on. Gas began to leak, alarms were triggered, and the platform was rocked by a huge explosion.

At this stage there were probably only a few casualties, but things were about to get much worse. Despite a mayday call from Piper Alpha, two neighboring rigs did not shut down their operations. Oil continued to be pumped into a communal pipe and toward the stricken rig. *You see where this is going.* Another enormous explosion rocked Piper Alpha and the rig fell into the sea.

It is likely that the magnitude of the disaster would have been much less had the neighboring rigs shut down immediately. But with the huge losses incurred by shutting down production on an oil rig, it was a case of profit before safety, profit before lives.

What's to be learned? When Madeleine Albright was asked what advice she would give to world leaders, she said, "I would tell them that what matters anywhere, matters everywhere." Better men and women than I have written about the galactic implications. But let's point the telescope at your company. What matters anywhere in your organization, matters everywhere in your organization. Organizations are webs of relationships. Each conversation, each meeting, creates a chain reaction, like a Rube Goldberg contraption.

You, all by your lonesome, are having an impressive impact on your world. Your conversations with your assistant affect his self-esteem and his impression of what matters to you, which he conveys in every conversation he has with all of the people in your world. Your conversations with peers affect their willingness to collaborate and cooperate with you when they could fake it if they wanted to. They pass on their opinions and experience of you to others in the company. Your conversations with customers, partners, and vendors ultimately win or lose the day.

Beach Ball Meetings

What to do? Stop *talking* about inclusion and engagement and start *including and engaging*! It may help to picture your organization as a huge beach ball as in Figure 15.1.

Each person in your company operates from a different stripe and experiences reality from that perspective. People in marketing, human resources, manufacturing, accounting, out on the loading dock—and let's not forget your customers—have different, perhaps competing perspectives. Blue, red, green, gold. What matters is not whose perspective is correct, but that everyone puts his or her brain on the table for all to see (assuming that they brought their brains with them).

Consider holding a beach ball meeting to bring all that brain power together.

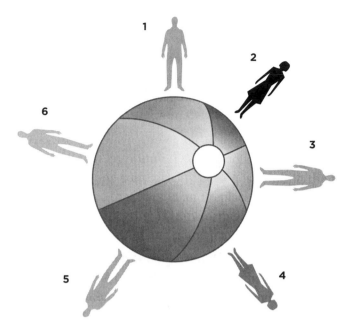

Figure 15.1 Beach Ball Model

Instructions for holding beach ball meetings are covered in detail in *Fierce Conversations* and *Fierce Leadership*. Here are the steps in brief:

- Think of a significant or recurring problem you wish to resolve.
- Write down the names of the people whose perspective will be important to understand in order to make the best possible decision.
- Prior to the meeting, send out any material invitees will need to review.

Hold the meeting. Thank everyone for coming and ask them all to turn off high-tech distractions likely to ring, hum, or vibrate, including laptops. Tell them that you want eye contact and deep listening. Talk them through the issue *quickly* to focus attention on the topic. Answer clarifying questions. Then say something like:

"I have defined the issue as I see it, what is at stake for us to lose or gain, as well as what I think needs to happen and why. Now I ask that you push back on anything I've said that doesn't match your view of reality. Tell me what I'm missing. Point out any fires that may be smoldering in our attic. That's how you'll add value to this meeting. My hope is to be influenced by you. I genuinely hope to be different when this meeting is over."

And mean it!

Make sure that you hear each team member's thoughts, concerns, ideas. Your goal is not to persuade them to your way of thinking, but to understand theirs. If you disagree with a comment or don't understand, don't say, "Yes, but . . ." Ask the person to say more and listen. If someone says, "I don't know," ask, "What would it be if you did know?" If someone says, "I have nothing to add," ask, "What would you add if you did have something to add?" Don't let anyone off the hook. Ensure that everyone speaks.

When you have heard from everyone, ask each team member to write down a concise answer to this question: "Having heard from everyone here, what is your strongest recommendation?" or "What would you do if you were in my shoes?" Have each person read his or her advice. Don't respond, except to say, "Thank you." After all participants have read their advice, ask them to sign their recommendations and give them to you so that you can follow up if you'd like more information.

Thank everyone for their contributions and tell them you will let them know your decision. And do so.

Beach Ball Meeting Results

Because beach ball meetings are far more engaging and productive than the meetings most of us are used to, the idea tends to catch on. Ultimately, inclusion and engagement become a way of life, what everyone does, threaded through every activity, every conversation, every meeting. Not top down or bottom up, but side by side. Listening to each other. Your organization cannot move toward success unless you act *in unison* to further what wants and needs to happen. Our power as individuals is multiplied when we gather together with common goals. It will be your collective intelligence and strength that makes positive change possible within your organization.

The instructions for a beach ball meeting are detailed in the online tool for this chapter.

It isn't easy—this looking beyond hard-wired assumptions and beliefs, welcoming competing perspectives. Some people aren't interested in listening to those who disagree with them, who are not from their world. But they will never grow because they just meet themselves over and over, entranced with their own forms, their own faces and ideology.

Employee engagement. A worthy goal that will remain just that—a goal—unless and until here and now, we create deep connection in this moment, with *this* person who is holding forth or sitting quietly, the one with whom we disagree, the one we haven't valued, haven't really *seen*. Until now.

About Fierce, Inc.

Fierce, Inc. is a leadership development and training company that develops conversation as a skill to drive measurable results for business and education. Our award-winning training has helped clients worldwide achieve higher levels of alignment, engagement, collaboration, partnership, and accountability throughout their organizations.

In addition, Fierce principles and methods are:

- *Results-Oriented.* Experiential training that leads to measurable ROI, improved engagement, and successful outcomes.

- *Flexible.* Leadership development and training tailored to your organization, available in instructor-led and online delivery methods.

- *Universal.* Principles and methods that translate across the globe, throughout your organization, from the front line to boardroom.

- *Immediate.* Practical, easy-to-learn skills that can be applied immediately.

Fierce, Inc. is home to multiple training offerings including Fierce Conversations®, Fierce Leadership®, Fierce Accountability®, Fierce Negotiations®, and Fierce Generations®. Its founder, Susan Scott, is the author of two national bestsellers: *Fierce Conversations: Achieving Success at Work and in Life, One Conversation at a Time* and *Fierce Leadership: A Bold Alternative to the Worst "Best" Practices of Business Today.*

Submitted by Susan Scott, Founder

Fierce, Inc.

101 Yesler Way, Suite 200

Seattle, WA 98104

(206) 787-1100

info@fierceinc.com

www.fierceinc.com

SECTION IV

DEVELOPING LEADERS

Introduction

The Corporate Leadership Council, an international organization representing corporate human resources executives, reports that 60 percent of its member companies are currently experiencing a leadership shortage. That's up from 40 percent just one year ago.

Many organizations are concerned about how to fill the leadership void they are currently experiencing and the huge drain they expect in the not-too-distant future. This loss is caused in part by the anticipated mass exodus of the baby boomer generation. Typical organizations have not prepared adequately for the knowledge and skill loss as leaders are about to slip out the door. Now developing leadership skills is high on the action list of many corporate human resources professionals.

The most important investment an organization may make is in the development and grooming of its future leaders. So this task is not taken lightly. The list of competencies is similar from one organization to another, although the forward-looking organizations link their leadership development plans to the organization's strategy, its culture, and its vision for the future.

The topics in this section could easily take up several books of this kind. These chapters are dedicated to setting the stage for a successful leadership development effort. All three seek to lay a solid foundation from which to springboard your own leadership development efforts or strengthen those you already have started.

- Chapter 16, "Developing Future Leaders" by ebb associates inc, presents a compelling rationale for why the responsibility of leadership development must lie squarely with the executive-level team. Six factors can predict the success of leadership development efforts in organizations. The chapter is accompanied by an assessment that can be downloaded on the website that accompanies this book.

- Chapter 17, "Awaken, Align, Accelerate®" by MDA Leadership Consulting, introduces a three-phase approach to leadership development and growth: awaken, align, and accelerate. The chapter is loaded with tips and implications for developing leaders.

- In Chapter 18, "Designing Great Leadership Development Workshops," Bluepoint Leadership Development delivers ten critical design features of an effective leadership development learning experience. The best part of this chapter is that you can borrow all of the ideas and implement them in your own leadership development program.

- This section's bonus activity is "Historical Orienteering," an activity presented by Sonoma Leadership Systems. The activity helps participants learn the best practices of leaders through the lens of past leaders. Tying leadership challenges to local history is brilliant.

Chapter 16

Developing Future Leaders

Whose Responsibility Is It Anyway?

ebb associates inc

In This Chapter

- A rationale for why the responsibility for leadership development must start at the top of an organization.

- Six factors that predict the success of leadership development efforts in organizations.

The most valuable investment any organization can make is in the development of its future leaders. The responsibility for this investment lies squarely with the executive team. This vital task ensures that leaders possess competencies to achieve the organization's strategy, continue to mature the organizational culture, and inspire the workforce.

Due to the baby-boomer exodus from the workforce, many organizations are poised to lose 30 to 50 percent of their key leaders in the next half-dozen years. In addition, organizations have been lax in developing people who will replace individuals in these leadership roles. At the same time, the expectation of essential leadership skill standards continues to climb. Senior leaders' positions have become more challenging, requiring a broader range of job experience and a surprisingly long list of competencies.

In addition to what we typically think of as required leadership skills, the next generation of leaders must be visionary coalition-builders; internationally astute; quick learners and fast implementers; highly creative; comfortable with change, volatility, and ambiguity; have an intimate knowledge of the changing customer needs; have the agility to revamp operations instantly; and must produce rapid results in all areas.

The breadth of these competencies indicates that every forward-looking organization should be asking itself, "What are we doing to prepare our next generation of leaders? Is our pipeline filled with sufficient talent to carry out our organization's strategy and to inspire the workforce? Who is at the helm of developing our new leaders? How are our key leaders involved? Is leadership development at the top of all of our leaders' action lists? And exactly what are these actions?"

Actions for Successful Leadership Development

Leadership development must start at the top so that all leaders have a role model. Leaders need to be clear about what they need to do and why. Six critical success factors distinguish organizations that are successful in developing their leaders. An organization's leaders are the key in each of these actions to ensure success. Ask these questions:

To what extent do our leaders:

- View leadership development from a strategic, future focus?
- Make improving quality of bench strength a top priority?
- Accept full responsibility for developing future leaders?
- Practice evaluating the results of leadership development?
- Value learning and development?
- Take a long-term, aligned, systemic approach to developing leaders?

Lack of support from current leaders is one of the key reasons that leadership development fails. If current leaders rate high on each of these six factors, a company's leadership development efforts are most likely thriving. Let's examine each of these factors.

VIEW LEADERSHIP DEVELOPMENT FROM A STRATEGIC, FUTURE FOCUS

Successful companies ensure that their leadership development efforts are strategically driven and see business strategies as inseparable from leadership development. Senior leaders examine the emerging issues and challenges and consider the unique skills required to resolve them. They see leadership development as a strategy as opposed to being a project.

Leaders must:

- Place as much rigor into the leadership development effort as they do in marketing, sales, or other key areas in the organization.

- Encourage discussions with future leaders about their strategic developmental needs.

MAKE IMPROVING QUALITY OF BENCH STRENGTH A TOP PRIORITY

The quality of leadership, more than any other factor, determines the success or failure of an organization. Leaders must candidly discuss the current and the future bench strength required. Does the organization have the leadership resources to achieve its strategic imperative given the current competencies on board?

With this in mind, identifying and improving the quality of leaders must be a top priority to ensure a filled pipeline of experienced employees ready to be placed in leadership positions. This includes recognizing the high-potential individuals and accelerating their development.

Leaders are responsible for developing a systemic process for identifying candidates for key leadership positions. Once candidates are identified, leaders provide opportunities for learning and growth. Research by RHR International Company shows that over 90 percent of senior teams are involved in identifying individuals with high potential (Kaiser, 2005). In addition, organizations need to learn what it takes to retain employees identified as future leaders once they have identified them and integrate that learning into the company's culture.

Leaders must:

- Initiate a candid discussion of skills required for the future among themselves.

- Create and support a systemic approach to identify high-potentials.

- Sustain a progressive retention plan.

ACCEPT FULL RESPONSIBILITY FOR DEVELOPING FUTURE LEADERS

It's easy for leaders to say, "I support the mentoring program" or "Rotational assignments are critical to a leader's growth" or "Leaders must be involved in employees' learning." It is quite another for leaders to set aside time on their calendars to meet a protégé for an early morning breakfast or to encourage their best employees to leave for a six-month-long, high-visibility project during the busiest season or to show up to facilitate a leadership class. The Leadership Reminder List presents ideas for what your leaders can do to develop future leaders in their departments.

Leadership Reminder List

❑ Are you spending one-third of your time strengthening the talent and growing leaders in your department?

❑ Are you and your key people held accountable for improving skills and knowledge?

❑ Do all of your employees have an individual development plan, and are your managers held accountable for them?

❑ Does your department regularly identify job rotation opportunities to give your upcoming employees experience and development?

❑ Do you have a robust mentoring and coaching plan for your employees?

❑ Do you mentor your direct reports on a regular basis?

❑ Do you regularly reach down several levels in search of possible talent?

❑ Do you have attrition data about your young managers and why they are leaving?

❑ Have you implemented a strategy to ensure that your best and brightest managers continue employment?

❑ Are you working with HR to develop an aggressive recruitment plan for top talent?

❑ Have you implemented a plan to deal with underperformers?

❑ Is leadership development and talent management one of your top priorities?

Leaders develop leaders. Senior leaders accept the important role they have of developing future leaders: owning and sponsoring development efforts. Leaders of successful organizations spend as much as one-third of their time in developing others. For example, Larry Bossidy (2001) states that, while at Allied Signal, "That level of [leadership] excellence didn't happen by accident. I devoted what some people consider an inordinate amount of emotional energy and time—perhaps between 30 and 40 percent of my day to hiring and developing leaders." Reportedly, Jack Welch, when he was chairman at GE, invested 30 to 40 percent of his time at Crotonville, GE's leadership development center. Welch believed that his most important job was motivating and developing GE leaders and future leaders. He felt so strongly about it that he spent about 50 percent of his time on people issues. He likened a leader's role to that of a gardener. "You have to go along with a can of fertilizer in one hand and water in the other and constantly throw both on the flowers." He noted that leaders, like plants, may need more fertilizer to ensure that they will fully blossom and that some need to be weeded out so the strongest can thrive and achieve their potential (Hymowitz & Murray, 1999, p. B1).

Leaders must:

- Schedule time to spend with potential leaders to assess their inherent leadership talent capacity, identify goals, and provide coaching, tools, and development opportunities.

- Coach before a new assignment using good questions and follow the assignment with a solid after-action review and feedback.

- Seek rotational assignments and special projects to provide real-world experiences for the best and brightest employees.

PRACTICE EVALUATING THE RESULTS OF LEADERSHIP DEVELOPMENT

Future leaders must deliver a competitive advantage; therefore, the goals for the current leadership development efforts must support the organization's strategy and produce results.

An organization's leadership must establish, track, measure, and evaluate clear goals for their organization's leadership development efforts. These may be different for every organization.

Leaders must:

- Determine how they will measure and evaluate their leadership development efforts.

- Design a measurement process that ties leadership development efforts to the bottom line.

- Hold each other accountable for developmental results.

VALUE LEARNING AND DEVELOPMENT

The most successful organizations value learning and development for all employees, not just leaders; the organization is committed to a life-long learning strategy. Learning is rewarded. In addition, standards for reaching leadership positions are clear to everyone in the organization.

Even more critical, leaders must be willing to admit that they do not know everything and actively participate in learning events. Finding opportunities to learn and grow provides an excellent model for the rest of the organization.

Leaders must:

- Model a developmental mindset, encouraging all employees to develop to their full potential.

- Establish a broad view of leadership development based on teachable moments that incorporate projects, assignments, mentoring, cross-functional experiences, and hundreds of other learning opportunities.

- Continuously attend to their own professional and personal self-development.

TAKE A LONG-TERM, ALIGNED, SYSTEMIC APPROACH TO DEVELOPING LEADERS

A successful leadership development program is aligned with the other aspects of the organization and prepares future leaders to cope with the challenges of the future. Every leader should ensure that the leadership development efforts are aligned with the organization's mission, vision, values, and strategic plan.

Senior leaders understand and accept that leadership development is a lengthy process. They ensure their involvement in establishing a common set of leadership values and standards that permeate everything the organization does, including recruiting, hiring, succession planning, and performance management. What does the organization believe about leadership development? A leadership development philosophy is a statement that defines the principles the organization espouses. A leadership development philosophy provides direction for those crafting the plan and a communication tool to help the organization understand leadership development.

Leaders must:

- Build leadership development into their strategic planning efforts.
- Lead by example.

You may predict your organization's success in implementing a leadership development effort based on the six factors using the Organizational Leadership Readiness Audit found in the accompanying online tools.

The Ultimate Goal

Whose responsibility is it to develop an organization's future leaders? The responsibility starts at the top. Support and development must begin in the C-level suite. Engaged senior leaders are best poised to recognize leadership gaps as an obstacle to the execution of strategy.

At a time when leadership development is recognized as a vital ingredient for organization success, the involvement of senior leaders in the learning and development of future leaders is a powerful decision by every organization. The function of leadership is to produce more leaders, not more followers. Senior leaders are the key to the success of producing the next generation of leaders who will ensure the success of the organization.

REFERENCES

Bossidy, L. (2001, March). The job no CEO should delegate. *Harvard Business Review*.

Hymowitz, C., & Murray, M. (1999, June 21). How GE's chief rates and spurs his employees. *The Wall Street Journal*, p. B1.

Kaiser, R.B. (2005). *Filling the leadership pipeline*. Greensboro, NC: The Center for Creative Leadership.

About ebb associates inc

ebb associates inc is an organization and leadership development firm that helps organizations work through large-scale change. The thirty-year-old company specializes in helping people work as teams to maximize their effectiveness. Customizing all services and products for individual clients, ebb associates conducts strategic planning and implements corporate-wide systems such as quality improvement, change management, reengineering business processes, and designing mentoring programs.

ebb associates has provided services to hundreds of public- and private-sector organizations to prepare them for the challenges of the new millennium through coaching, facilitation, training, and custom designing programs such as leadership development, creativity, customer service, speaking skills, internal consulting skills, training competence, communication, and conducting productive meetings. Elaine

Biech, founder, is the author or editor of more than fifty books and is particularly adept at turning dysfunctional teams into productive teams.

Submitted by Elaine Biech, CEO

ebb associates inc

Box 8249

Norfolk, VA 23503

(757) 588-3939

ebboffice@aol.com

www.ebbweb.com

Chapter **17**

Awaken, Align, Accelerate®—A Framework for Developing Leaders

MDA LEADERSHIP CONSULTING

In This Chapter

- A three-phase approach to leadership development and growth: Awaken, Align, and Accelerate.

- Rationale for applying the three phases for leadership development.

- Tips and implications for developing leaders.

To develop and grow—personally and professionally—leaders need to have an understanding of the skills they must acquire, focus on those most relevant to their work, and engage in the most beneficial development activities. This framework

Figure 17.1 The A³ Model

provides the structure for the Awaken, Align, Accelerate (A³) process—an integrated three-phase approach to leadership development and growth:

- *Awaken* potential by enabling leaders to gain insight into their impact and aspirations.
- *Align* individual and organizational goals by understanding the business context and connecting leadership development goals with business outcomes.
- *Accelerate* performance by challenging leaders to seek new experiences, gain additional knowledge, and practice key leadership skills and behaviors.

Awaken, Align, Accelerate is built on the interaction of two concepts: the talent pipeline and MDA's leadership competency model. When we constructed our competency model, we analyzed a variety of leadership competency models and incorporated our observations from thirty years of work with dozens of leaders in several hundred organizations. During that work we identified the need for a fresh, comprehensive, and practical approach to leadership development. The Awaken, Align, Accelerate framework is an ideal approach for leaders in developing themselves, leaders (and professional coaches) who coach others, and human resources leaders.

The Six Principles of Awaken, Align, Accelerate

Awaken, Align, Accelerate is based on six key principles that are integral to developmental success.

- *Business-oriented*: A business context is critical for leadership development. Understanding what is necessary for successful business performance will help you prioritize your efforts. With this in mind, you can go beyond simply achieving personally satisfying results to increasing your organizational impact and return on investment.
- *Insight-oriented*: What does "being a leader" mean in today's world? Leaders often use outdated perspectives on leadership rather than understanding how to make

the greatest impact. Self-insight, insight from others, and competitive insight will provide you with a comprehensive perspective on development. Leaders who use insight to better understand their impact and incorporate their personal motivation will see greater results.

- *Engagement-oriented*: Being vulnerable as a leader can be intimidating but also very liberating. Leaders who are transparent with their development goals help create a supportive development culture in their organizations. Ensuring that key stakeholders are aligned and involved is a fundamental ingredient for sustaining strong development results.

- *Action-oriented*: Experiential learning is the most powerful way to develop. Identifying and including meaningful on-the-job activities, experimenting with new behaviors, and reflecting on and learning from experiences are all key actions in creating significant development. When leveraging the latest leadership book or information from a development program, interpreting and applying the material to your real-world situation is the key to self-development.

- *Measurement-oriented*: Systems, processes, and tools can be powerful allies in reinforcing behavior change. The old adage, "What gets measured and rewarded gets done," remains true today. Strong development cultures hold leaders accountable for creating leadership development plans, measuring progress on goals, and holding regular development conversations.

- *Systems-oriented*: The organizational environment has a major effect on what, how, and whether leaders learn and develop. Organizations with a strong focus on individual learning and growth link their talent reviews, succession planning, and development systems together to create an integrated approach. Holding leaders accountable for having solid leadership development plans for their direct reports is a great starting point.

Applying Awaken, Align, Accelerate in Your Role

PHASE 1: AWAKEN YOUR POTENTIAL

The Awaken phase will help you understand your impact through evaluation of your leadership style, skills, and values. It involves assessing your current strengths and development opportunities, as well as identifying what you want to achieve. Through personal exploration and reflection, you will gain insight and awareness, providing the clarity and motivation needed for development. By investing time to increase your awareness of your performance and impact, you will more likely realize your full potential and become better able to contribute stronger results.

Self-awareness is a critical component of leadership development. Substantial research has been conducted to understand the dynamics and impact of individuals' self-knowledge and self-awareness. Generally, research findings support that improved self-awareness and insight leads to change and improved performance (Kluger & DeNisi, 1996) and that accurate and positive self-knowledge is related to a range of positive outcomes. For example, Judge, Erez, Bono, and Thoreson (2003) found that people with accurate, realistic, and positive self-concepts or "core self-evaluations" were more likely to:

- Perform more successfully in their work.
- Have higher levels of work motivation, persistence, activity, and productivity.
- Select more challenging jobs and find greater satisfaction in their work.
- Show stronger commitment to work and organizational goals.
- Be more effective at overcoming obstacles, solving problems, and adapting to organizational change. (Erez & Judge, 2001; Judge & Bono, 2001)

You can begin the Awaken phase with self-reflection and then circle back with others to determine congruence. To begin, answer the following questions (as honestly as you can):

- What has shaped you? Think about your relationships, education, and experiences.
- What has brought you to this point in your career?
- What have you learned about leadership?
- What are your values?
- What do you believe is your purpose as a leader?
- What do you bring to the leadership role in your organization?

How do others view your leadership style, performance, and results?

If you would like, you can supplement your thinking and reflection by completing personality assessments, a 360-degree feedback process, or candid interviews with others. Consider partnering with a human resource representative for access to such tools.

Know that the means and methods of obtaining feedback for improving self-awareness are critical. Studies have found that when feedback is timely, objective, focused on improving task performance, presented in a non-threatening way, and includes information about how one could improve, it is most likely to produce a beneficial effect (DeNisi & Kluger, 2000; see also Hattie & Timperley, 2007). When feedback is not timely, is too harsh, or is provided by someone whose sincerity or motives the feedback recipient may doubt, it is much less effective.

This speaks to the art of providing feedback to others and is an appropriate caution in the Awaken, Align, Accelerate model: the manner in which feedback is provided may make all the difference to your leadership development. After taking stock of who you are, your impact on others, and what you aspire to become, you can then move to the Align phase.

PHASE 2: ALIGN YOUR INDIVIDUAL AND ORGANIZATIONAL GOALS

The Align phase is where your personal development goals intersect with your business agenda—what the organization needs from you to deliver strong results now and in the future. By understanding the business context for your development goals and aligning them with business outcomes, both you and your organization will be positioned to deliver stronger results.

Theory, research, and practice have shown that employees with higher levels of job satisfaction and engagement produce stronger business outcomes and results for their organizations. In a meta-analysis of studies from thirty-six companies, Harter, Schmidt, and Hayes (2002) found that organizations that built an engaged and aligned workforce enjoyed higher levels of customer satisfaction and loyalty, profitability, productivity, and safety; and lower levels of employee turnover. Moreover, employees become more engaged when the expectations of them are clear, fair, rewarded, and when their values and goals are consistent with those of their organizations and their leaders (Macey & Schneider, 2008).

Focusing on the Align phase involves stating the desired outcomes of development at the individual, team, and organization levels. Alignment means coordinating what you have learned during the Awaken phase with what is expected by your organization. It is critical to know the context of your role—especially the strategic or business context—as well as how stakeholders expect you to perform. The outcomes of this phase will provide you with the business case and context for development.

Again, self-reflection will provide key insights. Begin by answering questions such as these:

- How could your strengths contribute to advancing your own goals? Your team's goals?

- How might your development needs hinder your success in achieving your objectives? Your team's objectives?

- How could your development contribute to better business performance and results?

Setting effective development goals is a start. Researchers have found that conscious goal-setting positively affects action by providing direction, energizing behavior, influencing persistence, and guiding people to the best strategies for goal accomplishment (Locke & Latham, 2002).

Engaging others in your Alignment efforts, especially those who understand what's expected from you as an employee and as a leader, should give you additional motivation to complete this phase. Once you have completed Alignment, you and your organization will be more powerfully committed to accelerating your development.

PHASE 3: ACCELERATE YOUR PERFORMANCE

The Accelerate phase involves designing and deploying intentional learning strategies that enhance leadership development and performance. This phase requires creating and executing a plan to ensure development actually happens. The action steps in the development plan should describe how you can gain new experiences, additional knowledge, and practice key leadership skills and behaviors. The objective is to help you obtain the best return on your developmental investment in the most efficient way possible. It is the how and when of development.

The findings from decades of study on goal-setting have shown that goals lead to improved performance when they are specific, challenging (but attainable), set collaboratively (or at least understood and accepted), and when feedback or knowledge of results is provided or available (Locke & Latham, 2002).

There is also a growing consensus that the best source of learning and development in adult work lives, especially for the development of leadership skills, is on-the-job work experience (McCall, 2004). An extensive research program sponsored by the Center for Creative Leadership has shown that new or novel work experiences that challenge leaders to stretch themselves and acquire new skills or new skill levels are the most beneficial for effective leadership development (McCall & Hollenbeck, 2002; McCall, Lombardo, & Morrison, 1988).

In particular, the most powerful learning experiences for leadership development (McCauley, Ruderman, Ohlott, & Morrow, 1994) are those that:

- Involve unfamiliar responsibilities.
- Create and lead organizational change.
- Provide high levels of responsibility.
- Work and influence people across organizational boundaries and over whom one has no direct control.
- Manage people from different cultural, racial, and ethnic backgrounds.

While there are many ways available to learn and develop, and the sheer number of options can be overwhelming, the best strategies contain the right mixture of challenge and support, balancing learning through new relationships, education, and experiences. The Accelerate phase will help you sort through your choices and keep you on your "growing edge"—where learning is maximized by being challenged—without becoming overwhelmed.

Key questions to reflect on in the Accelerate phase include:

- How do you need to learn?
- What sources of support and challenge are available to you?
- How will your change and growth be obvious or visible to others?
- Who will support and reinforce your change?
- How will your change be measured?

The Accelerate phase should encompass a number of specific activities, including targeted skill-building and practical learning applications. Simply performing one activity and gaining experience is usually not enough. A manager or coach can help you brainstorm and/or sort through options, if needed.

Applying Awaken, Align, Accelerate in Concert

In conclusion, it's important to commit to practicing all three phases—Awaken, Align, Accelerate—in concert. Otherwise, your efforts may be wasted or significantly less effective. For example, without focusing on awakening, you may lack effective or accurate insight into your leadership style and how it promotes or inhibits your effectiveness. Likewise, without alignment, you may focus on personal development without sufficient attention on how it affects the results of your team and the organization. Last, when acceleration is insufficient, you may let change happen, rather than intentionally making it happen. When all of these phases are used together, results are significantly stronger and no doubt have a more substantial impact on results much broader than the individual.

For those committed to leadership development—organizations, managers, executive coaches, and leaders themselves—five implications and lessons are clear:

1. To develop as a leader, you need insight and understanding about yourself. The right kind of self-awareness will help you perform better and embrace your development needs and opportunities.

2. Feedback can help you can gain increased self-awareness, but it must be provided in a way that is helpful and facilitative of learning.

3. Self-awareness is a necessary, but not sufficient, condition for change and development. Once you are aware of the need to change, you must focus on the developmental objectives that are aligned with and, most important, to the goals of your organization. Well-aligned development objectives will help you gain the skills your organization values and rewards; increased engagement, effort, and productivity will in turn lead to positive business outcomes and results.

4. Establishing specific, challenging development goals and plans will increase your motivation to develop. It is critical that you be involved in the creation of your development plan, in order to be the most committed to implementing it. You also need feedback about your progress and success to ensure you remain on-track and confident in your ability to continue to improve.

5. The field of adult learning and development tells us much about how to structure leadership development activities. Adults learn primarily from experience, and leaders learn most from on-the-job leadership experiences, especially those that involve the challenge of new leadership roles and responsibilities—provided they are not overwhelming. Plan accordingly.

The Awaken, Align, Accelerate framework is an ideal approach for leaders in developing themselves, leaders (and professional coaches) who coach others, and human resources leaders. The model provides you with a powerful development framework to achieve leadership success. Leaders who are development-conscious can act as catalysts for change within their organizations, working concurrently to develop themselves while revising internal processes or systems to drive stronger results. Be courageous, make development a priority, and lead yourself and your organization toward growth for the future.

REFERENCES

DeNisi, A., & Kluger, A.N. (2000). Feedback effectiveness: Can 360-degree appraisals be improved? *Academy of Management Executive, 14,* 129–139.

Erez, A., & Judge, T.A. (2001). Relationship of core self-evaluations to goal-setting, motivation, and performance. *Journal of Applied Psychology, 86,* 1270–1279.

Harter, J.K., Schmidt, F.L., & Hayes, T.L. (2002). Business-unit-level relationship between employee satisfaction, and business outcomes: A meta-analysis. *Journal of Applied Psychology, 87,* 268–279.

Hattie J., & Timperley, H. (2007). The power of feedback. *Review of Educational Research, 77,* 81–112.

Judge, T.A., & Bono, J.E. (2001). Relationship of core self-evaluation traits—self-esteem, generalized self efficacy, locus of control, and emotional stability—with job satisfaction and job performance: A meta-analysis. *Journal of Applied Psychology, 86,* 80–92.

Judge, T.A., Erez, A., Bono, J.E., & Thoreson, C.J. (2003). The core self-evaluation scale: Development of a measure. *Personnel Psychology, 56,* 303–331.

Kluger, A.N., & DeNisi, A. (1996). The effects of feedback interventions on performance: A historical review, a meta-analysis, and a preliminary feedback intervention theory. *Psychological Bulletin, 119,* 254–284.

Locke, E.A., & Latham, G.P. (2002). Building a practically useful theory of goal setting and task motivation. *American Psychologist, 57,* 705–717.

Macey, W.H., & Schneider, B. (2008). The meaning of employee engagement. *Industrial and Organizational Psychology, 1,* 3–30.

McCall, M.W. (2004). Leadership development through experience. *Academy of Management Executive, 18,* 127–130.

McCall, M.W., & Hollenbeck, G.P. (2002). *Developing global executives: The lessons of international experience.* Boston: Harvard Business School Press.

McCall, M.W., Lombardo, M.M., & Morrison, A.M. (1988). *The lessons of experience: How successful executives develop on the job.* Lexington, MA: Lexington Books.

McCauley, C.D., Ruderman, M.N., Ohlott, P.J., & Morrow, J.E. (1994). Assessing the developmental components of managerial jobs. *Journal of Applied Psychology, 79,* 544–560.

About MDA Leadership Consulting

MDA Leadership Consulting partners with organizations to strengthen individual, team, and organizational leadership. We help organizations identify the right talent to drive results, accelerate the development of leaders at all levels, and sharpen alignment between talent and strategy. By taking the time to understand our clients' needs, strategies, and challenges, we help them build a competitive advantage through increased talent acumen and leadership performance.

Submitted by Scott Nelson, EVP of Consulting Services, Partner; Jason Ortmeier, Director of Coaching Services; Robert Barnett, EVP, Partner

MDA Leadership Consulting

150 South Fifth Street, Suite 3300

Minneapolis, MN 55402

(612) 332-8182

info@mdaleadership.com

www.mdaleadership.com

Chapter 18

Designing Great Leadership Development Workshops

BLUEPOINT LEADERSHIP DEVELOPMENT

In This Chapter

- Ten critical design features of an effective leadership development workshop.
- Rational and ideas to ensure leadership development workshops are a wise investment.

Leadership development workshops are very expensive. And this is not just the cost of facilities, materials, trainers, and bagels. When a company takes twenty or thirty key contributors out of the organization for even one day, it is incurring a significant cost. If you are in the business of designing these workshops, ask yourself this question: Have I designed a workshop that is really worth this investment?

1. Research-Based Content

Unfortunately, the barriers to entry in this discipline are not very high. Many leadership workshops appear to have been created by a couple of guys in a bar in Milwaukee and recorded on the back of a beer coaster. The truth is that anyone can cobble together some interesting exercises and call their product a leadership development workshop. But what do these workshops really accomplish?

When designing a workshop, start with the end in mind. We know the outcomes of great organization leadership: alignment, commitment, retention, productivity, teamwork, and innovation, to name a few. While there is little mystery here, what many designers ignore is all the research that identifies the specific leadership behaviors, practices, and approaches that create these outcomes. A good leadership workshop is grounded in this research and, as such, equips the participants with the capabilities to immediately impact their organizations. Pick the top twenty-five books on leadership and study these well. Make sure you include authors like Drucker, Senge, Nanus, Heifetz, Kets De Vries, Bennis, Pinker, and Damasio.

2. Engagement

The frenzied pace that most managers face today has turned the otherwise calm, thoughtful, and eager participant into a skittish, preoccupied onlooker infected by a self-imposed form of ADD with one eye on his or her BlackBerry and the other eye on the door. It's not that these managers are disinterested in their professional development; they are simply products of today's frenetic organizations.

To capture and keep their attention, they must be first distracted and then entertained. While describing a good leadership workshop as distracting and entertaining may sound like a call to design a boondoggle, unless your workshop can successfully compete with the myriad of distractions facing today's managers, you will simply be providing a new place for them to fuss about the demons that are haunting them. Your participants will be with you in body but not in mind. The famous communications guru, Marshall McLuhan, made the connection even more direct with this statement: "It's misleading to suppose there's any basic difference between education and entertainment." Videos, stories, games, puzzles, debates, physical experiences, and colorful materials all play an important role in participant engagement. Use them liberally.

3. Storytelling

Humans don't tell stories just to be engaging or entertaining. Humans tell stories because it is the only way they can think. Neurologists agree that the information we hear, the emotions we feel, and the events we experience must be organized into stories in order for our brains to process these things and produce thought. And humans learn by creating new stories for themselves.

Every participant comes to your workshop with a unique leadership story. Early in the workshop, give them an opportunity to reflect on and tell their stories in some way and have them honored in the classroom. Images work great. Throughout the remainder of the workshop, challenge the participants to create new, bigger leadership stories for themselves. The greater the new story, the greater the development.

4. Feedback-Rich Environment

No learning device is more potent than feedback. Whether it comes from multi-rater assessments, group fishbowls, or one-on-one coaching sessions, feedback is a powerful stimulus for personal learning and change. And that's what leadership development really is: personal learning and change. Are your workshops rich in feedback? If not, the reasons may be largely the result of your own timidity and fears. Too often, designers assume that workshop participants cannot handle negative feedback. They are too fragile. They will somehow be irreparably damaged by the facilitator's words or by those of fellow participants.

Or you may be projecting your own insecurities onto the facilitators. They will lose control of the workshop. Emotions will run rampant. They will not be able to handle the resulting carnage. Give the participants and facilitators more credit. Be bold in creating opportunities for participants to see themselves through the eyes of others. They will learn things about themselves they would never have imagined and thank you for the gift.

5. Appreciation

The problem with many leadership development workshops is that there is an underlying assumption that the ideal leader needs to develop a predetermined set of corporate competencies while becoming some fantastic amalgamation of Mother Teresa, Martin Luther King, Jr., Gandhi, and Jack Welch. You should leave that notion with the boys at the bar in Milwaukee. Corporate culture and desired competencies rightly have a bearing on workshop design, and there is also much you can learn from the great leaders of the past.

However, the best workshops are based on the assumption that all participants come uniquely gifted for the challenge of leadership, and the role of the workshop is to help them identify and cultivate these gifts. It is not your job to help them become the next Steve Jobs but rather someone much more potent—the best leadership version of themselves. A workshop that is designed to help the participants accelerate the development of their natural strengths is much more potent than one designed to fix the participant or change him or her into the model corporate leader.

6. Intense Experiences

Thousands of workshop participants were asked to reflect on the following five items and select the one that had the most influence on their development as a leader:

- Reading and research
- Performance appraisals
- Coaching and mentoring
- Challenging on-the-job experiences
- Formal training programs

"Challenging experiences" was selected by over 90 percent of the respondents. Even though most designers are keenly aware of these findings, there is a great temptation to fill the workshop agenda with content that is largely extraneous such as succession planning models, managerial competencies, and corporate values. While the intention to provide material that can be applied back on the job is laudable, this information is largely ignored. People can read. Give them the content beforehand. Use the workshop as a learning laboratory where the participants are confronted with real leadership situations. Challenge them to lead at higher levels. Create a curriculum that exposes participants to intense experiences and allows them to experiment with new behaviors and approaches. This will accelerate their learning and development. (By the way, most savvy managers have read all the corporate tenets and many of the important books on leadership anyway.)

7. Peer Coaching

In the survey noted in item 6, "Coaching and Mentoring" always comes in second. One-on-one learning processes are very powerful because, for a period of time, it really is all about the individual workshop participant. Because coaching requires no content knowledge, any participant can effectively coach another with a little guidance from the facilitator. For those of you who make your living standing in front of a classroom being insightful, witty, and sage-like, it is a little difficult to accept the fact that the average peer coaching session is usually much more effective than your most brilliant lecture. Whenever possible, get your body and ego out of the way and let the participants talk to each other.

8. Self-Awareness

It has been said that leadership development is an inside-out game. I like the way Manfred Kets De Vries puts it: "Healthy leaders are passionate. They are very talented in self-observation and self-analysis; the best leaders are highly motivated to spend time in self-reflection" (*Harvard Business Review*, 2003). The leadership development workshop provides the perfect opportunity for the leader to step out of his or her chaotic schedule, put his or her job in neutral, and take a long, fresh look inward. After all, the only thing participants can work on to improve their leadership is themselves.

Put sufficient white space into the workshop design so the participant can personalize the learning. Most managers cannot remember the last time they spent fifteen minutes in complete silence to contemplate their own leadership journey. Give them the fifteen minutes.

9. Performance Breakthroughs

The most frequently voiced dissatisfaction with leadership workshops is the lack of application on the job. It's not because workshop participants do not want to change; it's just that real change is so difficult. The pressures of the job, lack of support from their managers, no time. The list goes on. Significant improvement in leadership effectiveness rarely occurs in one big leap. You won't see the freshly trained leader walking through the hallways wearing saffron-colored robes, musing about shared community values, and throwing rose petals on others. Change occurs incrementally and is fueled by short-term successes—a process that needs to start in the classroom.

Provide ample opportunities for the participants to actually step up their leadership in the classroom. Real change starts in the workshop, not back in the office. Start the habit of experimentation, incremental change, and learning application in the workshop.

10. Accountability for Learning

Great coaches know that they can best serve their clients by insisting that they take full responsibility for their own decisions, learning, and future. They often do this by kicking off their coaching assignments with a somewhat irritating question such as, "So, Sally, if nothing changes in your performance, what is likely to happen?" The coach knows that unless clients take personal accountability for their development, there will always be someone else to blame: their boss, their staff, their customer, or their mothers. So, too, with a leadership development workshop. The question that needs to be oft-asked in the workshop is this one: "So, George, what have you learned about yourself and what are you going to do about it?"

A great leadership development workshop can be the source of some of the most important learning in a manager's career. Is this the result of great facilitation? Most certainly. A great facilitator can turn almost any curriculum into an important learning experience. But it is also the result of thoughtfully considering the above design principles.

REFERENCES

Carpenter, E., & McLuhan, M. (Eds.). (1960). Classroom without walls. Explorations (Vol. 7, 1957). *Explorations in communication*. Boston: Beacon.

Coutu, D.L. (2004, January). Putting leaders on the couch. A conversation with Manfred F. R. Kets de Vries. *Harvard Business Review, 82*(1), 64–71, 113.

About Bluepoint Leadership Development

Bluepoint Leadership Development designs workshops and coaching programs that graduate leaders who have *the head* to think for themselves, *the voice* to inspire their organizations, *the heart* to serve others, and *the courage* to act when others will not.

We are recognized by our clients and our peers as one of the premier leadership development companies in North America. Our areas of expertise are advanced leadership, coaching, communication, and innovation. We are known for our engaging, highly experiential workshops that provide participants with advanced leadership practices and approaches that they can immediately use to positively impact their teams and organizations. Some of the world's leading corporations, such as American Express, GE, Qualcomm, Microsoft, and Intel, use our services globally to help their leaders create extraordinary alignment, engagement, productivity, and innovation throughout their organizations.

Submitted by Gregg Thompson, President

Bluepoint Leadership Development

101 Commerce Boulevard

Loveland, OH 45140

(905) 319-9920

info@bluepointleadership.com

www.BluepointLeadership.com

Historical Orienteering: Leadership Lessons from History

SONOMA LEADERSHIP SYSTEMS

History's greatest leaders give us tangible examples of exemplary leadership that we can learn from and be inspired by. A growing number of writers and educators are drawing from history to learn lessons from leaders in the past. Stories about historical leaders are a powerful, and often emotionally loaded, way to make concepts come alive and more accessible to most people. Real-life stories create images in the mind that store in memory more directly and easily than hard data. This Historical Orienteering activity integrates stories about leaders from history and utilizes The Five Practices of Exemplary Leaders® (Kouzes & Posner, 2007) as the research-based model for leadership to give participants an opportunity to see how past leaders exemplified these best practices:

- Model the Way
- Inspire a Shared Vision

- Challenge the Process
- Enable Others to Act
- Encourage the Heart

We conduct the Historical Orienteering activity in our Sonoma, California, Open Enrollment workshops. Sonoma is the birthplace of the State of California and also is in the heart of the world-renowned wine region. This orienteering type of activity explores a historical area and brings to life the leaders that shaped these places and made their mark 150 years ago. The activity is intended to give participants a chance to hear real-life stories, interact with their fellow colleagues, and learn leadership lessons. The experiential and fun nature of the activity ensures that what they have learned in Sonoma stays with them over time.

ACTIVITY OBJECTIVES

- To find parallels of challenges between historical leaders and leaders of today.
- To learn the best practices of leaders through the lens of past leaders.
- To better understand participants' personal leadership challenges and those of their colleagues.

INTENDED AUDIENCE

Supervisors, managers, executives, anyone in a leadership role. There should be at least eight people to create two teams. There is no upper limit as long as there is space and enough places of interest.

TIME REQUIRED

60 to 90 minutes.

MATERIALS AND EQUIPMENT

- Handouts with stories and questions for teams; see examples at the end of this activity.
- Compass for each team.
- Orienteering map with directions.
- (Optional) Smart phone with QR reader to view stories, audio, and videos.

PREPARATION

Prepare handouts in advance:

- Orienteering map with directions to stations.
- Printed out stories and questions for each team; see sample.

PROCESS

1. Explain to participants that orienteering is a sport that requires navigational skills using a map and compass to navigate from point to point. In this activity they will be given a simple map with directions, which they will use to find the designated stations. Tell them they will visit at least two stations. At each they will read a story about the place and leader from history on their handouts, answer questions, take notes, and be prepared to discuss on returning to the meeting place.

2. Divide the group into two (or more) teams of at least four people each.

3. Each team selects a team leader. The leader is responsible for making sure the group is at the right station and the assignment is completed: the team reads the story about the historical place/leader and answers/discusses the questions.

4. Tell the teams how much time they will have (suggested time: 15 minutes at each station). Tell them they should report back to the entire group when finished.

5. Each team leaves to navigate and meet at each of the stations to complete the assignments.

6. When teams return to the original meeting place, lead a discussion about the leadership lessons learned, relating your curricula.

INSIDER'S TIPS

- Determine in what area you want to do the activity, then research history and leaders from the area. An excellent source is *The Historical Marker Database* at www.hmdb.org/

- Join an orienteering club http://en.wikipedia.org/wiki/Category:Orienteering_clubs.

- Read about historical leaders and pick one or two that inspire you, then drop them into this orienteering activity. There is a wide range of choices, including Abraham Lincoln, Winston Churchill, Lewis and Clark, Sitting Bull, Clara Barton, and many others.

REFERENCE

Kouzes, J.M., & Posner, B.Z. (2007). *The leadership challenge* (4th ed.). San Francisco: Jossey-Bass.

About Sonoma Leadership Systems

Sonoma Leadership Systems provides a dynamic range of integrated leadership and team training programs, coaching, courseware, e-learning solutions, and implementation tools designed to inspire and develop exemplary leaders and teams at every level of your organization. Our vision is a "well-led world, one leader at a time."

Sonoma Leadership Systems creates breakthrough experiences for current and future leaders, from top executives and management to every employee. Through open-enrollment workshops and customized programs, we provide measurable, learnable, and teachable sets of behaviors that can be successfully integrated into your culture. As the number 1 provider of The Leadership Challenge® and consulting partner for The Five Dysfunctions of a Team®, Sonoma Leadership Systems helps you build a high-performing leadership and team culture that specifically addresses your organization's unique challenges and impacts your bottom line. Contact us to learn about our open-enrollment workshops and experience The Leadership Challenge first-hand or to bring this research-based program into your organization.

Submitted by Jeni Nichols

Sonoma Leadership Systems

835 Broadway

Sonoma, CA 95476

(707) 933-3882

ask@sonomaleadership.com

www.sonomaleadership.com

Sample Historical Orienteering Activity Handout

This activity is designed to give you a chance to become better acquainted with each other and with the past leaders and history of Sonoma.

The Sonoma Plaza is the largest of its kind in California. It was originally surveyed and laid out by General Mariano Vallejo in 1834 and has been dedicated as a National Historic Landmark. The City of Sonoma is known as the birthplace of the State of California. Past leaders in Sonoma played important roles in California history, which you will discover during this orienteering activity.

MEETING PLACE: THE BEAR FLAGGER MONUMENT (NORTHWEST QUADRANT OF THE PLAZA)

This bronze statue of a figure unfurling the California State Flag marks the approximate spot where American settlers staged an uprising against Mexican rule under General Vallejo on June 14, 1846. In the Bear Flag revolt, a group of local hunters and trappers took over General Vallejo's headquarters. This revolt, led by Captain John Charles Fremont, U.S. Army topographer, explorer, and trailblazer, ultimately led to California's entry into the union as a state. William L. Todd, nephew of Mrs. Abraham Lincoln, designed the flag, with the words California Republic and a rough illustration of a grizzly and a star, using rusty nails and blackberry juice. Todd's rendering of a bear wasn't very accurate, and Native Californians looking up at it were heard to say "coche," the common name for pig. The edict by the Bear Flag Party was short-lived. The new republic, with Sonoma as the capital, was under U.S. rule in just twenty-six days.

STATION 1. MISSION SAN FRANCISCO SOLANO SONOMA (NORTHEAST CORNER OF THE PLAZA)

The first, and now oldest, building in Sonoma, Mission San Francisco Solano, was constructed as part of the northernmost of the California mission system.

Historical Leader: Father Jose Altimira

Leadership Practice: Inspiring a Shared Vision

Father Jose Altimira was a young, ambitious, and impatient leader who had a controversial plan to replace the existing mission establishments at San Francisco and San Rafael with a mission in Sonoma Valley. Altimira was drawn to Sonoma Valley and called the area around San Francisco de Solano, "The Valley of the Moon," after the Native American observation that the moon in winter made seven successive appearances between distant mountains. He inspired a shared vision of dedicating a new mission to God's work, and under his leadership this mission was completed and dedicated in 1823.

Questions

- Five years from now, what will you be doing?
- What is your vision of the future for your team?

STATION 2 SONOMA BARRACKS (NORTH SIDE OF THE PLAZA ON SPAIN STREET)

In the early 1800s, California was part of Mexico, known as Alta California. The Mexican government sent twenty-seven-year-old Lt. Mariano Vallejo to Sonoma to secularize the mission, found the Pueblo Sonoma, and to establish headquarters of the commandant of the Frontera del Norte—the Mexican provincial frontier of the north—to mitigate the threat of Russian settlers in Northern California coming in through Mendocino County. The Sonoma Barracks were built to house Mexican army troops under the command of the leader, General Vallejo. From the barracks, more than one hundred military expeditions set out with the object of subduing the Wappos, Cainameros, or Satisyomis tribes, who more than once rose up and attempted to throw off Mexican domination of the country around Sonoma.

Historical Leader: Mariano Vallejo

Leadership Practice: Challenge the Process

Are you finding it difficult to face budget cuts? General Mariano Vallejo, a man credited with shaping early California, was sent by the Mexican government to Sonoma in 1835 to secularize the mission and found the Pueblo of Sonoma. He did all this with virtually no subsidizing from the Mexican government. He actually gathered resources to finance his own army garrison. Vallejo was also charged with mitigating the threat of Russian settlers in Northern California coming in through Mendocino County. He realized that the ties with Mexico were too loose, that California was an isolated outpost of the Mexican government, and that the future of California lay in close association and union with the United States. Because of the isolation of California, Mariano Vallejo learned to make his own decisions, serve as foreign minister in matters relating to the Russians to the north, and monitor and control the American immigrants and foreign traders. On June 14, 1846, General Vallejo was captured in Sonoma by the ad-hoc military group known as the Bear Flaggers in the Bear

Flag Revolt. He was imprisoned unjustly in Sutter's Fort. This story remains the central irony of his life—and provides a rich leadership lesson. In return for his friendship to Americans, he was treated like a criminal. Finally returned to Sonoma six weeks later, he found his immense Rancho looted of all its possessions: thousands of cattle, horses, and stores of all kinds had been taken. He was forced to begin anew. General Mariano Vallejo went on to become a proud American citizen, and when California joined the Union he served admirably in the Constitutional Convention and as a Senator in the State Assembly. As a delegate in making the first state constitution, he also laid out the design of the Sonoma Plaza, the largest in California. Certainly, the growth and progress made in California since that time attest to the great foresight of General Mariano Vallejo, a fine example of living the leadership practices of Challenge the Process.

Questions

- How have you challenged the process in a work situation to find resources?
- How do you celebrate your small wins (and large wins) with your colleagues and team?

Sample Historical Orienteering Activity Card

The historic story is featured on one side, with leadership questions on the back with QR code link for further study.

Station 1
Mission San Francisco
Solano Sonoma,
Northeast
corner of the plaza

Historical Leader: Father Jose Altimira

Leadership Practice: Inspiring a Shared Vision*:

**ENVISION the future
by imagining exciting
and ennobling possibilities**

**ENLIST others in a common vision
by appealing to shared aspirations**

*The Five Practices of Exemplary Leaders® Kouzes & Posner,
The Leadership Challenge 4th Ed.

Questions

- **Five years from now, what will you be doing?**

- **What is your vision of the future for your team?**

Sonoma Leadership Systems Historical Orienteering Activity

SonomaLeadership.com/Orienteering

SHAPING A VITAL CULTURE

Introduction

Whether you call it engagement, a respectful culture, a high-passion/high-performance environment, a motivating work environment, employee work passion, an inspiring climate, or a productive culture, there are certain organizations that evoke a desire to embrace them.

Leaders generally have a good sense of the culture of their organizations. Unfortunately, some may not realize how they can most effectively lead within the culture or that they can change the culture (with a good deal of work) if it would better for the organization.

To describe a culture, look around the organization to determine who seems to be accepted and who isn't and identify what it is about those who are accepted as compared to those who are not. Consider the kinds of behaviors that are rewarded, for example, getting along, getting things done. Notice what management attends to the most, for example, problems, successes, crises. Also consider how decisions are made, for example, by one person or by consensus. Are discussions held? Or are decisions made at all?

Finally, notice whether a close alignment exists between what the organization says it values, for example, creativity, innovation, or team building, as compared to what is actually experienced, for example, conformity or individualism. Clarity about values and what your organization represents saves a huge amount of energy that can be deployed productively in other places.

It is not a surprise, as Richard Whiteley states in his chapter, that the leader defines and reinforces the culture. Leaders emphasize what's important in the organization by communicating the organization's goals, disseminating and living up to the mission statement, talking about accomplishments, and reiterating expectations of the workplace. Leaders reinforce the culture by rewarding employees whose behaviors reflect the organization's culture and dissuading employees from continuing unwanted behaviors by delivering constructive feedback, verbal or written warnings, or, when necessary, firing them. Leaders model the behaviors that they want to see in the workplace. This is perhaps the most powerful way to influence the culture. For example, if you want to see more teamwork among your employees, then involve yourself in teams more often.

The culture discussions presented in the seven chapters in this section will inspire you to consider the shape of your culture. While each labels its culture differently, you will find similarities from one to the other—most notably, ensuring a productive and engaged workforce.

- Chapter 19, "Bringing the Twelfth Man Alive in Your Organization" by The Whiteley Group, taps into a sports phenomenon that can be evoked in organizations as well. The six leadership practices build a high-passion/high-performing work environment can be executed by anyone aspiring to be a great leader.

- In Chapter 20, "Creating a Culture of Employee Work Passion" by The Ken Blanchard Companies, you will learn about the company's most recent research and a description of their employee work passion model that goes beyond an engaged workforce.

- Chapter 21, "Owners and Renters" by the Center for Creative Leadership, provides employers with a solid rationale for hiring employees who perform as "owners" and the leadership factors that foster this owner mindset and culture.

- Chapter 22, "The Commercial Impact of Employee Engagement" by Performance Connections International, Inc., provides validation of the impact of an engaged culture as well as the role of senior management to maintain employee engagement.

- In Chapter 23, "Thank God It's Monday!," The Emmerich Group presents a tongue-in-cheek look at why employees are not satisfied. The managerial self-assessment is a tool to help you predict the ease with which a culture shift will occur.

- In Chapter 24, "Improving Workplace Cultures Through Respect, Service, and Safety at Work®," the Crisis Prevention Institute, Inc., shares a method for creating a policy for improving respect, service, and safety in the workplace.

- In Chapter 25, "Building Organizational Change Capability" by Being First, Inc., you will explore the process of building organizational change capability. Loaded with tools, assessments, and checklists, the chapter presents numerous ways to increase the capacity to change in an organization.

- The Exploring Culture Through the Canyon bonus activity in this section is one that you may want to try soon. Root Learning, Inc., provides an image to stimulate lively discussions about the challenges and opportunities in any culture.

Chapter 19

Bringing the Twelfth Man Alive in Your Organization

THE WHITELEY GROUP

In This Chapter

- Explanation of the "twelfth man" phenomenon.
- Six leadership practices that build a high-passion/high-performance work environment.
- Practical, implementable opportunities to create a positive climate and committed workforce.

There is a phenomenon in American football called the "twelfth man." What this refers to is that situation when the fans are so passionate, committed, and loud that they can actually affect the outcome of a game in favor of the home team. In effect, they become like a twelfth man on the eleven-player team. While most of us haven't experienced this as a player, my guess is that many of us, men and women alike, have at one time or another been part of a crowd whose enthusiasm was so great as to influence the results of an athletic contest. Just think, for example, of the energy, spirit, and compassion generated by the curbside crowds that help to keep exhausted marathoners running in Boston, London, or Paris when they feel as though they can't take another step.

When I reflect on this phenomenon and the many organizations I have had the pleasure of working with over the years, I have come to realize that the leaders in the really outstanding companies have figured out how to evoke a kind of twelfth player effect as well. I call it creating the high-passion/high-performance work environment. They are able to generate such excitement and commitment in the hearts of their people that not only do they establish great places to work, but they also gain unassailable competitive advantage. Culture as we know it is certainly part of the formula, but it seems to go beyond that. There is an intangible aspect to this twelfth man energy that you'll know when you experience it but will still have difficulty defining.

One example of this twelfth man situation occurred in the early years of Saturn, the GM spin-off that was established to win back market share from the small Japanese imports. Saturn was succeeding so well in executing this strategy that I decided to check out just how they were accomplishing such an impressive turn-around. At the time I was co-creating a video seminar with *Fortune* magazine on customer-centered companies, so I took this opportunity to grab a video crew and head down to Spring Hill, Tennessee, to see just how they were creating this early success. Part of the answer came in my interview with Saturn's president, Skip LeFave. I asked him what he believed was the most important element of his job. His response was immediate. Without skipping a beat he said, "That's easy. . . . My job is to create the kind of environment where individual excellence can emerge."

There it was. Some twenty years ago, one word offered by a successful CEO has stuck with me to this day. The word was *environment*. Without even knowing it, Skip was talking about the Twelfth Man effect. Feeling it in action that day confirmed my belief that one of the most powerful of leadership tools is to be an environment engineer. It is to intentionally establish a workplace climate that attracts the best people and enables them to give their best while having fun doing it. That is what the high-passion/high-performance work environment can achieve. It is like the twelfth man, an extra pair of hands working 24/7 to help make your enterprise successful.

Lou Gerstner, Jr., echoed the importance of this concept as he discussed some of the lessons he learned from orchestrating the extraordinary IBM turnaround. He said that going into that challenge he thought culture was one among a number of tools in his leadership kit that he would have to use in order to get the company back on track. When the dust settled, however, he offered another view: "Culture is not part of the game . . . it is the game!"

Anne Mulcahy, who engineered another exceptional recovery at Xerox, clearly understands the power of creating the right environment when she says, "Company culture is code for people." As elusive as it might be, if we look over the shoulders of paragons like Gerstner and Mulcahy, it becomes clear that creating the high-passion/high-performance environment is the responsibility of every leader in your organization.

It was the pioneering organizational climate work we practiced at The Forum Corporation in the early 1970s that put me on the track of thinking of the leader as responsible for creating a welcoming and stimulating place to work. My interview with Skip LeFave gave me a label that would help describe it, *environment*. Based on this background, I have arrived at the following definition of leadership:

> *Leadership is creating an engaging environment where people are willing and able to carry out the vision and strategy of the organization.*

This definition may contain more than meets the eye on a casual reading. First, not surprisingly, it identifies the leader as a creator of an environment that engages people. It also presumes that it is the leader's responsibility to cause the vision and strategy for his or her organization to be created and promulgated. The word "able" refers to resources, meaning it is the leader's responsibility to see that employees have the equipment, space, budget, support, training, and permission to do their jobs. "Willing" refers to free will or motivation. Here it is the leader's job to cause people to be fully and happily engaged in their work and the work of the enterprise.

There are a number of actions a leader can take in order to create the twelfth man effect. Many are covered in the excellent literature and training programs that are available today and aimed at improving leadership effectiveness. In the remainder of this chapter, I will suggest six leadership practices that may be less traditional but are powerfully relevant for today's rapidly changing and turbulent times. They are

1. Use "Cultural Moments of Truth" to Show You Mean Business

2. Tell the Truth . . . Hear the Truth

3. Be Present

4. Tell Stories

5. Be a Healer

6. Lead Yourself

1. Use "Cultural Moments of Truth" to Show You Mean Business

In the past decade, leaders have invested a great deal of energy in creating visions and values for their organizations. This work has been vital in supporting their employees as they are asked to direct their passion into company-related initiatives. People will work hard for a paycheck. They will work harder for a really good manager or leader. And they will work even harder for a cause. People will die for a cause. In organizations, the vision has become the surrogate for a cause. While we do not expect employees to lay down their lives for the shareholders, the vision, when properly created, will have a very powerful impact. In addition to the vision, a clear statement of values is equally important. This provides the non-negotiable behavioral guidelines for being a member of an organization.

The cultural moment of truth relates to the vision and values and can be a powerful tool for any leader. It is that time when there is a crisis or a significant decision to be made. How leaders act in that moment will have a highly leveraged impact on the kind of environment they create. In that critical juncture, do they live by the vision and values they have espoused? Or do they abandon them for expedient and sometimes even unethical solutions? The classic example of a cultural moment of truth is the oft-told story of how Johnson & Johnson handled the Tylenol incident. When faced with this extraordinary dilemma, the J&J executives were guided by their vision and values and strongly enhanced their reputation as an ethical and caring company in the eyes of their customers and, equally importantly, in the eyes of their own employees. Although the incident occurred in 1982, it has such power as a prototypical cultural moment of truth that it is still discussed and written about today.

While at Saturn, I asked Skip LeFave whether he had experienced any cultural moments of truth. He described how just after introducing their new line of automobiles they had a problem with about 1,850 of them and had to initiate a recall. How embarrassing. Here is the savior of the U.S. small car market featuring high quality at an affordable price and, WHAM! a recall. It was a kind of a public Ta-Dah . . . OOPS! What happened was a supplier provided bad coolant and the gaskets in the car engines were deteriorating. Saturn had three fix-it options: (1) recall the cars and replace the gaskets; (2) recall the cars and replace the engines; or (3) recall the cars and replace the cars! Option 3 carried a price tag of about $35 million. All three solutions would have worked. Now Saturn's number one value was "We are committed to creating customer delight." The top-level managers gathered to decide what to do and opted to bite the bullet and replace the cars. Why? Because their number one value was about delighting customers and they couldn't guarantee that somewhere down the road a customer would not have a problem caused by an unforeseen side-effect from the coolant incident. Because these executives put their number one value above all else, it took them just twenty minutes to make the decision! When faced with a gut-wrenching cultural moment of truth, the executives at Saturn stood by their espoused values and in so doing etched them forever into the DNA of the organization. Such is the environment impacting power of a cultural moment of truth.

More recently, no doubt there were many cultural moments of truth for British Petroleum in the horrendous oil spillage in the Gulf of Mexico. While the company's ad campaign featured service personnel expressing genuine concern for those affected by the disaster, it appears that in the early stages of the crisis some cultural moments of truth were missed.

Another dramatic and highly visible cultural moment of truth occurred on January 1, 2008. That was when Howard Schultz stepped back in as CEO of Starbucks. The company was on life support. Its stock had dropped from the high $30s to $6.81 per share. This downward spiral can be explained by the economic downturn, tougher competition, managerial arrogance, and undisciplined decision making. But the most compelling reason is that Starbucks lost its identity. Thirty-nine years of success allowed the executives to forget that the company's core values were around customers, employees, and the Starbucks experience.

Sixty days into his return, Schultz shut down the company for a day of retraining. In so doing, he was quite publicly saying mea culpa to his own staff and to the world. He went on a listening tour around the world to enable him to make decisions that were grounded in reality. He held a meeting of some eleven thousand U.S. store managers to ask their commitment to accept the challenge of the turnaround. The meeting cost almost $33 million at a time when the company was near bankruptcy. Most important, he did three things that helped him re-create the twelfth man energy and restore the trust of his employees and ultimately his customers: (1) he said, "I'm sorry," (2) he reenergized Starbuck's core values, and (3) he was brutally honest about the condition of the company and what he was asking people to do to recover. This combination of humility, clear action, and truth-telling turned the company around.

OPPORTUNITY 1: *Be aware of cultural moments of truth when they occur and use them to focus your decisions and reinforce your vision and values.*

---

2. Tell the Truth . . . Hear the Truth

Several years ago I had the pleasure of interviewing Jack Welch. He's a big believer in recruiting and retaining top talent and was aggressively involved in the hiring of senior officers while at GE. When I asked him what he looked for in a candidate, he said, "The four E's: energy, energizer, execution, and edginess." I understood the first three but asked for elaboration on "edginess." He explained that he wanted someone who would push back, speak his or her mind, and take a stand. He definitely wasn't looking for yes people. Perhaps agreeing with Mark Twain, who said, "Sacred cows make the best hamburger," Welch wanted to hear the truth and the whole truth, no matter how ugly or irreverent it may have been.

Regrettably, I believe Jack Welch's search for the truth is not universal. As I visit company after company, I am convinced that one of the greatest organizational wastes is employees not being edgy, not being willing to tell the truth. When people hide problems rather than solve them, the problems don't go away, they get worse. When people spend time in CYA (cover your a--) activities, their energy is inwardly aimed and certainly not externally or customer focused. This is pure waste. In addition, such a moribund cultural condition couldn't be farther from the power generated by the twelfth man phenomenon.

If truth-hearing is critical to creating the high-passion/high-performance work environment, why does it not occur routinely? Usually because the leader doesn't want to hear bad news, and all too often the messenger bearing such information is punished. It comes down to this simple dynamic. If you want people to tell you the truth, you have to be prepared to hear the truth . . . even welcome or reward people for bringing it.

At Starbucks, Howard Schultz has open forums where employees can meet and share what is on their minds. At one, a woman spoke so boldly others in the room tensed up a little only to have the moderator say, "I know how much courage it took to ask that question," and then with a smile, "No one is going to ask where you live." John Chambers at Cisco Systems walks the halls of his company and gives ice cream and candy to employees only in exchange for a suggestion on what he or the company can be doing better. And remember, hearing the truth is only half the equation. The other half is telling the truth, and as important as it is, it still makes many leaders uncomfortable today.

Now more than ever, leaders are being asked to be open and candid about their businesses. Transparency has become a buzz word, and rightly so, as they ask employees not just to do the work but to become their strategic partners in pursuit of the company's vision, mission, and strategies. They ask them to dedicate their time, talent, and emotional and physical energy to corporate pursuits. The least employees should expect in return is for leadership to let them know where the organization stands and where they stand as part of the organization. Whether it is an aberration in the company's direction or discussing a deficiency in a performance review, the need for leaders to tell the truth cannot be overstated. When Howard Schultz was preparing to address the eleven thousand store managers, he planned to tell it like it was even to the point that his advisors cringed, saying, "You're going to scare people if you're that honest." He told all and poured his heart out, even talking of love. Without truth-telling and truth-hearing, there is simply no chance for the twelfth man to have a home.

> **OPPORTUNITY 2:**   Have the courage to both tell the truth and hear the truth and reward others in your organization for doing the same.

3. Be Present

Last summer I was in Aspen, Colorado, to deliver a keynote presentation. As I approached the elevators in my hotel, I noticed there were several gentlemen in dark suits hovering around the alcove in which the elevators were located. The small shiny lapel pins and telltale earplugs suggested that these were security personnel. Sure enough, as I rounded the corner there was none other than Bill Clinton in conversation with a family who also appeared to be guests in the hotel. The woman was letting her feelings be known on some political issue that sounded trivial to me but obviously was not to her. As I waited for the elevator, I studied Clinton closely. I was only ten feet or so from him and, after a cursory nod to me, he returned to the woman and gave her his absolutely full and undivided attention. He appeared to be rapt, hanging on every word. He is legend for this kind of attentiveness and, having seen it close-up and in action, I was thoroughly impressed. He could give us all lessons in being present.

With the ever-increasing pace of business, long hours, increased complexity, and mind-boggling number of ways to connect electronically, it is easy to understand how effective, mannerly, face-to-face communication has suffered. The television ad that depicts two executives from the same company sitting next to each other on an airplane sending emails back and forth to each other epitomizes the problem.

I have long believed that one of the greatest gifts one human being can give to another is to witness the other with no bias, prejudice, or projections. This makes sense when you consider that one of the greatest fears of most people is that of being rejected. If you are earnestly sharing your point of view and I sigh, look at my watch, notice what is going on behind you, check my text messages, interrupt, and demonstrate other inattentive behaviors, it is indeed a form of rejection. Most likely you will feel blown off, marginalized, and not valued nor important. When people are feeling minimized or not valued, they certainly aren't going to contribute to the twelfth man dynamic.

Over the years when psychologists have conducted research to determine the deep wants of we human beings, being valued or appreciated always takes a place near the top. Purely and simply, one of the easiest ways to appreciate another is to be present with him or her. As a Japanese proverb suggests, "Say one word . . . hear ten words." This requires that you stop the chatter in your mind so you can attend to the other person and avoid the nonverbal distractions that signal you are not and don't care to be listening. Most leaders can do this; they just don't because they think it takes a lot of time. In the long run it doesn't because, after every interaction, communications are complete and don't need reruns. Plus, after every interaction, the other person feels heard and valued. Another culprit is the intrusive mind chatter that occurs while others are speaking. This happens when leaders mentally review their to-do lists and fret about problems that might be lurking around the corner. It takes true intention to quiet the mind when listening to another, but it is absolutely essential to embrace this discipline when creating the high-passion/high-performance work environment.

Garry Ridge is the CEO of WD-40 Company, an excellent organization where the twelfth man is alive and well. In addition to running a successful company, he teaches leadership at the University of San Diego and has co-authored a wonderful book with Ken Blanchard, *Helping People Win at Work*. We both serve on Ken's board, and at a recent meeting Garry shared his "Ten Traits of Leadership." One of them bears directly on being present. He says that outstanding leaders "are connected, aware, tuned in. They are particularly tuned in to the people around them and to subtle behavioral clues. They read a room well. They listen well. They have high EQ [emotional quotient/intelligence]!" Another executive who certainly would agree with Garry said to me, "I listen to understand . . . not to answer."

OPPORTUNITY 3: *Make the people around you feel valued and important simply by being present with them.*

---

4. Tell Stories

In recent years there has been a growing appreciation for the role of storytelling in organizations. In our research at Forum we found this to be particularly relevant for salespeople and leaders alike. We found that outstanding salespeople were able to present their solutions in such a way that their prospects could see themselves in the ownership scenario the salesperson created by, in effect, telling a story. Anne Mulcahy at Xerox understands well how this applies to leaders. She says, "By keeping in touch with your people, you've got to go out and work it. You've got to be able to communicate the story. You have to have the dialogue with your people so that there's a degree of ownership . . . that they know how they fit into the story."

It's not enough to do a good job of creating the vision and mission of your business or articulating your strategy. While all that is important, what is required is the context into which these are placed. Faced with the rapidly changing complex and uncertain world in which we operate, the people we employ want some sense made out of it all. They want the leader to bring stability to an unstable situation so that they can have confidence they are in the right place and working on the right things. In effect, they are looking for the big picture, and it is the leader's job to give it to them. Max De Pree, the former CEO of Herman Miller, understood this. He said, "It is important that we focus more on what we need to be than what we need to do. . . . People follow easily the leader who understands meaningful changes clearly connected to strategy" (De Pree, 1992, p. 142).

One form of storytelling is to actually document the history of the organization. In addition to marking significant dates on a time line, get the veterans to reminisce about the "good old days." Make the resulting product historically accurate, light in tone, with a lot of pictures and documentation of turning points or cultural moments of truth. The book can be given to employees to share with their families and used in recruiting and new hire orientation. After thirty years we took this on at Forum and in 2001 produced a beautifully bound 185-page book entitled *Forum Folklore: Unique Stories of Innovation and Inspiration*.

OPPORTUNITY 4: *Use storytelling to create the context for people at work and to portray a realistic picture of the future.*

---

5. Be a Healer

For the past eighteen years I have had the privilege of studying with a number of shamans. Shamans are healers from around the world and may be better known in the United States as medicine people. There is evidence that these fascinating individuals have been engaged in their healing activities for one hundred thousand years. I have a small practice in Boston based on their teachings. Also, as a result of my work, in 2002 I wrote a book called *The Corporate Shaman*. It is a fable that examines how some of the powerful practices used by shamans over the millennia might be applied to the world of business. One of the opportunities the book offers is viewing today's leader in a new role . . . that of healer.

The premise that underlies this idea is based on my experience in bringing some of these age-old practices to my clients. I believe an organization is first and foremost a group of people. No people, no organization. If this is true, then it is reasonable to assume that practices originally designed for an individual can work for an organization as well. For example, does an organization have spirit as does an individual? Perhaps that's what is meant by the phrase *esprit de corps*. Does an organization have a soul? My answer is "yes," and I am in good company. In his book *Onward*, Howard Schultz of Starbucks speaks of the soul of his company. In fact, the subtitle of the book is *How Starbucks Fought for Its Life Without Losing Its Soul.* If indeed an organization does have a soul, what happens to it when there is a layoff, an acquisition or merger, reorganization, the death of a beloved leader, the closing of a plant? It is at these times in particular that the conscious leader must assume the role of compassionate healer. What might that look like?

Howard Schultz understood that closing eight hundred stores and laying off 6,700 people would indeed be a serious wounding to the Starbucks soul. His healer revealed itself when he was asked why he came back. He said it wasn't to get the stock back up; it was because of "love." His first day back he stood in front of his employees and apologized. He made investments in his people at a time when the company couldn't afford them, saying, "There is no better investment we can make than in our people." He went on a worldwide listening tour, and he stated that "the lens we will use to continue to build the company with will be humanity." These are the actions of a healer.

In a segment of the ABC News show *20/20*, Diane Sawyer interviewed John Chambers, the CEO of Cisco Systems. He had just been named the best boss in America by one of the prominent business magazines, and she was finding out why. In discussing his former position at Wang, they touched on the downsizing during which he had to lay off five thousand employees. It was obviously a very heart-wrenching experience for him, as he said, "I'll do anything to avoid doing that again. It about killed me."

During that time he said he couldn't sleep, he didn't enjoy going to work, and he couldn't stop thinking about the people who were fired and the trauma that being out of work during an economic downturn would cause them. What impressed me was that, as he was saying these words, he welled up with emotion and tears came to his eyes. Here he was a captain of industry and leader of one of the world's most successful companies tearing up and still showing heartfelt compassion for the people he had to lay off many years earlier. That is the kind of caring and compassionate leadership that so many of our organizations need today.

This is particularly true when you look at an extreme example of alternative behavior as embodied in the callous actions of Al "Chainsaw" Dunlap some years ago. Al had a reputation as a turnaround specialist. One of his first and most predictable acts as a newly appointed leader was always to eliminate staff, hence the nickname "chainsaw." He was more effective at destroying companies than building them, and eventually the SEC sued him for exaggerating earnings and banned him from ever running a business again.

In his book, *The Power of Intention*, Wayne Dyer says, "Every single person on the planet has within [him/her] the potential to be a healer" (2004, p. 215). No doubt cultural anthropologist Angeles Arrien would agree. In her classic book, *The Four-Fold Way*, she offers four archetypes as guides for our understanding and managing ourselves. They are the Warrior, Visionary, Teacher, and Healer. I believe all four work wonderfully for those who aspire to lead. As reported in *The Science of Energy Healing*, Arrien believes healers have the following qualities:

- They pay attention to what has heart and meaning.
- They are skilled in the art of acknowledgement, acceptance, recognition, validation, recognition, and gratitude.
- They are able to sustain their own emotional and spiritual health while uplifting others.
- They hold the four qualities of the heart: full, open, clear, and strong.
- They have mastered giving and receiving to themselves as well as others.
- They have mastered the ability to connect.
- They harness the healing powers of storytelling, singing, dancing, and silence. (Gia Combs-Ramirez, undated)

6. Lead Yourself

"The hardest person to lead is yourself." So says Bill George, former CEO of Medtronic, current Harvard Business School professor, and author of *Authentic Leadership*. In a similar sentiment, charismatic speaker and founder of Wilson Learning, Larry Wilson, says, "You can't give away what you don't own." I couldn't agree more. It is from within one's self that outstanding leadership manifests. In the past, sound leadership was not quite at the premium or as challenging to master as it is today. Back then it was top-down, command-and-control, power- and position-based authority. The boss was the smartest kid on the block, workers did it because they were told to do it without reason or rationale—my way or the highway—and the communications flow was one way. All the leader had to do was extend last year's growth line to next year and follow the tried-and-true tenets of plan, lead, organize, and control. In those days it might not have seemed simple, but in hindsight it really was. How times have changed! Perhaps the new demands of leadership inspired consultant/author Tracy Goss to say, "Today's business leaders are reinventing everything but themselves. Unless executives realize that they must change not just what they do but who they are, not just their sense of task but their sense of themselves, they will fail."

A couple of years ago I attended a meeting at which Betsy Myers, who was then executive director of the Center for Public Leadership at Harvard, made a presentation. She indicated that the top three areas of focus for the Center's class members were conflict management, listening and, wouldn't you know, self-knowledge. This need to explore the inner landscape is catching on in business schools as relevant courses are being added to their curricula. WD-40 Company's Garry Ridge, who also teaches at the University of San Diego, dedicates one of his ten traits of leadership to "high self-esteem/self-worth." He says, "Leaders have to have a strong sense of self-worth. This brings the ability to accept failures and criticism."

After working with many different companies in numerous countries, I am certain of one thing regarding creating the twelfth man effect or the high-passion/high-performance work environment. It simply will not happen if the leader is not grounded in self-knowledge. Having the title, plans, control, funds, support, advisors, and even approval from above isn't enough. These factors can help, but what is needed is at least some of the following traits: openness, grounding, truth-hearing, sensitivity, compassion, listening, flexibility, humility, vulnerability, and empathy as well as decisiveness, toughness, clarity, courage, truth-telling, determination, and persistence.

So how does one gain self-knowledge?

First, start with a clear intention to do whatever work is required to achieve the personal growth objectives you choose. This includes a willingness to be vulnerable and at times step into the awkward and often humiliating space of the beginning learner where you have no idea what's going on and feel like a total bumbler. This can be humbling and create a good deal of dissonance for one who comes into the process with a splendid track record of success and career growth.

Ironically, I have found over the years that the people who are most open and willing to put themselves into situations where they may look awkward are the ones who are already exceptional leaders. An insatiable curiosity and willingness to embrace the attitude of a beginner might just have something to do with their success. This, of course, can involve some perceived risk. Max De Pree agrees. In what he calls a checklist for the attributes of a leader, vulnerability is number two of the twelve items. He says, "There is no such thing as safe vulnerability" (De Pree, 1992, p. 221).

Second, assemble a personal growth team to support you. This is your own board of directors for your personal growth. The chairman of the board could be an executive coach, fellow business person, therapist, or trusted confidante who will help you design your personal growth program. Other board roles that you may want to fill might include a *butt kicker* who will keep your feet to the fire on commitments you have made, a *cheerleader* who will always provide positive feedback on what's going well, and maybe a *Yoda*, a wise person who has walked the path you are about to embark upon.

There are hundreds of personal growth workshops, books, videos, and the like. You and your board can research which might be best for you and ask for recommendations and endorsements. Because quality is uneven in these offerings, you would do well to do a thorough check before committing to any one program. Workshops that provide feedback through validated self-assessment instruments and commentary from others can be very helpful.

The Twelfth Man Lives

Perhaps the hottest topic in business today is leadership. A staggering number of books on this subject are published every year. The reason, of course, is that there is a significant need for people who can operate comfortably and competently in this vital role. The dynamic, challenging, and constantly shifting circumstances leaders find themselves facing today are daunting. Perhaps that is why Betsy Meyers at the Center for Public Leadership said that "new leaders are like first-time parents."

Given these challenges, I would recommend to any new leader and the veterans as well that they consciously seek to create the twelfth man effect or high-passion/high-performance work environment in their organizations. Once accomplished, they will have a powerful asset that will work for them even when they are not at work. To achieve this, they would do well to embrace and master the six practices outlined in this chapter:

- Use "Cultural Moments of Truth" to Create the High-Passion/High-Performance Work Environment
- Tell the Truth . . . Hear the Truth
- Be Present
- Tell Stories
- Be a Healer
- Lead Yourself

The Final Word

Some may find these practices a little soft or new age-y. It would be pretty easy to write off "Be Present," "Be a Healer," or "Lead Yourself" as good for the "tree huggers" but not for real leaders. Executive Coach Shayla Roberts asserts that for many of her clients such bravado, when closely examined, turns out to be kind of a subconscious smoke screen that masks the executive's true fear of embarking on the inner journey. That said, one might be sincerely wondering, "How about good old goal setting, tracking the numbers, or leading by example like Teddy Roosevelt charging up San Juan Hill? Isn't that the way we get results in business?" The answer is yes and no. At Forum we determined through our best practices research that the so-called *soft* practices like knowing the capabilities of every member on your team, listening to others' opinions, or providing positive feedback to employees had a higher correlation with success than the more traditional *hard* practices such as setting aggressive goals, tracking progress against them, and creating strategy. William Peace presented a similar conclusion in his classic *Harvard Business Review* article, "The Hard Work of Being a Soft Manager," in which he states, "Soft qualities like openness and sensitivity are as critical to success as harder qualities like charisma, aggressiveness, and always being right" (2001, p. 6). In other words, in today's complex leadership environment, soft has become hard!

Turn to the online tools for this chapter for an individual exercise to create the kind of work environment that encourages commitment and enthusiasm.

RECOMMENDED READING

Arrien, A. (1993). *The four-fold way: Walking the paths of the warrior, teacher, healer and visionary.* New York: HarperCollins.

Bach, R. (1977). *Illusions: The adventure of a reluctant messiah.* New York: Dell.

Blanchard, K., & Ridge, G. (2009). *Helping people win at work: A business philosophy called "don't mark my paper, help me get an A."* Upper Saddle River, NJ: FT Press.

Sisodia, R., Sheth, J., & Wolfe, D.B. (2007). *Firms of endearment: How world-class companies profit from passion and purpose.* Philadelphia: Wharton School Publishing.

Whiteley, R. (2002). *The corporate shaman: A business fable.* New York: HarperCollins.

REFERENCES

Combs-Ramierez, G. (n.d.). Developing leaders, teachers. *The science of energy healing.* Retrieved 8/23/11 from scienceofenergyhealing,com.

De Pree, M. (1992). *Leadership jazz.* New York: Doubleday.

Dyer, W.W. (2004). *The power of intention: Learning to co-create your world your way.* Carlsbad, CA: Hay House.

Peace, W.H. (2001, December 1). The hard work of being a soft manager. *Harvard Business Review.*

About The Whiteley Group

The Whiteley Group is dedicated to helping individuals and organizations realize and expand their potential. This purpose is achieved by designing and presenting exciting and provocative speeches and workshops that are customized to each client's unique situation. The company is guided by three core values: create value, be authentic, and have fun. Topics covered are Creating the High-Passion/High-Performance Work Environment, Creating the Branded Customer Experience, Sales Through Service, Leading in Turbulent Times, and Meditating for Type A's.

Richard Whiteley is an entrepreneur, co-founder of The Forum Corporation, and founder of the Instructional Systems Association (ISA). He is a best-selling author of four books and a keynote presenter who has spoken to nearly one million people in thirty countries. He has received ISA's Service and Spirit awards and has been named one of the top one hundred consultants and best minds in leadership in the world.

Submitted by Richard Whiteley, Principal

The Whiteley Group

28 Atlantic Avenue, Unit 534

Boston, MA 02110

(617) 699-1141

Richard@whiteleygroup.com

www.whiteleygroup.com

WHITELEY

GROUP

Copyright © 2011, The Whiteley Group. Published by Pfeiffer, An Imprint of John Wiley & Sons, Inc. Reprinted by permission of The Whiteley Group.

Developing Talent for Organizational Results

Chapter 20

Creating a Culture of Employee Work Passion

THE KEN BLANCHARD COMPANIES

In This Chapter

- Definition of employee work passion.
- Description of an employee work passion model.
- Twelve work passion factors.

For years, researchers, organizations, and leaders have been grappling with both the challenge of how best to create a motivating work environment and the role of leadership in inspiring and maximizing the work passion and performance of others.

Several years ago, The Ken Blanchard Companies® began exploring these issues as well as the relationships between leadership, employee satisfaction, customer satisfaction, and organizational performance. The first study included the creation of a model we titled The Leadership-Profit Chain. This model was grounded in a literature review of hundreds of studies and meta-analyses from 1980 through 2005.

The study concluded that strategic leadership indirectly influenced customer devotion and employee work passion by establishing policies, procedures, vision, and values and that operational leadership directly influenced employee work passion and customer devotion through the daily operationalization of strategic leadership policies. The study also found that employee work passion, in turn, was a key factor in creating customer devotion and organizational vitality.

Further research allowed us to create a model of how employee work passion is formed, a definition of what employee work passion is, and a core set of factors that must be present in the organizational and job environment in order for employee work passion to be optimized.

Our initial research surfaced eight key factors responsible for driving employee work passion. These included meaningful work, autonomy, collaboration, fairness, recognition, growth, connectedness to colleagues, and connectedness to leader.

While these eight factors were not all-inclusive, they represented a majority of the influencers of employee work passion and accounted for approximately 64 percent of the variance that explained it.

A subsequent study was devoted to understanding what additional factors might drive employee work passion. A review of the literature produced a list of thirty-three possible factors. Using factor analysis, a final list of factors was narrowed to twelve. These included six of the original eight factors (growth, connectedness to colleagues, connectedness to leader, meaningful work, autonomy, and collaboration). In addition, some factors no longer correlated to the existing six, and new factors emerged. In the final analysis, recognition was replaced by feedback; fairness split into two new factors: distributive justice and procedural justice; and three new factors emerged, which were labeled workload balance, task variety, and performance expectations. This gave us the final set of twelve factors.

Regression analysis showed that each of the factors was interdependent of the others, and all must be present for employee work passion to be maximized. While there was no statistically significant ranking among the factors (meaning one was not more important than another), meaningful work was generally perceived to be the most present in the minds of our survey population, while procedural justice and growth were generally perceived to be the least present.

Through further statistical analysis, we learned that the factors could be grouped as either organizational factors, job factors, or moderating factors. Organizational factors are influenced by the organization's senior leadership, policies, procedures, and organizational systems. Job factors are influenced by aspects of the job, colleagues, or leader. Moderating factors influence an individual's perception of both organizational factors and job factors as identified in the listing below.

In addition to the twelve factors, five key areas of intent also emerged from our research. These include the intent to perform one's job well, the intent to remain with the organization, the intent to be a good organizational citizen, the intent to endorse the organization as a great place to work, and the intent to put forth discretionary effort. Intent is vital to understand and measure as it is instrumental in predicting behavior.

EMPLOYEE WORK PASSION FACTORS

Organizational Factors

Collaboration—the extent to which the organization encourages the sharing of ideas, teamwork, and collaboration on projects and tasks.

Distributive Justice—the extent to which resources, compensation, and workloads are fairly balanced.

Procedural Justice—the extent to which policies and procedures are consistently and fairly applied.

Growth—the extent to which there is support for current and future career growth.

Performance Expectations—the extent to which individuals feel that their work is compared to an agreed-upon standard and understand what is expected of them.

Job Factors

Meaningful Work—the extent to which people understand and resonate with the organization's purpose and believe they are working on projects that matter and produce positive results.

Autonomy—the extent to which individuals can choose how tasks are performed, are trusted to do their jobs, and have the authority to make decisions.

Feedback—the extent to which individuals receive adequate feedback on performance and are recognized for improvements and ideas.

Workload Balance—the extent to which individuals feel they have ample time to accomplish their work.

(continued)

Task Variety—the extent to which individuals feel that they have variety in both the type of tasks and the complexity of tasks.

Moderating Factors

Connectedness to Leader—the extent to which leaders make an effort to build rapport and personal and professional relationships.

Connectedness to Colleagues—the extent to which colleagues make an effort to build rapport and personal and professional relationships.

Intentions

Discretionary Effort—the extent to which the individual intends to expend his or her discretionary effort on behalf of the organization above and beyond agreed-upon requirements.

Intent to Perform—the extent to which the individual intends to do his or her job well and work effectively to help the organization succeed.

Organizational Citizenship Behaviors—the extent to which the individual is committed to supporting fellow workers and behaving in ways that are respectful, considerate, and sensitive to others.

Employee Endorsement—the extent to which the individual readily endorses the organization to others as a good place to work and as a quality supplier of goods and services.

Intent to Remain—the extent to which the individual plans to stay with the organization.

How Is Employee Work Passion Different Than Engagement?

We make several distinctions between the concepts of employee work passion and engagement. First, employee work passion is supported by a theory and model that explain how work passion is formed.

Second, *both* organizational and job factors influence an individual's level of employee work passion. Not simply one or the other. Engagement is generally associated with either job commitment (burnout, well-being, and others) or organizational commitment (intent to stay, endorsement, and others), but typically not associated with both. We feel employee work passion is better explained by social cognition, appraisal theory, and research—and encompasses both job commitment and organizational commitment; therefore, it is a different and more expansive concept than engagement.

Third, employee work passion measures cognition, affect, and intent, as opposed to measuring satisfaction. Engagement studies tend to measure employee satisfaction as "engaged," "disengaged," and "actively disengaged" but fail to measure "actively engaged." Measuring employee satisfaction on its own does not provide a measure of what the employee intends to do. Since employee work passion measures not only affect and cognition but also intention (and the degree to which individuals are actively engaged), it provides a clearer sense of how the individual intends to behave on behalf of the organization.

Understanding How Employee Work Passion Is Created—A Review of the Appraisal Process

In order to understand how employee work passion occurs, one must first understand the process an individual goes through in deciding to engage in a specific behavior. As stated earlier, much of the research does not take the full scope of this process into account.

Through deeper exploration of the literature, we began to incorporate significant ideas found in cognitive psychology. An individual's choices are driven by his or her understanding of how the experience or event being appraised impacts his or her well-being. Since all people are meaning-oriented and meaning-creating, they are constantly evaluating the environment from the standpoint of their own well-being and reacting rationally (cognition) and emotionally (affect) to those evaluations.

Cognition and affect go hand in hand, happening almost simultaneously, over and over, as individuals make sense of a situation to reach their conclusions about what is happening, what it means to them, how it will affect them, how they feel about that, what they intend to do, and, finally, what they actually do, all filtered through the lens of who they are. (See Figure 20.1.)

As one reviews the model, it is clear that the appraisal process begins with an assessment of the job and organizational environmental antecedents (the twelve employee work passion factors). During the appraisal process, an individual makes sense of how he or she feels about the extent to which the twelve factors are present in the work environment. It is the appraisal of one's environment that leads to a sense of well-being and coping with the presence of or lack of well-being that leads to the intention to behave in a certain way on behalf of the organization as measured through the five intentions. Intentions ultimately lead to either positive or negative behavior.

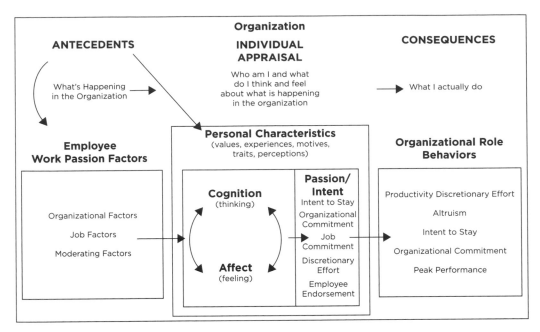

Figure 20.1   The Employee Work Passion Model

EMPLOYEE WORK PASSION DEFINED   *An individual's persistent, emotionally positive, meaning-based state of well-being stemming from continuous, reoccurring cognitive and affective appraisals of various job and organizational situations, which results in consistent, constructive work intentions and behaviors.*

Understanding How the Factors Influence Intent and Behavior

Much of our study in regard to what creates employee work passion has been focused on understanding which organizational and job factors are important to employees. Our research has also focused on which intentions and resultant behaviors are characteristic of individuals who are passionate about their work and their organizations. But it is just as important to understand the connections of specific factors to specific intentions.

Table 20.1 allows us to understand the relationships among the twelve employee work passion factors and the five intent scales. Using statistical analysis to analyze the connection between the intent scales (dependent variable) and the twelve factors (independent variable) enables us to understand to what extent the twelve factors influence the five intentions, which in turn influence behavior. It also allows us to understand which factors have the most impact across all five intentions. To interpret the correlation values, .500 represents a large correlation, .300 is a medium correlation, and .100 is a small correlation.

Table 20.1 shows that all twelve factors have a certain degree of correlation ranging from trivial or small to large. This supports earlier statistical analysis that allowed us to conclude that all factors must be present in order for employee work passion to be optimal.

For the purpose of this chapter, we will focus our explanation and rationale of the correlations by highlighting the larger correlations.

Table 20.1 Correlation Analysis Between Employee Work Passion Factors and Intentions in the Workplace

	Correlation Coefficients				
	Discretionary Effort	Intent to Perform	Employee Endorsement	Intent to Remain	Organizational Citizenship Behaviors
Growth	.460	.298	.545	.618	.345
Connectedness to Leader	.417	.305	.431	.417	.319
Connectedness to Colleagues	.513	.346	.450	.286	.506
Workload Balance	.137	.090	.243	.234	.190
Task Variety	.603	.520	.491	.359	.526
Performance Expectations	.388	.336	.465	.412	.345
Collaboration	.450	.376	.535	.468	.540
Meaningful Work	.488	.475	.505	.492	.477
Distributive Justice	.396	.262	.496	.519	.333
Procedural Justice	.511	.377	.635	.530	.476
Autonomy	.531	.390	.539	.524	.483
Feedback	.385	.338	.483	.454	.370

All correlations are significant at the 0.01 level

Discretionary Effort

An individual's intent to expend discretionary effort on behalf of the organization is directly influenced by all of the twelve factors. The top four, listed in order of both importance and correlation strength, are

1. Task Variety
2. Autonomy
3. Connectedness to Colleagues
4. Procedural Justice

WHAT THIS MEANS

This means that the extent to which individuals perceive that they have variety in their jobs and that they are doing different types of tasks that go beyond routine, have personal and professional connections to their fellow workers, perceive that policies and procedures are equitably applied to all, and have a certain level of autonomy in the way they approach their job all influence individuals' desire to exert discretionary effort in their jobs and on behalf of their organizations.

WHY

Task variety correlates to discretionary effort because people are more engaged, less bored, and more apt to go the extra mile when they have autonomy and variety in their roles. Individuals who have a greater degree of task variety are more inclined to exert discretionary effort because they tend to have a greater degree of interest in their jobs and they find work engaging.

Peer pressure can also play a role in influencing discretionary effort, so the more connected an individual is to his or her colleagues, the more likely that individual is to expend extra energy on behalf of the organization. Individuals who perceive that their colleagues are willing to expend extra energy on behalf of the organization are more likely to do the same.

Additionally, the concept of procedural justice (or the extent to which individuals feel involved in decisions that affect them and feel that decisions, policies, and procedures are equitably and fairly applied to all) influences discretionary effort because, if people perceive there is a lack of fairness in the work environment, they are inclined not to be fair or expend additional energy on behalf of the organization. On the other hand, people feel good about working extra hard when the organization they are working for treats them fairly. Research in the area of procedural fairness has shown that people are more willing to accept decisions when procedural fairness is alive and well in the work environment.

Intent to Perform

An individual's intent to perform at peak levels is directly influenced by all of the twelve factors. The top three, listed below in order of importance and correlation strength, are

1. Task Variety
2. Meaningful Work
3. Autonomy

WHAT THIS MEANS

This means that the extent to which individuals perceive that the work they do has meaning to the organization and that the work the organization does has meaning to the customers, the extent to which there is variety in their work and tasks, and the degree to which they have autonomy to decide how to best approach tasks all influence individuals' intent to perform.

WHY

In looking at the correlations, we believe that when individuals find meaning in their work, they are more compelled to perform the tasks and roles of the job.
Task variety influences intent to perform because the more that individuals feel their jobs contain variety, keep them from being bored, and include more than routine tasks, the more likely they are to work efficiently and effectively and to do their jobs well. Autonomy is correlated to intent to perform because most people want to have the ability to decide how their tasks are performed and to have the authority to do their jobs; the more this is the case, the stronger their intent to do their jobs well.

Employee Endorsement

An individual's intent to endorse the organization as a great place to work and to do business with is directly influenced by all of the twelve factors. The top three, listed in order of importance and strength of correlation, are

1. Procedural Justice

2. Growth

3. Autonomy

WHAT THIS MEANS

This means that the extent to which individuals perceive that policies and procedures are equitably applied to all, the extent to which they have growth opportunities in their roles and to grow within the organization, and the extent to which they have some amount of freedom when deciding how to approach roles and tasks all impact employee endorsement.

WHY

Endorsement correlates highly with procedural justice because fairness in the work environment is important to people and its presence causes people to form an attachment to the organization or group. This attachment makes individuals more likely to endorse and speak positively about their organizations. People want others they care about to come to work in a place that is fair, offers people a voice, and utilizes decision-making processes that focus on the benefit for all.

The connection between growth and autonomy and the intent to endorse the organization stem from people's need to feel that they can see a future for both their job and career growth and that they have the autonomy to make decisions about how they accomplish their work. This influences their willingness to endorse the organization as a good place to work and to recommend the organization to their family and friends, as well as to potential customers.

Intent to Remain

An individual's intent to remain with the organization is influenced by all of the twelve factors. The top four, listed below in order of importance and strength of correlation, are

1. Growth

2. Procedural Justice

3. Autonomy

4. Distributive Justice

WHAT THIS MEANS

This means that individuals' intent to stay with an organization is influenced by their perception that there are opportunities to grow within their current roles and within the organization; by their perception that benefits, resources, and compensation are fairly and equitable distributed to all; and by the degree to which they have autonomy to do their jobs.

WHY

We generally find that intent to remain with an organization has the lowest ranking of any of the intention scales. People see their intent to stay with an organization as a right and a statement of confidence in leadership as well as the organization. If individuals don't perceive that there are growth opportunities in the organization or that benefits and pay are not equitably distributed, their intent to stay diminishes over time. There is a prevalent school of thought that presumes it is an individual's relationship to his or her leader that is the key determinant of retention. While this relationship is important, it is not as important as the presence of growth opportunities, autonomy, and the presence of fairness or distributive justice. Procedural justice is also important in regard to retaining key talent. Leaders need to be careful that policies and procedures are consistently applied to all and that people are involved in the decisions that affect them.

Organizational Citizenship Behaviors

An individual's intent to be a good organizational citizen is directly influenced by all of the twelve factors. The top four, listed in order of importance and strength of correlation, are

1. Collaboration
2. Task Variety
3. Connectedness to Colleagues
4. Autonomy

WHAT THIS MEANS

This means that people's willingness to be valuable organizational citizens is influenced by the extent to which they feel connected to their colleagues, the degree to which they feel they have autonomy and variety in their tasks and their jobs, and the degree to which they feel that their work environments are collaborative.

WHY

Individuals who feel more highly connected to their colleagues and see their workplaces as collaborative tend to focus more on the welfare of the organization. This connection is due to the concepts of sportsmanship, fair play, and taking care of those they care about. Organizational citizenship is the goodwill that an organization keeps in the bank, which, in turn, offsets sabotage, stealing, and abusing organizational resources.

Task variety correlates to organizational citizenship because it has a sense of "justness" to it that makes individuals feel good about their roles, which, in turn, translates to feeling good about the organization. Additionally, a sense of task variety tends to make people feel more engaged about their jobs and therefore their organizations.

Autonomy connects to organizational citizenship because individuals are more invested in their organizations when their work has meaning and they have a certain amount of freedom to choose how to approach their projects and tasks. When individuals feel more invested in their organizations, they are more inclined to act in ways that benefit the organization.

Summary

While we know from our research that all twelve factors must be present in the work environment in order for employee work passion to be optimized, the data in Table 20.1 clearly shows that some factors are more influential than others in regard to intentions and their resulting behavior.

A caveat to the data and conclusions is that the analysis was conducted using a random sample of employees from many organizations. When we look at these same correlations within a specific organization and also compare organization-to-organization correlations, we find that culture is the most powerful influencer of how the twelve factors are represented and those results differ not only from organization to organization but also from the results of our national sample.

When looking to create environments that encourage people to have positive intentions in the work environment, organizations and leaders should examine the extent to which the twelve organization and job factors are present in their current cultures. In particular, leaders should ask themselves the following questions:

- To what extent does the culture allow individuals to find meaning in their work and their roles, and also in the organization's purpose?

- To what extent are policies, procedures, benefits, and compensation transparent and equitably applied to all?

- To what extent is the organization providing growth opportunities for individuals in their current jobs and in their careers? And do the feedback mechanisms allow individuals to improve and advance?

- To what extent are individuals clear about what is expected of them and have a reasonable amount of autonomy when engaging in projects and tasks? And are they provided opportunities to collaborate with others?

- To what extent are job roles balanced and reasonable with enough variety to challenge people to stretch and perform at optimal levels?

Employee work passion is an individual's persistent, emotionally positive, meaning-based state of well-being stemming from reoccurring cognitive and affective appraisals of various job and organizational situations, which results in consistent, constructive work intentions and behaviors.

Therefore, we recommend that organizations provide a sense of meaning beyond simply making a profit; the autonomy and flexibility for individuals to give their all at work; opportunities for growth, collaboration, and recognition; and a sense of connectedness. In addition, organizations must ensure that processes and procedures are fairly and consistently applied to all employees.

While it may seem daunting to address all twelve factors and to incorporate them into the workplace, organizations that support the development of employee work passion will be rewarded by passionate employees who are dedicated to creating devoted customers, achieving sustainable growth, and increasing profits.

RELATED READINGS

Nimon, K., Zigarmi D., Houson, D., Witt, D., & Diehl, J. (2011). Employee work passion: The assessment of a multinational. Manuscript submitted for publication.

Nimon, K., Zigarmi, D., Houson, D., Witt, D., & Diehl, J. (2011). The work cognition inventory: Initial evidence of construct validity. *Human Resource Development Quarterly, 22*(1), 7–33.

Zigarmi, D., Blanchard, S., Essary, V., & Houson, D. (2006). *The leadership-profit chain.* Escondido, CA: The Ken Blanchard Companies.

Zigarmi, D., Houson, D., Witt, D., & Diehl, J. (2007). *Employee passion: The new rules of engagement.* Escondido, CA: The Ken Blanchard Companies.

Zigarmi, D., Nimon, K., Houson, D., Witt, D., & Diehl, J. (2008). *From engagement to work passion: A deeper understanding of the employee work passion framework.* Escondido, CA: The Ken Blanchard Companies.

Zigarmi, D., Nimon, K., Houson, D., Witt, D., & Diehl, J. (2009). Beyond engagement: Toward a framework and operational definition for employee work passion. *Human Resource Development Review, 8*, 300–326.

Zigarmi, D., Nimon, K., Houson, D., Witt, D., & Diehl, J. (2011). A cognitive approach to work intention: The stuff that employee work passion is made of. Manuscript submitted for publication.

Zigarmi, D., Nimon, K., Houson, D., Witt, D., & Diehl, J. (In press). A preliminary field test of an employee work passion model. *Human Resource Development Quarterly.*

About The Ken Blanchard Companies

With more than three decades of helping leaders and organizations, more than eighteen million books in print, programs offered in more than twelve languages, and clients across six continents, The Ken Blanchard Companies® is recognized as one of the world's leading training and development experts. Our groundbreaking thinking and memorable learner experiences create lasting behavioral change that has measurable impact on the organizations with which we work—companies that wish to develop leadership capacity, improve workplace cultures, drive organizational change and strategic alignment, and become high performing organizations. Using a collaborative diagnostic process, we help identify each organization's unique needs and business issues, and then help to develop an appropriate leadership strategy to drive results and profits.

As the innovator of Situational Leadership® II—the most widely used leadership development system in the world—our behavioral models add a situational context to the training experience so individuals learn to be more productive in real-world scenarios and make the shift from learning to doing more quickly and effectively. Learning takes place through both instructor-led and virtual experiences offered by our worldwide network of consulting partners, trainers, and coaches. To learn more, visit www.kenblanchard.com.

Submitted by Dr. Drea Zigarmi; Dobie Houson; David Witt; Jim Diehl

The Ken Blanchard Companies

125 State Place

Escondido, CA 92029

(800) 728-6000

info@Kenblanchard.com

www.kenblanchard.com

Chapter 21

Owners and Renters*

Which Defines Your Organization's Culture?

CENTER FOR CREATIVE LEADERSHIP

In This Chapter

- The rationale for hiring employees who perform as "owners" not "renters."

- Three leadership actions that foster an owner mindset and behaviors.

Early in my career as a U.S. Navy pilot, I received an unexpected privilege—the chance to fly a $100 million, state-of-the-art airplane and lead a twelve-person crew. As a brand new lieutenant, I was surprised but delighted by this opportunity. What had I done to deserve it?

"It's because you're an owner, not a renter," my hard-charging commanding officer said. Every organization, even the U.S. Navy, had both types, he explained. Owners accept full responsibility even when it is not formally assigned, believe deeply in their mission, collaborate with others, take initiative, and hold co-workers accountable to the same high standards. Renters, meanwhile, approach their work with an "it's just a job" mentality, tend to make statements like "that's not my problem" and point the finger at others when things go wrong.

---

*A version of this article previously appeared on Forbes.com.

"Stack the deck with owners!" my commanding officer proclaimed. And also work hard, he cautioned, at remaining an owner. It was a label we needed to earn every day. His advice stays with me forty years later, and I've shared it recently with the women and men in my organization. I believe all workers should strive to see themselves as owners, no matter where they are in the organization. Give of yourself as if you own the company.

Owners have always been crucial to the success of any enterprise. In today's climate of volatility, uncertainty, complexity, and ambiguity (the "VUCA world" futurist Bob Johansen explores in *Leaders Make the Future*), they matter even more.

Every leader has the responsibility to foster the mindset and behaviors that serve as the foundation for an ownership culture. Attracting owners to our organizations and cultivating an ownership mentality in the employees we already have is often the difference between merely satisfactory efforts and great performance. In my experience, there are at least three primary ways of going about it.

Set the Right Example

First, we need to set the right example as leaders. The higher we sit in the organization, the more critical it is that we model the behaviors of real owners. Specifically, that means not shying away from accountability. It also means deflecting the credit from ourselves onto our colleagues when things go well. It's always tempting to hunker down in our organizational silos and try to hit our numbers, fight for resources, and look out for the immediate needs of our own teams and individual careers. Owners, however, try hard to span those boundaries, to make decisions and support causes that are best for the entire organization. As my colleague Chris Ernst, co-author of the recent book *Boundary Spanning Leadership*, has found in his work, game-changing, sustained innovation won't happen until an organization's entire workforce starts pooling its talents. Perhaps more than anything, though, setting the right example calls for exhibiting passion for your mission and your work.

At just thirty-three years old, Butler University's head basketball coach Brad Stevens rose to prominence in 2010 by guiding his underrated team all the way to NCAA men's national championship game. In 2011, he proved it wasn't a fluke, taking his team back to its second straight championship appearance. Stevens consistently gave all the credit to his team, remarking after one crucial victory that he had been outcoached but his players had done enough to win anyway.

Stevens, though outwardly calm, is regarded as an extraordinarily passionate and hard-working man, described by his own college basketball coach as one of the most self-less and team-oriented players he's ever seen. Those are qualities Stevens instills in his players, whose superior discipline and decision making create headaches for more athletically gifted teams. How invested is Stevens in his team's success? About a decade ago, totally committed to coaching the sport he loved, he took the major risk of quitting a good job with Eli Lilly to work for Butler's team—for free. His dedication impressed his bosses, who eventually made him a paid assistant and ultimately the head coach. After his breakout season last year, major universities courted Stevens with lucrative job offers. His response: signing a contract with Butler through the 2021–2022 season. That is the mark of an owner—someone who inspires ownership in others.

Provide Feedback

Beyond our own efforts to set the right example, we can also develop ownership in our employees by giving them a positive work environment, opportunities for personal and professional growth, and regular and direct feedback. We should praise our women and men for examples of ownership in action—and hold those examples up to the organization. Still, even our owners should not be above constructive advice. I've had smart, talented colleagues walk into meetings unprepared for questions to which they should have known the answers. I've quietly sent them back to their offices with instructions to do better next time—and they have. It's the kind of feedback superiors gave me in the Navy and in higher education—and which I still sometimes get from my board. As we tell our clients at CCL, feedback is a gift—especially when it's something we'd rather not hear.

It is also possible, meanwhile, to transform renters into owners. Here again, clear, consistent feedback is crucial. When we see employees underperforming, it's entirely appropriate to take them aside in a discreet, professional manner, point out concerns, and challenge them do better. Everyone, after all, deserves second and sometimes even third chances. If they respond positively and make improvements, you've helped put a colleague on the path to ownership.

And don't forget: feedback is a two-way street. About two years ago, we asked our staff at CCL for their views of our organizational culture. We learned, among other things, that our men and women wanted an executive team that's more engaged with and visible to the entire organization. Renowned executive coach Marshall Goldsmith, a good friend of CCL, recommended a process for doing this that has made our executive team members stronger owners in service of our clients and our mission. First, we decided on three key areas we needed to address as a team. Each month for a year we met to assess critically how we were doing with each of them. At the same time, each team member also picked two areas in which to improve personally. We regularly gave each other feedback on how we were doing there as well. This approach, which we still return to periodically, fosters candid communication and keeps us focused on getting better—both as a team and as individual team members. Most of all, this work fosters a sense of ownership that we hope will strengthen our overall culture.

Manage Talent

A focus on feedback connects closely with a third aspect of developing owners in our organizations—our overall approach to talent. The first trait to look for in assessing existing talent and recruiting new team members is a high level of engagement and performance. Engagement does not merely equate with logging long hours in the office. In fact, I never worry about how much time my organization's men and women literally spend in the office. I'm much more focused on what they achieve and the degree of energy they bring to their work.

Avoid people with a tenured mindset who feel deserving of a greater role and higher compensation regardless of performance. It also makes sense to add talent that is more focused on doing a superb job than padding the resume for the next career move. At the same time, we need to be realistic. As much as we don't want them to leave, some of our best people will take their skills and portable retirement plans and go elsewhere for an especially great opportunity. Their approach is to be an owner as long as their work is meaningful, challenging, and valued. When they leave for a new role, it is often with an attitude of, "That was a great experience, and I'm better for it." The organization is often better off, too, for having benefited from their talents. So we need flexibility in how we view ownership. After all, in a free-agent economy, it's not unusual for these very same owners to come back to our organizations later on and make a whole new set of contributions.

In the end, the surest way to judge our talent is by observing the demonstrated passion and commitment. When we've identified who our owners and renters are, compensation should be determined accordingly. Give promotions, training opportunities, raises, and bonuses to owners. Don't give them to permanent renters, who should not be encouraged in any way to stick around.

Remember: this is a high-stakes situation. Hanging onto renters will create a sustained drag on morale, innovation, and bottom-line performance. But a team made up almost entirely of owners will be unbeatable. Which way is your organization heading? And what steps can you take today to ensure it's going in the right direction now and well into the future?

About the Center for Creative Leadership

The Center for Creative Leadership (CCL) is a top-ranked, global provider of executive education that accelerates strategy and business results by unlocking the leadership potential of individuals and organizations. Founded in 1970 as a nonprofit, educational institution and focused exclusively on leadership education and research, CCL helps clients worldwide cultivate creative leadership—the capacity to achieve more than imagined by thinking and acting beyond boundaries—through an array of programs, products, and other services.

Ranked among the world's Top 10 providers of executive education by *Bloomberg BusinessWeek* and the *Financial Times*, CCL serves more than twenty thousand individual leaders and two thousand organizational clients annually, including corporations, government agencies, educational institutions, and nonprofit organizations. It is headquartered in Greensboro, North Carolina, with offices in Colorado Springs, Colorado; San Diego, California; Brussels; Moscow; Singapore; Pune, India; and Addis Ababa, Ethiopia. CCL's work is supported by five hundred faculty members and staff.

Submitted by John R. Ryan, President, CEO

Center for Creative Leadership

P.O. Box 26300

Greensboro, NC 27438-6300

(336) 545-2810

info@ccl.org

www.ccl.org

Center for
Creative
Leadership
www.ccl.org

Chapter 22

The Commercial Impact of Employee Engagement

PERFORMANCE CONNECTIONS INTERNATIONAL, INC.

In This Chapter

- Validation of the impact of an engaged culture.
- Role of senior management to maintain employee engagement.
- Factors that erode employee engagement.

Given the challenges in today's business climate, it's no surprise that employee engagement has surfaced as a vital organizational priority. Engagement is not solely an HR issue—it is a bottom-line business survival issue: the workforce must be fully engaged in order to work at full capacity.

Given the hype about engagement, we wanted to validate the impact of employee engagement on bottom-line business metrics such as revenue generation and corporate profitability. Specifically, the objectives were to:

- Clarify the impact of employee engagement on factors that influence revenue and profitability

- Develop a more business-driven way of thinking about employee engagement
- Articulate the role of senior management in maintaining employee engagement
- Identify current factors that erode engagement

Methodology

Much of the past research on workforce engagement was survey-driven and quantitatively informative but left too many important questions unanswered. Surveys alone, by definition, force respondents to select from a preset list of choices and don't allow them to offer their own broader perspectives on the issues. Our objective was to transcend this limitation by using interviews to supplement the quantitative data. Therefore, Performance Connections conducted a two-pronged quantitative and qualitative study. This two-pronged approach enabled us to not only identify data trends but also gain a deeper understanding of the engagement challenges corporate enterprises face and the potential solutions.

Over one hundred business professionals participated in the study, representing advertising, automotive, business services, consulting, education, financial services, healthcare, hospitality, technology, legal, medical equipment, manufacturing, print and internet media.

A Business-Driven View of Engagement

There is much confusion concerning the definition of employee engagement. Some argue that it is nothing more than motivation, which has been a topic of interest to business leaders since the beginning of the industrial revolution. The most universally accepted definition of engagement can be found in Figure 22.1.

When examining this definition, we at Performance Connections felt that, while useful, it lacked value and relevance and was removed from the challenges of the business world. In fact, we concluded that employees can exhibit engagement as it is defined above, but in a way that could be detrimental to the business.

For example, take the scientist or engineer who is committed to his work, spends long discretionary hours on one of his projects, and who has no interest leaving his company. He is engaged according to the standard definition. But if the project he is working on is his pet project and of little strategic value to the company, his form of engagement is not desirable.

Take the salesperson who has good relationships with her customers, is committed to spending time with them, works extra hard to get them what they ask for, and has

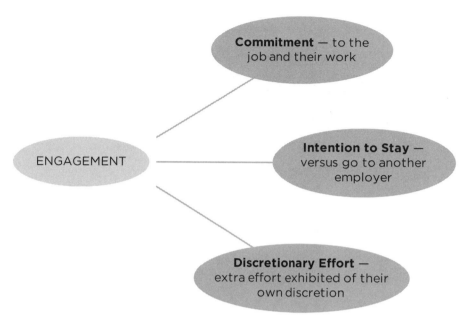

Figure 22.1 Defining Engagement

been in her job for many years with no intention of leaving. However, if she limits herself to interacting with the customers she knows well instead of also finding new customers and sells the old products with which she is familiar to the exclusion of the new products on which the company hopes to build its future successes, her form of engagement is also objectionable.

The current definitions of engagement fail to recognize this. A definition of engagement that is disconnected from the business—its vision, goals, strategy, and change initiatives—is of little value. We label this "aimless engagement." Given this, we were driven to develop a higher level definition of engagement that was

- More linked to the business
- Of greater relevance to senior management
- More operationally valuable

Performance Connections' definition of employee engagement is displayed in Figure 22.2.

We have labeled this "aligned engagement" because it reflects the alignment of engagement with the direction, strategy, and change efforts of the business. Aligned

- Engaged in, believing in, and *supporting the goals and strategy* of the business

- Feeling a *sense of belonging and pride* of affiliation with the business

- Discretionary effort *applied towards the fulfillment of company objectives*

- *Finding Value* (in the work they are doing), *Creating Value* (for the business and its customers), *Feeling Valued* (for their contributions)

- *Resilient and Change-Ready* — because in order to sustain engagement, employees must be ready to change and grow along with the business

Figure 22.2 Aligned Engagement

engagement is achieved in many ways, but most directly through three primary *engagement drivers*:

- *Accountability and Ownership*—Managing accountability for big-picture business results leads to increased ownership, which in turn results in aligned engagement.

- *Aligned Purpose*—Employees who have a strong personal sense of purpose are more engaged, and when their purpose is aligned with the direction of the business, the degree of aligned engagement is greater.

- *Change-Readiness*—Employees who are ready to change find it easier to continually re-engage in the business and its evolving directions, while employees who resist change find it impossible to be engaged and aligned with a rapidly changing business.

As the graphic in Figure 22.3 depicts, these three engagement drivers make up a system for aligned engagement deeply rooted in the business.

There is ample evidence from our study to support the validity and relevance of this enhanced business-driven definition of engagement:

- Can employees be engaged in the wrong things? We asked study participants whether employees could be engaged, but engaged in the wrong things, and 100 percent said yes!

- What percentage of the workforce is aimlessly engaged? We also asked them what percentage of their workforce was engaged, but engaged in the wrong priorities. Their answer: a whopping 33 percent, with some respondents reporting that up to

Figure 22.3 System for Aligned Engagement

90 percent of their employees fit into this category. This means that, on average, one out of every three employees is passionate about a set of priorities that are different from, and potentially even in conflict with, the direction of the business.

- What do we want the workforce to be engaged in? Specifically, we asked study respondents, "What do you want employees to actually be engaged in?" Their answers supported the importance of aligned engagement.

The first most frequently cited response: We want our employees to be engaged in taking care of our customers. The comments included:

- Customer service, internal and external
- Anticipating customer needs
- Making a difference with each customer/employee touch point
- Serve customers in a way that keeps them coming back
- Determine better ways to service our clients
- Exceed expectations
- Create the brand experience

One study participant stated it clearly and simply, "We want a client-service culture in which everyone comes up with better ways to serve our clients" (Laura Bridge, vice president of client services, Navicure, Inc.).

Tied for the second most frequently cited response: We want our employees to be engaged in making a bottom-line contribution and executing corporate strategy, which included:

- How we save and make money
- The success of the firm
- Hitting the metrics of the business
- Growing the business
- Engaged in the strategy of the business
- Committed to the company mission
- Sustaining the corporate culture

The third most frequently cited response (although significantly less often than the first response) was productivity, which included:

- Getting results
- Being productive
- Making better decisions

Cited less frequently but still of note:

- Ownership for the projects they are working on
- Quality output
- Their own professional growth
- Collaborating across business lines
- Pride of affiliation

None of the opinion leaders said that they wanted their employees to be motivated or committed in general. Each respondent linked engagement to a business anchor—to some end state the company was trying to achieve. Given this, the pursuit of engagement disconnected from the business is folly at best. Businesses must instead:

- Recalibrate their engagement assessments to focus on aligned engagement, not free-floating generic engagement
- Focus on not just building ownership for personal job success, but the success of the larger enterprise

- Ensure that employee passions are aligned with strategic direction
- View an engaged workforce as a tool to be a dominant marketplace player as opposed to being a separate competing priority

Commercial Impact

Given this more enlightened view of engagement, there is both direct and inferential data, as displayed in Table 22.1, that shows how aligned engagement, or the lack thereof, affects different business functions in various ways.

Table 22.1 How Engagement Affects Business Functions

Function	Less Engaged Employees	More Engaged Employees
Sales	Less prospecting for new customers[i]	Excited about acquiring new customers
	Reduced proactive selling	Proactive contacts with customers
	Less enthusiasm for new products and markets[ii]	Commitment to new products
		Higher readiness to change
	Impact	**Impact**
	Slow down in revenue generation	New revenue streams
	Missed sales goals	Reach and exceed sales goals
	Lost sales opportunities	Faster revenue and uptake of new products
Service	Lower service levels	Passionate about service
	Slower problem resolution	Faster problem resolution
	Less ownership of the customer experience	Ownership for the entire customer experience
	Holding on to old systems and processes	
	Impact	**Impact**
	Reduced repeat business	More repeat business
	Customer attrition	Greater customer retention and profitability
	Competitor inroads	Positive word-of-mouth advertising

(continued)

Table 22.1 How Engagement Affects Business Functions (*Continued*)

Function	Less Engaged Employees	More Engaged Employees
R&D	Less innovation	More innovation[iii]
	Less continuous improvement	Ongoing continuous improvement
	Stuck in old patterns	More customer-focused solutions
	Impact	**Impact**
	Fewer new products	New revenue streams
	Lag in the market	Stable revenue from current updated products
	Eroded customer perception	Beat competitor sales
Operations	Reduced quality	Commitment to quality
	Lower output	Always think about getting better
	More errors	
	Impact	**Impact**
	Costly mistakes	Increased customer confidence
	Missed deadlines	Higher output
	Fewer repeat customers	More return business
		Higher operating margins

[i]Six Misconceptions, What You Don't Know About Increasing Sales, Performance Connections International, 2003, indicating that acquiring new customers is in the bottom five areas of sales effectiveness for most firms.

[ii]Expansion into New Markets, A Benchmark Study, Performance Dimensions Group, 2009, indicating that it takes years to successfully expand into new markets for most businesses.

[iii]Engaged Employees Inspire Innovation, Gallup Study, 2006, which shows that 59 percent of engaged employees strongly agreed with the statement that their current job "brings out [their] most creative ideas." On the flip side, only 3 percent of actively disengaged employees strongly agreed that their current job brings out their most creative ideas.

Engaged employees in these critical functions believe they make a greater impact on the business, and that becomes a self-fulfilling prophecy. Specifically:

- Eighty-four percent of highly engaged employees believe they can influence the quality of products the company produces; in contrast, only 31 percent of less engaged employees believe they can.

- Seventy-two percent of engaged employees believe they can affect the customer experience, in contrast to only 27 percent of less engaged employees.

- Sixty-eight percent of engaged employees believe they can impact profitability through cost control, in contrast to a meager 19 percent of less engaged employees (Towers-Perrin, 2008).

Given this, it's not surprising to conclude that higher levels of engagement enhance revenue and profit performance. Several studies validate this:

- Businesses with greater employee engagement and alignment with the business strategy have measurably higher levels of revenue growth, market share, profitability, and customer satisfaction (Workplace Institute, 2009).

- Best Buy reports that if a store's engagement score increases by a tenth of a point (on a 5-point scale), that store will increase profits $100,000 that year (Flander, 2008).

- Companies that invest in talent management and engagement yield 27 percent greater shareholder returns (Michaels, Handfield-Jones, & Axelrod, 2001).

- Lower levels of engagement result in 2.01 percent reduction of operating margin and a loss of 1.38 percent in net profit margin (ISR, n.d.).

- Higher levels of engagement lead to an increase of 3.74 percent in operating margin and 2.06 percent increase in net profit (ISR, n.d.).

- High engagement companies improved 19.2 percent while low engagement companies declined 32.7 percent in operating income over a 12 month period (ISR, n.d.).

- There was a 13.7 percent improvement in net income growth over a one-year period for companies with high employee engagement, while seeing a 3.8 percent decline in net income over the same period for companies with low employee engagement (ISR, n.d.).

- Companies with high employee engagement also demonstrated a 27.8 percent improvement in EPS growth, while companies with low employee engagement reported an 11.2 percent decline in EPS over the same period (ISR, n.d.).

- Organizations ranking in the top quartile of engagement had EPS growth of 2.6 times the rate of those that were below average (Gallup, 2007).

- Business units that have higher levels of engagement deliver 36 percent more operating income than other business in the same company that have lower levels of engagement (Engren, 2008).

In the final analysis, many of the revenue factors link back in some way to *the customer*:

- Are they happy with the quality of your products/solutions?
- Do they plan to buy again from you?
- Will they resist competitor attempts to lure them away?
- Will they stick with you over time?
- Will they act as ambassadors for your brand when speaking to other potential customers?
- And most importantly, do they feel well taken care of by their provider?

In light of this, we sought to understand the degree to which workforce engagement affects customer engagement. We asked respondents whether they were concerned that reduced levels of engagement affect the way employees take care of customers and affect the customer experience.

As you can see in Figure 22.4, only 13 percent were not worried about this, leaving 87 percent concerned to some degree that reduced levels of engagement affect how well employees take care of customers.

Is there any question that the customer experience impacts revenue? Data from a recent Forrester report, "Customer Experience Boosts Revenue," should dispel any doubts. This study indicates that, when comparing businesses in the bottom and top

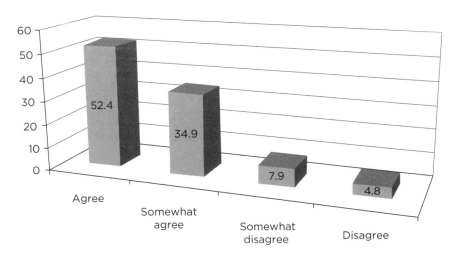

Figure 22.4 The Impact of Engagement on Customer Care

Developing Talent for Organizational Results

quartile of managing the customer experience, top quartile businesses have customers who are significantly more:

- Willing to buy more products
- Reluctant to switch to a competitor
- Likely to recommend the business to potential customers

In order for businesses to survive and thrive, they must not only focus on the mechanics of the business, but also on their workforce. Failure to do so will result in a measurable reduction in revenue and earnings, as well as customer satisfaction, repeat business, and market share. All link back to the lack of engagement.

Engagement is not an all-or-nothing proposition; it is a matter of degree. The greater the percentage of a company's workforce that is aligned and engaged . . . the greater the likelihood a business can predict favorable revenue and profits.

The effort to align and engage your people represents only a fraction of the cost of delayed or compromised strategy fulfillment, missed mission critical goals, lost customers, eroded market share, and reduced revenue.

Consequently, this makes engagement not only a vital HR issue but also of concern to those people at the helm of your company.

Engagement and Strategy Alignment

Given the business-driven definition of aligned engagement, we sought to clarify how engaged and aligned employees are with their company's strategy. To help us measure aligned engagement, we used a tool we created, the Performance Connections Strategy Alignment Ladder. This tool, shown in Figure 22.5, defines the different levels of alignment a workforce can have with their company's business strategy.

We sought to identify what percentage of the workforce, for the average company, is on each rung of the cumulative ladder. Furthermore, we recognized that there might be different degrees of alignment with the employees' department versus alignment with the larger enterprise, so we also investigated this potential gap, as shown in Figure 22.6.

Several factors influence where an employee, team, department or entire division fall on the Strategy Alignment Ladder:

- *The Proximity Effect:* In general, there is greater alignment with the employee's department than with the company overall. We call this the "Proximity Effect"— the closer the operation is to the employee, the greater the degree of alignment.

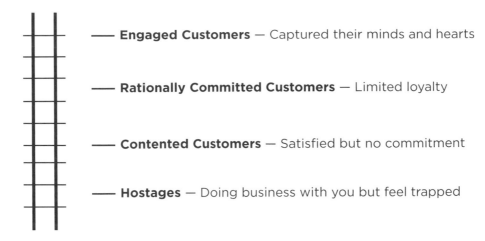

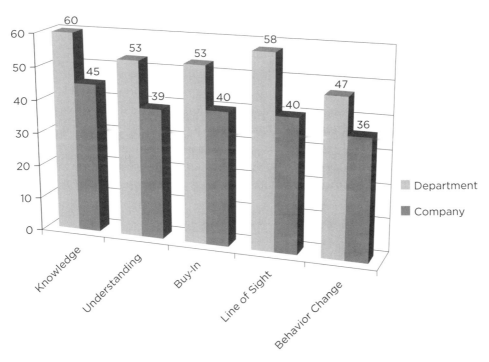

Figure 22.5 Performance Connections Strategy Alignment Ladder

Figure 22.6 Strategy Alignment

Developing Talent for Organizational Results

- *They Don't Know the Strategy:* Less than half of employees know what their company's strategy is. This is quite striking and spells difficulty for any business that wants its workforce to pull the company forward to reach strategic goals and objectives.

- *Disconnected:* Approximately four out of every ten employees understand the rationale and buy into their company's strategy, leaving six out of ten being disconnected from the strategy, indifferent, or even negative about the strategy.

- *Understanding Why:* Those who understand the rationale for the strategy also appear to buy into it and see their connectedness to it. We heard this from study participants who reported that the same people who really understand the "why" behind a strategy are more likely to agree with it and have a line of sight connection.

- *Fully Engaged in Strategy:* Only about one in three employees are fully engaged with their company's business strategy and prepared to change their behavior to support the execution of the strategy. This leaves two out of every three employees resisting the changes required to operationalize the company's vision.

- *Within Department:* Even within their own departments, less than half of employees are ready to change their behavior to support the fulfillment of department goals.

The implications of this data are significant. This explains why so many businesses struggle to fulfill their strategic goals and that, even if successful, take way too long to arrive at their destination. The *strategy alignment gap* reflected in this information may be a reflection of several factors, described below.

LACK OF ACTIVE AND STRATEGIC COMMUNICATION

Some senior leaders simply don't see the value in proactively and frequently communicating their company's mission, vision, and current strategy to employees. Supporting this is one study of over 700 HR managers who report that most of their "leaders are not well trained to engage the workforce" (IC4P, 2007).

FALSE ASSUMPTIONS

Some senior leaders do a good job of communicating their vision and strategy to the upper and middle management teams, but in some cases, those same senior leaders wrongly assume that their message is getting translated down to the entire organization. In those same organizations, middle managers mistakenly assume it is the senior leaders' job to translate strategy, not theirs.

CRITICAL MASS DRAG

When a critical mass of the workforce is disconnected from the business strategy, it puts a measurable drag on the business attempts to grow. In the best case, the speed to strategy ROI is slowed dramatically. In the worst cases, major change efforts implode, supported by the fact that only 30 percent of organizations report that they manage change effectively (Institute for Corporate Productivity, 2008).

Executive Influence

Executives have significant influence over workforce engagement. In one short town hall speech, they can disengage large segments of the workforce with a public comment about a significant change that employees perceive as negative. One study indicated that the actions of senior managers have the greatest weight of all factors that influence engagement (Melcrum, 2005). Given their significant impact on engagement, we investigated several elements of the executive/engagement connection.

DO EXECUTIVES CARE ABOUT ENGAGEMENT?

Our research indicates that:

- Ninety percent of executives care about employee engagement.
- In 7 percent of the cases, the executive concern for engagement was variable.
- In 3 percent of the situations, executives simply were indifferent to engagement. To quote one executive speaking about his peers, "The focus here is more on making budget (sales goals) and the mechanics of the business; not on the people."

WHY DO EXECS CARE ABOUT ENGAGEMENT?

When asked why they care about engagement, executives provided the following responses, presented in rank order:

- *Productivity:* Executives care about engagement because they see that engaged employees are more effective, better at their jobs, more productive in their work, more agile, produce greater sales, have higher efficiency and produce a higher quality output. "In order to accomplish our goals and remain competitive, we need to be nimble and efficient. That can only happen if we have a highly engaged workforce" (Russell, n.d.).

Developing Talent for Organizational Results

```
┌─────────────────────────────┐
│  1. Increased Productivity   │
│  2. Fulfill Brand Promise    │
│  3. Maintain Morale          │
│  4. Talent Retention         │
│  5. Achieve Objectives       │
│  6. Key to Survival          │
│  7. Empowerment              │
└─────────────────────────────┘
```

Figure 22.7   Seven Top Reasons Executives Care About Engagement

- *Brand Promise:* They recognize that their customers will be better taken care of by engaged employees, leading to higher levels of customer satisfaction and fulfillment of the brand promise.

- *Morale:* They want to maintain a family feeling in the company.

- *Talent Retention:* Recognize that engaged employees are easier to retain.

- *Achievement of Corporate Objectives:* See the link between engagement and goal achievement.

Also mentioned, al though less frequently, were survival and empowerment, and one trend watcher said, "Because it's a hot topic." During the interviews, a number of themes emerged concerning executive attention to engagement:

- *Passion or Easy Way Out:* Some senior executives are passionate about engagement and recognize that "their success as leaders is dependent upon it," while others say the words but don't follow through on their actions and would like to "know the quick and easy solution to sprinkle on the organization."

- *Full-Time Engagement:* There was a greater interest in engagement for the full-time workforce than part-time employees or subcontractors.

- *In the Dark:* Certain execs who don't have access to engagement data about their workforce don't really know how engaged or disengaged their employees are.

- *Insights:* One executive observed, "If I had two employees equally talented, but one was more engaged than the other, I would get much more from the engaged employee" Moyer, n.d.). Another executive stated, "We can see a shine in the eyes in the people who are engaged. We are looking for people who have talent but also we look for the shine in their eyes."

The Commercial Impact of Employee Engagement

In light of the significant impact executives can have on engagement, we also queried interview participants about how effective their executive team is at engaging the workforce. The study (see Figure 22.8) participants reported that:

- Thirty-five percent of executives are good at orchestrating engagement.
- Fifty percent are fair at managing engagement.
- Fifteen percent are poor at inspiring engagement.

This means that 65 percent of the senior execs are fair to poor at inspiring engagement, a troubling finding given that the senior exec has a significant ability to enhance or erode engagement. Several interesting comments emerged during our interviews on this topic:

- *Distracted Attention:* "At times our executives are excellent at inspiring engagement, and during other times it's secondary for them with other issues being more important and diverting their attention."
- *Controlled by the Environment:* "We [executives] are reactive to issues instead of anticipating them and being strategic. The environment dictates to us how we spend our time."
- *Inconsistent Messaging:* "Our executives only get a passing grade because they are not consistent in their messages—we get a different message each month."
- *Remote Disengagement:* "Our executives' engagement effectiveness is limited to our local site. They have no knowledge of how to affect engagement remotely."
- *Don't Share the Vision:* "The executives in our firm only do a good job of this 50 percent of the time. They don't communicate or share enough with lower-level

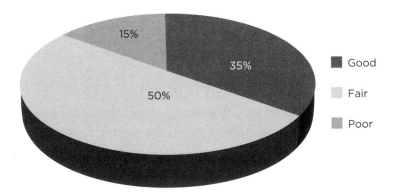

Figure 22.8   Executive Effectiveness in Orchestrating Engagement

employees so the employees don't feel included. They don't share the strategy with employees and don't show them the macro vision."

- *The Layer Challenge:* "Because there are so many layers down, even the best-intentioned senior manager can send a message and it won't get translated down. This is why someone can work in one department and feel engaged and then go to another department and feel disengaged."

- *Positive Exception:* "Our CEO does a fairly good job of blogging with details that bring life to his messages. He uses live streaming video messages during all-hands-meetings and does a town hall meeting wherever he goes. He has his own passion for the business. He gives enough information to satisfy employees but not put the company at risk."

Senior executives are required to balance the interests of multiple stakeholders and various forces that, on the surface, often have very different and even contradictory goals (Berg, 2005). When an executive sees employee engagement as just one more of many concerns to juggle, the engagement priority competes for attention, energy, and resources and falls to the lower end of the priority list. Those executives who recognize that engagement is not a standalone factor but rather an *enabler of business results* place it side by side with the businesses' most important priorities even and especially in difficult times.

Building and sustaining an engaged workforce must be treated as one of the most important executive competencies and imperatives if an organization is to be competitive in an aggressive marketplace earmarked by uncertainty and customer caution.

Factors That Erode Engagement

As part of our research, we investigated the actual factors that erode engagement. These are listed in rank order below:

ANYTHING THAT HAS A NEGATIVE IMPACT ON COMPENSATION

Mentioned most often, this includes a variety of issues such as:

- Salary freezes
- The perception of unfair compensation practices
- Unclear bonus criteria/no bonuses
- Not being compensated for discretionary effort
- Lack of adequate income

- Forced distribution performance rankings that push 50 percent of the population into the midpoint especially when everyone is working extra hard and smart during difficult times

NEGATIVE LEADERSHIP

This includes:

- Strong-arm dictatorial management tactics/hierarchical leadership
- Management by fear/overly critical managers
- Upper management that does not support employees, listen, or change their own behavior when required
- Senior managers who don't reach out to employees
- Perceived lack of integrity in leaders
- Executives who visibly don't care about the people who work for them
- Lack of trust in senior management who do not keep their promises or follow through on initiatives resulting in having a leader that people are not proud of and cannot rally around

LACK OF RESOURCE SUPPORT/EMPOWERMENT

Not having enough time, too few people to do the job right, insufficient funding and lack of tools to get the job done, competing priorities, no decision authority, excessive policies, and not being backed-up/supported when there is a short fall. As one study participant said, "When smart competent people can't make decisions on their own, you run the risk of creating disengaged employees"(Barnes, n.d.).

UNREALISTIC GOALS/EXCESSIVE WORKLOAD

This includes:

- Unreasonable goals resulting in employees who feel they are not going to meet their objectives
- Unclear and/or conflicting goals
- Long hours, burnout ,and lack of work/life balance

One study participant said, "We have such long hours that sometimes we don't go home and just sleep in the office." Another said, "With excessive workloads, people get miserable and it's contagious."

One study validated this challenge, indicating that employees are so worried about losing their jobs that 50 percent of U.S. workers say they would be willing to work eighty hours a week just to keep their jobs (Barnes, n.d.).

THE FAILURE TO COMMUNICATE

This reflects the failure to communicate the rationale for key decisions or not communicating at all or placing a greater focus on communicating shortfalls rather than good news. As one study participant put it, "When decisions come out of nowhere and employees are not in the communications loop, there is a much higher risk of disengagement"(Edelson, n.d.).

COMPANY NON-PERFORMANCE

This includes:

- Lower revenue and declining margins
- Cost reductions
- Repeated downsizing
- Fear of job loss (validated by a study saying that from 46 percent to 71 percent of the workforce is worried about job security) (CyberArk, 2008)
- Working harder but feeling they are losing ground
- Taking away small cost factors that have the impact of being symbolic (like reimbursement of broadband access at home)
- Consistently falling below goals—"never feels like we have a win"

One study participant observed that "Businesses needs wins for people to be motivated."

LACK OF RECOGNITION

This includes the lack of recognition even when employees are taking the right actions or demonstrating excellent performance, and leaders who not only fail to recognize the team, but worse, take the credit for themselves.

POOR CHANGE MANAGEMENT

This reflects:

- Change that is mismanaged

- Employee opinions that are not valued during change
- Employees who are not included and involved in change
- Lack of understanding of the driving forces behind the change

LACK OF VISION CLARITY

This includes:

- Unclear vision and direction for the company
- Lack of single purpose in the business
- Feeling that the company is going in the wrong direction

  Also cited, although less frequently, were:

- *Lack of Fairness*—In policy administration; holding people accountable
- *Routine Work*—Doing the same thing repeatedly, uninteresting work
- *Misaligned Metrics*—Metrics that prevent improvement or reinforce the wrong behaviors
- *Unclear Performance Standards*—Unclear what success means in the job
- *Lack of Career Path*—"Employees unplug when they don't see a career path, especially younger generation employees" (Cutrer, n.d.)[1]

Summary

The old standbys have fallen away. Today's workforce is worried and perhaps even feeling betrayed by the institutions and leaders who were formerly trusted to protect their livelihoods. With confidence in authority at an all-time low, business leaders are also feeling the burden of these unprecedented times in the new economy.

Survival and the "new normal" have necessitated a short-term focus, manifested in such actions as reducing staff and costs and pushing employees as never before to squeeze productivity. Ironically, these attempts to strengthen the business have the exact opposite effect if performed without a conscious awareness of the impact on workforce engagement.

The best leaders are balancing short- and long-term needs and creating purpose and hope in an envisioned future as well as the moment. Leaders and businesses that can mobilize an engaged workforce around their strategy—a workforce that is change-ready and emotionally invested in company success—have the competitive upper hand to optimize revenue and seize marketplace opportunities.

REFERENCES

Barnes, C. HR Director, Member-Driven Technologies. (2008). Executive Research Interview.

Berg, D.N. (2005, Spring). Senior executive teams: Not what you think. *Consulting Psychology Journal: Practice and Research, 117.*

Bridge, L. VP, Client Services, Navicure, Inc. (2009). Executive Research Interview.

Cutrer, A. VP HR, & Flynn, A., Retail Training Manager, Red River Bank (2009). Executive Research Interview.

CyberArk. (2008, December). The global recession and its effect on work ethics. Internet Research Report. www.cyber-ark.com/pdf/Ethics-Survey-Results.pdf.

Edelson, A. VP, Pennsylvania Hospital, (2008). Executive Research Interview.

Engen, J. (2008). Are your employees truly engaged? *Chief Executive.*

Flander, S. (2008). *Terms of engagement: J. Kalkman, Best Buy VP of human resource capabilities.* Palm Beach Gardens, FL: LRP Publications.

Gallup (2007). *Employee engagement.* Washington, DC: Author.

Institute for Corporate Productivity. (2007). *Building an engaged workforce.* Seattle, WA: Author.

Institute for Corporate Productivity. (2008). *Taking the pulse: Managing change.* Seattle, WA: Author.

Institute for Corporate Productivity. (2009, January). *Forecast for the 2009 workplace.* Seattle, WA: Author.

ISR/Towers Watson. (2008). *Providing a rock solid link between employee engagement and business performance.* New York: Author.

Melcrum Inc. (2005). Employee engagement: How to build a high performance workface. Research report. London: Author.

Michaels, E., Handfield-Jones, H., & Axelrod, B. (2001). *The war for talent.* Cambridge, MA: Harvard University Press.

Moyer, J. VP of HR, SMART Modular Technologies. (2008). Executive Research Interview.

Russell, S. Director, Corporate Learning and Development, Capital District Physicians' Health Plan. (2008). Executive Research Interview.

Towers-Perrin. (2008). *Employee engagement.* New York: Author.

About Performance Connections International

Performance Connections' leading-edge and complete range of workforce and customer engagement solutions unlock workforce potential and create new organizational value. A global training/consulting firm, we have been bringing unique competencies to an impressive range of clients across industries for over fifteen years, with success being our defining criteria.

Our unparalleled Engagement curriculum includes skills, business processes, and tools that ensure that the behaviors and strategies people acquire through training are sustained on the job. Our templates allow clients to customize to individual and business-unit needs. We are instructional design and performance improvement experts, providing clients with measurable behavior change and business results. Our programs are based on cutting-edge behavioral science research and best practices of top performers and successful companies, all to ensure clients receive systematic and consistent solutions that work. The founders, Herb Cohen and Bruce Fern, are instructional systems industry leaders and continue to be deeply involved and committed to client relationships by understanding client business needs and adding value.

Submitted by Herb Cohen

Performance Connections International, Inc.

39 Brook Farm Road, Suite 108

Bedford, NY 10506

(914) 244-0400

hcohen@perfcon.com

www.performanceconnections.com

Chapter 23

Thank God It's Monday!

How to Convert Disengaged Employees Into High-Performance Teams

THE EMMERICH GROUP

In This Chapter

- A tongue-in-cheek look at why employees lack workplace satisfaction.
- Managerial self-assessment to predict a successful culture shift.

Does anybody ever say "Thank God it's Monday" anymore?

Not many. According to the Conference Board, we are currently experiencing a twenty-two-year low in employee satisfaction. And the downward spiral is consistent.

How bad is it? A 2006 Gallup study categorized 71 percent of U.S. workers as "disengaged." That's bad enough. But fully 17 percent—more than one in six employees— are *actively* disengaged. The energy vampires (and we've all been one at least once, so don't get *too* pious here) are looking for ways to plot revenge. No wonder work isn't working.

And it gets worse. The last round of layoffs left those remaining with twice the work and half the friends. According to Salary.com Inc., more than 60 percent of those who have jobs say they actively looked for alternative employment last year.

So who's to blame? Well, that's complicated. Let's explore this.

Remember your first day of work? Your shirt was pressed. Your shoes were shined. You told your mama you were going to set the world on fire.

And then it happened. Two weeks went by, and you discovered you work with a bunch of "dweebs." Yep, imperfect souls everywhere. Whiners. Complainers. Brown-nosers. Passive aggressives. Excuse-makers. Gossips. And all of them shooting wildly toward mediocrity.

So you made a decision that it just wasn't worth it. You lowered your sights, and you've been bringing your "dweeb self" to work every day since, accepting things as they are, since you can't do a thing about it anyway. Hopeless resignation. Learned helplessness.

You think I'm wrong? Let's explore. Seems there are three groups responsible for this mess.

Who's at Fault 1: Executives

HOW DID EXECUTIVES DESTROY THE LEADING PREDICTOR OF FUTURE GROWTH AND PROFITABILITY?

Let's start with the possibility that the executive team is to blame. That's right. They can definitely own some of the fault in at least three ways: educating their people about job expectations, celebrating successes, and creating a safe workplace. Let's look at each one.

Reason 1

Their people have NO idea where the target is. Recent surveys indicate that less than 10 percent of employees have clearly defined outcomes and expectations from their work. That wouldn't be so tragic if not for *BusinessWeek* research showing that between 87 and 97 percent of six thousand employee respondents at all levels said they were currently performing in the top 10 percent!

Math issue or perception issue? Either way, that dog won't hunt.

So the delusional masses all think they're hitting the cover off the ball—yet they couldn't even tell you what the ball LOOKS like because leadership hasn't made it clear.

And they're ticked off. Why aren't they getting raises, advancing, getting oohs and ahhs from management? Why? Because they're not performing, but they don't know it!

Developing Talent for Organizational Results

Yep, that's a formula for madness. Each worker thinks he works for the boss from hell, and the boss is bummed about the performance . . . but there is no clear direction or expectations. So that unhealthy dance will continue until both parties drop dead from heartbreak.

Reason 2

Not only do they not know what the targets are, there is no visibility or celebration of those targets if they DO hit them. Neuroscientists have proven we're pretty simple beings. When we do good things and are celebrated, we form new neural pathways, changing the brain's electrical map. The more it happens, the more we're changed. It's like a muscle that is developed that now wants to create more success. If we repeat that celebration daily, so many new neural pathways take over that our confidence to repeat success is normalized. If we do good things but "nobody says nothin," well, we stop doing those things. No new neural pathways. No repeated behavior.

The problem is, work's just not fun enough. You have a bunch of walking stiffs—let's call them the "emotionally constipated"—who are taking themselves seriously and their results lightly. That's messed up.

What if instead we took results seriously and ourselves lightly? In fact, by taking ourselves lightly, we're more likely to take results seriously.

Ever been to a fourth grader's soccer game? It's a study in human dynamics. A weird transformation comes over the parents. The same folks who are loving, kind, it-takes-a-village-to-raise-a-child, Zen-like parents of the year become she- and he-devils with the fourth graders on the opposing team as the enemy. That's right. Little Jimmie from across the street is now the rival cause he's wearing blue today. But your team, those sweet, innocent, can-do-no-wrong angels, are the "chosen ones." Why? Because they're YOUR team.

When the game isn't on, you love those adorable kids on the other team. But on the field, they're the enemy, and the gloves are off!

What happened here? Why do we need to make the other team the bad guys so we can be the good guys? Don't know. It just works that way. WE want to be on the winning team, no matter what.

Now how can you use this funny little fact about human psychology to advance the results of your organization? Easy.

What if you put teams together in which each person receives points for hitting the critical drivers for his or her job? Maybe the teams are cross-sectional so you build bridges across the organization—a much better idea than pitting departments against each other, by the way.

Thank God It's Monday!

Then what if the results were visible every day, and you party down to celebrate the winners each week? Performance would skyrocket in . . . well, a week. You have to wonder how they miss this stuff in the MBA curriculum. Mind-boggling, isn't it? People want to play games and win. So why deprive them—especially if it will create miraculous results breakthroughs?

If you really want performance, not only do the teams compete, but the big prize happens when ALL the teams hit their numbers. Now the celebration is massive and the prizes are fun, fun, fun! At that point we've changed the culture to one where we don't see the other teams as the enemy. It's one big happy family, and it's about the WHOLE team winning. Your people now leave their homes and instead of saying, "Mommy has to go to work, now," say "Mommy's going to go play now. See you at 5:00. Love you."

Your Hoopla Team®—a team with the purpose of rolling out moments of truth, values, and critical driver contests—runs these contests and keeps the organization on the rails of measuring, coaching, and celebrating progress on the critical drivers of the organization, and suddenly—quite easily, in fact—results transform.

Reason 3

The leadership teams are missing the mark because they haven't created a safe workplace.

They have no understanding of the unwritten, unproductive "agreements" the company is operating from and how to change those agreements.

For example, most have an agreement that says, "If you don't create the targeted result, an excuse will be a lovely replacement, and then you're off the hook." Written or not, that's a bad agreement to make.

Another agreement: if something isn't right, just whine about it.

Have you ever seen a job posting that said, "Looking for an account exec who has mastered the skill of complaining about anything and everything to people who can't do a thing about it?" Me neither. So why is the workplace teeming with those who master that skill set? Unconscious agreements, that's why. (For help on creating productive agreements, go to www.ThankGodItsMonday/tools.)

Executives are well schooled in budgeting, spreadsheets, and analysis but are missing the single most important part of their jobs—*managing the culture*. Culture is the leading predictor of future growth and profitability, yet *nobody teaches executives how to master culture.*

If as an executive you start to replace the "crazy-making" agreements of gossip, passive-aggressive behaviors, and whining with healthy agreements like "You have a moral obligation to solve problems and directly approach those who have the capacity to make those changes with a list of well-thought-out ideas," things can actually change. If you actually follow through and acknowledge those that do and confront those who don't, those new agreements stick.

Then and only then do people get that you *mean it*.

In twenty-one years of watching powerful and sustainable performance breakthroughs happen, I can tell you that the clear bell-ringer, the moment that turns things around, is the moment executives stop delegating culture and realize that it is their number-one role. There are other ways executives get in the way of performance breakthroughs . . . but let's move on to managers.

Who's at Fault 2: Managers

WHY THE MIDDLE MANAGEMENT BREAKDOWN IS EPIDEMIC: WHY VISION AND STRATEGY RARELY MEET EXECUTION

What makes executives crazy? Managers—especially those who don't manage people and processes.

I was an abysmal manager, too. As soon as I mastered my technical job, I was promoted—and I instantly realized I had NO idea how to manage. I received the three-step management development program most receive upon their first promotion to management: (1) here's your desk, (2) here's your phone, and (3) good luck.

Didn't work too well.

Let's see how well-prepared you are to manage a performance breakthrough:

RATE YOUR HIGH-PERFORMANCE MANAGEMENT COMPETENCY I.Q.

Rate your performance in each of the areas below on a scale of 1 to 5 as follows:

1 = never

2 = occasionally

3 = with some regularity

4 = pretty frequently

5 = almost always

Here we go, complete honesty now, and no cheating off your neighbor:

1. My team members all know their internal and external customer service standards, and they are measured and celebrated on those standards regularly.

2. I have worked with my team to define a clear and purposeful vision of what extraordinary looks like and asked for a commitment from all that they will make it happen.

3. Meetings have actionable agendas distributed in advance, discussion is outcome-based, and each person walks out with a clear list of who needs to do what by when so that results happen after every meeting.

4. I do one-on-ones with my team members at least every two weeks (preferably weekly), where we review the critical drivers and results from the last two weeks, coach performance on those, and set clear outcomes for the next two weeks.

5. I communicate with my team members to make sure they understand their critical drivers (visit www.ThankGodItsMonday/tools to get more information on defining critical drivers) that create the critical results, and they each report weekly, monthly, and quarterly with transparency about where they are on those numbers. There is no place to hide.

6. When someone on my team is behind on a critical driver, he or she is clear about the need to communicate to me his or her "massive corrective action plan" to bring the project or outcome back on track.

7. I am actively intolerant of crazy-making behaviors like gossip, mind games, cliques, and bullying, and my team members all know I will hold them accountable to bringing their higher selves to work.

8. I have incorporated regularly scheduled celebrations about critical drivers and results: daily huddles, weekly and quarterly celebrations.

9. All my team members have performance development plans and a clear understanding that the responsibility to learn and grow is on their shoulders.

10. My commitment to grow my team members to be better people is obvious to them through the coaching, educational opportunities, and daily interactions that help people develop their ability to act and think with good character.

Add up your score. If you scored 20 or less, put yourself on management life support! Start by focusing hard on anything that scored a 1 or 2.

If you scored 21 to 30, you are obviously doing *something* right—but not enough. Find the weak spots and get to work.

If you scored 31 or higher . . . well, you're certainly doing better than I did as a first-time manager! But that's not a high enough bar to power an extraordinary culture shift. Get busy fixing what needs fixing. Use this quiz as your guide.

By the way, you can download this quiz from the book's online tools.

Thank God It's Monday!

Who's at Fault 3: Employees

WHY EMPLOYEES CAUSE LAYOFFS, DESTROY COMPANIES, AND MAKE THEIR CO-WORKERS SICK

Okay, that was fun. We blamed the bosses. And now you know why you are disengaged. But wait. Organizations only thrive when EVERY person takes 100 percent responsibility for the result. And if you're going to play a role in the breakthrough, "The Victim" isn't the role that will get you an Oscar.

When I saw my attorney (who I thank goodness haven't talked to for at least a year) at a Twin's game this spring, it was clear he was enjoying the summer baseball brew. Slightly under the influence, he asked, "Roxanne, you still working with companies to help them get their employees to act like grown-ups?"

"Well, that's not exactly what I do," I said. "I help businesses double growth, profits, and service scores in a few months. I get the needles moving quickly for them. The employee stuff is just a part of it. Why do you ask?"

He smiled. "After thirty-five years of practicing law, I have only heard business owners say one thing on the day we close the sale of their business: 'I didn't sell for the money.' I used to be shocked by that. They also didn't sell because they stopped loving the business. You know what every one of them says on the day of closing? They sold because they couldn't wait to get away from the employees."

Well then, that's interesting. There probably IS some fault on the employee side. Let's put THAT under the microscope.

There's an old country song my cousin played every year at the holidays: "Ya done stomped on my heart . . . and you mashed that sucker flat."

Well, that's how it feels to be in the workplace some days. Our souls are stomped on.

People's behaviors seem childish, unkind, and self-consumed—a bit like adult daycare.

So the responsibility of every team member is to put on grown-up pants and bring that higher self to work every single day. It's a choice. We only act like children in the workplace because we don't stop to reflect on how unattractive it is when adults fail to hold their behaviors to higher standards than children have.

Managers spend an average of 37 percent of their workday dealing with poor performers and bad behaviors. Imagine how much would be available for raises and bonuses if that hole in the bottom of the bucket wasn't creating the need for layoffs.

So employees have a role. First, they have to understand that they choose their attitudes moment by moment. Just because life isn't perfect—and it never is—that

Developing Talent for Organizational Results

doesn't give them the right to pout, sabotage, hold back, or otherwise give free rein to their destructive behaviors.

Next, employees must take responsibility for getting a crystal-clear understanding of their critical drivers and report on those on a weekly basis. It's not okay to play the victim card and complain incessantly about the long hours you're working while you're missing the targets—*even if your boss didn't give you those targets*. Take the initiative yourself. Lay out what you think the targets are, get agreement from your boss, then take aim and fire. You won't hit every target every time. Demonstrate integrity and transparency by letting your boss know what you hit, what you missed, and what your corrective action plan is to improve your aim.

Most important: as an employee, you have the right and even the moral obligation to understand that leadership is not a position—it's a way of being. And YOU can be the one who brings enlightenment to your workplace by showing others the way.

About The Emmerich Group

Roxanne Emmerich,
New York Times bestselling author, is founder and CEO of The Emmerich Group, a leading business transformation firm that helps companies get results beyond what they even dreamed possible.

Based on Roxanne's experience as three-time Entrepreneur of the Year recipient, her firm helps companies solve one of these three problems:

- Increase the speed to the stated profit and growth goals by 50 percent.

- Bring the one out of three dollars currently lost due to employee disengagement (average, according to Gallup) back to the bottom line within three months.

- Double service scores within sixty days and high-profit accounts within one year.

She has spoken and consulted to the leadership of many of the largest and most respected companies in the world, including Verizon, Merck, and Lockheed, but is best known in banking, having worked with half of the top 1 percent performers. *Successful Meetings* magazine listed Roxanne as one of the top twelve most-in-demand speakers in the country.

She is the author of many books, including the *New York Times* bestseller, *Thank God It's Monday! How to Create a Workplace You and Your Customers Love.*

Submitted by Roxanne Emmerich, CEO

The Emmerich Group, Inc.

9521 West 78th Street, Suite 120

Eden Prairie, MN 55344

(800) 236-5885 or (952) 820-0360

Roxanne_Emmerich@EmmerichGroup.com

www.EmmerichGroup.com

Chapter 24

Improving Workplace Cultures Through Respect, Service, and Safety at Work®

CRISIS PREVENTION INSTITUTE, INC.

In This Chapter

- Creating a culture of respect, service, and safety at work.
- How to create a policy framework that prioritizes respect, service, and safety.

- *"Her anger was not warranted given the situation. Customers get upset, but she was beyond upset and it got personal."*
- *"She was being rather quiet—not talking with anyone for weeks."*
- *"He was odd; I felt uncomfortable around him since the first day he came here."*
- *"Was there a way to make that area more secure? Something bad was bound to happen."*

- *"Something was not quite right with those two."*
- *"He said he was going to file a report, because no one should be treated that way."*

We may read or hear these types of statements in the aftermath of a critical workplace incident. But every day, many critical incidents and crisis situations are prevented in workplaces because when these same types of statements are made, *one* word changes. Read the above statements again and replace the word *was* with the word *is*. Does your workplace culture invite and support proactive *is* discussions?

A proactive culture that commits to preparedness has a clear protocol for expressing these feelings as they become concerns. Each employee is made aware of this protocol in orientation and understands expectations regarding where, when, and to whom he or she should convey such concerns. This preparedness is important not only to avoid the "worst case scenario" violent incidents. Anxiety, anger, hostility, fear, and intimidation can also cause significant damage to people and organizations. These human emotions and feelings may be brought into the workplace or emerge as a reaction to change or personality conflicts at work. Resulting behaviors and attitudes infiltrate workplace cultures and impact not only safety, but also productivity, wellness, performance, commitment, satisfaction, and service.

Three Guiding Words

There are three words that, if regularly and thoughtfully considered, can guide people to be part of solutions rather than part of problems that escalate situations at work.

- *Respect* involves treating others with courtesy and preserving their dignity.
- *Service* involves meeting commitments and maintaining professionalism.
- *Safety* involves preventing and responding to danger, risk, or injury.

The culture change within an organization begins and evolves when these three words become expectations between:

- Employer and employee
- Leadership/supervisors and employee
- Co-workers
- Customers and all employees

Respect, service, and safety is a philosophy that can be woven into the fabric of a workplace culture to prevent crisis situations and ultimately improve or even save people's lives.

Crisis as Opportunity

In the Chinese language, the word "crisis" includes the character for the word *danger,* plus the character for the word *opportunity.* Without a doubt, crisis moments are times of danger. But they are also dynamic opportunities to facilitate resolution and change. Since 1980, the Crisis Prevention Institute (CPI) has worked with thousands of organizations and touched millions of employees through training programs aimed at seizing those opportunities while putting procedures in place to prevent and de-escalate situations. By implementing training in this important area as an ongoing process, organizations have built and maintained cultures in which employees successfully balance responsibilities relating to respect, service, and safety. There is no single factor that can be added to any workplace that will make it immune to conflict or crisis. There is no quick fix. But there are ways to frame expectations, policies, and even discussions that are relevant and empowering.

Key Ingredients

How employees interact with other employees and customers is a significant ingredient in the workplace culture recipe. In turn, the culture of a workplace impacts the way people feel and act. It is an integrated experience with behaviors and attitudes responding to behaviors and attitudes. Other ingredients include policies and how they are translated to procedures that are consistently implemented. Supervisory practices, leadership, and communication channels also flavor the workplace culture. It is one thing to say a workplace culture promotes the mission and values statement displayed on the wall. It is another thing when values such as respect, service, and safety come to life every day in a workplace because of the purposeful attitudes and actions of the employees.

A Tool to Emphasize a Culture of Respect, Services, and Safety

The policy and procedure development tool outlined in the following pages organizes a policy framework that prioritizes respect, service, and safety. While there are various organizational policies and procedures that are related to these values (for example, complaint procedures, harassment policies, and emergency response), this framework recognizes what is at the core of all of them, their interconnectedness, and the critical significance of employee attitudes and behaviors. The tool is organized into four parts: an overview of the three inter-related words and sections that expand specifically on respect, service, and safety. Examples of employee expectations, organizational support, and procedures to translate these values to actionable workplace behavior are suggested.

This tool can be used by leadership as a way to evaluate the organization through the lens of these critical areas. It can also be used to identify workplace training needs, as a discussion resource for work teams, or as a template for policy creation.

Each workplace has unique issues relating to respect, service, and safety that should be incorporated into the template where relevant. Information is presented as guidance or introduces sample language to stimulate thinking. Examples are general, to be modified for workplace specifics as appropriate.

I. OVERVIEW

Values or Mission Statement

The organization's mission statement may reflect values relating to respect, service, and safety and can be included here.

Respect, Service, and Safety as Organizational Values

Sample language could include something like the following:

> "The XYZ Organization's mission can be best carried out in a safe, respectful, service-oriented environment in which employees feel respected and are respectful to one another and customers. XYZ is committed to providing an atmosphere in which everyone feels safe and secure, and workplace disruptions are prevented or defused in early stages with minimal anxiety. XYZ places great value on an employee development process that translates our mission and policies to procedures and exemplary work practice. This policy reflects the organization's expectations relating to respect, service, and safety issues in the workplaces. Training relating to these issues is provided annually to all employees to assure information and skills needed to meet expectations are provided. This training includes information on:
>
> - Recognizing signs of anxiety, discontent, irrational thinking, and emerging aggression.
> - Respectful communication.
> - Defusing verbal altercations.
> - Problem solving difficult situations.
> - Giving bad news.

- Identifying quality improvement opportunities in the aftermath of unusual incidents.

- Emergency response procedures, including/violence response procedures.

- Documentation and incident reporting.

"XYZ relies on the efforts of all employees to maintain an environment of respect, service, and safety in order for the organization's mission to be carried out with integrity."

II. RESPECT

Provide a definition that includes workplace specifics such as the following:

"Respect includes attitudes and behavior that:

- Convey honesty, integrity, and the absence of personal bias.

- Honor the dignity and worth of all people.

- Demonstrate empathic approaches in listening and speaking.

- Show consideration when interacting with co-workers and customers.

- Recognize the talents and contributions of co-workers.

"XYZ relies on its employees to interact cooperatively and respectfully with one another in order to meet the needs of customers and create a productive work environment. Clear, respectful communication is essential for the diverse work teams necessary for our business. Interactions with customers may occur in stressful situations. Practicing the utmost respect in all interactions will help prepare us for these situations."

Define the expectations/responsibilities of employees, including organizational or job-specific expectations. Examples might include:

- Actively listen to the point of view or concerns of others.

- Express yourself politely.

- Avoid using offensive language.

- Show courtesy to others.

- Welcome the opinions of others.

- Avoid encroaching on the personal space of another.

- Use care and caution around the property of others.

- Offer accurate information when needed.

- Strive for win-win resolutions.

- Avoid gossip or communication framed to disrupt employee relations.

- Honor the privacy of others.

- Create an environment in which people feel valued.

- Communicate respectfully with all customers and co-workers.

- Respect the rights of others.

- Respect customer opinions even when complaints seem unwarranted.

- Report customer complaints to your manager.

Define the support from the organization and management/supervisory team including details of what is in place to assist employees in meeting expectations. For example, supervisory support, communication systems, team meetings, performance reviews, and training. Sample language might be

"XYZ's organizational chart outlines a flow of communication for all employees. If your direct manager is not available to you when you need assistance with a concern or a conflict, contact the manager on duty. Employees are invited to submit agenda items for team meetings and are encouraged to raise issues and questions relating to specific scenarios that impacted responsibilities and expectations."

Expectations/Responsibilities of Managers

Examples might include:

- Communicate necessary information so that employees can perform job duties effectively and efficiently.

- Provide for channels of communication that minimize confusion.

- Set an example for positive communication.

- Recognize strengths as well as growth areas and offer support to help build strengths and aid in development.

- Provide opportunities for employees to contribute ideas and express concerns openly.

- Convey expectations in a nonjudgmental manner.

- Maintain confidentiality relating to personnel policies.

- Provide constructive criticism in private.

- Post expectations of customer behavior where visible and refer to as necessary.

- Provide advance notice of change in operations or routines, and assure details are communicated to employees and customers as necessary.

This section may also include your organization's efforts to communicate expectations of customers or vendors. Examples might include:
Signs are posted at points of entry noting:

- Visitors are invited to convey concerns or complaints in writing or can request to speak with a manager.

- Individuals who appear intoxicated will be asked to visit the organization at another time.

- Boisterous behavior and offensive language are not allowed.

Issue Notification/Evaluation Process

While procedures are communicated in a variety of ways (postings, employee handbooks, training, job descriptions, operations manual), this section should offer clarity on how employees are expected to notify management or human resources about issues/concerns and what the process will be for evaluating those issues/concerns.
Examples:

- Requests for supervisory consultation forms are available on the organization's intranet. Employees concerned about unresolved conflict with another employee or a customer should complete and forward this form to the director of human resources.

- Complaints from customers are reviewed with employees for development purposes at each supervisory meeting.

Related Policies or Procedures

Other relevant organizational policies or procedures related to respect should be referenced for review. Examples might include:

- Employee conflict resolution or alternative dispute resolution procedures.

- Employee grievance procedures.

- Harassment policies.

- Employee assistance program (EAP).

- Staff development and training.
- Code of conduct/employee behavior at work (dress code, language, smoking, alcohol/drug use).
- Team meetings and communication with co-workers.
- Employee property storage.
- Employee posting procedures (types of displays that are allowed and where).
- Organization's communication procedures (organizational postings, organization-wide meetings, memos).
- Electronic communication policies (email, Internet use, cell/smart phone, computer).

III. SERVICE

Provide a definition of "service." Sample language is provided below, but you should use language specific to your workplace.

> "Service is the assistance we provide to customers and the manner in which needs are met. Our service objectives aim to:
> - Assure the customer feels valued.
> - Provide efficient responses to needs, concerns, and requests.
> - Create a comfortable environment.
> - Recognize the importance of timeliness.
> - Convey interest and accessibility.
> - Incorporate customer voice and perspective.
> - Exceed customer expectations.
> - Make appropriate referrals to meet customer needs.
> - Convey the importance of customer satisfaction.
> - Problem-solve situations without complication."

Expectations/Responsibilities of Employees

Add organizational or job-specific expectations. Examples might include:

- Learn and understand customer needs and expectations.
- Complete work promptly and accurately.

- Arrive on time to avoid any service delays or interruptions to business.
- Listen carefully to the customer.
- Protect customer property.
- Report unusual occurrences that may negatively impact customer experience.
- Discuss customer complaints with supervisors.
- Don't argue with customers.
- Communicate quality improvement suggestions to management.
- Share relevant information with co-workers.

Support from Organization and Management/Supervisory Team

Detail what is in place to assist employees in meeting expectations. For example: supervisory support, communication systems, team meetings, performance reviews, and training. Examples might include:

- Employees are issued cell phones to maximize communication efficiencies during off-site assignments.
- Individual and team meetings are held each month and focused on a service issue or experience.
- Exemplary service recognition is posted on the organization's website.

Expectations/Responsibilities of Managers

Example might include:

- Promptly share information regarding what is learned about customer expectations and needs.
- Implement necessary recruitment and hiring efforts to assure capacity meets customer needs.
- Listen to staff perceptions and experiences about service issues.
- Intercede in complex customer matters or concerns to allow staff to focus on providing exemplary service.
- Promptly respond to customer complaints.
- Advise staff about complaint resolutions as soon as possible/feasible.

Addressing Issues/Concerns

While procedures are communicated in a variety of ways (postings, employee handbooks, training, job descriptions, operations manual), this section should offer clarity on how employees' issues/concerns will be addressed.

Examples might include:

- Customer service issues are addressed by supervisor at the start of each shift.
- Managers are paged with an identified code to intervene in customer disputes.

Related Policies or Procedures

Other organizational policies or procedures related to service should be referenced for review. Examples of service policies or procedures may include:

- Documentation.
- Report writing.
- Responding to customer complaints.
- Continuous quality improvement measures.
- Conflict resolution.
- Employee etiquette and behavioral expectations.
- Customer service policies (wait time, phone-on-hold time).

IV. SAFETY

Provide a definition of "safety." Sample language is provided below, but you should use language specific to your workplace.

> "All employees have responsibilities to minimize risks and to prevent hazards, disruptions, violence, and other crisis situations. Consistency in our approaches to safety risks is aligned with regulatory guidance [*reference any relevant guidance or laws*] and our appropriate responses can keep people safe, as well as limit damage or liability.
>
> "Awareness is extremely important for the prevention of disruptions and for maintaining safety in the workplace. A thorough understanding of our emergency response procedures is a requirement of employment and is reviewed in annual training and emergency drills."

Expectations/Responsibilities of Employees

Add organizational or job-specific expectations. Examples might include:

- Prompt reporting of potentially hazardous situations (environmental, personnel-related, customer-related).

- Behavior and attitudes that maximize safety for customers and employees.

- Reporting of personal safety concerns that may impact the workplace (such as restraining orders, threats, domestic violence situations, or conflicts with co-workers) to assure plans are in place to prevent potential crisis situations.

- Documentation of critical incidents and proper use of incident report forms.

- Adhering to the organization's security policies.

- Abiding by internal security procedures relating to building access, identifications, monitoring, visitor screening, loss prevention, and shift change protocol.

- Monitoring the environment continuously and consistently.

Support from Organization and Management/Supervisory Team

Details of what is in place to assist employees in meeting expectations can be described here. For example, supervisory support, communication systems, team meetings, performance reviews, and training. Examples might include:

- Leadership meets quarterly to review all incidents impacting safety and all safety-related policies and procedures.

- Workplace violence policies are reviewed annually with each employee.

- Security cameras and external monitoring is in place for employee and customer safety.

- Panic alarms are located at designated locations and convey emergency to police department immediately.

- An emergency response team is trained and members are available on each shift.

- Reporting procedures are carefully reviewed with each employee.

Expectations/Responsibilities of Managers

Examples might include:

- Evaluate environmental safety regularly.

- Respect employee confidentiality when personal safety risks (such as domestic violence, restraining orders, and threats) are reported.
- Initiate employee conflict resolution procedures within [timeframe] of conflict issue identification.
- Initiate debriefing of critical incidents within [timeframe].

Procedures

While procedures are communicated in a variety of ways (postings, employee handbooks, training, job descriptions, operations manual), this section should offer clarity on how employees carry out these procedures. Examples might include:

- Employees scan their identification tags upon entering and exiting the building.
- All visitors are required to sign in and be escorted by the employees they are meeting.
- Emergency response buttons (located at each work station) send a silent notification to the police and/or the manager on duty (depending on pre-determined code). Specific response procedures are practiced and provided in writing to employees in training and during review sessions.

Related Policies and Procedures

Other organizational policies and procedures related to safety should be listed. Examples of relevant policies and procedures include the following:

- Emergency evacuation procedures.
- Violence response procedures.
- Emergency response procedures.
- Visitor policies.
- Building access policies.
- Regulatory compliance policies (OSHA, state and local requirements, etc.).
- Safe handling procedures.
- Heavy equipment procedures.
- Safety issue reporting procedures.
- Building safety check procedures for open/closing times.
- Severe weather plans.

The shell of this Policy and Procedure Development Tool can be found in this book's online resources.

About CPI

CPI is an international training organization committed to best practices and safe behavior management methods that focus on prevention. Through a variety of specialized offerings and innovative resources, CPI educates and empowers professionals to create safe and respectful work environments. By doing so, they enrich not only their own lives but also the lives of the individuals they serve.

The cornerstone of CPI is the *Nonviolent Crisis Intervention*® program, which is considered the worldwide standard for crisis prevention and intervention training. With a core philosophy of providing for the *Care, Welfare, Safety, and Security*SM of everyone involved in a crisis situation, the program's proven strategies give human service providers and educators the skills to safely and effectively respond to anxious, hostile, or violent behavior while balancing the responsibilities of care. In response to business demands for adaptable solutions to manage potentially disruptive or even dangerous situations, CPI developed the *Prepare Training*® program. The strategies taught in this program have been effective in reducing the frequency and severity of these situations, increasing employee confidence and morale, and fostering a culture of *Respect, Service, and Safety at Work*®.

Submitted by Judith Schubert, President

Crisis Prevention Institute, Inc.

10850 W. Park Place, Suite 600

Milwaukee, WI 53224

(800) 558-8976

UK: 0800 89 1874

IRE: 1800 55 8077

AUS: 1800 55 3247

jschubert@crisisprevention.com

www.crisisprevention.com

educate. empower. enrich.

Chapter 25

Building Organizational Change Capability

This Century's Competitive Advantage

BEING FIRST, INC.

In This Chapter

- A process for building organizational change capability.
- Tools, assessments, and checklists to establish a change capable culture.
- Stimulating considerations to build the capacity for organizational change.

"Your success in life isn't based on your ability to simply change. It is based on your ability to change faster than your competition, customers, and business."

—Mark Sanborn

Organizations that excel at change have a competitive advantage. They capture market opportunities, innovate, improve, acquire, downsize, rebrand, restructure, and implement new products, services, and technologies better than their competitors. Unfortunately, research shows that most organizations consistently underperform at change, with 60 to 70 percent of all change efforts failing to deliver their intended results. These dismal success rates have persisted for over a decade, costing organizations millions of dollars in wasted investment and lost opportunity.

Change is not going away. Improving your organization's ability to change, and building the required conscious change leadership capability throughout your enterprise, can become profound competitive advantages. In this chapter, we explore how to build such change leadership capability and the power of approaching change consciously as a strategic discipline. This entails not only building your leaders' and internal consultants' awareness, knowledge, and skills about change, but also the organizational systems and infrastructure that will enable change to be led more effectively—forever. You will find several online tools provided with this chapter to help you identify your organization's need for building change capability and how to tailor this work to fit your organization's unique needs.

The Leverage of Building Change Capability

Change capability is the ability of an organization to plan, design, and implement all types of change efficiently, with committed leaders and stakeholders, so desired business and cultural results are consistently achieved and integrated seamlessly into operations to deliver maximum ROI.

Figure 25.1 shows how building change capability positively impacts your organization. In the diagram, A Work denotes your core business mission and activities, that is, everything your organization does to provide value to customers. B Work is all of the change efforts you undertake to improve your A Work, making your organization the best it can be. C Work is consciously improving your ability to do B Work. In other words, C Work is improving your ability to improve, to change, to transform. C Work is consciously building change capability so you continually improve the results you get from change. Remember the statistic of the 60 to 70 percent failure rate? C Work stops the failure and maximizes results from change. Building change capability, or C Work, requires change leadership training and development, and treating change as a strategic discipline. Let's address each in turn.

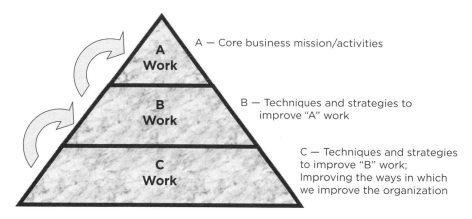

Figure 25.1 The Leverage of Building Change Capability (ABC Work) Model

Training and Development in Change Leadership

Building change capability requires commitment, resources, and time. It starts with increasing executive, management, and employee change knowledge and skills through training and development. Executives must learn what it takes to lead the various types of change in their organizations, especially transformational change, which is the most complex and disruptive. They must learn how to sponsor change effectively, beyond the typical "bless and delegate" mode of traditional—and non-effective—sponsorship.

Change project leaders and their team members must develop solid competence in the process of change: planning, designing, and implementing the best solutions in ways that the end-users both want to make the change and are capable of succeeding in it. They must also assess and address the cultural and human dynamics that will make that solution work on the ground.

Managers must learn how to carry out change in their operational areas, including how to deal with people's reactions to change and how to engage employees to build commitment and ownership of the changes. Workers must learn how to adapt to change, make the changes relevant and meaningful, and contribute to successful outcomes.

All of this requires a serious commitment to training and development, including real-time change project application that goes beyond the classroom. Action learning, ongoing feedback, learning clinics, and on-the-ground support and consulting are critical. Communities of Practice and Centers of Excellence can provide vital ongoing coaching, mentoring, development, and sharing of best practices. Together, this wide range of development beyond traditional classroom approaches will improve your track record in leading change.

Review the key change leadership competencies in the list that follows. Check those you believe need to be improved in your organization. If you check over ten, then building a change leadership training plan is critical to your current and future success at change.

KEY CHANGE LEADERSHIP COMPETENCIES

- How to establish clear change governance: leadership roles and responsibilities, decision making, interfaces with operations, change infrastructures.

- How to build and communicate the case for change and desired outcomes so they are understood by all stakeholders.

- How to accurately scope change initiatives to include organization and technical initiatives as well as required cultural, behavioral, and mindset changes.

- How to develop a realistic change strategy—owned by the sponsors and leaders of the change—that clearly outlines how the change effort will be led.

- How to create a multi-directional change communication plan that engages, informs, and catalyzes two-way dialogue from stakeholders.

- How to develop a stakeholder engagement strategy that involves stakeholders from the start, and ensures they have a voice and a stake in the change they are expected to make.

- How to cause and sustain required mindset and behavior changes in both leaders and employees.

- How to turn stakeholder resistance into commitment and positive contribution

- How to create an effective change process plan that properly sequences change activities.

- How to establish and sustain critical conditions for successful change.

- How to determine required resources.

- How to set realistic timelines.

- How to determine and ensure adequate capacity for change on top of operational workloads.

- How to establish effective mechanisms for making rapid course corrections to your change plan.

- How to ensure and sustain executive alignment and commitment to the change

---

Change: The New Strategic Discipline

Virtually all key functions in organizations—finance, marketing, sales, human resources, and information technology—are established as strategic disciplines to ensure they function consistently at the highest levels of performance. Strategic disciplines embrace management protocols, proven methods, and best practices that ensure they fulfill the needs of the organization. Today, change is as mission-critical as these other functions and must be embraced and set up in similar fashion. Seeing change leadership as a strategic discipline moves it beyond simply a skill set to develop and promotes it to a vital function of the organization that has equal impact on success as do other key functions. In similar fashion, information technology was not treated as a strategic discipline in the 1980s. Now, virtually all of the Fortune 500 have a chief information officer, and IT has become as critical to success as marketing or finance.

Five key strategies exist for creating change as a strategic discipline: (1) identifying and managing an enterprise change agenda; (2) having one common change *process* methodology; (3) establishing change infrastructures; (4) building a strategic change center of excellence for all change practitioners; and (5) creating a strategic change office. We will describe each in order, although sequence is not implied here. You will quickly see that they fit together as an integrated approach, where the fifth strategy, the strategic change office, coordinates all of them.

Read each description first for understanding, and then consider the possibility for creating any of them in your organization. You may find that your leaders have an appetite for one or more of the disciplines. Start with those and then build from there after you begin to demonstrate value. Establishing change as a vital function—a strategic discipline in your organization—can be a two- to five-year undertaking.

1. ENTERPRISE CHANGE AGENDA

An enterprise change agenda names the most important change initiatives required to execute your organization's business strategy. Its purpose is to identify, capture, coordinate, and monitor the major changes underway or planned in your organization, ensuring their strategic relevance to business success. It may or may not include less significant changes underway or planned, depending on your capacity to monitor them. Its intent is to focus on mission-critical changes for the enterprise as a whole and its primary businesses.

You may be familiar with project portfolio management—a method for collectively managing a group of current or proposed projects. While similar in concept, the enterprise change agenda is owned by the senior executives and designed to address the organization's strategic changes. Its focus remains high-level—appropriate to executive oversight. The specifics of project objectives, timelines, resource requirements, risks, and interdependencies are handled by a strategic change office (if you create one), project change leadership teams, and other mechanisms within your organization's change infrastructure, described later in this chapter. If you have a project portfolio office that serves the executives, tailor the enterprise change agenda as an extension of it.

In most organizations, the decision to establish the discipline of an enterprise change agenda belongs to the senior executive team. Ideally, you would recognize its value before its absence overwhelms the organization. It can counteract the pervasive chaos, "project of the month," and costly capacity issues that leaders inadvertently create by initiating untold numbers of changes and pet projects. The agenda ensures that change does not get out of control and gives leaders greater strategic oversight and accountability for priority changes. It also helps them weave a cohesive story to communicate to stakeholders and the workforce about where all of the change activity is leading and the outcomes it needs to produce.

The change agenda assists your organization and executives to ensure five critical success requirements are addressed. You will find the change agenda assessment with this chapter's online tools. Discuss the tool with your executives to assess your need for an enterprise change agenda.

The organization's change agenda is built by identifying and grouping change initiatives currently underway or planned in four categories, from the most strategic to operational:

- Strategic importance to business success
- Enterprise-wide impact

Developing Talent for Organizational Results

- Function- or business-line specific
- Operational requirement

Identify the change efforts within each category, and cluster them to assist with prioritization. Review your available resources and contracted services, and then ascertain whether you have adequate capacity for the change efforts within each level.

The creation of the enterprise change agenda typically follows the organization's strategic planning process and precedes your operational planning cycle. Because new change efforts may arise in any of the categories throughout the year, revisit the agenda periodically to ensure that it is still relevant and accurate. If you put in place a chief change officer (see number 5 below), he or she oversees the agenda and coordinates its use and accuracy throughout the year. If not, then appoint one of your executives to do so. Organizations that have large autonomous business units may have each business create and monitor its own change agenda, aligned with enterprise requirements. This makes reporting on each business unit's annual change priorities, progress, and resource usage easy. These issues may be added to your scorecard.

2. COMMON CHANGE PROCESS METHODOLOGY

We are not surprised when we do change audits for clients and discover that they have multiple change methodologies used across their organization. Often, when new leaders come into an organization, they bring their familiar approaches with them. Some change models address start-up, some people issues, some just implementation, some engagement, and some communications. All are pieces of the overall picture that a change process methodology must provide. Intentional or not, these various change models, concepts, and terms often end up competing and conflicting, confusing both employees and change leaders who work on multiple efforts. They make it difficult to coordinate across initiatives and measure progress in common terms or metrics.

Note also that some organizations have no distinct approach to change at all. With each change effort, they reinvent the change process, wasting enormous effort and often creating confusion. This negates much of the opportunity to learn from past changes and expedite current and future ones. The absence of a shared change process model is costly and a clear sign of poor change leadership capability.

A common change process methodology overcomes these challenges and produces many positive outcomes that you cannot achieve with multiple approaches to change or bolting on change management services. Consciously determining and using one common change methodology across your organization is critical to building change capability. Does your organization have one preferred change model? Does it have many?

You can assess the effectiveness of your change models with another tool found online. It lists critical attributes of an effective change model. Use it to help you select the best model for your organization. Have your organization's change leaders rate your model(s) on each of the items and discuss the consequences and risks you face based on your results. Pay particular attention to the items you rate 3, 2, or 1. Ideally, you will select one model that fulfills all of these criteria for success.

The model we recommend is The Change Leader's Roadmap, shown in Figure 25.2. It rates high on every item above and is designed to be an organization's one common change process methodology. You can learn more about it at www.change leadersroadmap.com or by reading our book, *The Change Leader's Roadmap: How to Navigate Your Organization's Transformation* (Ackerman Anderson & Anderson, 2010).

3. CHANGE INFRASTRUCTURES

Change infrastructures are standard structures and practices for designing, implementing, and monitoring your organization's change efforts. They underlie the work of change, making it clear, consistent, and manageable. All strategic functions in your organization have such infrastructures. Think about your IT, finance, marketing, or HR functions. They all have standard practices, methods, templates, and ways of ensuring high-level performance and outcomes. Those methods and practices are structured, overt, accessible, understood, and used by all professionals in that function. Each of them is trained and held accountable for applying those standard practices to his or her areas of responsibility. Over time, those "infrastructures" are refined and developed to produce best practices to ensure the highest results. This is all possible because the methods and practices are common to everyone engaged in that function.

The purpose of developing change infrastructures is identical to other strategic disciplines: to support your organization to deliver optimal results from change by establishing and using overt, commonly used structures and practices that optimize change execution and accelerate time-to-results. Once established, these infrastructures become the baseline for people to increase their change leadership effectiveness and build your organization's change capability.

Change infrastructures include standard roles, templates, and methods for governing your change initiatives, as well as common practices for setting up, orchestrating, and overseeing their effectiveness. When you establish a common change process methodology, it will become your most significant change infrastructure. The Change

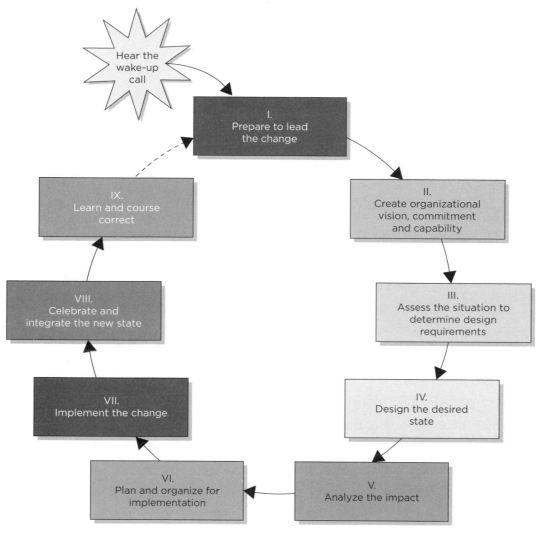

Figure 25.2 The Change Leader's Roadmap Model
Copyright © 2012 Dean Anderson and Linda Ackerman Anderson.

Leader's Roadmap is designed so that each task can become a change infrastructure by providing guidance on best practices for executing that task. Our clients use these to optimize and then standardize how their change leaders and consultants design and execute change. Over time, these become best change practices for their entire organization. Standard change tasks are included in the sample list of change infrastructures

Building Organizational Change Capability

below. You can use this list as a checklist of possible infrastructures your organization may wish to create.

Sample Change Infrastructures

❑ Practices for creating your case for change

❑ Criteria for establishing project outcomes

❑ Templates for building change strategy

❑ Mechanisms for change governance, including roles, team charters, and decision making

❑ Conditions for success

❑ Measurements of success

❑ Practices for project launch and on-boarding team members

❑ Practices for developing multi-directional change communication plans

❑ Methods for building stakeholder engagement strategies

❑ Expectations and methods for rapid course correction

❑ Expectations and mechanisms for multiple project integration (for example, "air traffic control")

❑ Change leadership competencies: skills, knowledge, behaviors, and mindsets

❑ Roster of best practices and change tools for all key tasks in your common change process methodology

❑ Universal support mechanisms for communications, feedback, and information management, such as intranet sites, project software, and communication protocols

Which change infrastructures are important to implement as standards in your organization?

Make key change infrastructures known and available to anyone involved in leading change in your organization. However, beware of the fear of mandated standards. Leaders and change consultants can easily balk at the idea of standard approaches unless you demonstrate the wisdom in using them. Make the enterprise benefits overt, and engage users in helping develop and refine your infrastructures. Ultimately, your change leaders and consultants should "own" these infrastructures and be held accountable for making them best-in-class.

4. STRATEGIC CHANGE CENTER OF EXCELLENCE

Many organizations have internal change consultants, and specialists. These professionals are found in different departments in different organizations, including organization development, organization effectiveness, change management, quality, process improvement, Lean, Six Sigma, IT, HR, and project management. Each adds its own value in its own way, depending on the discipline.

The most common scenario we see in organizations is that leaders call on these services when they happen to see a need, often too late in the process to ensure clear foresight or prevent predictable people or process problems. Many leaders, operating on autopilot, simply do not see the need very often and, when they do, miss significant opportunities for how best to apply these talents. Most of the existing services offer a piece of what is needed, but challenges arise because no one is looking after all of what is needed. To make matters worse, these resources often compete among themselves to be used on major change efforts. The end result is that the organization does not receive its full value from these resources.

Consider the following: Who has an eye on the organization's strategic change needs? Who keeps conscious, proactive attention to ensuring that the organization sets up its mission-critical change efforts for success from the very beginning? Who oversees that the level of change expertise needed is being developed and used in the best ways? Who ensures that there is effective collaboration among these various change resources for the good of each change effort and the entire enterprise? Someone must, or breakthrough results can never occur.

These needs and the complexity, cost, and potential benefit of enterprise transformation have generated a need for a Strategic Change Center of Excellence in many organizations. This center of excellence is comprised of the organization's major change resources, many of which are listed above. Most large organizations have all of this consulting expertise in place, at their headquarters and in their business lines. The center is a way of organizing, networking, and training them for the best and highest use across the enterprise. The center need not house all of these resources; rather, it supports them, accesses them, develops them, and deploys them as needed. The center's charter is to create a new breed of change consultants, devoted to the overall success of the enterprise, no matter what their expertise or where they live in the businesses.

The center can play many different value-added roles. Key roles are listed in this chapter's online tools. You may use this tool to determine the potential value proposition that creating a Strategic Change Center of Excellence would deliver for your organization.

VALUE PROPOSITION FOR A CHANGE CENTER OF EXCELLENCE

Rate each of the statements below and, for each, assess how much you believe it would add value to your organization's ability to succeed at change. Use a 5-point scale, with 1 being "of low value" and 5 being "of high value." In other words, a 1 means, "We don't really need this," while a 5 means, "We desperately need this." Add the scores. A total of more than 75 means that a Strategic Change Center of Excellence may provide great value to your organization.

_____ Identify all internal change resources so we know what skills we have and which we need.

_____ Provide access to a central pool of the most highly skilled internal consulting resources for use on major change efforts.

_____ Determine complementarities and duplication of our change resources.

_____ Ensure consistency among all of the change resources and their approaches, thereby providing the best and most aligned guidance on change.

_____ Provide temporary or "loaned" resources where the organization needs them most.

_____ Provide a centralized function for developing the highest level of change leadership and consulting that the organization needs to succeed.

_____ Identify, build, teach, and ensure the use of the organization's common change process methodology and change infrastructures on major change efforts.

_____ Identify, build, and distribute best change practices.

_____ Pilot new change practices before rollout.

Developing Talent for Organizational Results

____ Provide "case management" learning clinics and showcases for others change leaders and internal consultants during any phase of change.

____ Match junior resources with more experienced senior resources to ensure a consistent pipeline of development within the organization.

____ Help address cross-boundary/cross-business integration needs relevant to producing the highest results from change.

____ Help match change resources to demand.

____ Create a voice for change capacity audits and reality checks.

____ Maintain a list of qualified external vendors to support internal change capacity and capability building as needed.

____ Surface critical risk factors, issues, and needs for course correction from all levels of the organization engaged in major changes.

____ Advocate for realistic conditions for success on how changes are set up and led.

____ Input to and facilitate changes in culture and leadership style affecting key change efforts' success.

____ Provide coaching to executives as they lead their change efforts.

____ Give stakeholders a single point of access to request change resources on projects.

5. THE STRATEGIC CHANGE OFFICE (SCO)

Addressing change as a strategic discipline to build superior change capability all comes together in establishing a Strategic Change Office. This is a pioneering concept that represents the current cutting-edge of change disciplines—a wave of the future that will become more common over the next decade. The SCO is the key strategic discipline for ensuring results from change, managing your enterprise change agenda, building superior change capability, and sponsoring your Strategic Change Center of Excellence. As you read about this function, imagine having an SCO in your organization and its impact on change results, change leadership, and change capability.

The SCO is a senior executive function that oversees the success of change across the entire enterprise. It is led by the chief change officer (CCO), who sits on the executive team. This positions the SCO to ensure that the right change initiatives are launched to drive the business strategy, advocating for what is needed to maximize results on these mission-critical initiatives, and ensuring strong change capability throughout the organization. The SCO raises the priority level of the oversight and support of change from somewhere down in the organization—usually in a program management office—up to the C-suite. It houses your Strategic Change Center of Excellence, which enables it to access the most skilled resources, services, and methods for all major change efforts.

The SCO does not "own" all of the priority change initiatives; rather, it creates the conditions for them to be optimally successful! The SCO leader and its consultants partner with the executive sponsors of key initiatives to support those leaders to accurately scope and successfully launch their change efforts. The executives still own the decisions about what needs to change to implement their business priorities and the strategic decisions about how they are run. But instead of simply naming change projects and handing them off to project teams, the executives first engage with the SCO to ensure there is adequate capacity and capability to succeed.

SCO consultants work closely with each executive sponsor to create a change strategy that clarifies change governance, potential integration with other initiatives, scope, pace, and a true picture of the resources and time required for the change effort to deliver on its promise. The SCO helps assess the impact of the change on current operations and people, so other executives can know early on what impacts they will have to deal with and when. The SCO then secures professional change support from the Strategic Change Center of Excellence, the organization's content experts, and/or external resources to define and mobilize the effort according to its priority, desired outcomes, resourcing, and requirements.

The SCO enables change leaders and project team members to have far greater access to the executive suite when critical change-related issues emerge. Being knowledgeable about all the large change efforts in the organization, the SCO can more easily get the right senior leaders to engage in key strategic change issues, such as the impacts of taking on any new change, how it will or will not tax capacity and resources, what priority and level of urgency it has, what organizational activities can be stopped or modified to address capacity constraints, issues with external consultants, and what will be required of the executives collectively to ensure results. The SCO has the authority to capture the executives' attention when any of the change efforts—or the organization's capacity to deliver on them—are at risk. With this intelligence, the executives have far more capability to ensure the effective implementation of their own individual initiatives, enterprise-wide efforts, and, more importantly, the organization's collective business strategy.

The following list describes what the SCO is responsible for and the value it brings to the organization. You may wish to use some of the items to make your case for establishing an SCO, to shape its function, and to evaluate its benefit to the organization.

Functions and Benefits of the SCO

- Increases the speed and lowers the cost of change.
- Ensures major change efforts are directly linked to business strategy.
- Ensures that executives understand the implications of launching major change efforts before they make such decisions.
- Ensures the enterprise change agenda is appropriate, realistic, and vital to driving the right strategic changes.
- Ensures executive commitment is maintained throughout the lifecycle of each change effort.
- Ensures that the organization has the capacity to succeed in its change agenda.
- Ensures executive accountability for proactively leading change efforts until full ROI is achieved.
- Ensures that top change efforts have priority selection for staff and resources.
- Ensures effective course corrections of major changes.
- Ensures that executives have a peer to support them in modeling desired behavior and walking the talk of change.

- Ensures efficient access and best use of the organization's change expertise and resources.

- Ensures the best use of external consultants.

- Optimizes execution of enterprise culture change and leadership style strategies.

Summary

Developing change capability and conscious change leadership requires a significant investment in training and developing people and building organizational infrastructures, systems, and processes that support change execution. A key is treating change as a strategic discipline within your organization and giving it the same type of study, standards, and application you give to other strategic functions.

Conscious change leaders seek more than success in their change projects. They also pursue building change capability as an outcome of their leadership. They consciously use their change projects as laboratories of continuous development for all involved. They build and use their organizations' strategic change infrastructures and systems to continually expand their organizations' ability to change. In other words, they are always engaged in "C" work—improving the way in which their organizations change.

Building world-class change capability in your organization can be a critical path to sustained success, and a 21st century competitive advantage.

REFERENCE

Ackerman Anderson, L., & Anderson, D. (2010). *The change leader's roadmap* (2nd ed.). San Francisco: Pfeiffer.

About Being First, Inc.

For thirty years, Being First, Inc. has specialized in one thing—*maximizing results from change* for clients from all industries, government, and large nonprofits. We ensure successful change projects, specializing in organization transformations that require breakthrough business results along with profound shifts in culture, behavior, and mindset. We build world-class change leadership capability in our clients, develop their change skills, and license our change methodology and tools for enterprise use. We provide career-changing self-mastery training and high-performance team development in support of transformational outcomes, with a special emphasis on developing co-creative cultures based on accountability, collaboration, and optimal performance.

Our services include change leadership training, consulting, coaching, executive team development, consultant certification, change audits and assessments, and licensing our change methodology and tools. Check out our two leading-edge books on organizational change: *Beyond Change Management: How to Achieve Breakthrough Results Through Conscious Change Leadership* and *The Change Leader's Roadmap: How to Navigate Your Organization's Transformation*.

Submitted by Linda Ackerman Anderson; Dean Anderson

Being First, Inc.

1242 Oak Drive, DW2

Durango, CO 81301

(970) 385-5100

deananderson@beingfirst.com

lindasaa@beingfirst.com

www.beingfirst.com

www.changeleadersnetwork.com

Bonus Activity V.1

Exploring Culture Through the Canyon

ROOT LEARNING, INC.

CANYON CONTEXT

This Learning Map visual represents the challenges most organizations face as they try to execute strategy. The Canyon exercise can be used with any organization, any team, and at any level within that organization.

OBJECTIVES

- To discuss the elements that foster engagement and form a culture.
- To explore the responsibilities, roles, challenges, and opportunities that all employees face.
- To discuss the critical importance of creating a clear line of sight between colleagues and the company's vision, values, and strategy.

INTENDED AUDIENCE

Directors, managers, and front-line employees within any organization. Small groups of six to ten people at a time can experience a Learning Map® module experience. The group is big enough for a variety of ideas and small enough so everyone can take an active part.

TIME REQUIRED

One to two hours, depending on group discussion.

MATERIALS

- A copy (or copies) of The Canyon image (available with this book's online tools). You may use one large illustration or multiple small ones so everyone can see.

AREA SETUP

A space large enough to accommodate a table, chairs, and six to ten people.

PROCESS

1. Welcome participants to The Canyon exercise and explain the reason they are here. State that they will discuss the importance of employee engagement and what we can do as an organization to bridge the canyons between leaders, managers, and individual contributors.

2. State that, during this dialogue, they will explore the challenges that many organizations face in engaging their people to execute strategies. Have them look over the entire visual and describe what they see. Allow everyone an opportunity to say something. Allow two or three minutes for them to point out images, and then move on.

3. Say, "Let's start with a problem that is increasingly challenging for organizations today. Read the Top Measures That Matter information on the chart at the top left." You may wish to ask for a volunteer to read the chart.

4. State that these studies by Ernst & Young tell us that investors believe that the "execution of strategy" is more essential than market position, innovation, or even the quality of strategy itself! But we also know that 90 percent of all strategies are not optimally executed within organizations. Ask, "In your experience, why is this happening?"

5. Ask them to read the News Flash at the left. "In your experience, does this ring true? Why or why not?"

6. State, "Let's look at some reasons why strategic change may fail due to people issues. According to the *Gallup Management Journal,* employees fall into three categories: Engaged, Indifferent, and Disengaged. Read the percentages on the cliff wall labeled Employee Engagement. What are some characteristics of each employee category?" If you wish, write responses on a whiteboard or flip chart.

7. State: "Engaged employees feel connected to their company, work with passion, drive innovation, and move the organization forward. What do you think is the percentage of employees at our company who consider themselves 'engaged'?"

8. Continue to draw participants into the discussion with these comments:

   - "Indifferent employees devote time—but not energy or passion—to their work. Actively disengaged employees aren't simply unhappy. They actually work to undermine the accomplishments of their co-workers. What do you think is the percentage of our employees who consider themselves either 'indifferent' or 'actively disengaged'?"

   - "According to Gallup (undated), actively disengaged employees in organizational cultures cost the U.S. economy alone $300 billion per year in lost productivity. How much do you think indifferent and disengaged employees cost our organization per year? How do these employees impact our ability to execute strategies successfully?"

   - "Consider the market and workforce trends shown on the tornado. What impact will these trends have on our ability to engage employees in the future?"

   - "Let's see how the challenge of engaging and aligning people plays out throughout all levels of our organization. Read the coordinating quote bubbles that span leaders, managers, and doers." *Facilitator Note:* You may wish to ask one person to read the leader quotes, another to read the manager quotes, and one more to read the doer quotes. These should be read in order (leader, manager, individual contributor) and by color: blue, purple, then green.

   - "Consider our vision, strategy, and value proposition. Do we have a clear, concise, and aligned interpretation of our strategic plans?"

   - "Do we have a clear plan and commitment to consistently execute our strategy throughout the organization?"

   - "Now, let's think about our broader organization. What are the key strategies we are trying to bring to life?"

   - "To do this, what knowledge must be transferred to our managers and front-line employees? What capabilities must be developed at each of these levels?"

   - "The majority of workers attribute only 10 percent of their own job proficiency to formal training—courses and books. Even with a strategic plan in place, it's essential to communicate that plan in a way that will engage our employees. The first way to foster that engagement is to provide opportunities to internalize

Bonus Activity V.1

learning. This is done best in ways that allow employees to apply their understanding in complex situations."

- "As an organization or team, where are our most significant canyons?"
- "What can we do to build bridges over these canyons?"
- "If we were to redraw this picture after we've bridged the canyons, what should it look like?"
- "What are the most important actions we can take to address these canyons and redraw the picture?"

9. Address any concerns that have been raised, if you can. If you don't know the answers, ask a volunteer to investigate and report to the group, or take this on as a personal task. Thank participants for sharing their ideas.

REFERENCE

Gallup. (n.d.). *Employee engagement survey*. www.gallup.com/consulting/52/employee-engagement.aspx.

About Root Learning, Inc.

For more than twenty years, Root Learning has partnered with the world's leading Fortune 1000 companies to help activate, execute, and sustain strategic imperatives throughout their organizations. Root Learning brings a unique blend of strategic consulting and proprietary creative engagement methods to solve meaningful business problems where people are the critical lever to success. Root Learning's talented global team of one hundred has connected millions of people, deployed thousands of strategies, and helped more than seven hundred organizations worldwide, including PepsiCo, Taco Bell, Starbucks, Hampton Hotels, Delta, General Motors, Dow Chemical, and Prudential Insurance.

Submitted by Jim Haudan, CEO, Chairman

Root Learning, Inc.

5470 Main Street

Sylvania, OH 43560

(419) 874-0077

sales@rootleaning.com

www.RootLearning.com

INVIGORATING YOUR TRAINING PROCESS FOR RESULTS

Introduction

According to the American Society for Training and Development's (ASTD) 2010 *State of the Industry Report*, U.S. companies spend $126 billion annually on employee learning and development programs. Above all, leaders seek results, so measuring your organization's development based on business results is a fundamental of success for training.

Business goals such as profitability and mission accomplishment must be identified as the target goals for measuring training—whether your organization's portion of the $126 billion has been invested wisely and has a return on its investment.

You can begin to explore potential return on investment even before you implement any training. Ask management for input:

- Will the selected development methods result in learning?
- Are the knowledge and skills the correct ones to perform the task, carry out the role, and achieve results?
- Have other employees been successful using these methods?

Ask highly skilled employees their impressions:

- Does the design incorporate learning preferences acceptable to your colleagues?
- Does the design focus on the right skills or knowledge?
- Have any skills been omitted?
- Are the materials, documentation, and content clear and correct?

Asking these questions may give you a head start on measuring by ensuring a good design.

Focusing on measuring training results is important right from the start. The strong emphasis on achieving results in training comes through in all seven of the chapters in this section. Invigorate your training and development by incorporating ideas from some of these experts.

- Chapter 26, "Getting More from Your Investment in Training" by RealTime Performance, presents the rationale and five factors required for creating a learning culture. It includes before, during, and after intervention strategies to ensure results.
- In Chapter 27, "Does Your Organization Have It Backwards?" the Kirkpatrick Partners present a practical three-step approach to delivering training that supports organizational goals. They emphasize putting business results first when designing and delivering training.
- Chapter 28, "Design the Complete Experience" by the Fort Hill Company, presents the four phases of learning necessary to improve performance: prepare, learn, transfer, and achieve. The chapter's checklist guides you through step-by-step.
- Chapter 29, "Engaging All Learners in an Age of Information Overload" by Herrmann International, uses the Whole Brain model to design and

deliver training that appeals to a diverse audience with specific focus on learning through technology.

- In Chapter 30, "Behavior Changes That Stick," Forum shares a process to ensure that learning is sustained and applied to attain desired organizational results.

- Chapter 31, "Reinforcement" by MOHR Access, reminds us of the importance of management follow-up reinforcement to training to ensure transfer of learning. The reinforcement strategies are practical and easy to implement.

- In Chapter 32, "Take Courage," Beyond ROI, Inc., uses the imagery of competing in an Ironman triathlon to present the compelling reasons for measuring training results. The five measurement guidelines offer good advice to a novice as well as to someone experienced to the business.

Chapter 26

Getting More from Your Investment in Training

REALTIME PERFORMANCE

In This Chapter

- Rationale for creating a learning culture.
- How an organization can optimize the training experience.
- Five factors for creating a learning culture.

The goal of creating and delivering training is to help learners attain new knowledge, perspective, and skills to enable higher levels of individual and organizational performance. Much has been written about the various aspects of learning design, theoretical models, facilitation, materials, and all of the components that make up a successful training intervention. Most people in training today focus on the learning event itself, because that is where the learning happens. It is not, however, where the business impact happens. Too often in creating and delivering training we ignore the organizational and cultural factors that reside outside the learning event. Ultimately, the cultural and organizational factors dictate the extent of business impact that your training will achieve.

The Opportunity

U.S. companies spend $134 billion annually (http://store.astd.org/Default.aspx?tabid=167&ProductId=19786) on employee learning and development programs. When interviewing participants who have attended these programs, we generally find they have a good time, enjoy meeting people from throughout the company, and appreciate a break from the normal routine. Many of these participants even pick up new skills and knowledge and, when pressed, will claim their experience was valuable and worthwhile. However, when we dig deeper, we discover very few participants apply their learning to achieving important business goals.

In fact, research studies peg the average number of employees who apply what they learned to achieving business results at between 10 percent and 20 percent of participants in training programs (http://stephenjgill.typepad.com/performance_improvement_b/2010/11/mckinsey-discovers-what-we-already-knew-about-training-impact.html). This means that 80 to 90 percent of participants are not applying the training in any significant way. If companies invested in training with the same rigor and analysis they apply to investing in equipment and software, there would be dozens of MBAs crawling through every training department in search of inefficiencies. Can you imagine, in this day and age, a manufacturing plant with a quality defect rate of 80 percent? That is exactly the level of quality most organizations accept today in their training programs.

Missed Opportunity

If you talk with the 10 percent to 20 percent of managers who actually apply what they learned, you will find they often achieve tremendous results. One sales manager we interviewed who attended a relationship-selling workshop attributed closing a $15 million office systems deal with one of his customers to newly learned skills. Consider, for a moment, that the relationship-selling course included nine other participants, each with territories and accounts similar in size to that of the successful sales rep. If everyone in the course was able to apply the new relationship-selling skills to close a $15 million dollar deal then, at least theoretically, this company would generate an additional $135 million in revenue.

If you are skeptical of this $135 million missed opportunity, assume for a moment that it is off by 10x. That is, the true missed opportunity here is closer to $13.5 million. Does that not still warrant further investigation and beg the questions: What about all of the other sales managers who could be achieving that kind of result and are not? Were they not at the same training? Did they not experience the same quality learning event? What is preventing these learners from applying their new skills to achieve business results?

Organizational Factors

When trying to determine why learners are not successfully applying what they learn, training departments often turn to the training event itself. We have all heard excuses about mediocre facilitators, poorly designed content, and useless exercises. However, from our research, most participants find today's learning events highly engaging and educational. When we ask learners what is preventing them from being successful, most point to organizational factors that reside largely outside of the classroom.

In this chapter we explain why organizations are failing to get the most they can from training and what they can do to fix the problem. And we tell you from research and our own experience how to optimize your investment in training programs.

The following real-life case studies highlight the important role organizational factors play in helping or preventing an employee from applying new skills toward achieving business goals.

Sam's Story

Sam is a systems engineering manager for a technology services company. He has been with the company for seven years and has eight systems engineers reporting to him within the mid-range commercial business group. His boss nominated Sam to attend the company's new leader development program. Sam's boss didn't say much about his reasons, other than that this was a course that Sam hadn't attended yet and it looked like an opportunity for Sam to "sharpen" his leadership skills. Sam showed up at the first day of a three-day off-site workshop without a clear understanding of the purpose of the program and what he was supposed to learn and do differently. However, the facilitator was especially engaging and Sam had a "terrific experience." He met many new people from other functions and business units, and felt that he "learned a lot." At the end of the third day, Sam gave the workshop the highest rating on the evaluation.

Immediately upon returning to his office, Sam told his boss about how the workshop emphasized the value of cross-functional teamwork. Sam's boss responded by warning him that trying to collaborate with the marketing and sales groups would be a waste of time. Sam's boss pessimistically stated that those departments didn't understand systems engineering—and furthermore, his previous attempts at collaboration with sales and marketing had failed. After that remark, Sam didn't try to apply any of the content from the new leader development program.

When interviewed about the program six months later, Sam could not recall anything that he had done differently since participating in the program that had contributed to enhanced business results for his business unit or for the company.

Carla's Story

Carla is the shift supervisor for a call center at a large hotel. She supervises three to four people each shift. In many cases, Carla and her employees are the first people to have contact with the property's guests. Carla was asked to attend the company's new three-day diversity workshop. Before going to the program, Carla met with her boss, who had already participated in the workshop, to discuss how the experience could benefit Carla, her team, and the hotel. Together, they identified some goals and outcomes that would contribute to their success.

The workshop was a powerful, life-changing experience for Carla. She discovered some blind spots in her treatment of others. After the workshop, she met with her boss again and they talked about applying what Carla had learned in the workshop to making her team more effective. These goals were made part of Carla's performance review.

One example of learning was Carla's interaction with an employee who had a "smart mouth" and a "bad attitude" talking to guests on the phone. Before attending the diversity workshop, Carla was on the verge of firing this employee. After the workshop, Carla agreed with her boss to change her approach and give the employee another chance. She met with the employee, praised her first for the things she had done right, gave her feedback, and then asked her about what kind of help she needed. The employee confided in her, saying, "I learn differently than other people." Carla discovered that all of the bravado and "over-talking" was the employee's way of compensating for her difficulties. Once this came out, Carla was able to figure out how to help this employee become successful. Now they work well together and the employee has become one of Carla's best operators. Carla successfully retained a valuable employee.

Beyond Training

Sam and Carla are examples of how organizational factors affect the impact of training. In terms of content and process, the new leader development program attended by Sam and the diversity workshop attended by Carla were both exceptional programs. Each event met the highest standards for adult learning. The programs had clear, meaningful goals, interactive and engaging facilitation, opportunities for participants to share individual experiences, and small team interaction to build interest and commitment. These learning events received very high ratings from participants. Even so, our stories of Sam and Carla show how factors beyond the workshop made all the difference. Sam was unable to achieve any significant business results, while Carla applied her new skills to retain a valuable employee.

When we ask managers why relatively few people are showing evidence of success from training, they mention conditions outside of the learning event, such as:

- Senior management does not understand the value of training.
- Our training department is not involved in strategic business planning.
- Our training budget has been cut severely.
- Employees are not learning what they need to learn to be successful.
- Training programs are isolated events with little follow-up.
- Employees are not given the opportunity to apply everything they learn in training.
- We don't have a way of measuring the extent to which training is having a positive impact on our organization.

Before, During, and After Learning Interventions

We have evaluated the results of some of the best leadership development, business acumen, team-building, and supervision skills programs in the field, and it is always the same. Unless something is done before, during, and after the program to support learning and its application, there is very little impact on the bottom line of a business. What we are suggesting here goes way beyond a little pre-training information packet and post-training reflection. Organizations must confront all of the factors that prevent learning from contributing to business success.

Adults do not learn in a vacuum. They need to believe that they can improve, and they need to believe that what is being taught will be useful to them. They need to care about the knowledge and skills they are learning. They need to practice what they've learned soon after being exposed to the new material, and do this in an environment in which they won't be criticized for being less than perfect. They need to apply the knowledge and skills to meaningful work. They need feedback. They need to feel recognized for what they have learned. And finally, they need to see meaningful results from their actions.

Imagine taking a golf lesson without being committed to improving your golf game. Or imagine not picking up a club again for months after the lesson or, when you do play again, not keeping score and not having anyone observe your game and give you feedback. It's unlikely you would improve your game very much. You might remember a few things from the lesson that could help your game, but you would not be maximizing the value of the lesson. You would probably be better off skipping the lesson altogether and avoiding the frustration. Even if Tiger Woods were the instructor, you wouldn't learn very much. However, this is what managers are often asked to do. They are asked to attend leadership training and development programs with little preparation, little support, minimal practice, no follow-up, and no feedback. And then the program is blamed for not bringing about the change that is needed.

Too often managers find themselves being parachuted into an instructional drop-zone. All of a sudden they are tapped to attend the latest and greatest training. Without preparation and without a plan for follow-up and follow-through, they are told to go to "Lean Manufacturing," "Seven Habits," "Good to Great," "Customer Loyalty," "One Minute Manager," or some other hot program. Most hot programs offer useful content that would benefit anyone, but they are wasted efforts if the other key elements of learning are not in place. That is why these programs go from hot to cold so quickly, which causes the program-of-the-month phenomenon in organizations. Employees attend and perhaps enjoy the experience (especially if held at an attractive location) and, in the short term, report that the program was beneficial and they liked talking with the other participants. Then, over time, their behavior and, more importantly, organizational performance do not improve. Still wanting change, executives and the HR department begin to look for the next big thing.

Companies today can no longer afford to rely on these isolated events to make a difference, whether a one-day skill-building workshop or a year-long leadership development institute. Maybe there was a time when companies could offer these events to employees without concern for results. Today, resources are too precious. You must make sure that you are maximizing the impact from every performance intervention.

Wanted: A Learning Culture

This means that, rather than a culture of events, you need a culture of learning, one that supports ongoing learning throughout your organization. In a learning culture, the normal behaviors, customs, expectations, and goals are all oriented toward learning and performance improvement. After conducting hundreds of studies of the impact of performance improvement programs, we have concluded that to create and maintain this culture, five factors must be present:

- *Alignment:* Align learning with strategic goals.
- *Anticipation:* Anticipate success.
- *Alliance:* Create a learning alliance between learner and supervisor.
- *Application:* Apply learning immediately.
- *Accountability:* Hold learner and organization accountable for business results.

The 5As Framework Audit found in this book's online tools will help you identify the areas in which your organization is strong and the areas where your organization's learning culture could be strengthened.

About RealTime Performance

Founded in 1999, RealTime Performance delivers online training products to develop company leaders. The products enable companies to cost-effectively assess leadership skills, make targeted recommendations for performance improvement, and empower employees to create and share development plans to achieve business goals. The company's flagship web-based training product, Inspire, provides a self-directed means for employees to manage their career development, giving them access to knowledge and skills at the point of need. If you would like help applying the 5As Framework at your organization, or implementing the 5As Framework audit, contact RealTime Performance. Read more in the book *Getting More From Your Investment in Training: The 5As Framework*.

Submitted by Sean P. Murray, CEO; Stephen J. Gill

RealTime Performance

603 Stewart Street, Suite 800

Seattle, WA 98101

(206) 749-9000

seanm@realtimeperformance.com

www.realtimeperformance.com

Chapter 27

Does Your Organization Have It Backwards?

KIRKPATRICK PARTNERS

In This Chapter

- Using Kirkpatrick's model to maximize training results by focusing on business results.

- How to put "business results" first when designing and delivering training.

Attracting, developing, and retaining top talent is critical for maximizing business results. Correspondingly, many organizations identify top talent retention and development as strategic goals. This approach should be rethought. Strategic goals should represent what the business was created to produce or deliver. No business is actually in business to retain or develop their top talent; it is simply a means to an end. True business goals like profitability and mission accomplishment should be identified as the target for initiatives. Retaining top talent is a collateral benefit; it could be considered applause for a job well done.

There is tremendous pressure on training and learning to produce measurable results. This pressure has resulted in many training departments resorting to reporting what they can indeed quantify and measure—things like the number of participants in training classes, hours of training, and post program customer satisfaction scores. Unfortunately, these so-called results have little or no relationship to what matters to an organization: maintaining and increasing profitability and accomplishing the highest level mission.

There also seems to be a misconception about what training alone can actually accomplish. Some organizations apply training, as if a bandage, any time there is a talent issue, and assume that some time in the classroom will heal the wound and fix the problem. Training professionals often know that this won't work, but they lack the stature in the organization and relationships to hold the necessary conversations before training is selected as the panacea for the problem of the day. So the training professionals continue to conduct the requested training, sometimes knowing that it will have little or no positive effect on the problem.

This chapter presents a simple yet effective approach to talent development that will support the highest level results of any organization, no matter the size, type, or sector. There are just three steps:

1. Focus on business-level results.

2. Realign training resources to support on-the-job learning and performance.

3. Make formal learning efficient and tactical.

Step 1: Focus on Business-Level Results

Any successful talent development initiative starts with clear definition and understanding of the most important organizational outcomes. It is important to note that talent development itself is not an organizational outcome; it is a required component that will support it. With this in mind, talent development initiatives can be focused so that the effort and resources expended actually do impact the highest level results the organization needs to accomplish. This focus maximizes results and minimizes resources employed.

This can be accomplished by using the Kirkpatrick Model (Figure 27.1) in reverse during the planning phase: starting with Level 4 Results, then moving backward to Level 3 Behavior, then considering Levels 2 and 1. The balance of this chapter describes this process.

Using the Kirkpatrick Model in reverse during the planning phase eliminates two common problems found with many initiatives: too much focus on training and learning and not enough focus on on-the-job performance and application of what was taught.

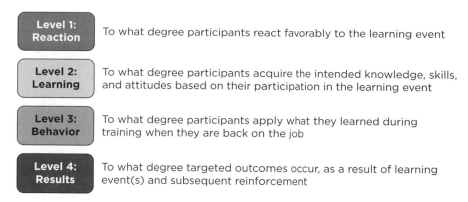

Figure 27.1 The Kirkpatrick Model

Many well-meaning initiatives start with Level 1. This is evidenced by current statistics: 78 percent of all programs are measured at Level 1, 49 percent at Level 2, 25 percent at Level 3, and 7 percent at Level 4 (ASTD, 2009). These figures illustrate the first problem well: when there is not a plan that starts with the highest level result as the goal for initiatives, organizations spend most of their time, money, and resources on training and fail to support on-the-job behavior, where help is needed the most.

Another challenge that starting with the four levels in reverse can eliminate is myopically focusing on training as the solution itself to the problem. For example, if there is a training program designed to teach participants to resolve conflicts efficiently and diplomatically, the overall goal of the program should be linked to better working relationships that are more productive that yield higher output; this all contributes to company profitability. Stating the overall goal as teaching participants to resolve conflicts diminishes the overall importance of the initiative and keeps it stuck at Levels 1 and 2. Examples of appropriate organizational level results to which initiatives should be targeted include increased revenue, cost savings, customer satisfaction, brand recognition, earnings per share, and market share.

Another important component of this step is resource allocation. The time, money, and effort available for the initiative have to be in line with expected impact on the highest level results. In other words, high expectations will require a high level of resources.

As basic and simple as starting with the desired end result in mind sounds, this first step is where many initiatives become misguided. Research by Jack and Patti Phillips revealed that in a study group of ninety-six CEOs, only 11 percent of them

Does Your Organization Have It Backwards?

are currently receiving data on Level 3 Behavior, while 61 percent of them want those metrics in the future. Even more troubling, only 8 percent of them reported that "our programs are driving our top five business measures in the organization," while 96 percent of them said this is critical to future success (Phillips & Phillips, 2009).

Frustration with the seeming inability to relate a single training class to a high-level organizational mission is common. Leading indicators help to bridge that gap by providing short-term observations and measurements that suggest that critical behaviors are on track to create a positive impact on the desired results.

LEADING INDICATORS: *short-term observations and measurements that suggest that critical behaviors are on track to create a positive impact on desired results*

Strategic business results by their nature often take several quarters or even years to be manifested. They are also lofty in nature. Leading indicators show stakeholders, managers, and training participants whether the initiative is moving in the right direction. They bring organizational results down to a level than can be grasped and embraced by every company employee. They also provide data to confirm if training and reinforcement are working or require modification.

Step 2: Realign Training Resources to Support On-the-Job Learning and Performance

Once a suitable organizational-level goal is determined, the next step is to identify the Level 3 behaviors. These are termed "critical behaviors" because they are the few, specific actions, which, if performed consistently on the job, will have the biggest impact on the desired results.

Critical behaviors are supported by required drivers: processes and systems that reinforce, support, monitor, and reward performance of the critical behaviors on the job.

The New World Kirkpatrick Model diagram (Figure 27.2) visually depicts the relative importance of each of the levels. Level 3 is the most important in accomplishing organization goals, and is therefore in a large bulls-eye configuration.

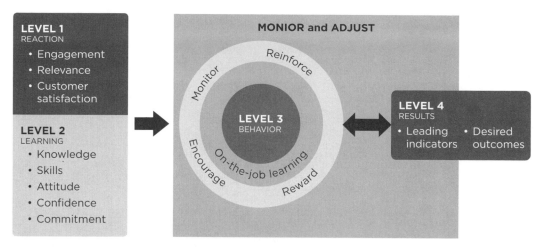

Figure 27.2 The New World Kirkpatrick Model
© 2010–2011 Kirkpatrick Partners, LLC. All rights reserved.

> **REQUIRED DRIVERS:** *processes and systems that reinforce, support, monitor, and reward performance of critical behaviors on the job*

Organizations that put a strong emphasis on the reinforcement of training through accountability and support can expect as much as 85 percent transfer of learning to behavior. Conversely, companies that rely primarily on training events alone achieve around a 15 percent application rate (Brinkerhoff, 2006).

Required drivers (Figure 27.3) are the key to accomplishing learning transfer. They decrease the likelihood of people falling through the cracks or deliberately crawling through the cracks (if they aren't interested in performing the required behaviors). These reinforcing processes and systems cannot merely exist; they must be actively executed and monitored.

Support of on-the-job behaviors has unfortunately received a bad rap for being difficult and expensive. Based on the variety of required drivers available, it is neither difficult nor expensive to execute an on-the-job support plan. Training and business professionals should together review the learning transfer statistics and come to an agreement during the planning stage of an initiative to determine who will perform and measure each driver.

Does Your Organization Have It Backwards?

Support	Reinforce	Follow-up modules	Refreshers
		Work review checklist	Job aids
		On-the-job training (OJT)	Reminders
		Self-directed learning	Executive modling
	Encourage	Coaching	Mentoring
	Reward	Recognition	Pay for performance
		Bonsuses	
Accountablity	Monitor	Action learning	Action planing
		Interviews	Dashboard
		Observation	Work review
		Self monitoring	Survey
		KPIs (Key performance indicators)	

Figure 27.3 Required Drivers

Step 3: Make Formal Learning Efficient and Tactical

Today almost 50 percent of the training evaluation budget is spent measuring Level 1. Add to this the 23 percent spent on Level 2 testing, which has little correlation to the training participant's ability to later perform the task on the job (ASTD, 2009). The end result is that a disproportionate share of resources is spent in areas with little direct organizational value.

Focus training on teaching participants what they need to know to confidently perform the desired on-the-job behaviors. Get rid of the rest. This tactical approach will focus the resources required to support on-the-job performance. This is where the most impact can be made on the bottom line, by actually ensuring that the most critical behaviors are performed reliably. From there, results will happen, and collateral benefits like increased talent retention and employee engagement come with the package.

Failure of training graduates to perform the desired behaviors on the job is often inaccurately diagnosed as lack of skill, so they are sent back for more training. In reality, only about 10 percent of learning transfer failure is due to training; 70 percent or more is due to something in the application environment (ASTD, 2006).

Level 2: Add Confidence and Commitment

Two new dimensions have been added to Level 2 learning to help to close the gap between learning and behavior: confidence and commitment.

Confidence is defined as "I think I can do this on the job." *Commitment* means, "I intend to do this on the job." Addressing these issues during training brings learners closer to the desired on-the-job performance. It can proactively surface potential application barriers so they can be resolved. Gathering evaluation data on confidence and commitment also provides the information needed to diagnose the root cause if learning transfer is substandard. Some of the most common causes of lack of confidence and commitment are

- Lack of clear expectations
- Unsupportive or toxic supervisors
- A culture of non-accountability
- Conflicting and confusing priorities
- Lack of ongoing learning resources

METHODS TO INCREASE LEARNER CONFIDENCE AND COMMITMENT

- Describe how the training supports highest organizational goals in communications before and discussions during the event. Make sure everyone involved knows the importance of applying what they learn when they are back on the job.
- Allow enough time for skills practice during training.
- Near the end of a session, facilitate a discussion about what it will be like to apply the new skills on the job. If anticipated barriers are mentioned, work collaboratively on solutions.
- Include a question about confidence in the after-course evaluation form, for example, "To what degree are you confident that you will be able to apply what you learned?"

(continued)

- If an underlying pattern in responses points to shortcomings in job culture or environment, surface these issues and try to address them quickly so the training has a chance of succeeding.

Level 1: Focus on Engagement and Relevance

The current investment in gathering Level 1 reaction data is far greater than the importance this level dictates. Many reaction sheets include phrases that start with, "The facility was. . ." and "The facilitator was. . . ." These types of questions ask training participants to give opinions about trainers and training rather than how the event prepared them to perform a new task on the job. Engagement and relevance reflect the higher purposes of measurement at this stage and should be the focus of post-course Level 1 questions.

> **ENGAGEMENT:** *Some learners are demotivated by the mindset that they are being sent to training by their supervisors. This creates a lack of self-responsibility that transcends the learning experience and follows them back on the job. Level 1 evaluation questions can set the stage for learner responsibility if they are phrased as learner-centric questions instead of trainer-centric.*

Examples of learner-centered Level 1 evaluation questions include (Assume the use of a 4-point scale, from strongly agree to strongly disagree):

- I was fully engaged during the workshop.
- The classroom was free of distractions so I could focus on the course.
- The knowledge of the facilitator added richness to my learning experience.
- I will be able to apply what I learned in class on the job.

By transforming Level 1 questions to be as learner-centered as possible, participants will find more value in their training experiences. It will lead them to take both their learning experience and Level 1 reaction sheets more seriously.

> **RELEVANCE:**   *Relevance is also of vital importance for learning, application, and ultimate value. When training participants are clear about why they are learning the information and how they will be expected to apply it on the job, there is a much better chance of on-the-job application and contribution to organizational results. Here lies an opportunity not only to find out useful information about relevance, but to weave in other evaluation methods besides a survey immediately following a program.*

METHODS TO MEASURE LEVEL 1 RELEVANCE

- Use formative methods to ensure that participants see the relevance of the material during training.
- Use questionnaires, and individual and group structured interviews.
- Consider delayed administration, as participants moving into new situations cannot give informed opinions about relevance until they have a chance to apply the information.
- Query line managers, subject-matter experts, and program observers in addition to participants.

The New "Business Results First" Approach

Table 27.1 shows a side-by-side comparison of how many organizations are approaching their talent development initiatives, either with training in the lead or with the approach outlined in this chapter—business results leading the way.

Table 27.1 "Training First" Versus "Business Results First"

Process	Old "Training First" Approach	New "Business Results First" Approach
Step 1: Focus on business level results	Business leaders only involved to approve defined training program in the budget. A simple training needs assessment may be used to determine what needs to be trained.	Business and training leaders together define initiative scope and negotiate expectations and targeted impact on results. Necessary resources and level of effort required are also negotiated up-front.
Step 2: Realign training resources to support on-the-job learning and performance	Training professionals don't concern themselves with what happens on the job; it is the responsibility of the employee and their supervisors. Training professionals just hope that training "sticks."	Training professionals work with the business to develop required drivers and a plan to support them. Business units prepare to support training participants in application efforts when they return to the job. Training professionals offer continuous and on-demand learning opportunities for employees and conduct targeted Level 3 evaluation.
Step 3: Make formal learning efficient and tactical	Training professionals design and develop (or purchase) training materials. Each course is treated with equal importance. The goals are that participants like the training and actually learn something. Pre-training work may be sent to participants as indicated.	Business and training professionals make deliberate determinations as to what specific interventions will best solve business problems and challenges. Training professionals design programs that point participants beyond the course to on-the-job performance expectations and resulting bottom line contribution. Training professionals include elements of confidence and commitment in Level 2 evaluations and learner-centered components of relevance and engagement in Level 1s.

Your Flag in the Ground

Maximizing results through talent development is a goal that every organization can accomplish. The key is in the journey. By starting with results, focusing on employee behaviors through support and accountability, and then laser-focusing training on the critical behaviors, results will be maximized with minimal resources employed. The collateral benefit is that talent development happens along the way, and retention also occurs. Why? Because this process helps each employee to see his or her role in the big picture, shows why they are important, and helps them to be successful every step of the way. This is what makes talented employees want to work hard, contribute to the organization, and stay to see their work come to positive fruition.

Check out this chapter's online tools to support your next step.

REFERENCES

ASTD. (2006). *State of the industry: ASTD's annual review of trends in workplace learning and performance. Alexandria,* VA: Author.

ASTD. (2009). *Value of evaluation study.* Alexandria, VA: Author.

Brinkerhoff, R.O. (2006). *Telling training's story: Evaluation made simple, credible and effective.* San Francisco: Berrett-Koehler.

Phillips, J., & Phillips, P. (2009, August). Measuring what matters: How CEOs view the success of learning and development, *T+D.*

About Kirkpatrick Partners

Kirkpatrick Partners is proud to be the One and Only Kirkpatrick® company, and the only provider of authentic Kirkpatrick® products and programs. The company carries on the work of Don Kirkpatrick, Ph.D., and the Kirkpatrick Model. Kirkpatrick Partners offers training, consulting, impact studies, and books and other written resources on the Kirkpatrick Four Levels and related concepts. Kirkpatrick Partners, LLC, was established in 2008 to respond to a growing need for companies to rationalize the resources dedicated to training.

Kirkpatrick Partners is firmly grounded in the principles that Don Kirkpatrick created over fifty years ago. Don remains active in the company as a presenter, consultant, and the honorary chairman. Jim, Don's son, is a senior consultant with the company. Don's daughter-in-law, Wendy, is the founder and managing director. Kirkpatrick Partners proudly continues to reinforce the importance of the Four Levels around the world. In addition, the newer Kirkpatrick Business Partnership Model and Kirkpatrick Foundational Principles underpin all products and programs the company provides.

Submitted by James D. Kirkpatrick; Wendy Kayser Kirkpatrick

Kirkpatrick Partners

124 N Rock Hill Road

St. Louis, MO 63119

(443) 856-4500

information@kirkpatrickpartners.com

www.kirkpatrickpartners.com

Chapter 28

Design the Complete Experience

FORT HILL COMPANY

In This Chapter

- Four-phase model for developing talent.
- How to design the complete learning experience to achieve business results.
- Ideas to ensure transfer of learning to a higher performance level.

Developing talent that produces organizational results is a long-term process. It takes time and a carefully planned development pathway that includes a mixture of structured and informal learning as well as developmental experiences and assignments. Formal leadership and managerial development programs are important components of the process, but too often they are treated like isolated events, rather than as part of a continuum.

In researching our book, *The Six Disciplines of Breakthrough Learning,* we discovered that the organizations that obtained the greatest return on their training investments were those that designed the *complete* learning experience—including what needs to happen before and after class—rather than just focusing on the event itself. We realized that learning programs need to include four phases—preparation, learning, transfer, and achievement—if they are to most effectively support talent development. We present here a four-phase model and a checklist for the complete learning experience that have proven valuable in designing and reviewing learning programs by those charged with developing talent for organizational results.

The Complete Experience

No one disputes the importance of developing talent in today's environment, in which competitive advantage depends much more on human capital and know-how than on bricks and mortar. Yet most companies continue to approach development as a disconnected series of events that start and end at the classroom door. A recent study by McKinsey & Company concluded that "to improve results from training programs, executives must focus on what happens in the workplace before and after employees go to class" (DeSmet, McGurk, & Schwartz, 2010, p. 1). In other words, having great leadership and talent development programs is not enough. Organizations need to consider the entire *learning path*—which Williams and Rosenbaum define as "the complete sequence of learning activities, practice and experience required to become independently productive in a function or task" (2004, p. 5).

In our research of the most effective learning practices, we identified six disciplines (the 6Ds®) that differentiated high-impact from lower-impact programs. The second of these is D2: Define the Complete Experience. By that we mean going beyond the ADDIE instructional design model, which focuses primarily on the learning even itself, to embrace the learner's complete experience. The evidence is clear: what happens before and after a learning event determines its ultimate success.

Four Phases of Learning

The process of turning learning into improved performance has four phases (see Figure 28.1).

Active learning needs to occur in all four phases if a program is to be successful in developing talent for organizational results. Each of the four phases is described below.

PHASE I—PREPARE

Whether participants transfer new skills and knowledge to their work—and thus improve their performance—is influenced by what happens during the preparatory Phase I, long before formal instruction begins. Participants arrive at a corporate educational program with assumptions about its expected value. These assumptions strongly influence their willingness to devote time and energy to learning. Particularly important in this regard is the influence of the participant's manager. A pre-course

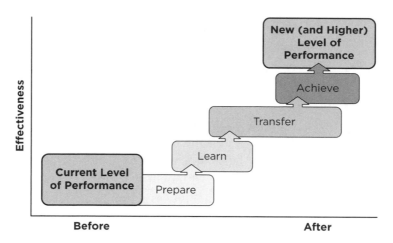

Figure 28.1 The Four Phases of Learning Necessary to Improve Performance

discussion between the participant and his or her manager has a powerful salutary effect on the subsequent learning and application and therefore should be encouraged—or ideally, required.

Phase I learning also includes background reading, online exercises, assessments, and other experiences that help accelerate and enrich the learning that takes place in the formal or structured Phase II.

PHASE II—LEARN

The second phase of learning is the structured learning phase, whether in person, online, or blended. By and large, organizations do a good job of planning and executing this aspect of development, although most programs contain too much content and insufficient time for practice with feedback. In terms of planning the complete experience, the critical issues for Phase II are to:

- Ensure congruence between the learning experiences and the ultimate business outcomes sought.
- Build on and reinforce the preparatory work of Phase I.
- Use instructional methods that are appropriate to the required behaviors and skills (not just PowerPoint lectures!).
- Honor principles of adult learning.
- Make the transition between training and on-the-job application strong and seamless.

Design the Complete Experience

PHASE III—TRANSFER

The leading reason that training often fails to improve performance is inadequate learning transfer. In most corporate programs, the training itself is well-designed and executed; the amount of learning is often substantial. But talent is developed, and performance improves, only to the extent that new skills and behaviors are transferred and applied to the work of the individual and firm. As we like to say: "The real work begins when the course ends." And that is the weak link in most training programs. Responsibility for learning transfer falls in the no-man's-land between the development organization and line management, with neither taking real ownership for providing the structure, support, and accountability essential to achieve enduring change.

Development professionals don't control the post-training environment to which participants return. But as Bill Amaxopoulos, leadership program manager for the Chubb Group of Insurance Companies, put it, "We owe it to them to have a major influence over that environment" (Wick, Pollock, & Jefferson, 2010, p. 95). Building learning transfer (Phase III) strategies into development programs not only serves the participants better, but it is also in the best interests of training and development professionals themselves. Management doesn't distinguish between failure of learning and failure of learning transfer. When the performance of someone who attended a development program fails to improve, management concludes that "the training failed"—even if the real problem was in the transfer climate.

We feel strongly that development professionals must take greater ownership of Phase III and exert more influence on the post-course environment. Transfer and application (Phase III) should not be thought of as something that happens *after* a program; it is an integral and irreplaceable part of the process. Learning transfer is action learning in which people continue to advance their understanding, skill, and knowledge by applying the nascent learning from the instructional phase to real-life problems and objectives. "In connecting training to how people really learn, you need to focus not just on what they need to learn, but also on the practice and experience they will need to achieve a high level of performance" (Williams & Rosenbaum, 2004, p. 18).

Strengthening transfer and application—the third phase of learning—requires providing both accountability and support. Participants in development programs should be educated on the research regarding the importance of learning agility as a criterion for further advancement (Eichinger, Lombardo, & Capretta, 2010). They should be held accountable for improving their performance by putting what they learned into practice as a prerequisite for future developmental opportunities. That requires a mechanism for periodically following up with participants after training to remind them of the need for application and a system to track their progress. The advent of online learning transfer support systems, like *ResultsEngine*®, has greatly simplified this process in recent years and made learning transfer support practical for a broad range of development programs.

The other key element in ensuring learning transfer is providing performance support in the form of job aids, online systems, coaches, access to experts, and so forth, to help participants master new skills and behaviors. Do not underestimate the power of simple checklists and reminders. Gawande (2009) found that a simple, three-part, nineteen-item safe surgery checklist reduced surgical complications and deaths by more than one-third, saving hundreds of lives and millions of dollars in healthcare costs. Benefits were seen in the world's most advanced hospitals as well as in developing countries, demonstrating that performance support benefits even highly sophisticated practitioners.

The point here is that to maximize the value of talent development, the learning transfer period has to be planned and executed with the same care as has been traditionally afforded to instruction; Phase III learning needs to be a conscious part of the overall design.

PHASE IV—ACHIEVE

The final phase of the learning cycle is to assess participants' achievements. There are two key concepts to Phase IV: (1) that there is a defined end point for a given cycle and (2) that it *assesses and celebrates* individual performance.

There are three solid reasons for including assessment as part of the overall learning design:

1. It makes expectations explicit.
2. It establishes a clear goal line for the learning experience.
3. Assessment is, itself, a learning experience; feedback is essential for continued development.

Assessment of achievement at a point weeks or months after training is the new finish line for learning. Program participants should be informed at the outset how and when their ability to use their new knowledge and skills will be assessed. Ken Blanchard told us the story of how, when he was a young assistant professor, he used to give the students a copy of the final examination on the first day of class. Other faculty objected, but Ken persisted, arguing that since the final examination represented what he felt was most important for students to take away from his course, then it only made sense to let them know that from the beginning so that they would energize and focus their learning accordingly. We should do the same for participants in corporate development programs: let them know at the outset what is expected and when it will be assessed.

The other reason to include this fourth phase of learning is that assessment itself is a learning experience. Assessments reinforce learning by requiring participants to retrieve and process the information long after the original learning occurred, which, in itself, is reinforcing. A well-designed assessment provides vital feedback to learners on what they have achieved as well as what they still need to work on.

Defining an end point for a learning cycle affords people the satisfaction of reaching a milestone. It harnesses the power of intrinsic motivation, which is a very powerful force for change, as Daniel Pink demonstrated repeatedly in his best-selling book, *Drive*. For these reasons, we believe that defining an end point at which participants' achievements will be assessed, recognized, and celebrated should be part of the complete learning experience design.

Checklist for the Complete Experience

The following checklist will help you ensure that you have designed a *complete* learning experience, one that will contribute significantly to your organization's commitment to talent development. Use it as a final "pre-flight checklist" similar to the ones that pilots use to ensure no critical step is overlooked (for a discussion of checklists in aeronautics and elsewhere, see Gawande, 2009). It can be used to evaluate and enhance programs developed internally as well as those supplied by training providers. A copy of this checklist is available in this book's online tools.

Phase I—Preparation

	Element	Criterion
☐	Selection	The selection or enrollment process makes sure the "right people are on the bus"—meaning those with appropriate job experience and responsibilities to benefit from the program.
☐	Invitation	The invitation is clear and compelling. It explains the business rationale for the program, summarizes its content, and sets expectations for its subsequent use.

☐	Preparation (participants)	There is meaningful preparatory work—reading, exercises, simulations, feedback, etc.—that will help maximize the time spent in the learning program itself.
☐	Preparation	A pre-program meeting with the participant's manager is strongly encouraged (ideally, required). Guidelines and worksheets for that meeting are provided to both managers and participants.
☐	Preparation (managers)	Managers are provided an overview of the program, its objectives, the business needs being addressed, and guidelines for their role in maximizing learning outcomes.

Phase II—Instruction/Learning

	Element	Criterion
☐	Use of Pre-Work	The preparatory work is an integral part of the program—so much so that those who do not complete it are at a disadvantage (or ideally, are not allowed to attend).
☐	Value Chain	There is a clear understanding among the design team and facilitators on how each component relates to the desired behaviors, capabilities, and expected business outcomes. These links are made explicit to the learners.
☐	Relevance	Relevant examples, stories, simulations, discussions, and so forth are included to help learners see how the material applies to their jobs. The achievements of prior graduates of the program are used to help underscore its utility.
☐	Practice	The agenda provides adequate time for learners to practice the desired skills or behaviors with supervision and feedback.
☐	Process Check	End-of-course evaluations include assessment of whether learners perceived the utility and relevance of the program and feel prepared to use it to advantage in their work.

Phase III—Transfer and Application

	Element	Criterion
☐	Support	There is a plan and resources committed to ensuring that learners can receive help in applying new skills and knowledge.
☐	Manager Involvement	Participants and managers are strongly encouraged to meet following the course. Guidelines are provided for those meetings. Ongoing manager involvement is facilitated.
☐	Accountability	Processes are in place to periodically remind participants of their obligations, hold them accountable for progress, and recognize superior effort and accomplishment.
☐	Process Management	There is a process and system in place to allow learning professionals to monitor, support, and manage the learning transfer period.

Phase IV—Assessment and Evaluation

	Element	Criterion
☐	Assessment	The finish line or "final exam" is defined as on-the-job performance weeks or months after the instruction. The expectations for on-the-job application have been clearly communicated to the participants. There is an assessment plan in place and participants know what it is.
☐	Evaluation	The "conditions of success" have been discussed and agreed on with the sponsors. There is a plan to collect, analyze, and report credible and compelling evidence of impact.
☐	Communication	There is a plan for communicating the results of the program to key stakeholders.

Summary

In today's knowledge economy, ongoing talent development is more critical than ever to an organization's ability to survive and thrive. Formal training will continue to be an important part of development programs. To be effective, however, training must be viewed as only one aspect of the full "learning path" to proficiency and it must be managed as a process rather than an event.

Highly effective development organizations practice D2—they design the *complete* learning experience, not just training events. That is, they explicitly *plan and manage* all four phases of learning to maximize the amount of learning that is transferred to the work of the individual and company in a way that accelerates development.

REFERENCES

DeSmet, A., McGurk, M., & Schwartz, E. (2010, October). Getting more from your training programs. *McKinsey Quarterly*, pp. 1–8.

Eichinger, R., Lombardo, M., & Capretta, C. (2010). *FYI: For learning agility.* Minneapolis, MN: Lominger International.

Gawande, A. (2009). *The checklist manifesto: How to get things right.* New York: Henry Holt & Company.

Pink, D. (2009). *Drive: The surprising truth about what motivates us.* New York: Riverhead Books.

Wick, C., Pollock, R., & Jefferson, A. (2010). *The six disciplines of breakthrough learning: How to turn training and development into business results.* San Francisco: Pfeiffer.

Williams, J., & Rosenbaum, S. (2004). *Learning paths: Increase profits by reducing the time it takes to get employees up-to-speed.* San Francisco: Pfeiffer.

About Fort Hill Company

Fort Hill is a consulting, training, and learning technology company that focuses exclusively on helping organizations and individuals put learning to work and prove and improve its impact. We are committed to the proposition that learning creates competitive advantage for individuals and organizations, provided it is properly targeted, supported, and applied.

Fort Hill defined the 6Ds˚: The Six Disciplines of Breakthrough Learning and developed *ResultsEngine®*, the first online learning transfer management system—which has since been used to accelerate the development of more than 150,000 learners in fifty countries. Fort Hill also provides advice and consultation on best practices in program design, execution, measurement, follow through, and marketing to help organizations enhance the beneficial impact of their learning and development efforts.

Submitted by Calhoun W. Wick, Chairman, Founder; Andrew McK. Jefferson, CEO; Roy Pollock, Chief Learning Officer

Fort Hill Company

1013 Centre Road, Suite 103

Wilmington, DE 19805

(302) 651-9223

wick@forthillcompany.com

www.forthillcompany.com

Chapter **29**

Engaging All Learners in an Age of Information Overload

HERRMANN INTERNATIONAL

In This Chapter

- Developing effective learning for time- and attention-strapped learners.
- Using the Whole Brain® Model to design and deliver training that appeals to a diverse audience.
- Choosing the right blend of online and offline delivery approaches for optimum engagement, retention, application, and reinforcement.

With the rise of social media, virtual classrooms, cheaper and more readily accessible technology solutions, and new approaches to just-in-time training and reinforcement, our options for designing and delivering learning have multiplied dramatically in recent years. But so many choices, coupled with a learning population that is increasingly pulled in numerous directions and dealing with a constant barrage of information and messages, mean that learning—no matter how it's delivered—can become one more distraction. When your audience is already dealing with information overload but you need to deliver important new skills and knowledge, how can you sort through the options and harness them effectively to achieve your outcomes? As this chapter will demonstrate, the key is to start with looking first at what we know about how people think and learn.

The tips and exercises provided in this chapter will help you develop Whole Brain® Learning—learning that reaches all learners as intended—using both traditional and new tools to their best advantage so you can reach better and lasting results. It's a perspective that will allow you to create an end product that connects more effectively with a diverse audience. In fact, the Good Science Studio team at Microsoft Game Studios used similar exercises to develop *Kinect Adventures*, the game that ships with Kinect for Xbox 360. Their goal was to develop a game that would appeal to everyone in the family, using our Whole Brain® system as a framework for design and decision-making. You can use the system to design and deliver learning that cuts through the clutter, generates buzz, and gets results.

Delivering Learning to Overloaded Brains

In the past few years, we've learned a lot about how brains work and how people learn, and the result has been an ongoing revolution in communication and learning—especially electronically. The arguments continue. Although we know that using technology in communication and learning can be a positive step forward, in what ways is it getting in the way of learning? And when it comes to our ability to process and retain information and new learning, is the on-demand instant access that technology affords a good thing, or is it part of the problem?

Let's begin with two fascinating but possibly troublesome concepts that are very much a part of the world we now live in. First, we know that we ask our brains to multitask, and technology enables some serious multitasking. Although the brain is designed to be linear in its processing, when we ask our brains to task-switch by shutting down one function temporarily and choosing another, we slow down our mental processes, which can lead to up to a 50 percent longer processing time and possibly up to a 50 percent error rate (Medina, 2009; Rogers & Monsell, 1995). In the tiny fraction of a second that we switch, it is believed that there is a mini squirt of adrenaline—enough to make devoted multitaskers become almost addicted to the constant stimulus of a new message. In fact, if they're not deluging the brain with an array of different activities, they can actually feel bored. The explosion in the use of social networking sites in such a short time frame is a testament to this phenomenon.

That brings us to the second concept: the need to have uninterrupted processing time for retention of critical content. When I was a French translator, I spent my day rapidly translating between French and English, but by day's end, I had no idea what I had actually said. Because my brain was consumed with the translation task, I didn't have any mental energy left to soak up the content. When we engage the brain by task-switching, either with one or more technologies or simply from the increased workload and responsibilities many are having to deal with on a daily basis, we will miss things and lose retention. The content I was translating was of low importance to me, so there was little consequence. However, when we have critical content that must be absorbed and processed and moved to long-term memory, we need to plan for processing time and protect learning time, reinforcement, and energy to allow the brain to do that essential work.

Given all that, we also know that technology contributes many positives when it comes to learning and communication. Consider the following four areas where technology can help solve challenges we face:

Technology allows us to offer options. That means we can give people what they need, how they want it, and when it's best for them. The trend toward learner-centric learning, as opposed to what's most convenient for an organization to create and provide, reflects the understanding that when you're able to deliver the learning as it's needed in the way your learners prefer to receive it, you can improve engagement and application. The more flexible options you have in your toolbox, the better.

Technology facilitates staggered learning. Staggered learning refers to learning that takes place over time, with processing breaks in between, as opposed to the all-in-one download of learning in one sitting. Brain studies continue to demonstrate the value of staggering your learning over time for significantly improved reinforcement and retention. Online communities, personalized learning follow-up, and other approaches make this much easier to accomplish, and we will continue to see a trend of usage of online technologies before, during, and after the core programs.

Technology helps us reach those who were once unreachable. Whether you use social media or not, it's clear that technology brings people together in ways that were once impossible. Electronic connections are easing the isolation of virtual workers, giving them a chance to stay connected across geographies, time zones, and generations. Face-to-face interaction is great, but having instant access to people who would otherwise be on their own has many advantages, too. We need to understand the positive implications of our virtual reach, scope, scale, and touch that just weren't possible before. Although technology has its limitations, we have an opportunity to harness its possibilities and accomplish outcomes that are different but still useful. For example, technology-based learning is often rated as feeling more comfortable and "safe" for more introverted learners, and it may even neutralize some cultural challenges when working with global teams because it allows them to concentrate more fully on what they are hearing, rather than being distracted by culturally different nonverbal signals that can confuse the message in a face-to-face situation.

Technology encourages innovative thinking. When my company partnered with IBM to deliver debriefings of participants' Herrmann Brain Dominance Instrument® (HBDI®) profiles via an online simulation and blended solution instead of solely face-to-face, we were concerned the technology wouldn't be able to duplicate the richness of the live one-on-one debrief. This is often a very personal and emotional experience for the participant, as it explores the person's personal thinking preference data, how those preferences may shift under stress, and what the implications are for the person's work and everyday interactions and productivity. While the profile data reveals the results from the 120-question HBDI® assessment, the debriefing ensures the participant is understanding and interpreting the results correctly. It is also what allows the person to see how he or she can get the full benefits of that knowledge, setting the stage for a system that drives better thinking in everything the person does. We couldn't settle for "almost as good."

But once we got out of our own way, we found that the technology would enable us to add enhancements that weren't possible in a face-to-face setting. The benefits included instant access to data on demand, the ability to stop and start any time, a personalized simulation allowing the participant to learn about the data in a virtual group experience online, a simulated environment reflecting the cultural diversity of the global participant audience, and feedback presented in a highly individualized and "safe" way for the learner. These are advantages we couldn't even conceptualize before.

All of these points—the positives as well as the challenges—have implications for how we deliver learning in today's always-on, increasingly virtual, hyper-thinking world.

Learning Designed with the Learner in Mind

The availability and applicability of technology-related learning tools, combined with the need for the three S's of scope, scale, and speed, have contributed to the now ever-broadening field of blended learning, where learning is made available in a wide range of media and modalities (online, classroom, formal, and informal workplace, offline, and others). By its very design, blended learning makes use of multiple learning platforms and processes, providing variety and options for many different types of learners who are often dispersed. It's a very brain-friendly approach when done well, and as new technologies become available, the options for creating an ideal blend continue to grow.

A challenge is that the field has emerged organically, starting from stick-on hybrids of content repurposed for multiple platforms that were not really designed for the platform per se. Just because something is built does not mean the learning will be effective across delivery mechanisms. e-Learning, for example, got a bad reputation early on because it often consisted of poorly repurposed content on a different and inappropriate platform.

Current research shows that in order to achieve good blended learning results, there are three essential questions to answer:

1. *Learners:* What is the best method for the target audience?

2. *Learning Design:* What is the best instructional model and delivery method for the content?

3. *Learning Environment:* What is the best method to meet your organizational constraints and requirements?

Each one of us as a learner is a unique human being with a unique learning style. Consider your own experience: You likely did much better in some subjects than others; surely you responded much more to some teaching methods than others; finally, you retained some material more accurately and for a longer period of time than other material delivered in a different way.

There's a reason for that. Our unique learning style is the result of the brains we were born with combined with the years of experience that have developed into our own distinctive learning styles over the course of our lives. So we're drawn to certain methods, materials, and areas of focus. It's not about competence; rather, it's about our *preferences.*

A recent study at Yale College in Wrexham, North Wales, demonstrates how we can use this understanding of people's learning styles and preferences to improve learning outcomes. The College used the Herrmann Brain Dominance Instrument® (HBDI®) and Whole Brain® Model as a means of identifying high and low learning preferences in order to find appropriate strategies to address learning challenges and low performance. The results of the study showed that this learner-centric approach, learning designed to better meet the preferences of the learner, increased students' achievement scores, motivation, and enjoyment. Students felt more involved in the learning process itself and had a better connection to the material, even though they may have previously had difficulty with the subject matter (May & May, 2010).

While every learner is different, our thirty years of research into these thinking and learning styles has shown that, taken as a whole, the world is a composite

A **Learns By**	**Learns By** D
Acquiring and Quantifying Facts Analysis and Logic Thinking Through Ideas Building Cases Forming Theories	Taking Initiative Exploring Hidden Possibilities Relying on Intuition Constructing Concepts Sythesizing Content
Learns By	**Learns By**
Organizing and Structuring Content Evaluating and Testing Theories Practice Implementing Content B	Listening and Sharing ideas Integrating Experiences w/Self Moving and Feeling Emotional Involvement Harmonizing w/Content C

Figure 29.1 Whole Brain Learning Considerations
© 2011 Hermann International

of different learning preferences, crossing the traits described in the Whole Brain® Learning Considerations model displayed in Figure 29.1. This means that any population of more than one hundred learners will represent distinct differences in their individual learning and thinking styles. Since each learner population will be diverse in their learning, the most effective training design and delivery methods will take into account an approach that works well across those differences.

The concept of Whole Brain® Teaching and Learning provides the basis for bridging the gap between the unique individual learner and the design and delivery of the learning. With a Whole Brain® approach, as outlined next, you'll be able to better reach and engage with diverse learners, improve their retention, and deliver memorable—rather than forgettable—learning experiences in an increasingly cluttered, fragmented work environment.

Step 1: Understand Your Learners

Review the Whole Brain® Learning Considerations model and think about the populations you serve. How are they different? Similar? If you think of each of these quadrants as four different people learning how to drive a car, imagine how each might approach the process.

Mr. A., Allan, would want to relish the technical aspects of driving, would be very comfortable with the mechanical issues, and would approach the challenge quite logically. Ms. B., Barb, on the other hand, would be ready and organized, enjoying the steps as they progressed: Sit in the vehicle, adjust the mirrors, attach her seat belt, etc. Mr. C., Carl, would be thinking about the fun he will have with his friends and spend time talking and chatting throughout the whole lesson. Ms. D., Deb, might be imagining the freedom she will have, all the places she will see and experience, and doesn't seem too worried about the procedures.

As a driving instructor, you might have all four of these students, and certainly may prefer teaching one or more over others. Fortunately, we are not limited to a one-quadrant perspective, but are "hard wired" to be whole. There is "wiring" representing massive connections that allow for direct interaction between these different specialized areas. The good news is that each learner does have access to all four quadrants, meaning that any given learning design will have the potential to reach him or her, even if it is not in the person's preferred style. The even better news is that when you are able to effectively plan for a very diverse audience, you can look for ways to use your blended options and appropriate technologies to provide different platforms for learning as well as diversity for your learners.

If you were designing a blended learning program for the above four (albeit stereotypical) characters, you could easily use the different platforms and options available to best meet everyone's needs.

More often than not, we do not know the preferences and styles of our learners. Thus, when in doubt, design using a Whole Brain® approach—chances are you will have that diversity anyway. Keep in mind that you will also need to think about other differences, including how introverted or extroverted the audience may be. In general, extroverts will want more interaction, either online or face to face. Introverts may be more comfortable with a self-study option. Generational differences may also come into play, especially as they relate to comfort with technology.

There are other aspects to audience diagnosis, including size and location of the audience, technical skills, and need for support. To ensure you don't overlook any critical areas, use the Whole Brain® Model to guide your own thinking. Answer each of the questions below (also organized by importance to quadrant) to explore other key aspects of your target audience and begin developing a learner profile.

Consider these style differences first:

1. *Assumed Learning Styles:* Across all four quadrants: A, B, C, and D.

2. *Introvert/Extrovert:* Assume both unless other information is available.

3. *Generational Aspects:* Expect differences unless you know otherwise.

A. QUADRANT (ANALYTICAL, TECHNICAL, AND QUANTITATIVE ISSUES)

Aspects to Consider

- *Are learners technically astute?* It is critical to know how comfortable your audience is with the technology solutions you may be considering. Keep in mind that culturally diverse audiences may have very different levels of technical skill. The lower the skill level, the greater the need for training on the platform and/or favoring non-technical options. In addition, bandwidth varies greatly around the globe; make sure all of your learners can actually access your type of learning.

- *How many learners are there?* Large numbers of learners may require more scalable online solutions (make sure the infrastructure can support it!). Small numbers may allow for less scalable, offline solutions.

B. QUADRANT (ORGANIZATIONAL, DETAILED, PLANNING ISSUES)

Aspects to Consider

- *How much time is available for learning?* Several studies have shown that online solutions can be up to 30 to 40 percent faster. Keep in mind that there are lots of variables that can impact those outcomes, especially available time in the workday, management support for the learning, and access to technology after hours if that is a requirement. If the learners are learning in their non-native language, you have to build in extra processing time as the brain is working overtime. Staggered learning will allow for a better learning experience when more time is needed.

- *How consistent is the knowledge level among learners?* Online systems can provide a pre-test assessment to allow for better alignment between learner, knowledge level, and the learning process. You can provide the basic theory in an online format for those with less knowledge and save time and effort on the part of learners who have greater knowledge. That translates into less wasted time and more value-add content for each learner.

C. QUADRANT (INTERPERSONAL, EMOTIONAL, SUPPORTIVE ISSUES)

Aspects to Consider

- *How motivated are your learners?* The more motivated your learners are, the easier it will be to sustain the learning process and achieve compliance with a self-study type program. Less motivated learners will need more support that can be provided through online facilitators, communities, mentors, or face-to-face workshops. Also keep in mind confidence and comfort with technology that can get in the way of motivation! Face-to-face interaction (online or classroom) may allow for better management of the motivation issues if they are present.

- *How supportive is the culture toward learning?* Workplace environments are increasingly demanding and may leave little time for the learning to take place, particularly with so much information bombarding employees every day through emails and other communications. Where and when will your learners be learning? The more you can work with local management to gain buy-in and support for the learning experience, as well as to provide follow-on workplace initiatives, informal learning options, and other opportunities that take into consideration the workplace realities, the greater chance your learning program will be successful. Will learners have support for taking the time to attend a face-to-face program? Participate in an online learning experience? Keep in mind the need for our brains to have time to reflect on the content for it to really stick.

D. QUADRANT (STRATEGIC, "BIG PICTURE," INTEGRATIVE ISSUES)

Aspects to Consider

- *How widely dispersed are your learners?* The greater the geographic scope, the more economical online solutions will be. Note, however, that online collaborative synchronous approaches (happening at the same time) may present a challenge when scheduling and navigating time zones. This solution can, however, provide an effective solution when face time is needed and travel is not an option.

- *How global or culturally diverse is your audience?* Cultural diversity often (but not always) goes along with geographic dispersion. Any online approaches should include a closed captioning option if the learning is in non-native language. The global consistency that comes from an online option is often a reason for selecting that choice. When face-to-face learning is an option or a priority (over efficiency), other benefits will emerge as different cultures may get to know each other more deeply than when online. Make sure your design process takes into account the global diversity of your learner population by building in culturally appropriate situations, references, names, etc. In any case, build in more time for "cultural translation" to occur for learners.

Step 2: Think About Your Learning Design

Now that you have analyzed your learners, your learning design and key learning points require the same. Just as in any learning design, you have to design the instructional approach(es) and delivery methods you will use to teach those critical learning points.

For the purposes of this overview, I will not discuss the front-end diagnosis of the type of learning but rather the selection of options and methods available to best engage the brains of your learners.

Epic ("Blended Learning in Practice," www.epic.co.uk) suggests three main categories of delivery methods and their respective lists, which I have annotated.

FACE-TO-FACE/WORKSHOP

Learning experiences that are not online and most often involve interaction, such as those in Figure 29.2:

- Lectures/presentations
- Tutorials
- Workshops/seminars
- On-the-job learning/training
- Role play
- Simulations
- Conferences
- Tutoring
- Coaching
- Mentoring
- Feedback
- Manager as developer
- Projects (action learning and other)
- Informal
- Apprenticeships
- Shadowing
- Job rotation
- Communities of practice

- Site visits
- Action learning
- Informal learning

INDIVIDUAL LEARNING METHODS AND RESOURCES (OFFLINE)

Learning experiences that do not require interaction:

- Reading (e-books, books, magazines, newspapers, articles, and so forth)
- Workbooks

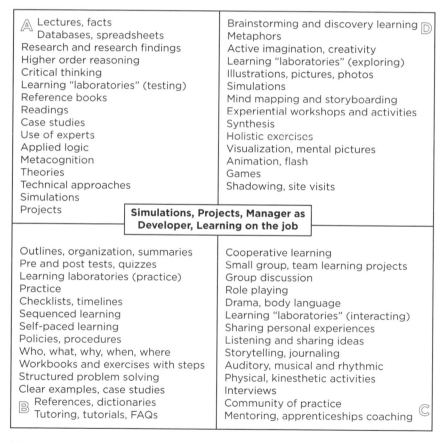

A Lectures, facts
   Databases, spreadsheets
Research and research findings
Higher order reasoning
Critical thinking
Learning "laboratories" (testing)
Reference books
Readings
Case studies
Use of experts
Applied logic
Metacognition
Theories
Technical approaches
Simulations
Projects

Brainstorming and discovery learning D
Metaphors
Active imagination, creativity
Learning "laboratories" (exploring)
Illustrations, pictures, photos
Simulations
Mind mapping and storyboarding
Experiential workshops and activities
Synthesis
Holistic exercises
Visualization, mental pictures
Animation, flash
Games
Shadowing, site visits

Simulations, Projects, Manager as Developer, Learning on the job

Outlines, organization, summaries
Pre and post tests, quizzes
Learning laboratories (practice)
Practice
Checklists, timelines
Sequenced learning
Self-paced learning
Policies, procedures
Who, what, why, when, where
Workbooks and exercises with steps
Structured problem solving
Clear examples, case studies
B References, dictionaries
   Tutoring, tutorials, FAQs

Cooperative learning
Small group, team learning projects
Group discussion
Role playing
Drama, body language
Learning "laboratories" (interacting)
Sharing personal experiences
Listening and sharing ideas
Storytelling, journaling
Auditory, musical and rhythmic
Physical, kinesthetic activities
Interviews
Community of practice
Mentoring, apprenticeships coaching C

Figure 29.2 Face-to-Face and Workplace Learning Methods: The Whole Brain® Way
© 2011 Hermann International

- Keeping a journal
- Review/learning logs
- Audio files, MP3s, and CDs
- Videos and DVDs
- TV
- Radio and music

ONLINE TECHNOLOGY METHODS AND RESOURCES

Electronic online learning experiences, such as those in Figure 29.3:

- Interactive learning programs (off -the-shelf and custom)
- Performance support (EPSS)

Figure 29.3 Locator Map
© Herrmann International

- Simulations
- E-tutoring
- E-reading
- E-coaching
- E-mentoring
- 360-degree feedback
- Email
- Bulletin boards
- Discussion forums
- Text chat
- Twitter
- IM (instant messaging)
- Application sharing
- Audio conferencing
- Video conferencing
- Webinars
- Virtual classrooms
- Cisco TelePresence/virtual meetings
- Searching knowledge bases
- Data mining
- Document sharing and file retrieval
- Ask an expert
- Blogs
- Vlogs
- Search engines
- Websites
- Social networks
- User groups

- E-commerce sites
- Second Life/alternative reality
- Online communities
- Gaming
- Videos such as YouTube

Our research has shown that different design and delivery approaches improve and facilitate learning for each of the four specialized quadrants of the brain. The two models show different design and delivery approaches by quadrants for online and face-to-face/workshop learning. Use them as a guide in creating the optimum blend of approaches across the online and offline spectrum as well as the four quadrants.

Step 3: Put It All Together in the Context of the Reality of Your Learning Environment

An important secret to successful blended learning initiatives, particularly as we consider how quickly the technology is changing and how the next big thing is always around the corner, is to do a reality check. It is very easy to get caught up in the spell of the technology options available. I have a colleague who calls this the dancing hot-dog syndrome: using technology that is totally unrelated to the learning just for the sake of the "coolness" of the technology.

Depending on your own thinking preferences, the growing list of options technology gives us may seem exciting or overwhelming. Either way, take a step back and focus on the two to five approaches that will best serve your design, your audience, and your organization—within its constraints. Keep it simple and always, always keep the brain in mind. You are, after all, a learner yourself. Put together a Whole Brain® team to help you evaluate your options and think this through. Then do your own reality check, such as the one that follows.

REALITY CHECK

Ask yourself and your team:

- Does this make sense?
- Will people really do this?

- Will the learning environment support it?
- Is this good learning design?
- Have we tested this?
- Do we need live interaction? If so, when and why?
- Does the technology add value or create distractions?

Use technology only when it offers the best way to facilitate learning for your audience and your learning environment. You want to ease, not add to, the information overload.

A World of Choices

This rapidly evolving learning environment means we have an obligation to rethink what we've always done and how we've done it. This doesn't mean we throw out all the old ways, but now we have so many more options that let us actually *anticipate* learner needs, and we can adapt, using internal social networks as well as face-to-face and online methods. It's not just a challenge—it's our responsibility to continue to push our thinking in a much more complex world of choices. The Whole Brain® Model gives us the system for organizing and harnessing those choices in a smart way to obtain exponentially better results.

Thinking and learning are the new currency in the age of the knowledge worker, and yet it's becoming that much more difficult in our always-on, fragmented environment. Everything you can do to help your learners better target their thinking, invest their attention more efficiently, and leverage their Whole Brain® Thinking skills more effectively will not only deliver results for the individual but for the organization as a whole.

Practice It!

Now you are equipped to think about how you would design a Whole Brain® blended learning solution for the learners we met earlier: Alan, Barb, Carl, and Deb. Keep in mind what you know about the environment, the learners' attention, and the vast amounts of information they have to process as new drivers.

1. How might you leverage the options available?
2. What would you do to ensure you address the learning styles of each participant?

3. What other issues do you need to take into consideration?

4. What would you add to a typical "driving lesson" to make it an even richer learning experience?

5. Where might technology be helpful and where might it create a distraction or potentially interfere with the learning?

Now apply it to your learning situation: Select a program you know well. Using the models provided above as checklists, evaluate it from a Whole Brain® perspective.

REFERENCES

May, C.H., & May, P.H. (2010, April 15). *Spotlight on learning: Using the HBDI® to improve learning, process, quality and outcomes at Yale College.* Wrexham, Wales. www.hbdi.com/Resources/Research/Yale-College-Wales-Using-the-HBDI-to-Improve-Learning-Processes.

Medina, J. (2009). *Brain rules.* Seattle, WA: Pear Press.

Rogers, R.D., & Monsell, S. (1995). Depth of processing and the retention of words in episodic memory. *Journal of Experimental Psychology: General, 124*(2), 207–231.

About Herrmann International

Because better results demand better thinking, Herrmann International gives organizations the system and tools to outthink, outpace, and outperform the competition. The company's Whole Brain® Thinking system is a comprehensive yet practical method that can be easily embedded into an organization's culture, learning programs, day-to-day practices, communications, and customer-facing initiatives to optimize thinking across the business. With better thinking, Herrmann International clients are able to reduce costs, sell more, innovate faster, and develop and retain top talent.

Used by nine out of ten of the Fortune 100, the Whole Brain® Thinking system includes the Herrmann Brain Dominance Instrument® (HBDI®) thinking styles assessment, the HBDI® Certified Practitioner program, instructor-led and online learning programs, job aids, facilitation resources, design tools, and consultative services. Since the company's founding in 1981, Herrmann International experts have continually engaged in research on the brain, thinking styles, and how thinking impacts organizational effectiveness. Today, they are regularly called on to share their insights with the media and present educational keynotes and sessions for major corporations, events, and conferences around the world.

Submitted by Ann Herrmann-Nehdi, CEO

Herrmann International

794 Buffalo Creek Road

Lake Lure, NC 28746

(828) 625-9153

ann@hbdi.com

www.hbdi.com

Chapter 30

Behavior Changes That Stick

Sustain to Attain Results

THE FORUM CORPORATION

In This Chapter

- Process to ensure learning is sustained and applied to attain desired organizational results.
- Suggested sustainment activities to close the learning/doing gap.
- Importance of identifying owners who are responsible for embedding behavior changes.

Traditionally, organizational learning and development interventions have focused on the visible, concrete, "main event" components of learning: virtual or face-to-face programs or workshops that introduce new concepts, skills, tools, and behaviors. However, a significant component of the learning intervention—the ongoing sustainment and reinforcement of the new knowledge and behaviors—is often neglected or overlooked. Failing to sustain and reinforce desired behavior changes is like neglecting to provide appropriate nourishment and support to a food crop. The neglect results in a less-than-full yield—a marginal return on the original investment. In terms of learning, this means that participants won't retain the knowledge learned, will fail to act in new ways, and, ultimately, will not master and apply new behaviors.

DEFINITIONS

Sustain (verb): *To supply with sustenance.*

Attain (verb): *To reach a goal with effort.*

Sustain to attain: *To supply nourishment and support over time to strengthen new skills and behaviors.*

Forum has partnered with many clients to implement targeted sustainment plans designed to help improve the uptake of new behaviors and processes in the workplace. Our experience shows that for these plans to be successful, they need to fit with the learning environment, with the nature of the work, and with the work styles and capabilities of the target audience. This chapter outlines our sustainment approach: how we've worked with clients to move from a mindset of "spray and pray" event-based learning to one of "sustain to attain" as outlined in Table 30.1. Our approach includes assessment of the learning environment, identification of ownership levels, and choosing sustainment activities that fit the learning environment and the ownership level.

Table 30.1 New Ways to Sustain Behavior Change

From "Spray and Pray"	To "Sustain to Attain"
One-off follow-ups after formal learning interventions	Multiple touches at multiple levels over time
Bolt on: Sustainment is added as an afterthought to the rollout of the "main learning event"	Dovetail: Sustainment activities weave through—short, medium, and long term
Push approach that repeats, restates, or drills key concepts	Pull approach that challenges and supports application

Traditional media: print, audio, video transmissions	Multiple media: Web 2.0 collaboration
Random or poorly defined ownership of sustainment activities	Defined ownership at three levels: organizational, management, and individual
Follow-up to track achievement of learning goals	Engagement to support, extend, and expand application and impact

Assessing the Learning Environment

A farmer looking for a rich yield examines the environment (weather patterns, temperatures, soil) before planning how to nourish and sustain a new crop. Similarly, organizations should think about the environment for learning whenever they embark on an initiative that requires changing behaviors in the workforce. There's a significant range of conditions in organizations that can impact choices about how to support/improve adoption and mastery of new knowledge, skills, and tools.

To better understand the conditions, Forum uses a learning environment assessment (LEA) to diagnose the current actions to support learning on the job that are prevalent in an organization. This assessment identifies what learning practices, processes, and tools currently exist in the workplace and then evaluates them at three levels: organizational, work group, and individual.

CASE IN POINT: TRANSFORMING SALES BEHAVIORS

One year into a significant change program to improve its sales force effectiveness, a leading U.S. beverage company took stock of its situation. The initial phases of the initiative had included alignment work, rollout of skills development workshops to all salespeople, and the restructuring/revising of sales processes. The company was committed to helping salespeople change their behaviors and deliver a more consultative approach to working with customers.

Sales leaders knew they were facing a possible stall in the initiative, specifically the danger of "flavor of the day," in which people pay attention to the initiative in the early stages of rollout but then slip back to old habits and ways of working. To address this, the company executed a sustainment plan to support people in applying the new behaviors and skill sets. The plan consisted of a variety of simple, hands-on activities to reinforce and support salespeople as they applied new skills and tools back on the job.

Six months into the sustainment phase, one tenured manager described the impact and uplift as follows: "These sustainment activities have helped us to move from obligation and 'We have to do this' to commitment and 'I get it! This stuff does work!'" Change happens over time, and people need support and sustainment activities to help them change behaviors. A "sustain to attain" approach improves the application of new knowledge and skills back on the job.

Picking the Right Owners

In the "spray and pray" world of performance improvement initiatives, organizations fail to define who specifically they expect to drive the behavior change and application of new skills and tools. It's assumed that everybody has a role, with the manager population implicitly central in supporting individual learners back on the job. As usual, when "everybody" owns it, "nobody" owns it.

In the "sustain to attain" approach, Forum uses the learning environment assessment to define the primary- and secondary-level ownership of sustainment activities. These owners are selected from the three levels below, which are further described in Table 30.2.

- *Organization drives:* The learning and development organization invests in centrally driven reinforcement activities and events.
- *Leaders lead:* The ownership and responsibility for sustainment and reinforcement work lies primarily in the hands of managers of participants.
- *Learners seek:* Sustainment efforts are in the hands of the individual learners. They select what they will do and how to sustain what they are learning.

Table 30.2 Three Ownership Levels

Organization Drives	Leaders Lead	Learners Seek
Centralized approach that creates a "push" out to users: multiple elements centrally executed	Leaders/managers of participants model, coach, and support learning for their employees	Individuals find opportunities and support to sustain the learning, based on their own initiative and network
Benefits: Consistent, reliable, aligned	Benefits: Active modeling and coaching	Benefits: Fit to individual needs
Drawbacks: Requires dedicated support resources and investment; assumes "message sent is message received"	Drawbacks: Relies on expertise of managers and on managers' prioritizing development of their people	Drawbacks: Variable interpretation—participants may not prioritize their own development

Once the primary and secondary owners have been identified, the appropriate sustainment activities can be chosen to fit with the ownership.

Choosing Sustainment Activities to Fit the Learning Environment and the Ownership Approach

Our experience and work with clients who take the "sustain to attain" approach to performance improvement reveal four categories for sustainment activities as identified in Table 30.3.

Examples ("I See It"): Activities in this group help learners see and know what they should be applying back on the job. These activities demonstrate and show people what successful application of the behaviors looks like. They provide relevant and regular examples, in a structured way, over time, to help learners see clearly what it looks and feels like to successfully master the new behaviors and tools.

Table 30.3 Categories of Sustainment Activities

Examples: "I See It"	Line of sight between actions and impact
	Models of what "great" looks like
	Stories that illustrate how to get to "great"
	Refreshers on knowledge, skills, behaviors, tools for great performers
Assessments: "I Need It"	Rating of current effectiveness
	Monitoring of improvements
	Identification of specific goals for ongoing improvement
	Active reflection on cause-and-effect relationships
Opportunities: "I Do It"	Deliberate practice as part of existing job
	Stretch assignments as part of existing job
	Temporary assignments (inside or outside workplace)
	Coaching/teaching others
Supports: "I Live It"	Recognition and acknowledgment that build confidence
	Future-focused feedback that builds competence
	Discussions that challenge, inspire, and validate
	Coaching that drives continuous improvement

Assessments ("I Need It"): Assessment activities uncover gaps in performance and opportunities for improvement. These activities allow the learner, line manager, coach, and organization to rate current performance and then use the feedback to establish and/or update improvement goals.

Table 30.4 Specific Sustainment Activities by Ownership Level

Sustainment Activity Categories	Three Ownership Levels		
	Organization Drives	Leaders Lead	Learners Seek
Examples: "I See It"	Refreshers, Reconnects/ Results Stories, Expert Demonstrations	Leader-Led Skills Clinics, Results Stories, Demonstrations	Job Aids/Tool Kits, Reference Materials, Role Models
Assessments: "I Need It"	360-Degree Behavior Surveys Impact/ Application Survey, Business Case	180-Degree Behavior Surveys, Manager Observations, Coaching Conversations	Self-Assessments, Active Reflection, Requests for Feedback
Opportunities: "I Do It"	Action Learning, Temporary Assignments, Leading Learning Assignments	Delegation, Stretch Assignments, Team Projects	Goals/ Action Plans, Deliberate Practice, Requests for Assignments
Supports: "I Live It"	Coach on Demand, Communities of Practice, Recognition Awards	On-the-Job Coaching, After-Action Reviews, Recognition	Self-Coaching, Peer Support, Learning Network

Opportunities ("I Do It"): Deliberate practice is at the heart of behavior change. Opportunities for application of new skills and tools don't have to amount to "ten thousand hours," but they do need to be more significant than a couple of notes in an action plan at the end of a formal workshop or e-learning event. The nature of the work determines to what extent deliberate practice needs to be in a safe or simulated environment or whether practice drills can be done on the job.

Supports ("I Live It"): Activities in this group include significant catalysts for change. Affirmation and encouragement are often underrated but have been shown to be highly significant in helping people to make a change in behavior and move through any short-term performance dip on the way to lasting performance improvement.

The four categories of sustainment activities can be defined more specifically by mapping them against the three levels of ownership. The resulting matrix in Table 30.4 defines a menu of sustainment activities available. The activities that are in the primary ownership column should be the focus of the sustainment plan.

Going the Distance: Communication Planning and Systems Integration

While the sustainment activities strengthen application of new behaviors and tools on the job, companies can also close the gap with a comprehensive communication plan and a strategy for linking performance/behavioral expectations to other human resource systems.

The communication plan should define what the targeted message will be over time and identify the optimal method or technology to drive communication (for example, communities of practice, learning groups, coaching the coaches, email communication, or the use of an internal portal or intranet). The communication plan ensures that there are deliberate "touches" to people a number of times so that the messages stick. It also creates clarity so everyone understands his or her role and what resources are available to support and reinforce learning.

Where appropriate and realistic, Forum has assisted clients in connecting learning initiatives to broader human resources systems. These include performance management, talent assessment, reward and recognition, and talent development processes related to job assignments and job rotations.

Seeking Expert Help

On the surface, the idea of transforming learning events into learning systems that include deliberate and broad sustainment plans may not seem too complicated.

Table 30.5 Developing a Targeted Sustainment Plan

Current Program Review			*Targeted Sustainment Plan:* Activities and owners to reinforce and maximize behavior changes
	Diverge: Identify potential sustainment activities	*Converge:* Identify best fit activities, given program and learning environment	
Learning Environment Assessment			*Strategic Changes:* Systems updates to embed behavior changes

A variety of externally developed tools and processes can help companies migrate from traditional event-based learning to "sustain to attain" approaches. Forum has developed a six-step process for building targeted sustainment plans, displayed in Table 30.5.

Using this process, we work with clients, typically in a one-day workshop, to define their sustainment plans. We work with key sponsors and stakeholders to complete the learning environment assessment, select ideas for sustainment, and identify best-fit activities for the sustainment plan. The outcome is an approach that ensures that additional yields can be obtained for the individual and for the organization.

The Execution Edge

While many learning and development departments consider sustainment an optional investment, it is important to understand that for the individual learners, sustainment activities back on the job are the real activators for change. They can close the knowing-doing gap that exists between knowing the value of skills and behaviors and doing something real to apply them on the job.

Sustainment is the phase in which the learning translates into new, improved behaviors and performance. Without nurturing, kernels of knowledge and rough skills won't translate into insight and mastered behaviors. Organizations need to put the focus on reinforcement and sustainment activities that get behaviors to stick, drive performance improvements, and yield individual and organizational returns on learning investments.

Developing Talent for Organizational Results

About Forum

Forum is a recognized global leader in linking learning to strategic business objectives. Our learning solutions help organizations effectively execute their business strategies by focusing on their most important asset: their people. We provide clients with practical and research-based advice and tailored programs that mobilize employees, accelerate business-initiative implementation, and improve agility. Forum's forty-year legacy as a pioneer and thought leader continues with the release of our latest book, *Strategic Speed* (Harvard Business Press).

In learning solutions, bricks are the content—the programs. Forum's "bricks" are research-based, modularized, and among the best in the business. But it is our "mortar"—*how* we work with clients—that helps us, and our clients, win. What does that mean for you? Quite simply, no single classroom event is going to get you the results you seek. It's how you construct and tailor the whole learning solution that creates something great and accelerates results within an organization. Forum is unique in our ability to mobilize world-class resources against complex client needs, delivering top-quality content in an expertly designed, expertly implemented, scalable solution.

Forum's approach to achieving results for our clients is different because we implement learning solutions that really move the needle. We perform deep assessments and engage with senior leaders to align the solution with the strategy. We drive core and consistent individual and group behaviors across complex, global organizations. We offer modularized content that can be tailored easily and quickly. And we focus on sustaining learning through coaching, reconnect sessions, action learning, and our new Speed to Mastery™ web-based reinforcement system.

Submitted by Vivien Price; David Robertson

The Forum Corporation, World Headquarters

265 Franklin Street, 4th Floor

Boston, MA 02110-3113

(800) FORUM.11

(617) 523-7300

info@forum.com

www.forum.com

Chapter 31

Reinforcement

Making Great Training Pay Off

MOHR ACCESS

In This Chapter

- Importance of management follow-up reinforcement to training.
- Five-step reinforcement discussion strategy for supervisors and managers.

"Raise your hand if you've been in the industry for five years, ten . . . , and so forth." We train managers who have often been in their industry for many years. It's not unusual to have people who have been with a particular company and even in the same position for ten, twenty, or even thirty years. If the group I'm training is more senior, I'll start the session by asking that very question. Then I ask, "Why are you here in a training session? Aren't you done learning yet? Why not? When does training end?"

The answer, of course, is that it doesn't end. The reasons participants give for being in training, even with experience, are the ones that keep businesses innovating, changing, and evolving. New competitors edging into your market, customer expectations rising, the need to find more cost-effective ways of doing the job, and so on are all reasons that drive the need to learn—every day. And yet, many of them, ourselves included, still use the same approach and leadership behaviors that we have for many years, even after attending a training session.

How many times have you attended a conference or session where the presenter was terrific? You probably took lots of notes and nodded throughout the presentation. You laughed, smiled, were engaged, and thought this was the best session ever. And then you went home. Back at work you struggled to remember the key points and tried your best to implement at least one of them!

Getting someone to learn something or gain insights from a training session is fairly straightforward. Getting that person to actually use what he or she has learned after the training is far more challenging and complex. Let's take a closer look at one tool that is key to ensuring that new behaviors are used back on the job, reinforcement.

Reinforcement

When a company has identified a skill gap or need for training, there is a substantial amount of time spent *before* any training is done analyzing who to train, how, when, and by whom or in what format, for example, e-learning, distance learning, virtual classroom. Weeks or even months might be spent on this portion of preparation alone, not to mention the amount of time for actual development of new material to be used during the training. Once those initial questions are answered about the population and training approach, there's the logistical side of getting ready, which might include reserving outside facilities, making travel arrangements, defining equipment needs, and so on. There might be a separate implementation plan that has to be worked out for national or global implementations as well as measurement criteria to assess impact. Planning and preparation for training can require a substantial amount of time and resources.

Assuming the actual training content is on target and has been developed with a credible learning design, either internally or with help from outside training professionals, you are finally ready to begin delivery of the training. The facilitation and/or delivery of training is fairly concise, almost blast-like when it finally reaches the audience.

While the training department or whoever is responsible for this training has been immersed in this project for some time, the participants might be having the experience of being dipped into a torrent of information for a very short period of time. Is there a way to involve them sooner? Using participants to help develop content does increase their personal buy-in. Unfortunately, this typically involves only a small percentage of the overall audience. When a company is embarking on a major initiative that requires training, it's important to remember that *training is change*. And we all know how much participants like change. Since there will be a new expectation, a new norm for performance and/or method to performing their job, reinforcing that new norm even *before* managers come to the training is essential. A Level 1 assessment at the end of the training gives you a sense of how confident or relevant the training was. It doesn't tell you whether people are going to use it.

The Manager's Role

When we're working with a client who is charged with doing a training initiative, one of the early questions we like to ask is: "What is the role of senior managers in developing their people?" The question almost always evinces some kind of reaction: a knowing smile, a frown, or nodding in agreement. What comes next is not always as encouraging. Many clients understand the importance of what happens back in the field, but they also know that senior managers are rarely interested and/or fully equipped to reinforce what was learned. Not to mention having the time to reinforce it.

Training of any kind is just the beginning. In order to receive a full return on the investment of time, money, and effort involved in being away from the field, it's critical to have planned follow-up and reinforcement. Managers often look to their supervisor's behavior to set their own priorities. Do they really want me to use what I learned? Is it really as important as they said? Will anybody notice if I don't change to the new norm?

The role of the senior manager is to ensure that what was trained actually is used. It's the best way to maximize productivity of any training. A specific follow-up strategy to reinforce any training you ever do is displayed below. This is a sequenced strategy that needs to be done in order. Make sure that each step is fully explored and discussed before moving to the next step. It will give you an opportunity to intentionally focus your senior managers' discussions with their direct reports about how to get the most out of the tools and skills they just learned. Have them use this within ten days of any team member attending a training session. Your senior managers' ability to coach and strengthen the leadership of others will produce clear, measurable results.

REINFORCEMENT DISCUSSION STRATEGY©

1. Discuss the importance of strengthening skills/tools that were trained and the impact on business results.

   - **Tip:** This step emphasizes the need to strengthen use versus waiting until it's a problem that needs to be corrected. Look for reinforcement opportunities often.

2. Ask your direct report to review any commitments made during the training for using what was presented.

   - **Tip:** Many training programs have commitments built into the material. Start here before adding more actions.

3. Ask your direct report to share results created so far with what they learned and what additional support they need from you.

   - **Tip:** The intention of providing training is to create a positive impact on the business and relationships.

4. Ask your direct report to summarize next steps and come to agreement on what each of you will do to keep use of new skills/tools a priority.

   - **Tip:** You should hear your report's "voice" here more than yours. Let the person think through next steps to create more ownership.

5. Reinforce your direct report's willingness to grow and apply new learning; set a date for follow-up.

   - **Tip:** Much of what the person may have learned is new. It will take time to make it his or her own. Encourage even small steps in the right direction.

Consider these questions as you prepare for your reinforcement discussion.

1. What will you say to discuss the importance of strengthening their skills and the impact on business results? Consider the possible reactions.

2. How will you ask them to review their commitments?

3. How will you ask them to share results created so far? How will you ask what additional support is needed from you?

4. How will you ask them to summarize and come to agreement on what each of you will do to keep the new training a priority?

5. What will you say to reinforce their willingness to grow and apply new learning? When will you follow up?

Research has shown that, when someone has a follow-up conversation with an employee about training the employee recently attended, the likelihood of that training being used is increased significantly (Bush, 1984). Just the fact that the person is asked about it, not even tested or required to prove competency, is enough to encourage him or her to begin to apply what was learned. When training sessions end, the facilitator's work may be finished, but the participants' work has just begun. The end of a session is the beginning of new behaviors and use of new tools and skills learned.

Think back to the last time you learned something new. Were you perfect after the first lesson? Probably not. What you had were fundamentals that required practice and attention. Who better to follow up and reinforce your efforts, as clumsy as they may feel, than your senior manager? It sends a powerful message that the expectation for change is strong and he or she has your back. Reinforcement not only ensures better results from more consistent use of training. It also builds trust and strengthens a critical coaching role your senior managers play every day. Reinforcement makes great training pay off again and again.

And the next time you ask participants to raise their hands because they've been in the industry in excess of a decade, you will know for sure that the session is not the end of their learning.

REFERENCE

Bush, R.N. (1984). Effective staff development. In *Making our schools more effective: Proceedings of three state conferences*. San Francisco: Far West Laboratories.

About MOHR Access

MOHR Access is a retail training and consulting company that teaches interpersonal skills that drive results. We focus primarily in five key topic areas with nationally researched programs, including retail negotiation, multiunit management (leading from a distance), store leadership, recruiting & interviewing, and sales training. Our national network of consultants can deliver one of our programs onsite or develop fully customized solutions for any type or size of retailer. We also conduct public sessions of some of our programs around the United States during the year. More information about those sessions and our offerings can be found on our website.

Submitted by Michael Patrick, Founder, President

MOHR Access

38 Oak Street

Ridgewood, NJ 07450

(201) 444-4100

info@mohraccess.com

www.mohraccess.com

Chapter 32

Take Courage
Measurement for Mere Mortals
BEYOND ROI, INC.

In This Chapter

- Compelling reasons for measuring training results.
- Five measurement guidelines.

Your company has invested thousands of dollars in a major talent development effort. The feedback is positive. Expectations for results are sky-high. But now, how can you actually measure the impact and organizational results? A brief measurement story is a good place to start.

I've not been this scared since I was a kid. Picture this. It's a beautiful morning at the beach. The sun rises over the ocean. Waves roll toward you from the horizon. You wiggle your toes in the cool sand and look up. A helicopter circles overhead. Your heart is pounding and your stomach is tied in knots.

You glance at those around you. Of the two thousand people around you, a few are chatting and smiling, but most are silent. Tension and fear are etched on their faces.

Your excitement is mixed with anxiety because you've been working, planning, and anticipating this day for twelve months. This is it. Your final exam. Welcome to the starting line of the Ironman® Triathlon. This is the ultimate measurement.

I'll never forget those long moments before the starting gun at my first Ironman. What a reality check! I was about to be held accountable for everything I'd done in the previous year. This included every lap in the pool, every mile on the bike, and every step on the track. It included every bite of food, glass of water, and hour of sleep. On this day, it all counted and it all mattered.

The Ironman is like truth serum. You must complete a 2.4-mile ocean swim, a 112-mile bike ride, and 26.2-mile marathon run—all in the same day—before midnight. There's no faking it. There's no place to hide.

Ironman racing has taught me the incredible power of accountability and measurement. You see, there's no way I'd train that hard, or eat that well, when left to my own devices. I'll choose pizza over broccoli any day. Only the certainty of an Ironman race day could provide sufficient motivation for me to follow an arduous year-long training plan.

There are obvious parallels to the realm of training measurement. In order to perform to our full potential, we all need a measure of accountability. That's why a key ingredient to getting great results from training is, in fact, letting people know they're going to be held accountable in the future. Otherwise, will they take it seriously?

Another parallel is facing the fear of the unknown.

Even with sufficient training, there are no guarantees you'll finish an Ironman. After completing three Ironmans, I've learned there are just too many outside variables: heat, wind, waves, flat tires, bee stings, muscle cramps, and the like. Similarly, measuring the results of a training initiative involves a certain degree of risk. Your first measurement project can be intimidating. There are, in fact, outside forces that can affect the results (we can control for most of them).

But which is worse? Receiving feedback on where to improve, or receiving no feedback at all? Your measures of success must match your goals. After every Ironman, at least one person back at the office asks, "Hey, Scott, did you win?" I look them square in the eye and say, "Absolutely." That's because my list of goals for the race have little to do with crossing the finish line first. That's just not realistic, given my age and genetics. Instead, my definition of victory is specific to my situation: get into shape, meet new people, relieve stress, explore my limits, learn some hard lessons, have fun, and finish without dying. These specific goals provide me multiple measures of success, and more than one reason to celebrate (especially the part about "finishing without dying").

There are many legitimate business reasons for investing in training and development—beyond generating an ROI (return on investment) statistic. I believe the obsession with ROI has totally missed the point. We're NOT in the business of training. We're in the business of transformation. Our mission both lofty and eminently practical: to change lives and help to grow the business.

It's time for a change in thinking about measurement. The truth is that, unlike doing an Ironman, the measurement starting line is very wide and the race is not reserved for the genetically gifted few. Ordinary people with no special training are conducting meaningful measurement and revolutionizing their organizations in the process. You can, too.

Over the last two decades, I've had the privilege of completing more than eight hundred measurement projects with firms as diverse as Hewlett-Packard and PepsiCo; from Novartis to Monster.com. Large or small, all of these organizations valued—and had attempted—some form of training measurement. A few succeeded brilliantly. Others displayed conviction and technical know-how but stumbled short of the finish line.

What follows are five measurement lessons "learned the hard way." They have proven to be invaluable guideposts for line management and training functions alike.

Lesson 1: Focus on the Business

You've heard often that effective performance development must be linked to the goals and objectives of an organization. It's true. That principle is called "alignment," and it also applies to measurement. Strong alignment is the genesis of all successful measurement.

Now every measurement project we launch with our clients begins with a detailed view of their business goals, challenges, and needs. That sounds deceptively simple. In practice, most failed measurement efforts lack a clear connection to the desired business outcomes. There is a critical distinction between training goals, challenges, and needs and business goals, challenges, and needs as compared in Training vs. Business: A Critical Distinction

---

TRAINING GOALS VS. BUSINESS GOALS: A CRITICAL DISTINCTION

Examples of Training Goals	Examples of Business Goals
Develop a comprehensive curriculum	Grow revenue 18 percent
Provide best-in-class blended learning	Cut expenses 25 percent

(continued)

Facilitate thirty hours of training per employee annually	Reduce turnover from 22 percent to under 10 percent
Ensure evaluation scores of 9.0 or higher	Increase customer satisfaction by 10 percent
Get a 5:1 return on each training dollar	Develop the next generation of leaders

Merge a newly acquired division into the corporate culture.

Both line and training functions tend to see performance measurement on their own terms. Why does that happen?

One reason is that the training group will focus, often exclusively, on measuring participant reaction (smile sheets) and classroom learning (pre- and post-tests). That's familiar territory for professional educators. If, by chance, the initiative fizzles, then evidence that "learning has taken place" is a tempting defense. That approach may suffice for technical or product training, but it doesn't fly for tracking the effects of service, leadership, or selling skills development.

I recently asked a group of ten training directors from the divisions of an $80 billion corporation about their measurement efforts over the last twelve months. Most had tracked participant reaction and classroom learning (Kirkpatrick's Levels 1 and 2), but only two divisions had linked training to new behaviors (Level 3). None had quantified the actual business results (Level 4).

The measurement efforts of this corporation were, in fact, typical of those I've encountered in other organizations. Tried-and-true smile sheets and pre- and post-tests are valuable tools, but meaningful measurement requires that you have greater insight into the driving business issues.

Another problem is that business leaders tend to develop bottom-line myopia. They want to measure performance development solely by monthly or quarterly numbers, sometimes to the exclusion of all other indicators of performance.

One line executive at a large, high-tech company focused primarily on tracking closed deals. "To win in this market, our people need to be better negotiators," he said. He was right. But a deeper analysis revealed a more complex picture. His division's margins had slipped, competition had increased, and discounting had become a crutch that account executives used to close deals. Major accounts expected and received deep discounts, so the company's desire to retain these clients sustained the vicious cycle of discounting.

In that case, we discovered that the critical measure of the company's negotiation skills training was not the amount of closed business, but rather the reduction in the use of the competitive allowance.

Together, line and training functions must dig deeply into the underlying forces that affect revenue, customer or client relationships, and business results. There are no shortcuts.

How will you know your measurement project is focusing on the business results? One sure sign occurs when the director of training and the head of a division meet to talk about improving performance and growing the business. If that sounds unlikely, keep reading.

Lesson 2: Build a Bridge Between Line and Training Functions

Meaningful measurement requires collaboration. Once you have a strong focus on the business issues, you have a foundation for building a relationship between line and training functions. So why doesn't it happen more often? I've observed an almost universal tendency: Training professionals don't initiate enough, and line executives don't participate enough.

For example, the training professionals at a medical equipment company asked me to help them devise a way to track the bottom-line impact of their new training initiative. I suggested that we get input from the vice president of the division on what to measure, but they resisted. They said, "We want to have this done before we go to him." Okay, so we just want to surprise him and hope we guess right?

Beware of attempting measurement in a vacuum. Often, the training group is made solely responsible for measuring the effects of performance development. Training professionals may try to select specific measures and collect sensitive data on their own. Without insight and involvement from the executive team, they're just guessing. What's more, they're forced to cajole other departments for data and resources. Frustration is a common result. For example, the accounting department at a major telecom company actually refused to provide the training group access to the necessary sales numbers.

What about line executives? There's a major difference between management support and management involvement. For example, busy executives at a bio-tech firm were extremely supportive of training: they rallied the troops and signed the checks. But they were reluctant personally to invest time and become involved in measurement efforts. The business owners wanted to see results, but the measurement effort stalled. How was that problem solved?

We put on a pot of coffee, brought together the line and training functions, and walked away with specific business objectives linked to the training. Measurement then focused on key business issues, such as growing revenue in the twenty top accounts and insulating them from competitive threats.

Instead of pointing fingers, training professionals have the responsibility to initiate aggressively, and it's the responsibility of line executives to participate actively. In every case of successful bottom-line measurement I've seen, both line and training functions were deeply involved in tracking progress toward common goals.

Lesson 3: Look for Progress, Not Proof

Nothing keeps organizations from attempting measurement more than a proof mentality. If your objective is to track the impact of training, I've found that absolute proof is impossible—and totally unnecessary.

At a recent conference, I had the opportunity to talk with Dr. Donald Kirkpatrick, father of the Four Levels of Evaluation. I asked him, "Since you introduced the Four Levels way back when, have you ever seen indisputable proof?" Without hesitation, he said, "No, I've never seen it." But he quickly added, "I've seen a lot of good evidence, though."

For pharmaceutical companies seeking FDA approval of a new drug or for physicists exploring the laws of nature, the search for proof is appropriate and necessary. Such empirical researchers appropriately ask: "Is there an indisputable relationship here?" But those of us charged with performance improvement should ask: "Are they using it?" and "Is it helping?"

Throughout this chapter, you've seen the phrase "tracking progress" used to describe training measurement. The word *progress* is the Latin root of the English word evolution (rerum progressus). Ultimately, the idea here is to track the progress, or evolution, of an organization from its current state to a new, more productive, and more efficient future state. In measurement, we're simply gathering evidence that progress is taking place.

Listen to the discussions in your management meetings. People are asking, "Will we make our numbers this year?" "Is customer retention improving?" They're looking for indicators of progress toward a goal. The real questions to be answered by measurement are "How has this helped?" and "In what ways?" That common-sense approach works beautifully.

For example, the direct sales force in one mid-size telecommunications company was plagued with extremely high turnover (80 percent) and dreadfully low performance. The new vice president of the division said, "It was painfully obvious to me that we had a big problem." Part of his company's solution was to implement a consultative selling skills program.

Three months into the performance development effort, our tracking showed that the company's sales reps had steadily increased their productivity by 42 percent. A group of new reps achieved their quota in just two months, rather than the usual six months or longer. The turnover rate fell steadily to an acceptable 28 percent, well below industry norms. When compared to the baseline and to reps not yet trained, those were compelling signs of progress.

Along the way, the company also trained managers to coach more effectively, tweaked its compensation plan, and reinforced new skills consistently. All of those factors undoubtedly contributed to the stellar results. We never proved that the sales training worked, but, as Kirkpatrick would say, "We found a lot of good evidence." The management team was thrilled.

Tracking progress, not obtaining proof, takes pressure off of the people doing the tracking and shifts it onto the people doing the performing, where it belongs.

Lesson 4: The Client Is Probably Already Doing Measurement

There is a widely held perception that bottom-line measurement is arduous and expensive. That's not surprising. So often, we've heard that Level 4 measurement is the most difficult by far. But the training world is discovering that it's just not true.

Recently, I was swapping notes with the Ph.D. responsible for measurement at a major U.S. computer company. He had successfully completed four bottom-line tracking projects, three more than planned. As we talked after a meeting, he confided, "I've realized that it's easier than doing a survey." I agree.

You can complete a fairly rigorous analysis of bottom-line performance before lunch, with a spreadsheet and a cup of coffee. It's possible IF you align performance development with the business, IF the line and training folks work together, and IF your aim is to track progress—not obtain proof. And finally, IF you tap into pre-existing data, solid results are easily within your grasp.

Most organizations are swimming in data. These days, companies maintain tracking systems for sales and service activity, inventory, scheduling, accounting, and prospect management. Additionally, there are ISO 9000 standards, MBOs, and performance reviews. In essence, every organization under the sun is already doing measurement.

The good news is that all that wonderful data already exists. The challenge is to select a few key performance indicators that are linked to a performance development initiative. How? Here's one example: Last year, in our work with a major consulting firm, we faced a mountain of options for the bottom-line measurement of negotiation skills. To make matters worse, the firm had extremely sophisticated internal data systems. After several hours of fruitless guesswork, we set up a meeting with the director of finance. We asked, "What do the senior partners look at on a monthly basis to monitor the health of the business?" With his answer, we hit pay dirt.

He unveiled a list of thirteen metrics rolled up every month to the managing senior partners. From that list, two key measures were associated directly with the firm's negotiation skills training. They included rate-per-hour and percent-of-standard-rate billed. By comparing those numbers before and after the workshops, we tracked the firm's progress toward greater profitability.

A good rule of thumb is to always look for the data currently being used to manage the business at the executive level.

For example, I frequently ask an executive for a sample of his or her monthly reports, or what's on his or her "dashboard." If that information is important to this leader, then it's critical to performance and is most likely accurate. That's a powerful way to develop alignment between a measurement effort and the life-pulse of an organization.

But what if the data used by the leadership team is not enough for tracking progress? There are alternatives, as you'll see in Lesson 5.

Lesson 5: Track and Connect, Cause and Effect

The most common question I hear when working with clients to develop bottom-line measurement is: "What should we track?" The simple answer is cause and effect—a principle that applies to any type of performance development.

Revenue, for example, is the result of something. We consider it to be a lagging indicator—or an effect—of performance in the field. In contrast, leading indicators—or causes—of revenue are building new customer relationships, qualifying opportunities, presenting solutions, and closing business. The powerful distinction between leading and lagging indicators pinpoints the most strategic measures of performance. When combined with deep insight into business issues and knowledge of the specific metrics used by a company's business leaders, it takes the guesswork out of tracking progress.

Here's another example: I met with both the director of sales and the training coordinator at a major electronics company to develop bottom-line measurement. The company's business goals included increasing revenue by 20 percent and maintaining current levels of profitability. The business challenges included an over-reliance on demonstrations to sell products. In addition, the reps were getting trapped at the technical level and had limited influence with actual decision-makers.

The company decided to implement a consultative selling skills program. Our team selected two leading indicators and two lagging indicators from data available on the company's contact management system and accounting system.

The leading indicators included the level of sales contacts and tracking how often an actual decision maker was present for system demonstrations. The vice president lamented, "We have a tendency to demo for the janitor." More importantly, improvements in those metrics would result in progress toward the revenue goal.

The lagging indicators included tracking increases in the size of the systems sold (in dollars) and changes in the ratio of product presentations to closed deals (win rate). Those measures were both manageable and highly strategic. Objectives that sound like "galvanizing," "synergizing," and "energizing" may be well-intentioned, but they're nearly impossible to measure. By tracking both causes and effects, we ensure that a measurement is grounded in the most tangible behaviors and outcomes.

Simple, meaningful measurement gives training and development staying power in an organization. The best approach is to simplify. Just one or two leading and lagging indicators of improved performance may be all that are needed to run the race and cross the finish line a winner.

About Beyond ROI, Inc.

You may be discouraged by the cost and complexity of showing a return on investment (ROI) from training programs. Beyond ROI assessment and measurement is simple, relevant, and actionable. We help companies "Get the credit you deserve, so you can get the funding you need™."

Over the last two decades, Beyond ROI Founder Scott Watson has designed and delivered more than eight hundred assessment and measurement projects with companies like Microsoft, Cisco Systems, ExxonMobil, Dell Computer, Hewlett-Packard, and Accenture. These companies are looking for solid evidence of business results—not excuses. Today, we've moved beyond traditional measurement models like Kirkpatrick's Four Levels of Evaluation and return on investment (ROI) calculations. The key lies in linking actions to outcomes.

Submitted by Scott Watson, Founder

Beyond ROI, Inc.

5850 Town and Country Boulevard, Suite 1003

Frisco, TX 75034

(214) 872-1100

scott@getbeyondroi.com

www.getBeyondROI.com

TIMELY TRAINING TECHNIQUES

Introduction

The world of training has changed dramatically over the past decade.

A premiere training professional stays on top of the timely topics—not just content and delivery methods, but also information that is critical to your organization's success.

Content changes rapidly in some areas, not so in others. For example, staying on top of the technology in your organization may require you to rework content between every training session. Conversely, communication is a perennially in-demand topic, though even communication requires regular upgrades, such as how to write effective emails (see the first bonus activity in Section I).

Delivery is changing. Business simulations, virtual classrooms, podcasts, on-demand courses, and mobile learning all require staying in tune with new methods. Matching the right delivery strategy to the right content is a new challenge. No matter what your facilitation role, it is exciting to maintain (or gain) expertise in all.

Your organization's needs change also. A new role you may have is ensuring that wisdom is transferred as experienced people leave your organization. When your organization's strategy changes, you have to be ready to change with it by knowing which competencies are required to achieve the organization's goals. You may find yourself needing to conduct a "training triage" or two.

Don't be satisfied with merely good. Discover what it takes to be a great training professional. The five timely chapters in this section ensure that you will look at your training with a fresh perspective. The content in this section varies widely from how to be a better facilitator to how to teach wisdom to ways to improve your online learning events.

- Chapter 33, "The Seven Separators of Great Facilitation" by Leadership Strategies, presents seven attributes that separate great facilitators from good facilitators. The tips and suggestions incorporated throughout the chapter are easy to build into any delivery.

- In Chapter 34, "How to Teach Wisdom," The Steve Trautman Company delivers a solution for organizations that are concerned about the transfer of tacit knowledge as many senior people leave for retirement, taking with them a wealth of knowledge and skills as they walk out the door.

- Chapter 35, "Maximum Value from Simulations" by Insight Experience, is about how to increase the impact of using business simulations during training. Choosing, structuring, and creating learner accountability are addressed.

- Chapter 36, "Virtual Classroom . . . *Real* Results" by Development Dimensions International, Inc. (DDI), sheds light on how to create a compelling training experience for participants. Use the seven elements to ensure more effective planning for your next virtual classroom experience.

- Chapter 37, "Training Triage" by VisionPoint, presents a plan that is efficient for busy organizations as they identify and implement the competencies required of a high-performing workforce. The workforce model can be used as a roadmap to create a high-performing workplace, as well as a model for diagnosing workforce problems.

Chapter 33

The Seven Separators of Great Facilitation

LEADERSHIP STRATEGIES

In This Chapter

- Seven attributes that separate excellent facilitators from good facilitators.
- Suggestions and tips to improve facilitators' skill level and increase their effectiveness.

What separates great facilitators from good ones? You typically know within fifteen minutes, and often sooner, whether a facilitator has what it takes to make it worth your time to sit through a training class or a facilitated session. Of course, every training facilitator must know the content, be able to communicate clearly, and deliver the learning points effectively. Yet, there seems to be something that distinguishes the best facilitators from the rest of the pack. Can we identify a set of skills that separates great facilitators from good facilitators? The answer is a resounding yes.

Figure 33.1 displays The Facilitator's Methodology™, the structured process for facilitation that we train facilitators to use based on ten fundamental principles and over one hundred specific techniques and tools. It is through this work with facilitators who have had a wide variation in proficiency that we have identified the Seven Separators—key skills that seem to separate top facilitators from average ones.

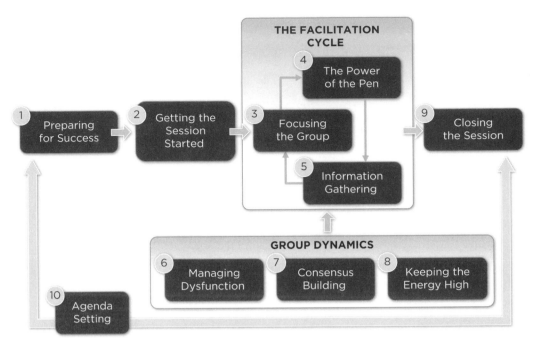

Figure 33.1 The Facilitator's Methodology™

It takes numerous skills to be a great facilitator or trainer. But for trainers who are already good at the mechanics, focusing on these seven skill areas will increase their facilitation excellence.

Separator 1: Level 3 Energy

Energy is a primary separator that differentiates great facilitators from good ones. Whether training a group in a week-long program or facilitating a quality team that meets for two hours once a week, great facilitators know that it is important to establish and maintain a high energy level. Why set the energy level high? High energy does three important things, which we call the "three Es of energy."

- Energy engages the group by getting their attention, gaining their interest, and keeping it fun.

- Energy energizes the topic. The facilitator's energy around the topic suggests to the participants, "This must be important because the facilitator seems to be excited about it."

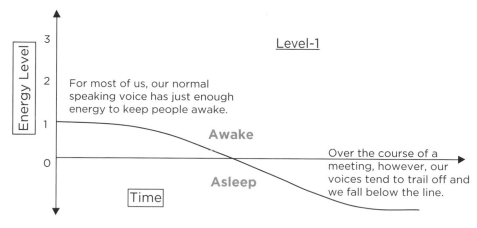

Figure 33.2   Level-1 Energy

- Energy elevates the facilitator in the eyes of the participants. Simply put, high energy projects confidence. Unfortunately, the complementary perception is also true: facilitators with low energy are *perceived* by participants as having low self-confidence!

How do you project energy from the start of a session? The first words out of your mouth establish the energy level for the session. Consciously set your energy level high by ensuring that you speak your first words at the appropriate level.

In the diagram in Figure 33.2, the zero line represents the division between being awake and asleep. Most of us normally speak with just enough energy in our voices to keep people awake. We call this your level-1 voice. If you start a session at your level-1 voice, however, over the course of the session the energy in your voice will tend to fall off dramatically. As a result, you will typically end up well below the zero line.

Let's say you raise your energy to level-2. Your energy level at the beginning of the session will be sufficient. But once more, over time, it will fall off below the line, as shown in Figure 33.3. To maximize your impact, start your session at level-3 energy, two levels above your normal speaking voice. In this way, when your energy trails off, you will likely fall back to your normal speaking voice.

Separator 2: Starting Questions

In most training sessions, there are specific times during brainstorming or listing exercises when the facilitator asks a question and is looking for the group to provide

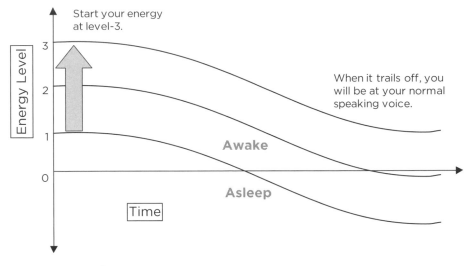

Start your energy at level-3.

Energy Level

3

2

1

0

When it trails off, you will be at your normal speaking voice.

Awake

Asleep

Time

Figure 33.3 Level-3 Energy

considerable input. Good facilitators figure out what questions they want to ask. Great facilitators are very conscious that the way they ask "starting questions" will greatly influence the quality of the responses. So they ask starting questions that draw a vivid image of the answers.

As an example, take a look at these two different ways of asking about problems with meetings in Table 33.1.

The question on the left is a "Type A" question. It asks what the facilitator wants to know. The question on the right is a "Type B" question. It creates an image that the participants use to visualize their answers.

Why are Type B questions better in most cases? When you ask Type A questions, you may very well get silence because people are trying to create an image in their heads—the one that you didn't create for them. When you ask a Type B question, people can "see" their answers and are very quickly able to respond with information that is directly on the topic. By asking a Type B question, you avoid silence and make it much easier for your participants to respond.

How do you ask Type B questions every time? Consider the following.

1. Step 1: Start with an image-building phrase ("Think about . . . ," "Imagine . . . ," "If . . . ," "Consider . . . ").

Table 33.1 Type A and Type B Questions

Type A Question	Type B Question
The next thing we are going to talk about are meetings. What are the typical problems you have seen in meetings?	Think back to the last few meetings you have attended. Think about the problems with those meetings, the things that went wrong, the things that made you say, "We have got to run better meetings here." What are the typical problems that you have seen in meetings?

2. Step 2: Extend the image to the answers by giving at least two phrases that allow the participants to see their answers.

3. Step 3: Ask the direct, Type A question. Now that they see their answers, ask the direct question that prompts the participants to respond with their answers.

Great facilitators ask better questions that result in them receiving better answers, nearly all the time.

Separator 3: The Opening—Inform, Excite, Empower, Involve

Good facilitators know that it is important to open a session well. However, great facilitators treat the opening as one of the most important parts of the session. For example, when executives walk in the room, they have the power. Great facilitators know that they have at most fifteen minutes to get the executives to transfer their power over to the facilitator. When that transfer of power happens, the participants sit back and allow the facilitator to lead them.

When that transfer doesn't happen, it can get ugly. Typically, the nice executives will simply ignore you. They will answer emails, hold side conversations, or find other ways to use their time. The not-so-nice executives may begin fighting you: they may object to what you are doing, try to hijack the agenda, or point out the many reasons why the meeting is a waste of time. So it is critical that the transfer of power happens.

To influence the transfer of power within the first fifteen minutes of the session, practice four important actions: inform, excite, empower, and involve.

Inform	Let the participants know the purpose of the session and the product to be produced.
Excite	Clearly define the benefits of the session to the participants by answering, "What's in it for them?" Use the words "you" or "your" at least four times to ensure that the benefits are participant-focused.
Empower	Describe the role they will play or the authority that has been given to them.
Involve	Involve them immediately through an engagement question that furthers the session purpose.

Good facilitators typically do the "inform" well, but barely "excite" at all. Great facilitators recognize that a key in the opening is getting people excited and involved right way. What follows is an example of the inform-excite-empower-involve process.

Good morning. It is my pleasure to be with you today in this Masterful Meetings course.

- **(Inform)** *Our purpose over the next two days is to provide you with tools and techniques that will help you ignite a meetings revolution in your organization. When we are done, you will have your own master plan for not only improving your meetings, but also for transforming the meetings throughout your entire organization.*

- **(Excite)** *This would mean you would no longer waste your time in useless and unnecessary meetings. And the meetings you do attend would be purposeful, focused, and results-oriented. This is your opportunity to address one of the biggest areas of waste happening in your organization and get back valuable time for doing the things that are important to you.*

- **(Empower)** *Each of you was hand-picked by your area leader as the person in your organization to whom he or she would look to lead the charge in transforming meetings. The area leaders believe you have the vision and execution skills to make it happen.*

- **(Involve)** *Before we start, I would like to build a list of the different problems that you have seen with meetings in your organization. Think back to the last few meetings you have attended. Think about the problems with those meetings, the things that went wrong, the things that made you say, "We have got to run better meetings here." What are the typical problems that you have seen in meetings?*

Separator 4: The Why

When it comes to training programs, good facilitators understand the concepts and can explain clearly what to do and how to do. Great facilitators, however, recognize that, to achieve high levels of learning transfer, participants need to understand and buy-in to the "why." When participants understand why something is important, they are much more likely to take the necessary steps to begin doing the desired behavior outside the training classroom.

The earlier description of Separator 2: Starting Questions provides an excellent example of the what, how, and why in operation, as shown in Table 33.2.

By giving the participants the "why" for each tool or technique introduced in the classroom, the facilitator helps create a foundation for positive change.

Separator 5: Directions—PeDeQs

When giving directions, good facilitators explain what is to be done and are often surprised when people don't understand. Great facilitators know that in giving directions, they have to do the six things, which we call PeDeQs, listed in Table 33.3.

As an example, suppose you are training on a new performance review process and you want the participants to identify the problems that occur in the old process.

Table 33.2 The What, How, and Why

What	Ask starting questions that draw a vivid image of the answers.
How	Step 1. Start with an image-building phrase ("Think about . . ." "Imagine . . ." "If . . ." "Consider . . .").
	Step 2. Extend the image to the answers by giving at least two phrases that allow the participants to see their answers.
	Step 3. Ask the direct, Type A question. Now that they see their answers, you ask the direct question that prompts the participants to respond with their answers.
Why	When you ask Type A questions, you may very well get silence because people are trying to create an image in their heads—the one that you didn't create for them! When you ask a Type B question, people can "see" their answers and are very quickly able to respond with information that is directly on the topic. By asking a Type B question, you avoid silence and make it much easier for your participants to respond.

Table 33.3 The PeDeQs for Giving Directions

Purpose	Give the overall purpose of the activity.
Example	When appropriate, use a simple example, outside the topic area, that helps participants understand how to complete the activity.
Directions	Give general directions using verbal pictures and gestures.
Exceptions	Give specific exceptions and special cases.
Questions	Ask for questions.
Starting Question	Ask a starting question that helps participants visualize the answers.

Along with identifying the problems, you also want to identify the symptom and root causes for each of the problems.

To give your PeDeQs, you might say the following:

- **(Purpose)** *We will identify the problems, symptoms, and root causes related to the performance review process.*

- **(Example)** *For example, if we wanted to drive our car, a problem might be a flat tire. The symptom might be that there is no air in the tire. The root cause might be that I haven't put air in the tire for a while. What else might be a root cause?*

- **(Directions)** *Well, we're not driving a car. We are analyzing the problems with the performance review process. Here's how we will do it. First, we will list all the problems we can think of. Then, once we have identified the problems, we will determine the symptom and root cause for each.*

- **(Exceptions)** *Now there are a few other things you need to know. While we are discussing problems, you may come up with a root cause. I will place it in the root cause list until we identify the problem related to it. After we list all the problems and are talking about symptoms and root causes, you may mention a problem, and I will add it to the bottom of the list.*

- **(Questions)** *Any questions?*

- **(Starting Question)** *Okay, think about our last performance review cycle. Consider the things that were real problems, the things that frustrated you, and the things that worked very poorly. What are some of those frustrating problems with the current performance review process?*

Have you ever heard participants say, "I don't understand what you are asking us to do" or "Why are we doing this?" or "Could you explain that again?" If so, it is likely that you did not give your PeDeQs.

Separator 6: Engagement

Good facilitators understand the importance of keeping people engaged. So they will break up their presentations by asking questions, using fun games, or having people do things in small groups. However, great facilitators understand the importance of not wasting time on games or other activities just for the sake of engagement. They treat every moment in a session as precious and are intentional in selecting engagement activities that are purposeful. They have a wide variety of engagement activities from which to choose. They select activities that are carefully aligned to achieve a specific purpose that furthers one or more key objectives of the session. You may wish to use one of the engagement strategies shown in Table 33.4.

Separator 7: Dysfunction

Average facilitators understand that dysfunctional behavior by participants can derail a facilitated session. Therefore, they may be a bit fearful of dysfunction. They often ignore the early forms of dysfunction and hope and pray that the dysfunction goes away quickly should it occur. Great facilitators know that hope is not a strategy! During preparation, they seek to identify potential dysfunction and take steps in advance for conscious prevention, early detection, and clean resolution of dysfunctional behavior.

- *Conscious prevention*—To consciously prevent dysfunctional behavior, great facilitators ask questions about the individual participants to identify dysfunctional potential, such as people who are not in favor of holding the session, those who are on unfavorable terms with one another, or those who stand to lose something if the initiative is successful. Based on the information gained in preparation, great facilitators execute dysfunction prevention strategies such as adding specific ground rules and having conversations with people in advance.

- *Early detection*—Throughout the session, great facilitators actively look for the early signs of dysfunction, such as participants who are not speaking, side conversations, participants who complain, or participants whose body language may indicate uneasiness with the session, such as folded arms, legs crossed, or bodies leaning away from the center of the room.

Table 33.4 Sample Engagement Strategies

Name	Type	Brief Description
Brief Encounters	Generating ideas	Participants individually identify a question on which they desire input. Over a twenty-minute period, they have brief, one-on-one encounters with fifteen to twenty others to gain input on their question and provide input to others.
Dump and Clump	Generating ideas, Categorizing	Participants work in teams for two-to-four minutes to brainstorm responses to a question (dump); the responses from all teams are grouped into categories for further discussion (clump).
Elevator Speech	Summary	Participants write individual thirty- to sixty-second summaries of their experiences or key learnings from a session.
Future Letter	Action planning	Participants write letters to themselves identifying actions they will take based on the session. Letters are mailed to participants at a future date.
Jeopardy	Learning review	Using the popular game show format, participants select "answers" and provide the questions that relate to each answer.
Last Person Standing	Generating ideas, List reduction	Participants work in teams for two to four minutes to brainstorm responses to a question; team leaders post one response at a time on a common chart but are eliminated if they post a duplicate; last person standing will be from the team with the most unique responses.
More or Less	Action planning	Participants identify what they must do more of and less of based on a change or new strategy.
Rotating Flip Charts	Breakout review	Following a breakout session, the teams rotate from flip chart to flip chart, reviewing the work of other teams and identifying areas of agreement and disagreement using a specific documentation approach.
Start/ Stop/ Continue	Action planning	In response to a change or new strategy, participants identify what they will start doing, stop doing, and continue doing.
Whip	Reflection	The facilitator uses a rapid round-robin format to have participants express their reactions to an idea or event; responses are limited to one, two, or three words.

- *Clean resolution*—Should a dysfunction occur, great facilitators quickly recognize it and have specific strategies for addressing the common dysfunctions such as dropouts, nay-sayers, loud-mouths, whisperers, and door slammers.

What separates great facilitators from good ones? We find that great training facilitators are significantly more effective in these seven areas than good ones. Fifteen years ago, many thought that a flip chart and a pen was all you needed to be a good facilitator. Today, we know it takes considerably more. Please join us in our efforts to continually raise the bar on facilitation excellence. If you would like to determine whether you are a good or a great facilitator, visit this chapter's online tools for a self-assessment.

About Leadership Strategies

Leadership Strategies—The Facilitation Company is the number one meeting facilitation and facilitation training company in the United States. Through FindaFacilitator. com, clients have access to more than five hundred facilitators who can lead sessions in strategic planning, issue resolution, process improvement, team building, and a wide variety of other group sessions to help organizations improve results.

In addition, the Atlanta-based organization also offers more than a dozen facilitation-related training courses, including their flagship courses, *The Effective Facilitator, The Facilitative Consultant, Leadership Through Facilitation, Facilitating Strategy,* and *Facilitation for Trainers.* Leadership Strategies offers public, open enrollment classes in numerous cities throughout the United States, Canada, and Australia. The organization also provides private, on-site classes to corporations, nonprofit organizations, and government agencies around the globe. Michael Wilkinson, managing director, is the author of *The Secrets of Facilitation, The Secrets to Masterful Meetings,* and *The Secrets to Masterful Planning* and is the primary author of *The Effective Facilitator.*

Submitted by Michael Wilkinson, CMF, Managing Director

Leadership Strategies

56 Perimeter Center East #103

Atlanta, GA 30346

(770) 454-1440

michael.wilkinson@leadstrat.com

www.leadstrat.com

Chapter 34

How to Teach Wisdom

Transferring Tacit Knowledge on the Job

THE STEVE TRAUTMAN COMPANY

In This Chapter

- Importance of transferring wisdom in the workplace.
- Four-step process to transfer tacit knowledge to another person.

As a long-time and successful employee, you have undoubtedly been asked at some point along the way to train co-workers on the job. For instance, you might have been asked to be a mentor or to allow someone to shadow you. Experienced workers are asked to transfer knowledge to ramp up new employees, cross-train existing employees who are changing roles, improve consistency or quality, and to prepare for their own departures when they change roles or retire. This training must include more than teaching the steps involved in doing the work. It has to incorporate the "secret sauce" that makes you great at your job and uniquely qualified to do it: wisdom.

In my work on peer mentoring and knowledge transfer and in my book, *Teach What You Know*, I've written extensively about how experts can break their jobs down into manageable chunks, explain the steps to someone else with deference to learning styles, test to see whether the information was learned, and then give feedback on the resulting work. The tools my colleagues and I have developed have proven very effective in teaching the parts of each job that are easily broken into steps, but some have argued that true wisdom is too slippery and ethereal for such common-sense solutions. In this chapter, I'd like to outline some ideas to prove otherwise.

Transferring wisdom or tacit knowledge is a problem that can be solved with the right tools and some focused effort on the part of the experts, their co-workers, and managers. Here's the thesis: You can't replace the wisdom gathered over many years, but you can reduce the amount of time it takes someone to begin *acting wisely*.

Wisdom in the Workplace

Nowhere is the need to transfer tacit knowledge more evident than in companies that must begin replacing an aging workforce. According to a 2010 global workforce study, at least 90 percent of respondents in every sector expect retirements to *significantly increase* the loss of knowledge and expertise (Career Partners International, 2010). In some areas, 35 to 50 percent of workers will be eligible to retire in the next five to ten years. A major defense contractor did an internal study of the critical skills of its 6,500 engineering employees in the United States. Of those nearing retirement, they identified about 13 percent whose departure would have some *measurable impact* on business performance. Even with a faltering economy slowing the pace of their departure, this group will not be able to work forever. And the generation replacing them is smaller and more mobile than their elders—a fact that makes a quick ramp to productivity even more important.

The prospect of replacing so many long-time employees may be too overwhelming for some organizations, or perhaps they believe the issue will work itself out. That could be why they don't yet have plans. The truth is that, like most problems, this one can be broken down into realistic tasks, measurable goals, and practical solutions.

Examples of Wisdom and Tacit Knowledge

Veteran employees often lament that it's very difficult to share the wisdom they've accumulated with others. This type of tacit knowledge seems too amorphous and too dependent on years of experience to be teachable. After all, how can an experienced project manager say what she's looking for as she "takes care" of her team or a long-serving account executive explain how to "build a relationship" with a prospective

Developing Talent for Organizational Results

CEO? How can the research scientist describe thirty-five years of testing methodology or the chief engineer describe how he can "envision" a complex system that won't be fully developed for years? How can anyone impart all those years of trial-and-error experience to someone else?

These stories play out every day all over the world in many flavors, but all with some version of the same problem: How does an expert explain something that he or she has been doing forever, especially when it isn't a straightforward skill like changing a tire?

In my work, I've seen many examples of the need to transfer tacit knowledge. For this chapter, I'd like to take a look at an example that happens to be about transferring wisdom and tacit knowledge around marketing. I know that marketing isn't everyone's thing but, then again, neither is inventing the next biodegradable version of the Ziploc® bag or choosing the sugar for the next gummy/chocolate or biscuit at Cadbury (both real clients). As you read this, remember that the point isn't that we're talking about marketing but rather that everyone has expertise, knowledge, and wisdom that can be transferred.

Transferring Unique Marketing Skills

A colleague of mine had a successful career in marketing and was finally ready to leave her position. She had hired her replacement, but due to budget cuts, her firm was unable to afford an experienced marketer who would have come with all the marketing skills that she had developed after twenty years in business.

She called me and wanted to know whether I could help show her how to bring her new replacement up to speed quickly so as to add value to the company as soon as possible. She called me because she knew I had a specialty in knowledge transfer; she had a critical business need to solve but no idea how to go about transferring her accumulated knowledge and wisdom to another person.

I agreed to help and set up an appointment with a task list in hand. Here's how I approached the challenge.

STEP ONE: BREAK THE WORK INTO MANAGEABLE CHUNKS

The first step was to have her break her work down into the major components and make a simple list of these "silos" she knew the new marketer should know about. She came up with this list in a few minutes:

- Brand management and differentiation
- Social media

- Sales and marketing collateral
- Website
- User documentation
- Data management
- Public relations

Everyone agrees that siloed knowledge is a bad thing. The only way to break down the silos is to write them in a list like the one above and work methodically to ensure there is sufficient bench strength in each area. In this case, I asked my client the areas for which she was the "go-to" person, and she quickly made this list. This can be done for any role, team, or whole company. As is often the case, the list she created shows the real breadth of her role, which happens to include more than just the traditional marketing function that would have been in her formal job description. Note the "user documentation" as an example.

STEP TWO: ASK THE APPRENTICE WHAT SHE ALREADY KNOWS

Then I asked her to test her new hire's existing experience and thinking. She asked the new hire to go down the list and describe what she was already doing with each of these major "silos" of issues. We found that, since the apprentice already had a good deal of online experience, a couple of the silos such as website and social media were already familiar, but the others were not. That helped us decide where to start and made her discussion with her apprentice more efficient.

STEP THREE: BREAK EACH SILO INTO TASKS AND SKILLS

After considering the work at hand and the new hire's relative experience, my colleague decided to focus on the Brand Management and Differentiation silo for her first knowledge-transfer exercise. I had her make a list of what she does to manage the corporate brand. Here's the list she came up with for this specific silo.

1. Document the home brand in the Brand Book.

2. Analyze current collateral relative to brand.

3. Create and write "on brand" collateral for:

   a. Investors

   b. Homeowners

    c. General public

    d. Real estate agents

    e. Home buyers

4. Analyze and respond to Google Analytics.

5. Ensure new projects follow the four branded "must-haves."

6. Train any new employees and subcontractors on brand conformity.

In order to make this list, I asked my colleague to say all the things she *does* relative to branding. I had her follow three rules that help make the most specific, actionable list possible. These three rules are

1. Start with a verb.

2. Check to see whether the apprentice can go "do" everything on the list. For example, you would never say, "Go *understand* Excel" to an apprentice, but you would say, "Go create a Pivot Table in Excel." This will help you make sure you've chosen clear *skills* and not just general competencies.

3. Break the skill into chunks so that each one can be explained in one hour or so.

STEP FOUR: PREPARE TO TEACH EACH SKILL FROM THE LIST USING THE WISDOM QUESTIONS

Next, I had my colleague take each of the skills from the list above and spend five to ten minutes preparing to explain each one, making notes and deciding what was important. This represented the core body of "branding wisdom" that she felt was the most important to transfer to this new hire as quickly as possible. I had her make a list of all the tasks and skills for each silo and then use a subset of the Wisdom Questions (see below) to guide preparation. Each of the questions gets to a piece of the wisdom and tacit knowledge that my colleague learned over the years. She chose the questions that she thought were important enough to cover for the topic at hand. Remember, we weren't trying to tell the new hire everything. We just wanted to get the best advice out, put together in a quick, clear, and practical framework. You can find the list of Wisdom Questions in this chapter's online tools.

Here is a subset of the wisdom questions that my colleague chose. I wanted her to be able to explain these to the new employee:

1. The steps involved and why each is important.

2. The top three things that often go wrong.

3. The relationship between x and y (how the pieces fit together).

4. How to troubleshoot the three most common problems.

5. Who is/should be involved/affected/consulted and why.

6. Three best practices for this topic.

7. Where to find resources (docs, people, samples, websites, etc.).

8. How you know when you're in over your head.

9. The relevant historical issues to consider.

How the Wisdom Questions Work

Each of the questions above is designed to get at the information that experienced people carry around in their heads all the time. The difference between an expert and a novice apprentice is that experts have complete and thoughtful answers to each of these questions; the "right" answers that make their experiences valuable. If apprentices can learn to answer some of these questions, then that is a measure of whether they have learned. The opposite is also true, and perhaps even more telling. If the apprentice *cannot* answer these questions, then we know for certain that knowledge has not been transferred and the apprentice is not ready to go to work.

SAMPLE ANSWERS TO THE WISDOM QUESTIONS

What follows is a snapshot of how we prepared my colleague to talk to her apprentice about branding and differentiation. We chose to use questions 1, 2, 3, 7, and 9 from the wisdom questions list and then wrote up some notes (see below) before meeting with the new hire. Remember, we weren't writing a book on "branding," so her thoughts may appear a little cryptic, but they provided a useful backdrop for both the discussion that followed and the new hire's own notes and plans coming out of that. Here is how we sketched out answers to the questions:

Question 1: The steps involved in documenting branding and why each is important

- List the unique characteristics of the products that represent the underlying customer value proposition.

- Research competitive products. (Who is out there and what are they doing?)

- Fill out the positioning framework. (How does your product serve the target customer? What problem does it solve? What are the top three benefits to your customer? How is it different? What evidence proves your 3 benefit statements?)

- Develop a distinctive voice or other mechanism to tell your story.

Question 2: The top three things that often go wrong

- Jumping to design before doing research.
- Doing it without professional help.
- Getting stuck here because it can be more fun and easier than some of the other work.

Question 3: The relationship between the brand and the rest of the staff

- Brand is not just run out of marketing department.
- The full company must understand the brand promise and be able to share it verbally and in written form.
- Your job is to provide the proper messaging and tools so that others can help implement the brand.
- There are best practices that have already been established in the company. These are documented in the investor binder.

Question 7: Where to find resources (documents, people, samples, websites, and other items)

- Use my designer Gretchen to design; her contact info is. . . .
- Use Mike to do legal research on name and logo; here is his contact info. . . .
- Here's a file from someone who has used a competitor. You should research them.
- Here's the contact information of a colleague who does product performance consulting and you might find some synergies.
- The investor binder, pages 215–260.

Question 9: The relevant historical issues to consider

- This company had two years under a different brand name so here are some legacy issues:
  - Many people still associate us with the old name so we have to transition with mention of it in certain marketing pieces.

- We have to revise many documents, including legal and marketing ones, so you should always run a check to ensure the naming is correct.
- This is the year when we will become profitable, so we have to envision a world where we can actually spend money on branding expertise.

With this outline prepared, we spent an hour or so meeting with the new hire, talking over this aspect of the business. We just moved down the outline, telling stories and giving examples from experience. The apprentice asked a number of questions to make sure she had enough information on each of the points to begin to work. They took a similar approach to each of the other topics, with my colleague preparing briefly so that she didn't overwhelm the new hire or miss any important points, and then using a dialogue as the primary mechanism for transferring experiences. By the end of each session, the new hire successfully answered the five wisdom questions for the skill.

Example of the Difference This Made

After that first discussion on branding, my colleague told me that the process already helped her new hire a great deal. She mentioned the answer to Question 2 as one example. When the new hire thought about how she would have tackled the collateral issue without the advance advice, she imagined starting the process by opening up a desktop publisher and focusing to design the brochure. This would have meant learning how to use the software that came packaged with her computer, then trying to figure out where to begin writing the copy, followed by heading to Kinko's for printing. Since she likes design, she imagined staying on that project too long because it was fun—neglecting more pressing matters.

All of that might have happened *before* she realized that was using marketing language that didn't focus on the core value proposition, that didn't set her apart, followed by working in a software program that really wasn't compatible with the higher end printing process she would ultimately need. The simple wisdom my colleague shared as mentor saved days or even weeks of trial and error. This wasn't dumb luck. The time was saved because we thought through some of what my colleague knows (her wisdom) and she shared a very specific piece of it.

Epilogue

Within six months, my colleague's new hire was functioning at roughly the level one would normally have expected after about five to seven years. Now, she might tell you that is because she's just that much smarter than most, and she might be right. But it could also be that an organized mentor had shared just enough of her wisdom to give her a head start.

Teaching wisdom may sound a little lofty at first, but the good news is that wisdom and tacit knowledge can be packaged and delivered with just a little thought and preparation. If experienced people work to organize a little and then answer some version of the questions asked above, they could reduce the cycles required for others to begin acting wisely.

REFERENCE

Career Partners International. (2010). *2010 mature workforce survey*. Chapel Hill, NC: Author.

About The Steve Trautman Company

At The Steve Trautman Company, we are knowledge transfer experts. We provide business executives with the simplest, most relevant, and quick solutions for knowledge transfer. We understand that knowledge transfer isn't just on-the-job training but also moving the wisdom and tacit knowledge of critical professionals into the heads and hands of their co-workers. For nearly two decades, our proven tools have helped Fortune 500 and 1000 companies—in industries such as high tech, manufacturing, finance, energy, government, and communications—assess risk, internally share knowledge, and reduce the loss of talent and experience. We've rolled out large scale and enterprise-wide projects for blue-chip clients such as Boeing, Nike, Microsoft, Electronic Arts, Zynga, Kodak, Honeywell, Southern Cal Edison, FMI Mining, the U.S. Armed Forces, and more.

What sets us apart from other firms is our ultra-clear, practical framework for risk management in the areas of human capital and workforce talent—and our nearly twenty years of experience. We know knowledge transfer. Founder and principal Steve Trautman has been a pioneer of the field since the early 1990s, when he developed the first company-wide knowledge transfer/peer mentoring program for engineers at Microsoft. Today his three-step knowledge transfer solution is the recognized gold standard for corporate America. This process will typically allow organizations to retain and cross-train in more than 90 percent of their unique knowledge. We show our clients how to mitigate such workforce risks as aging and/or departing experts, slow ramp-up to productivity of new hires, and employees with siloed or trapped knowledge.

Submitted by Steve Trautman

The Steve Trautman Company

4302 Burke Avenue North

Seattle, WA 98103

(206) 547-1775

info@stevetrautman.com

www.stevetrautman.com

Chapter 35

Maximum Value from Simulations

INSIGHT EXPERIENCE

In This Chapter

- How to select an appropriate business simulation.
- How to structure a simulation based on how the time is used.
- Suggestions for creating learner accountability following a simulation.

Simulations are a terrific way to engage adult learners. They offer rapid feedback; they demonstrate tasks and relationships; they put learning in a business context. Those are the reasons that simulations of all types are the cornerstone of many leadership development programs. The business value of the learning experience, however, only occurs when learners use a new perspective and engage in new behaviors back on the job . . . and when those actions impact the business performance and improve results. These can be both positive reinforcement (doing new things) or negative reinforcement (stop doing destructive things). Either way, the business value of a simulation occurs not at point of learning but at point of application.

Too often, simulation learning experiences end at the "aha" moment and leave the opportunity for business impact unaddressed. There is often a gap between the engagement and energy of the simulation-based learning experience and application back on the job. However, the good news is that this gap is usually triggered by one of three easily addressable design issues. For a simulation to have maximum value to your learners and your business, you need to:

1. Choose the right simulation,

2. Structure the learning experience appropriately, and

3. Create learning accountability through specific, not generic, application activities.

1. Choose the Best Simulation for Your Needs

There are numerous business simulations on the market. Broadly, the definition of a simulation is simply "a structured learning environment that allows learners to try skills before applying them in real life." Simulations can range from a paper-based walkthrough of a new process; to data entry simulations of IT systems; to board games; to complex behavioral case studies with individual roles for participants to play; to computer-modeled environments for team or individual learning. Each creates a different type of learning environment, suited to different learning objectives.

The first critical decision a program designer faces is "Which one?" There are multiple dimensions for selection of a business simulation. However, the three most important are

- *Learning Objective Fit*—Will this experience focus learners on the skills or concepts they need to take back to the job?

- *Complexity and Feedback Structure*—Will the simulated backdrop of the experience and the information generated as a result of behaviors or decisions reinforce the learning objectives or undermine learning because of poor fit?

- *Duration*—Can the experience be conducted in the time available?

If any of the three of these elements isn't suitable for your organization's needs, the long-term impact of the learning experience will be jeopardized from the start.

LEARNING OBJECTIVE FIT

Because business simulations are so integrative, learners can take insights from the experience at many levels. In a way, that is a powerful safety valve for program designers, because you can be confident that every participant will learn *something* from the experience. However, clarity about the consistent insight or skill you want to address across the learning population can dramatically increase the long-term business impact of the experience.

In general, there are five types of learning objectives that business simulations address as described in Table 35.1.

Business simulations are often selected based on how closely a simulation model mirrors your industry. A better place to start is to clarify and focus on the learning objectives. The more clearly you can articulate the objectives for the experience, the better selection you will make (obviously!). There is a depth/breadth tradeoff: the broader the learning objectives, the greater the tendency for the outcome to be awareness instead of action.

Table 35.1 Five Types of Learning Objectives

Learning Objective	Experience Will Focus on
Discrete Business Skills	How to do something, for example:
	Analysis and diagnosis
	Decision making
	Strategic thinking
	Risk assessment and management
	Goal development
	Interviewing and feedback
	Project planning and tracking
	Scenario planning
	Presentation skills
Process Steps and Sequence	How an activity evolves over time, for example:
	Who is involved, in what roles
	Key handoffs
	Critical decision points and appropriate decision criteria
	Measurement of performance at various stages of the process
	Links among the process steps to the overall outcome
	These learning experiences could focus on:
	Operational management
	Business planning processes
	Customer service and support

(continued)

Learning Objective	Experience Will Focus on
Business System Interplay	How business decisions impact results in a complex operating system, for example:
	Setting, communicating, and executing strategy
	Collaborating across organizational boundaries to deliver results
	Leading teams and projects in a matrix organization
	Handling ambiguity and uncertainty
	Functional dynamics
	Managing through change
Team Dynamics	How a group works together to tackle an issue, for example:
	Structure and tools for team process
	Diagnosis of team effectiveness
	Contributions/roles of individual players
	Stages of team performance
	In these learning experiences, the task itself is less important than the dynamic created by the team working on it. However, the outcome of the task creates valuable pressure on team performance and a metric for linking team interactions to business outcomes.
Personal Behaviors and Skills	How individuals participate in business decisions and team dynamics, for example:
	How effectively individuals communicate ideas
	How individuals engage in group decision making
	How individuals' personality styles influence their contribution to the team performance and results
	A simulation can be a remarkably effective forum for direct peer feedback, particularly if the group is comprised of peers who do not work together back on the job. A simulation can create a realistic environment that enables individuals to demonstrate their strengths and opportunities for improvement.

APPROPRIATE SIMULATION STRUCTURE: TENSIONS, COMPLEXITY, AND FEEDBACK LOOPS

With clear learning objectives in place, the next criterion to consider is the simulation structure. Program designers often look for simulations that closely mirror their marketplace or industry or their process or their IT system. However, it is really three elements of the simulation model that will drive the fit and impact of the simulation to your needs.

First, does the simulation reflect the critical tensions that challenge learners back on the job? The value of a simulation is often to conceptualize the issues. Removing the specific details of your company or industry can sometimes actually help learners see the big picture dynamics more easily. While in some cases high fidelity to the details of your business is important, the key criterion is to look for an experience that highlights the tensions that drive your business. Are you a service or product business? Is your organization trying to balance local needs with global operations? Is your business model based on a post-sales revenue stream? Is your business capital-intensive? Labor-intensive? What is the cost structure of your business and which investments offer the greatest leverage? How consolidated or dispersed is the competitive marketplace? A fictional simulation can be as effective as a highly realistic customized one, as long as the tensions that make decisions difficult and outcomes unpredictable are realistic to your business.

Second, is the complexity in the simulation in the right place? If your learning objectives are to teach strategic analysis, then the competitive marketplace in the simulation should offer rich details and sufficient complexity to challenge learners as they apply analytical tools. With that focus, there may be little to no need for detail and complexity about the supply chain and production planning. In fact, complexity in the wrong places can distract learner attention and undermine the learning process. Alternately, if your learning objective is to provide individual feedback about a learner's skills in working with a diverse organization, there should be richness in the mix of employees in the simulation setting. Make sure the complexity maps to what you want learners to learn.

Finally, one vital element of any simulation is the feedback it provides. Look at the form and focus of the feedback generated by the simulation. Does it highlight the dynamics that are important to your learning objectives? While there is important learning through the process of the simulation, that learning is reinforced by the business results or other feedback that the simulation offers. A simulation chosen to reinforce learning about team dynamics should have some form of structured feedback on the interplay of the team activities to the business results.

DURATION

Simulations can be short (two to four hours), focused (one or two days), extended (over two days), and in some cases, intermittent (run in cycles over multiple days or weeks). The length of the experience impacts how much information participants can absorb and how many different learning objectives the experience can address. Often, compressed simulation experiences compromise the business impact because they attempt to do too much in too little time. Program designers need to make conscious, disciplined choices about the learning objectives, complexity, and duration of the simulation experience. If time is short, look to limit the complexity and focus on one significant insight. In shorter learning experiences, it is essential to allocate adequate time for debriefing and reflection, as well.

2. Structure the Learning Experience

Driving maximum business impact from a simulation requires more than simply selecting the right simulation model. Adults learn by doing, but increasing the impact on business results requires additional reflection, practice, and focus on how to use the learning back on the job. All simulation experiences include some time to discuss the results and what happened. The risk is that debriefings focus solely on the "What happened?" and/or the "What did we learn?" as opposed to the "So what?" insights of application.

The time allocation in a simulation experience has to provide adequate time for learners to translate their insights into action. Interestingly, in the time-challenged environment of most leadership development programs, this is the activity that is most often shortchanged or left unstructured. When left to participants to do application as "homework" or "follow on" thinking after a program, this translation simply won't happen. Three design elements help ensure that the learning experience creates the foundation for back on the job action:

- Opportunities for participants to fail and retry with the application of new skills and ideas through multiple learning cycles in the simulation
- Time during the experience to reflect (ideally, at multiple points in the process) and dialogue to refine application ideas with help from others
- Structure for the reflection to push learners to go beyond initial ideas and deepen their plans for action

The flow of a simulation-based learning experience is somewhat standard—present and digest background information, discuss and decide on key choices, receive feedback on the choices, and repeat the cycle. The power of a simulation is that it compresses time and enables learners to see the impact of their actions. Simulations enable learners to understand causality with new perspectives. However, that learning value is enhanced when participants have the opportunity to repeat the cycle: to try, succeed or fail, assess, and try again. Learners will understand, and be able to apply, concepts more deeply if they are challenged to apply them repeatedly through the simulation process. There is great learning value in the experience of failure and recovery, and in the shifting perspective of what Chris Argyris (1991) calls "double loop learning."

In addition to ensuring that the experience design allows for multiple cycles of learning and practice, designers also need to consider the time allocation in the experience. The energy and engagement of decision making in a simulation can be seductive and, particularly if there is pressure to add complexity to the simulation model, time can be over-allocated to the decision-making activity. However, the insights and learning from the experience occur during debriefings and reflection. Decisions that take fifteen to twenty minutes to make could trigger sufficient insights and ideas for an hour-long learning discussion.

Although there is no single formula, program designers should consider the mix of learner time during a simulation experience across four categories as depicted in Figure 35.1.

Reflection activities can be interspersed throughout an extended simulation or can be a culminating activity. The enforced pause will enable learners to step back from the experience and synthesize their insights. In extended simulations, these reflection

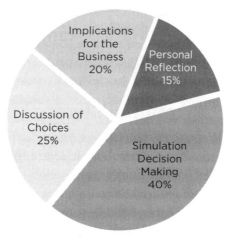

Figure 35.1 Target Time Allocation

Maximum Value from Simulations

pauses can reinforce the double loop learning cycle outlined above. Learners can identify areas of focus for successive decision-making rounds and be aware of their progress in applying new skills.

Reflection activity is often challenging for learners, who are accustomed to a fast pace of interactions and interruptions in their daily work. Initial reflection activities may not be well-received, but the learning design can reinforce engagement by asking learners to compare insights with one or two other participants. It is important to encourage learners to reflect on both their successes and their "misses" in performance in a simulation environment. Learners can over-focus on mistakes, and can thus miss insights about causality from their successes.

Finally, while open-ended reflection questions create a broad window for learners to frame their insights, more targeted questions can help ensure that all learners in a group focus on understanding specific dynamics or tasks. The more specific the questions, the more actionable the learning will be. For example, consider the difference between:

- Option 1: What have you learned about using ROI analysis to evaluate investments? and

- Option 2: What information do you need to ensure that an ROI analysis is valid?

Structured reflection should include broad, open-ended questions; targeted specific questions; and questions that encourage the learner to translate insights back to their role or job situation. In structured reflection, learners should be challenged to consider the business impact of their insights. Simply learning about the importance of communicating strategy is a useful insight. However, considering what to do differently to communicate strategy to their team, and then how that behavior will drive better business results, is a more thoughtful and, in the end, impactful activity for learners. The program design needs to encourage learners to make those links.

3. Create Learner Accountability and Reinforcement

Business impact happens back on the job—in the business. For a simulation experience to deliver results, the actions and ideas developed during the learning session need to be supported back on the job. Interestingly, reinforcement and support for simulation-based learning can be more difficult than other methodologies because the insights are individualized—not everyone has the same "aha's" from a simulation-based learning experience. However, that's no reason to skip this step, although many organizations do.

Application is the responsibility and choice of the learner in the end. The program designer can create incentives to help support the learners' work after a simulation session. The simplest incentives encourage activity (and assume that business impact will follow). Application and retention rates for learning activities increase significantly simply by setting the expectation that there will be follow-up of some sort (Martin, 2010). So encouraging participants to post updates on a discussion board or to report their activities to a peer or leader are both means to encourage application.

To deepen learner accountability to do something, design the reinforcement to go beyond reporting and be interactive. Pairing learners with a peer and scheduling periodic check-in conversations can create milestones that reinforce the good intentions participants have created as they leave the classroom or learning session. A more formal follow-up with a learning coach or supervisor increases the visible commitment to the learner and encourages more consistent action and impact as a result.

Reporting and discussing activities ("Here is what I have done") achieves only one level of business impact. The true business value is often more elusive, but requires developing measures of business impact, and ultimately, business value. Figure 35.2 displays this progression.

To truly "up the impact" of any learning experience, but particularly a simulation-based experience, learners need to commit to new activities and have an expectation about how those activities will impact business performance. If that commitment can be combined with a process to measure and track the impact on the business and ultimately the business value, the learning will become self-reinforcing.

As learners see the value of their learning in practice, there is an opportunity to deepen the learning and impact from a simulation experience in two ways. First, the

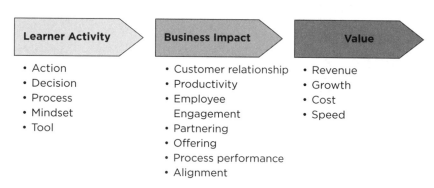

Figure 35.2 Turning Activity into Organizational Value

program can be designed to provide additional information and context to learners as they continue to apply insights in action. Online learning and communities of practice can provide additional tools and insights as learners continue to apply new ideas back on the job. The ultimate reinforcement of the business impact of new actions is to aggregate the measures (even anecdotally) to provide collective reinforcement of the new skills in practice. Making the collective value of a new approach visible ("We've applied this process diagnostic tool to fifteen core processes across the company with an 8 percent improvement in operating costs as a result") creates momentum for the learning and incentive to sustain a new behavior in practice.

There is a spectrum of ways to create learner accountability and reinforcement. Even the simplest (reporting on activities) can shift the business impact of a simulation-based learning experience in positive ways.

The bottom line: use simulations—often. They engage learners, build energy in learning programs, and create powerful sticky insights about ideas and concepts. As a learning methodology, simulations offer a unique way for employees to share their ideas and insights with each other. As a result, learning can be accelerated beyond the individual to a team and a broader group of employees. All these dynamics create a great starting point for business value: for employees to act differently back on the job and improve business results. However, to get the value, you need to design the simulation learning experience with the impact in mind. It's a design investment that will generate impressive returns. You may download a checklist for designing an impactful simulation from this book's online tools.

REFERENCES

Argyris, C. (1991, May-June). Teaching smart people how to learn. *Harvard Business Review.*

Martin, H.J. (2010). Improving training impact through effective follow-up: Techniques and their application. *Journal of Management Development, 29*(6), 520–534.

About Insight Experience

Insight Experience develops dynamic business simulation-based learning experiences that accelerate leadership development and strategy execution for the world's leading businesses. We work directly with clients and strategic partners to impact performance at all management levels across industries globally. Our offerings include business simulations in a wide range of formats and durations, focused on a variety of topics: Leadership and Strategy Programs, which we tailor to our clients' needs; and Strategy Implementation Workshops, supported by custom simulations.

Our simulations create a unique environment for participants to develop, integrate, and apply *both* business and people skills to become more effective leaders. We believe effective leadership in the current global business environment demands more than business acumen, functional expertise, and strategic thinking skills. Today's leadership challenges *also* require exceptional interpersonal and communication skills to engage and inspire others to achieve significant business results.

Submitted by Amanda Young Hickman, Founding Partner

Insight Experience

152 Commonwealth Avenue, Suite 20

Concord, MA 01742

(978) 369-0639

info@insight-experience.com

www.insight-experience.com

Chapter 36

Virtual Classroom . . . *Real* Results!

DEVELOPMENT DIMENSIONS INTERNATIONAL, INC. (DDI)

In This Chapter

- Best practices for implementing a virtual training session.
- Suggestions for creating a compelling virtual learning experience.
- Seven elements for effective planning for virtual classrooms.

The traditional corporate classroom has remained relatively unchanged for as long as most of today's trainers have been training. (How many business functions can make that kind of claim?) But facilitators at every stage of their careers should expect their classrooms to change dramatically in the coming years. With tightened travel budgets and teams becoming more geographically dispersed, classrooms are being taken to the web, and virtual deliveries are more and more prevalent. However, in spite of distance, companies still want peers from various locations to share experiences and skill practices with each other. This presents new challenges and considerations when approaching a virtual classroom implementation.

The first place to start is to think about the reason for training; start with the end in mind. Maybe you need better coaches, or leaders who can successfully lead change. In almost any scenario, you're looking to change behavior to accomplish your specific goal. To truly build skills and achieve behavior change in the virtual classroom (that is, learning delivered via a web-conferencing platform to learners in multiple locations) requires a high level of interactivity and engagement to keep learners' attention, drive knowledge acquisition, and deliver effective skill building and application on the job.

Best Practices to Successfully Implement Virtual Classrooms

Virtual classroom courses offer the best of both worlds: the ability to interact with others in real time, while minimizing time off the job and travel costs. The good news is that web conferencing technology and instructional techniques are now at the point where we can deliver engaging "soft skills" training that leads to application and behavior change on the job. But several tactical and strategic changes must occur to make the most of this new technology.

WEBINAR MINDSET: DITCH IT

In most organizations, the use of webinars has been, and will continue to be, an important vehicle to bring people together and disseminate information to dispersed audiences. Webinars are an efficient way to communicate broadly, but usually are not engaging enough to hold attention long term. After our many conversations with training professionals who were exploring virtual classroom, a recurring theme emerged: many had lower expectations for learner engagement and outcomes. One person summed up this approach by saying, "Webinar training will never be as good as classroom, but it's all we can afford right now." We call this the "webinar mindset," and it might be the biggest challenge leadership development professionals face in deploying virtual classroom. We also ran into the webinar mindset when discussing class length.

Coming into training, many participants may anticipate a webinar-like experience. To maximize your session, you'll want learners who are ready to take part, not just listen. When planning your implementation, be certain to:

- Provide a clear message about the expectations of a virtual classroom course for both the learner and their leader.

- Differentiate a virtual course from a webinar—define how this training offer beyond what they are used to in this format.

CREATE A COMPELLING EXPERIENCE FOR THE LEARNER

Based on our research and testing, we advocate the following approach: create an interactive and engaging virtual classroom experience by using all of the features in your web-conferencing technology, optimizing instruction design for virtual delivery, and training trainers in the special skill set needed for engaging delivery. After all, boring training is boring regardless of modality, and there are ways to make virtual classroom just as engaging and powerful as traditional classroom training.

Learners often cite the face-to-face networking and interaction as a high-value part of any traditional classroom delivery. How can this continue—and even be enhanced—in the virtual classroom? Here are two best practices to ensure a compelling learner experience:

- *Purposeful engagement.* The idea is to use a web-conferencing platform to capture the understanding of the learners, to engage them with each other in discussion about the challenges they face, and keep them focused on the progression of the content. The tools also can be used to connect the content to everyday application by involving the learners in activities to show how they would apply concepts. For example, the chat feature seems to be a favorite among learners and is available in most web-conferencing platforms. It is a great tool for involving quieter learners, who may be hesitant to speak up. Also, most virtual conferencing interfaces allow you to easily break participants off into small groups through breakout rooms. These provide participants the ability to conduct skill practices or to have small group discussions. Learners appreciate going from a classroom of fifteen or more people to a quiet chat room with two or three of their peers to discuss and learn from each other.

- *Teach learners to use the tools.* If learners do not clearly learn the tools and feel comfortable about the way they are being asked to interact, they won't get involved. Like anything new, these tools may seem a bit intimidating at first, but you'll quickly see that they are quite intuitive and easy to use. Be sure to take the time to show participants how to use them. It's also good to think through in advance how to handle technical glitches or learners who struggle to pick up how to use the tools.

MASTER THE TECHNOLOGY (TIMES 3)

Obviously, technology is a core element of virtual classroom training, and while we don't want to get into too many details here, we have identified two key areas that require mastery. The first area is being prepared for technology problems during a virtual classroom session. Nearly every web-conferencing session we've attended or led (whether a traditional webinar, team meeting, or virtual classroom) has had some technology hiccups. Even with rigorous and diligent planning, it's inevitable. At a minimum, technology problems are disruptive and waste time, and, at worst, they will derail the program (we have first-hand experience with both situations).

To deal with technology problems quickly and keep virtual classroom training on track and on time, it's essential to have an expert technology assistant or manager (we call the role a "producer") assisting the trainer. High-quality virtual classroom training requires a number of technology systems, including Internet connectivity, audio, video, and the web-conferencing software, and the producer needs to be adept at handling problems with each of these systems. Does this add cost to virtual training? Absolutely, but it is nowhere near the cost of wasted time and disruption to the class that happens when the trainer has to deal with technology problems.

The second technology area is the web-conferencing software itself. Trainers (and producers) need to be proficient with all of the features of their system. They need to smoothly and seamlessly move and annotate slides, use and manage whiteboards, move learners to and from breakout rooms, and so forth. One more thing to add here: if you think you can bypass this step because you are only piloting virtual classrooms, or you are only planning to deliver one or two courses in this modality, please think again.

NOT ALL FACILITATORS ARE CREATED EQUAL

Anyone who has facilitated virtual classroom training will say it is significantly different from traditional classroom training. While many of the core facilitation skills are the same for traditional and virtual classrooms, their application is different. The two biggest challenges are the lack of visual cues (both from and to learners) and maintaining an appropriate pace. Good instructional and materials design (optimized for virtual classroom) will help with both of these challenges, but most facilitators will need to adjust how they involve learners, explain key points, ask questions, modulate voice and tone, and provide coaching and guidance. Most importantly, they'll need to make sure they keep an appropriate pace, moving from slide to slide, building to key points, continually interacting with learners, and managing learner comments and individual needs. What follows are several facilitation best practices and skill sets that make for an engaging and impactful virtual classroom delivery.

In our experience, not all facilitators are appropriate for the virtual classroom.

A good traditional classroom facilitator may not be a good virtual classroom facilitator. One factor to consider is how the virtual classroom facilitator communicates with (or without) impact—how they use their voices, change the pace of their speech, and, overall, how they engage using tone of voice.

In the traditional classroom, a good facilitator can tell through body language and eye contact whether learners are engaged and understanding the content. Many facilitators get satisfaction and energy from seeing their audience. The virtual classroom leaves much to the imagination. Therefore, a good virtual facilitator has to engage learners with his or her voice and use questioning techniques to gauge understanding and acceptance of concepts.

It's also important to make sure that the facilitator you have in mind wants to deliver virtual classroom courses. Some simply may not be comfortable with this mode of delivery, or they may need to shadow a few sessions to increase their confidence. As in any facilitation scenario, a confident, comfortable facilitator is a much more effective facilitator. Once you've selected your facilitators, plan to ramp them up for the experience. Allow time to explore the web interface, and set up some "dry runs" so they can practice using the tools. Co-facilitation is a wise investment. It allows one facilitator to sit and record feedback for the other and then switch roles.

Go Forth, Virtually

As you consider moving into the virtual realm of training, review the seven elements listed below to increase the effectiveness of your virtual classrooms. You may also wish to turn to the online tools section for more details and a checklist to guide you through the many questions.

SEVEN ELEMENTS OF EFFECTIVE VIRTUAL CLASSROOM PLANNING

Organizational Landscape

- Development strategy accountability
- Support from leadership
- Application of skills

Virtual Classroom Program Strategy

- Training details
- Program composition
- Business case
- Barriers

Learning Landscape

- Your partners/stakeholders
- Learners
- Physical environment

Logistical Issues

- Project team
- Registration
- Course materials
- Tracking, evaluation, and measurement

Technology

- Web-conferencing platform
- Network considerations

Facilitation

- Facilitators
- Producers

Delivery Considerations

- Course adaption/conversion
- Pilot sessions
- Session enhancements

As you can see, there are many things to consider to be successful with virtual classrooms. Will virtual classrooms be equally successfully in all organizations? Probably not. Some organizations' cultures are simply not conducive to this sort of high-tech training. If the initial test-run is marked by technical glitches and low learner engagement, you can be certain that virtual classroom won't get very far off the ground. Should organizations turn exclusively to virtual classroom for their training? Definitely not! However, when used correctly, virtual classrooms can be an effective complement to traditional classroom training, in the same way that web-based training is. Organizations should use these modalities as part of their overall blended learning initiative. DDI has always advocated that the magic is in the mix when it comes to training—virtual classrooms add another ingredient!

About DDI

For over forty years, DDI has helped the most successful companies around the world close the gap between where their businesses need to go and the talent required to take them there.

Our areas of expertise span every level, from individual contributors to the executive suite:

- Success profile management
- Selection and assessment
- Leadership and workforce development
- Succession management
- Performance management

DDI's comprehensive, yet practical approach to talent management starts by ensuring close connection of our solutions to your business strategies, and ends only when we produce the results you require. You'll find that DDI is an essential partner wherever you are on your journey to building extraordinary talent.

Submitted by Annamarie Lang, Senior Consultant; Mark Phelps, Manager, Publishing, Design & Media Services; Aviel Selkovits, Senior Consultant

Development Dimensions International, Inc.

1225 Washington Pike

Bridgeville, PA 15017

(800) 933-4463

info@ddiworld.com

www.ddiworld.com

Virtual Classroom . . . Real Results!

Chapter **37**

Training Triage

PRIORITIZE HIGH-PERFORMING WORKFORCE NEEDS

VISIONPOINT® PRODUCTIONS, INC.

In This Chapter

- Five principles and eighteen competencies of a high-performing workforce.
- Using the eighteen competencies with the most impact to quickly rectify training issues.
- How training can use a workforce model as a diagnostic tool and roadmap to achieve a successful high-performing workplace.

For more than a decade now, the training profession has been quietly under siege. The apparent casualties—shrinking departments and smaller budgets—are not the primary victims, however. The potentially more damaging threat is the marginalization of training at a time when the need for it has never been greater. Once routine, comprehensive corporate training has become increasingly rare. Organizations that once invested heavily in individualized training for all employees have significantly cut back in the wake of globalization and other socioeconomic forces. While many business leaders recognize the potential for an agile, innovative, and customer-focused workforce to offset the pressure from low-cost competitors around the world, training has become disconnected from the larger strategic mission in many organizations. Absent a clear, line-of-sight role, training has become overly compartmentalized and, in many places, is now at a relative standstill. In others, training is completely reactive, occurring sporadically on the heels of lawsuits and regulatory actions. Consequently, when training does take place, it is implemented in a departmental vacuum and contributes little, if any, sustainable business value to the organization.

Understandably, the obstacles to training are formidable and on the increase: "We don't have the time," "We can't take people away from their jobs," "There is not enough money in the budget." These barriers are real and cannot be underestimated. The irony is that few, if any, organizations would deny their need for training; they just don't have sufficient bandwidth to make it a priority.

> *In a training-averse environment, the most serious casualty in need of immediate attention is the high-performing workforce.*

Without a cohesive strategy to train individual employees for increasingly higher levels of personal effectiveness, organizations hit a performance plateau that is difficult to move beyond. Stagnation and decline become very likely outcomes in this scenario. Fortunately, the prognosis is not all doom and gloom. Combining the concept of triage with insights into competencies of high-performing employees helps to equip organizations to emerge stronger than ever.

Cracking the Code of High Performance

What exactly is a high-performing workforce? In simplest terms, it is one that consistently delivers business results, making it THE competitive advantage of an organization. A high-performing workforce can exist only if the majority of employees who comprise it are high-performing individual contributors. The successful whole can be broken down into what high-performing people do and how they do it.

In recent years, extensive research has focused on identifying a core set of principles, behaviors, and competencies that individuals must have to be considered high-performing employees. For example, in their book, *The Value-Added Employee*, researchers Edward J. Cripe and Richard S. Mansfield identified a set of thirty-one unique competencies through which individuals demonstrate proficiency and contribute to the effectiveness of their employer organizations. Some components of this set are timeless; others have emerged reflecting the impact of societal trends (for example, globalization, technology, high rate of change) on learning and development.

While competencies themselves are essential, they are not the only element in the high-performance equation. There are five principles central to fostering a high-performing workforce:

1. *Integrity*—Honesty and truthfulness in all situations and adherence to the highest professional standards, no matter the circumstances.

2. *Respect*—Personal responsibility to assume good intentions and work through problems with professionalism, civility, and fairness.

3. *Initiative*—Ability to anticipate problems, think through all potential consequences, and offer and/or implement solutions before issues escalate.

4. *Confidence*—Self-assurance and poise to act decisively (even when a decision is unpopular) and to ask for help when needed.

5. *Purpose*—Persistence, commitment, and drive to see the big picture and the ability to be flexible and understand what it takes to get there.

These principles reflect both the nature of the workplace and how employees operate within it. A high-performing workforce exists as a result of the successful combination of core competencies (what) and high-performance principles (how).

A tool in this book's online tool section provides an opportunity for you to reflect on your high-performing principles.

Finding a Path to High Performance

The very idea of training even one employee in a multitude of core competencies and high-performance principles is daunting; to entertain the notion of training an entire workforce borders on overwhelming. However, the difficulty does not negate in any way the value of doing so. What is needed is a way of pulling these components into a cohesive, manageable framework. That's where the concept of triage comes in, providing an analogous methodology for quickly assessing critical needs and pinpointing what must be done immediately to ensure the best possible outcome.

The concept of triage grew out of the need to make delivery of emergency care as effective as possible within incredibly dynamic environments and under serious resource constraints. Through the decades, triage has evolved as a body of knowledge, procedures, and statistically proven protocols. For the emergency and medical personnel for whom it becomes second-nature, triage provides a mechanism that enables them to focus quickly and accurately on the most critical needs in front of them. When applied to training, triage yields both a practical diagnostic tool and an accessible model for delivering training precisely when and where it is needed most.

Training triage calls for a rational, competency-driven training strategy specifically designed for development of a high-performing workforce.

Triage for Training

Fortunately, workforce training does not rise to the dramatic level of battlefield trauma, nor does it typically involve life-and-death decision making. Nonetheless, the practice of triage already has a widely recognized business role, that is, prioritizing projects on the basis of where funds and other resources can be best used, are most needed, or are most likely to achieve success. Certainly, that application is pertinent for allocating limited budgets and resources to training, but it needs something more. In order to harness the full potential of triage for training, a designated resource must be utilized for prioritizing needs and making quick decisions. And a system of guiding principles and protocols is required.

The first protocol of training triage is to ensure a manageable scope. Practically speaking, individuals have their own unique combinations of competencies with varying degrees of each. Thus, the goal of training an entire organization to become highly proficient in thirty-one competencies is simply unattainable. A more realistic approach is to focus training and development on a subset of competencies that research indicates offer the most profound impact on lifting overall performance.

The second protocol of training triage calls for a logical sequence in which competencies build upon one another. With manageability and practicality in mind, VisionPoint® has developed a model, displayed in Table 37.1, that bundles and disperses core competencies across four functional categories (managing self, managing others, leading teams, leading organizations) and considers the logical path to high performance.

Let's take a look at each competency—the definition, VisionPoint's point of view on why it is important, the contributing behaviors, and the necessary training focus to improve skills and overall performance. The eighteen competencies are presented in Table 37.2.

Now let's put this together. As represented by the High-Performing Workforce Model™ in Figure 37.1, training for increasingly sophisticated functions in managing and leading moves left to right and upward. The structure and flow of the model is such that each successive competency builds upon those previously acquired. The model's objective is to provide a diagnostic tool, a compass, and a roadmap all in one.

Table 37.1 Critical Competencies for a High-Performing Workforce

Managing Self	Managing Others
1. Develop high-performing work habits 2. Demonstrate integrity and professionalism 3. Exhibit interpersonal effectiveness 4. Take initiative 5. Influence others	6. Navigate organizational politics 7. Prepare for the future 8. Manage performance 9. Manage work processes 10. Manage customer experience 11. Manage risk
Leading Teams	**Leading Organizations**
12. Facilitate change 13. Develop and retain talent 14. Promote teamwork 15. Lead a culturally diverse workforce	16. Create customer loyalty 17. Drive innovation 18. Transform the organization

Table 37.2 High-Performing Competencies

Competency 1	Develop High-Performing Work Habits
Definition	The essential work skills and mindsets needed to maintain focus and ensure productive action while adjusting to a variety of workplace circumstances.
Point of View	An organization's ability to execute its strategy hinges on its employees' abilities to consistently maintain focus and take action quickly, efficiently, and effectively. High-performance work habits form the core of employees' abilities to maintain this focus and take action.
Main Contributing Behaviors	• Be clear on expectations (what, when, why, and how) • Use good time and information management • Be positive and proactive • Be accountable and flexible • Solve problems

(continued)

Table 37.2 High-Performing Competencies (Continued)

Competency 1	Develop High-Performing Work Habits
Training Focus	Training that emphasizes developing high-performance principles, contributing quickly, personal productivity, building professional relationships, creative problem solving, asking for direction and feedback, and navigating change.
Competency 2	**Demonstrate Integrity and Professionalism**
Definition	Regularly exhibiting actions and choices consistent with the required standards of behavior. Being a role model for the standards and holding others accountable.
Point of View	Organizations must minimize the potential for violations of laws, regulations, and, policies. In addition, to attract and retain high-quality employees, organizations must ensure a respectful working environment. Employees of high personal and professional integrity are critical in achieving both objectives.
Main Contributing Behaviors	• Recognize and model ethical behavior • Meet required Code of Conduct standards • Demonstrate respect and transparency in interactions • Keep promises to others (e.g., deliver work on time) • Acknowledge responsibility for both mistakes and successes • Hold self and others accountable for professional and ethical behavior
Training Focus	Training that emphasizes workplace etiquette, modeling professional behavior, taking personal responsibility, maintaining confidentiality, preventing harassment and discrimination, and living the organization's code of conduct.

(continued)

Developing Talent for Organizational Results

Competency 3	Exhibit Interpersonal Effectiveness
Definition	Being effective and productive in communications, interactions, and relationship-building with people from diverse backgrounds and experiences.
Point of View	Organizations can only execute strategy and deliver results if their employees can work together effectively and efficiently. Good interpersonal skills are needed to maximize productivity and minimize misunderstandings, conflict, and wasted effort, particularly as the workplace becomes more diverse and more global in nature.
Main Contributing Behaviors	<ul><li>Express ideas clearly and concisely</li><li>Demonstrate cultural competence</li><li>Listen actively</li><li>Demonstrate collaboration and teamwork</li></ul>
Training Focus	Training that emphasizes active listening, contributing in a meeting, clear and respectful communication, being a team player, embracing inclusion, and resolving conflict.
Competency 4	Take Initiative
Definition	Recognizing a need or opportunity and taking action without being asked to act.
Point of View	Leaders play a pivotal role in helping organizations quickly adapt to a constantly changing global marketplace. Leaders must proactively and responsibly look for ways to take advantage of opportunities, minimize risk, and improve the working environment.
Main Contributing Behaviors	<ul><li>Proactively seek opportunities to learn</li><li>Volunteer for increasingly challenging tasks</li><li>Actively seek feedback and opinions</li><li>Proactively identify potential opportunities or problems</li><li>Proactively offer alternative solutions or courses of action</li></ul>

(continued)

Table 37.2   High-Performing Competencies (Continued)

Competency 4	**Take Initiative**
Training Focus	Training that emphasizes seeing the big picture, anticipating and solving problems, receiving and implementing feedback, setting goals, and developing a personal learning plan.
Competency 5	**Influence Others**
Definition	The ability to persuade and motivate people to act on an idea or point of view.
Point of View	Successful execution of organizational strategy depends on the ability of leaders at all levels to persuade and motivate others to act in alignment with the strategy—even when no one is looking.
Main Contributing Behaviors	• Display confidence and poise in presenting facts and information • Adjust communication based on needs and preferred style of the audience • Build rapport • Explore ideas, suggestions, comments, and alternatives offered by others • Maintain composure and handle questions and objections comfortably • Gain commitment to decisions and courses of actions
Training Focus	Training that emphasizes persuasive and adaptive communication skills, reaching agreements, and managing upward.
Competency 6	**Navigate Organizational Politics**
Definition	Identifying and managing the impact of organizational dynamics (such as competing priorities and individual career aspirations) in order to interact effectively with peers and superiors and deliver results with integrity.

(continued)

Point of View	The organization is a human institution full of individuals with a diverse range of personalities, backgrounds, goals, aspirations, and often competing priorities. As a result, it is a "political" environment. Leaders must have the ability to navigate this environment and forge effective working relationships in order to ensure the success of their own area of responsibility, as well as the overall success of the organization.
Main Contributing Behaviors	• Solicit input on potential organizational impacts of actions and decisions • Build a network of influence • Treat peers and superiors with dignity, civility and respect • Manage perceptions and power image • Appropriately share success stories and acknowledge mistakes • Maintain confidentiality of discussions, disagreements, and decisions • Actively support organizational goals and decisions
Training Focus	Training that emphasizes understanding organizational dynamics, managing image and perception, championing a position with savvy communication, and dealing with unethical behaviors (such as sabotage, deception, and abuse of power).
Competency 7	**Prepare for the Future**
Definition	Having the ability to self-assess development needs and create personal training and action plans to develop the competencies that experienced leaders need in order to move up to senior level positions of leadership.

(continued)

Table 37.2 High-Performing Competencies (Continued)

Competency 7	**Prepare for the Future**
Point of View	In order to be effective, senior-level leaders must exhibit organizational-level strategic thinking; assert influence over events that lead to organizational improvements, and exhibit imagination, initiative and readiness to champion new ways to improve organizational culture and productivity.
Main Contributing Behaviors	• Exhibit organizational-level strategic thinking and decision making • Exhibit a deep level of understanding of how a business works • Communicate complex concepts and strategies with clarity and context to any level audience (internal or external) in both formal and informal settings • Use the organizational structure and processes to solve business problems • Gain commitment to action among competing stakeholders and priorities • Proactively seek opportunities to learn and to teach • Seek opportunities that enhance career development • Build organizational networks to enhance career goals
Training Focus	Training that emphasizes career planning, mastering mentoring, building a sphere of influence, evidenced-based problem solving, and C-suite networking skills.
Competency 8	**Manage Performance**
Definition	A broad set of analysis, problem-solving, and communication skills that enable the successful day-to-day direction of effort to deliver desired results.

(continued)

Point of View	A motivated, productive, and loyal workforce is the one element that competitors cannot duplicate and is the cornerstone of any organization's long-term success. A leader's ability to manage workforce performance effectively is the single most important factor in attracting and retaining a motivated, productive, and loyal workforce.
Main Contributing Behaviors	• Identify the profile of individual team members (strengths, areas needing development, career and personal aspirations, communication style, and others) • Identify and hire the right people • Set and communicate work quality and process expectations • Set and communicate goals • Coach to correct and improve performance • Evaluate performance • Document actions appropriately
Training Focus	Training that emphasizes the balance of all management responsibilities, giving and receiving feedback, conducting performance appraisals, practicing progressive discipline, motivating high performers, conducting effective job interviews, delegating with accountability, and communicating and managing expectations.

Competency 9	**Manage Work Processes**
Definition	Applying the problem-solving, decision-making, and leadership skills needed to identify and execute procedures that contribute to effective and efficient operations.
Point of View	As organization's work to maximize productivity with the minimum level of resources possible, efficient and effective work processes often mean the difference between positive and negative bottom line operations. In addition,

(continued)

Table 37.2 High-Performing Competencies (Continued)

Competency 9	Manage Work Processes
	effectively managing work processes positively impacts workforce morale and retention because there is less confusion, misdirection, and wasted effort.
Main Contributing Behaviors	• Utilize good time and information management skills and processes • Utilize a systematic, disciplined approach to leading meetings • Utilize a systematic process for making decisions • Manage workflow and quality
Training Focus	Training that emphasizes sound decision making, effective facilitation of meetings, managing team time and productivity, managing competing priorities, organization of information, improving work processes, and coaching for action.

Competency 10	Manage Customer Experience
Definition	The essential work skills and mindsets needed to maintain focus and ensure productive action while adjusting to a variety of customer-driven workplace circumstances.
Point of View	Effectively managing the customer experience leads to customer loyalty. When customers trust you they are more likely to collaborate in problem solving, provide input for innovative change, and seek you out as a resource and partner.
Main Contributing Behaviors	• Build trust through honest communication • Be clear on expectations (what, when, why, and how) • Use good time and information management • Be positive and proactive • Be accountable, flexible, and responsive

(continued)

	• Solve problems
	• Proactive allocate resources
Training Focus	Training that emphasizes developing high-performance principles, effective listening and communication, creative problem solving, and uncovering hidden needs.
Competency 11	**Manage Risk**
Definition	Taking the preventive and corrective actions needed to ensure a safe, compliant, and productive workplace, while limiting the legal liability of the organization.
Point of View	Organizations can be forced to pay significant dollars in fines, fees, and compensation awards due to violations of laws and regulations. In addition, violations can result in failure to win and hold business, decreased productivity, and failure to attract and retain high-performing employees. New leaders are on the front lines of an organization's efforts to manage this risk and minimize the damage when situations do arise.
Main Contributing Behaviors	• Follow the organization's standards, policies, and procedures related to workplace ethics, workplace safety, fiscal accountability, and employment practices • Communicate laws, policies, and procedures to employees and confirm understanding • Enforce laws, policies, and procedures consistently and fairly
Training Focus	Training that emphasizes leading with integrity, promoting a respectful workplace, understanding employment law, preventing harassment and discrimination, preventing retaliation and workplace violence, preventing abuse of power, and investigating a complaint.

(continued)

Table 37.2 High-Performing Competencies (Continued)

Competency 12	Facilitate Change
Definition	Minimizing disruptions to productivity, quality, and morale while adapting to change in the shortest amount of time possible.
Point of View	Change is inevitable, constant, and necessary for the success of the organization. Leaders play a central role in helping employees navigate uncertainty and adapt successfully and quickly to required changes.
Main Contributing Behaviors	• Personally navigate change in a way that sets a positive and productive example for employees • Clarify how and why a change impacts employees • Coach team members to identify day-to-day impacts of change, make informed decisions to commit to changes based on reality, stay in control of reactions and responses and take positive action to make change successful • Get commitment on how to move forward • Hold people accountable • Support changes in conversations with employees and fellow managers
Training Focus	Training that emphasizes navigating change as a leader, conducting a change analysis, implementing a change plan, being a change champion, and overcoming common change challenges.
Competency 13	Develop and Retain Talent
Definition	Providing the training, encouragement, and opportunities needed to enhance and expand an individual's skill set for the benefit of the person and the organization.
Point of View	Organizations are faced with the departure of a large number of experienced employees as baby boomers begin to retire. Proactive succession

(continued)

planning is vital to the future and continued success of organizations. In addition, organizations must provide the opportunities, training, and resources needed for career advancement in order to attract and retain high-performing employees.

Main Contributing Behaviors

- Diagnose strengths and developmental needs
- Facilitate intentional development plans with employee input
- Cross-train employees to broaden their experience
- Delegate for developmental reasons
- Provide the resources and encouragement to complete assignments
- Hold employees accountable for personal development

Training Focus

Training that emphasizes how to diagnose strengths and developmental needs, mentoring high-potential employees, coaching high-performing employees, and accountabilities for succession planning and implementation.

Competency 14	Promote Teamwork

Definition

Identifying and minimizing the challenges of hidden and recognized biases, assumptions about motivations, competing priorities, personal agendas and differing work styles to create an inclusive environment where individuals can come together and consistently deliver results.

Point of View

Organizations thrive on the combined wisdom and talents of their human resources. The cross-functional work team is a necessity and, in many cases, the primary method of getting work done in organizations. Effective leadership is critical to efficient, successful teamwork.

(continued)

Table 37.2 High-Performing Competencies (Continued)

Competency 14	Promote Teamwork
Main Contributing Behaviors	• Identify the profile of individual team members (strengths, development areas, career and personal aspirations, communication style, and others) • Facilitate a shared vision of goals and processes • Build group trust • Manage team dynamics • Facilitate disciplined decision making • Hold the team members accountable for results
Training Focus	Training that emphasizes setting and achieving team goals, building trusting team relationships, implementing team decision processes, leading virtual teams, managing team diversity dynamics, and dealing with dysfunctional team behavior.
Competency 15	Lead a Culturally Diverse Workforce
Definition	Creating an inclusive environment that attracts, retains, and utilizes the talents of a diverse workforce.
Point of View	Organizations must attract and retain a high-performing diverse workforce in order to thrive in a global economy. A diverse workforce brings the competitive advantages that spring from diversity of thought, viewpoints and experience. A diverse workforce also brings a level of complexity to everyday interactions. Leaders must have the skills to nurture the opportunities while managing the complexity.
Main Contributing Behaviors	• Model inclusive behavior, personally • Create environments of inclusion and respect for differences

(continued)

	• Champion recruitment and retention of a qualified and diverse workforce
	• Hold people accountable for respectful, inclusive behavior
Training Focus	Training that emphasizes creating cultural and intercultural competency, developing diversity maturity, leading a multi-generational workforce, leading a global team, mediating cultural conflict, and addressing micro-inequities in the workplace.
Competency 16	**Create Customer Loyalty**
Definition	Applying interpersonal and problem-solving skills needed to exceed customer expectations and build trust-based customer relationships.
Point of View	Organizations must attract and retain loyal customers, particularly in times of shrinking margins and expanding choices. The effectiveness at retaining customers is ultimately dependent upon every employee knowing how they contribute to customer loyalty and taking action to ensure the organization always delivers on its promises to customers.
Main Contributing Behaviors	• Build professional person-to-person relationships
	• Educate the customer
	• Manage expectations and keep promises
	• Exhibit emotional intelligence in dealing with challenging customers
	• Deliver quality and value
	• Be accountable
	• Recover quickly from mistakes
Training Focus	Training that emphasizes responsiveness and follow-through, personal responsibility, the fundamentals of customer service, dealing with angry customers, handling tough inquiries, and supporting sales.

(continued)

Table 37.2 High-Performing Competencies (Continued)

Competency 17	Drive Innovation
Definition	Creating an environment where people feel secure and can openly share ideas, think outside of the norm, and contribute to the growth and future development of the organization.
Point of View	Remaining competitive is rooted in innovative thinking and creative problem solving. An organization's ability to drive innovation will determine its capability to sustain and grow regardless of changes brought upon by economic, environmental, and personnel challenges.
Main Contributing Behaviors	• Creatively solve problems • Collaborate with others • Communicate positively • Make decisions in the midst of ambiguity
Training Focus	Training that emphasizes developing high-performance principles, strategic thinking, creative problem solving, effective communication, collaboration, and suspended judgment.
Competency 18	**Transform the Organization**
Definition	The ability to implement enterprise-wide change and align functions, work processes, and people.
Point of View	In an effort to be and remain competitive, the alignment of people and process, across all functions of the organization requires a strategic approach to change.
Main Contributing Behaviors	• Think strategically • Plan for the future • Translate vision into meaningful daily activities • Maximize diversity
Training Focus	Training that emphasizes developing high-performance principles, strategic decision making, maximizing diverse talents, organizational planning, and goal setting.

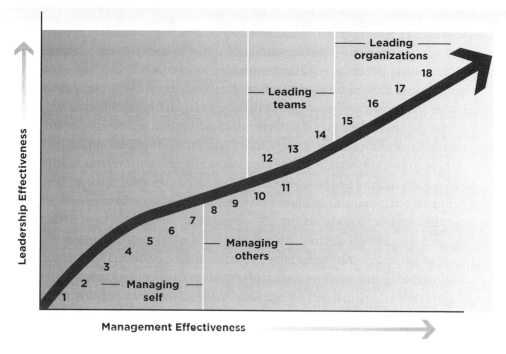

Figure 37.1 High-Performing Workplace Model™

Training Triage Applied

Let's apply the triage concept to two scenarios.

SCENARIO 1: INDIVIDUAL TRIAGE

Recently promoted from the rank-and-file, a new manager is having difficulty making the transition. Metrics used to monitor productivity in her department are down across-the-board by comparison to those posted under previous managers. In addition, two long-time employees have left the company and several others have either left or applied for transfers to other departments. The challenge: stop employee attrition while positioning the new manager for success.

Status: Training has been identified as part of the solution.

Action

1. Identify likely deficiencies among the manager's current competencies (aka, gap analysis) and determine the appropriate focus for training that will strengthen required proficiencies (aka, training prescription).

2. Scanning left-to-right across the model, the area most applicable to this scenario is Managing Others. Competencies in this category (8 to 11) include managing performance, managing work processes, managing customer experience, and managing risk. Given the manager's relative lack of experience, a likely starting point is in the first competency, managing performance.

3. Condensed from the knowledge base that supports the High-Performing Workforce Model™, the definition of managing performance includes a broad set of analysis, problem-solving, and communication skills that enable the successful day-to-day direction of others in the course of delivering desired business results from their combined efforts. And the training focus emphasizes the balance of all management responsibilities: giving and receiving feedback, conducting performance appraisals, practicing progressive discipline, motivating high performers, conducting effective job interviews, delegating with accountability, and communicating and managing expectations. Assessing the manager's skills and experience relative to each of these activities will help zero in on precisely what is needed immediately to help ensure her survival in the position.

4. In addition to Managing Others, the model can be referenced to assess and validate the manager's competency profile in the previous category, Managing Self, as it is entirely possible that gaps or deficiencies among critical competencies in this prior category could be contributing factors to the manager's lack of effectiveness. Looking at competencies 1 through 7 allows for evaluating the manager's work habits, professionalism, interpersonal impact, level of initiative, influencing ability, and savvy within the organization.

5. Based on the review of necessary competencies against the manager's performance, a targeted training prescription individualized for that manager can now be generated.

SCENARIO 2: ORGANIZATIONAL TRIAGE

In addition to its application to individuals, the High-Performing Workforce Model™ can be used to assess organizational competencies necessary for ensuring specified business outcomes. In this case, the organization is poised to implement a multimillion-dollar strategic initiative that will have far-reaching impacts on all employees. The success or failure of the initiative will depend on how well the organization adapts to change.

Status: Front-line and senior leaders have been asked to facilitate large-scale change.

Action

1. Identify likely deficiencies among the leaders and all employees (aka, gap analysis) and determine the appropriate focus for training that will strengthen required proficiencies (aka, training prescription).

2. Scanning left-to-right across the model, the areas most applicable to this scenario are Managing Self and Managing Others. Relevant competencies for all employees include initiative, influencing, political savvy, and future focus (4 to 7) and for leaders, facilitating change (12).

3. Focusing on the leaders first, the definition of facilitating change is minimizing disruptions to productivity, quality, and morale while adapting to change in the shortest amount of time possible. The training focus emphasizes navigating change as a leader, conducting a change analysis, implementing a change plan, being a change champion, and overcoming common obstacles/challenges to change. Skills and behaviors associated with this competency include coaching day-to-day impacts of change, taking positive action to make change successful, influencing others, and gaining commitment, holding others accountable and personally supporting the specific change.

4. Applying these insights, change leaders can assess their personal readiness to facilitate change and can also review the relevant skills and behaviors for the entire organization's overall readiness to execute by asking questions such as:

   - Are our employees change resilient?
   - Do our teams exhibit flexibility and accountability?
   - Do managers understand what is required?
   - Is the change plan sufficiently detailed?
   - Who are the identified champions for the initiative?

5. Based on the review of necessary competencies for both the change leaders and all employees, a targeted training prescription for an organization-wide initiative can now be generated.

What's Next?

In a profession with a long history of a "Ready! Fire! Aim!" approach, the bottom-line benefit of the High-Performing Workforce Model™ lies in connecting critical competencies directly to targeted training. The concept of training triage provides a new perspective on delivering the right training for the right reasons, to the right people at the right time.

As training and development practitioners, we can choose to hunker down in the trenches and wait for the siege to end. Of course, to do so is running the risk that we will emerge to find a workforce unprepared for the challenges of today and tomorrow. Or we can stay in the fray, rally the troops with core competencies and harness the true power of training.

About VisionPoint®

VisionPoint® develops ready-to-deploy media-rich content for all learning environments (e-learning, virtual classroom, and workshop) and offers access to its Training Assets Database (TAD™) to help clients quickly create and deploy their own training programs. VisionPoint's offerings help:

- Foster diversity and create cultural capability
- Boost productivity and increase efficiency
- Maximize performance and minimize risk
- Provide maximum flexibility for training delivery
- Increase the speed of training development
- Reduce the overall cost of training deployment

VisionPoint® is proud to be a GSA vendor and certified woman-owned business.

Submitted by Laura E. Bernstein, President, CEO

VisionPoint® Productions, Inc.

11112 Aurora Avenue

Des Moines, IA 50322

(515) 334-9292

(800) 300-8880

info@visionpoint.com

www.visionpoint.com

SECTION VIII

FOCUS ON INDIVIDUAL DEVELOPMENT

Introduction

Virtual classrooms allow training to be delivered to hundreds—even thousands—of people at the same time. Sometimes that's efficient; sometimes it's not. There will always be a need to have a focus on individual development, whether it is an individual development planning discussion, self-motivated discussions with mentors or coaches, learning in a small peer group, or discussing and acting on 360-degree feedback results.

Ideally, we would like to believe that everyone wants to be a lifelong learner. Word on the street has it that every 2012 college graduate will have upward of eight careers—not jobs, careers. If that isn't a strong argument for becoming a lifelong learner, I am not sure what is. Careers are in every individual's own hands—as Bev Kaye so eloquently states in Chapter 38. Organizations will always be there to support individual development, but the individual must *want* to be developed.

Helping individuals aspire to be the best that they can be may be where coaches, supervisors, trainers, mentors, and others need to start. This is hard work—for both the developer and the learner. But that cannot be a detractor. Hard work, continuous self-improvement, and a sense of building for the future create identity. From identify comes focus; from focus, success. Read more about techniques for self-improvement for a successful future in this section's six chapters. Be sure to top it off with the bonus activity at the end.

- Chapter 38, "Redirect the Development Dialogue" by Career Systems International, provides a foolproof process for helping managers refocus career discussions with employees. Even more important in this chapter are the suggestions for employees who desire career advancement.

- Chapter 39, "Building Your Business Acumen®" by Acumen Learning, addresses the importance of taking on personal responsibility for building business acumen. The seven steps are all doable by anyone desiring to develop this critical corporate skill.

- In Chapter 40, "Resilience—Build This Essential Personal Capability," Resilience Alliance addresses key elements and characteristics of personal resilience. Individuals will appreciate the importance of and payoff for increasing resilience in today's changing world.

- In Chapter 41, "The Promise of Peer Group Coaching to Develop High-Potential Leaders," The Eblin Group presents advice for starting a peer group coaching program. The advantages of this self-development process are many.

- Chapter 42, "Maximize the Results and Multiply the Impact from 360-Degree Assessments" by The Glacel Group, is the first of two chapters on 360-degree feedback. Practical advice about the logistics to consider prevents slip-ups later on.

- In Chapter 43, "How to Present 360-Degree Feedback Effectively," West End Consulting tackles the 360-degree process from a different perspective, discussing techniques to make the feedback more effective as well as exploring why people reject feedback.

- We are honored to present a bonus activity in this section by James Kouzes and Barry Posner. "Composing Your Personal Credo" assists individual learners to find their leadership voice and to determine what values they represent. We must all live by our values.

Chapter 38

Redirect the Development Dialogue

From Complaint to Action

CAREER SYSTEMS INTERNATIONAL

In This Chapter

- How managers can enhance career discussions with employees.
- Suggestions for employees who desire career advancement.

Like a fly on the wall, I could see that he was no longer listening. His eyes were focused on nothing, his mouth was snapped into a thin line, and there wasn't a hint of connection or interest in his body language. He was getting tense and his face showed the tightness of annoyance . . . maybe even anger. He seemed to drag himself though the rest of the meeting and I wondered whether he would make it to the end of the session without exploding. Another career development discussion and it was always the same story from his direct reports. Complain, complain, complain. . . . As a consultant and observer to this exercise, I could not blame this manager for being bored and anxious to finish the day.

I was observing the annual career development conversation marathon (sometimes called the individual development plan, or IDP), and things were not going well. In a few cases, folks came in prepared to discuss their career trajectory with a plan for moving forward. But in most cases, they came in to complain. Here's what I heard over and over.

- "Why didn't I get that promotion?"
- "When will my grade level be upgraded?"
- "I've been in the same job for eight months. What's up?"
- "How come I was passed over for that task force?"
- "When are you going to get me a mentor?"
- "I don't know what's happening in my organization."
- "I'm not doing what I like to do. What do you think I should be doing instead?"

An Old Story

These complaints should have ended a long time ago. But they continue. Employees are still in the dark about how to manage their own careers and believe that, somehow, their managers are in charge of them. They have not examined what's happening within their organizations, cannot name their interests or preferences, don't manage their own reputations, haven't created a personal "brand," don't know what their options are, and have no plans of action. They still believe they are entitled to move along and receive promotions, new responsibilities, and titles without plotting their own course.

Why are employees still waiting for managers and the company to do the work of figuring them out? We have online job postings that people peruse every day just to see whether something strikes their fancy. We do the same with web-based search engines and hope that our next move will appear on our desktops like a pop-up just for us. Sometimes it does; more often it does not.

What Every Employee Should Know About Career Development

- First, understand what's going on around you. Read company press releases, even if they don't apply to your area. Read the business journal that writes about your industry. Read the important bits from your organization's annual report. Get the picture for yourself. Ask what's happening and understand how it may affect you in your current work and future career.

- Second, understand yourself. Just because you do what you do, doesn't mean you love it or couldn't love something else. What are your interests? Your values? Your preferences? How important are they to you and what could you NOT live without?

- Third, figure out your brand. We all have them. Many were invented for us by those around us, and we may be unaware of our reputation at work. Find out how you're perceived (peer-ceived) by co-workers, friends, family. You may be surprised that your own image is not in synch with your reputation. Fix it, if you need to.

- Fourth, understand all the options you may have. Remember that moving up is not the only way to move in the organization. It may serve you well to move laterally in order to learn a new skill or gain experience in what may be a weak area for you. Even moving down is acceptable, as long as it serves your future. Course correct, if you've lost your compass.

- Fifth, put your own plan together. Use your manager, HR, colleagues, family, friends, and mentors to help you chart your own career plan. Make sure it's challenging, not altogether comfortable, somewhat flexible, and based on the truth about you.

Education Required

It has become necessary to teach a process to each and every manager and employee who focuses on his or her individual role in career development. These are separate, distinct roles, and each supports the other. Hold face-to-face discussions along with technology supported conversations to help make actions take hold. Smart HR leaders install sustaining processes to ensure longevity so the investment in development pays off. A development philosophy should also be introduced in your new employee orientation so that, from day one, employees are focused on what they can do for themselves and the company.

Turning Complaints Abound

Let's take a typical complaint list and surface some suggestions for a manager or coach who may want to turn those complaints around.

WHY DIDN'T I GET THAT PROMOTION?

Why didn't you get it? Was your experience lacking in something the job required? Did you pursue it? Make connections that could help you get it? Make sure you managed your personal brand to match the specs for the job? Sure, there was probably lots of competition for the position and maybe others who had longer tenure, but tenure isn't always the deciding factor. If you focus on the job you want and make sure you have learned what qualifications you'll need and clearly get those qualifications under your belt . . . you will make progress. The way to get the job you want is to do the one you have better than everyone else. And make sure the right folks know about it. If you really want it, make sure you do more than just stand in line to get it. Be aggressive, be prepared, and be visible.

I'VE BEEN IN THE SAME JOB FOR EIGHT MONTHS . . . WHAT'S NEXT?

What's the rush? Stay a while and grow where you are by truly taking time to learn your organization, learn your job, and develop a brand reputation. Make sure your reviews are excellent. Then get proactive and go after whatever you want. But don't expect the organization to move you along. There has been a recent movement in many school districts not to permit students to repeat grades or subjects, even though they have not met minimum requirements in competence. So kids are just pushed along, lagging further and further behind each year, but developing a spirit of entitlement to promotion. That just won't fly in the workplace.

Earn your way to the next job and you'll own your own success. Wait for someone to tap you on the shoulder and offer you a future and you might get lucky or you might wait for a very long time. Remember you don't "deserve" success . . . you are simply capable of it.

HOW COME I WAS PASSED OVER FOR THAT TASK FORCE?

Competition exists every day for every opportunity. And the more opportunity, the more competition for the best ones. Ask the leader of the task force what qualifications were important to the team. Ask how you could be on the short list for the next one.

Take pains to introduce yourself to current task force members and learn what's going on. Offer to participate as an ad hoc member of the team and offer your best talents to help them succeed.

WHY DON'T I HAVE A MENTOR?

Managing your own career also means finding your own personal teachers and coaches. Once you know where you're headed, surround yourself with people who will be honest, who are successful, and who are willing to share their experience and knowledge with you. Keep your sights reasonable. If you want Bill Gates to be your mentor, you will be disappointed. Here are a few guidelines. And after you've found a mentor—find more. One mentor is good, but multiple mentors are better.

- *Know what you want:* The more you approach others with a clear idea of what you want from them, the better your chances of getting it. Never ask just by saying, "Will you be my mentor?" Prepare yourself to tell him what you wish to accomplish, what you think you can learn from him, and why you chose him.

- *Know who's out there:* Create a web of relationships by developing diverse contacts, both personal and professional. You primarily want to identify individuals who can help you achieve your goals.

- *Know how others can help:* If you need an introduction to a potential mentor or coach, use your existing network to help make it happen. Perhaps it's your manager or someone for whom you worked previously. Remember, just as with any relationship, no one person can be everything to you. That's why a variety of mentors works so well.

- *Know the odds:* It takes effort to find a mentor. Not everyone is standing in line to mentor you. The most popular mentors are probably the ones at the top of your list. They're probably up to their ears in mentees, so keep an open mind. You must take the initiative, which means you need to know what you want and know how to ask for it. Have a Plan A, B, C, and D.

- *Know how to reciprocate:* Mentoring is no longer considered a one-way street. If you continually ask and offer nothing in return, you will not do as well as the person who—throughout the mentoring relationship—asks, "What can I give back? What can I do for you?" Think of ways to reciprocate and if you can't think of any, just ask. What goes around does come around. And around and around.

Redirect the Development Dialogue

I DON'T KNOW WHAT'S GOING ON AROUND HERE

Mergers, acquisitions, profits, losses, management shakeups, hiring freezes, layoffs, and promotions happen every day . . . and at lightning speed. It's hard to keep up, but if you wait for your manager to call a meeting to let you know, you may wait forever.

Manage this part of your career by becoming an independent researcher. Become active in a professional organization that not only serves your profession, but also your industry. Many professional organizations have SIGs (special interest groups) that serve a narrow group of their membership. Subscribe to magazines, newsletters, blogs, and so on that will keep you informed on your industry and profession. Sometimes we read about our company in the pages of *The Wall Street Journal* or *The Financial Times* long before any information is delivered to employees. Gain an advantage by reading business publications like *Fast Company, Fortune*, as well as your industry-related publications. Keep up-to-date on that world-wide web!

I'M NOT DOING WHAT I LIKE TO DO

We no longer need to remain with one career our whole lives. Many workers find that, after a time, what they used to love doing isn't their love anymore. What we wanted at age eighteen or twenty-two may not be anything like what we want at age twenty-seven or forty. There are so many choices and so much self-knowledge to acquire first, and having a process to use will be extremely helpful to most workers who find themselves falling out of love with their work.

Planning for Stimulating Career Conversations

The IDP conversation is a required career dialogue that is common to almost all organizations. Many organizations given it their own internal name and suggest times of the year that these conversations are to be held. Managers are expected to talk with each of their direct reports. Sometimes this is part of the performance management process; sometimes it is purposely separated.

Usually, there is room for improvement in these conversations and in the (vaguely) written forms that many managers submit. The tool in this book's online tool section can help managers structure the conversation so that all important areas of the career dialogue can be discussed.

Here's to YOU!

There's no secret formula. But there is a process that works, and it works for everyone who applies it. Know what's going on. Know who you are. Know what others think of you. Know your options. Know your plan and act on it. Organizations that provide a process to develop talent and allow workers to manage their own careers will have a continuous pool of developed talent from which to pull.

About Career Systems International

CSI has been a forerunner in the learning and development industry for over thirty years based on the thought leadership of its founder and CEO, Dr. Beverly Kaye. Our niche career development, retention, engagement, and mentoring solutions are offered in multiple modalities (facilitated live and virtual classroom workshops, blended, and self-paced web-enabled learning experiences) and can be tailored or customized to fit the particular culture and needs of our Fortune 1000 clients. These core offerings are backed up by an array of facilitated or stand-alone discovery tools, pre- and post-engagement surveys designed to identify opportunities for improvement and measure the return on investment, consulting and coaching provided by our cadre of certified subject-matter experts, and train-the-trainer certification processes.

Submitted by Beverly Kaye, Founder, CEO

Career Systems International

2400 Stafford Avenue, Suite 200

Scranton, PA 18505

(818) 995-6454

Beverly.kaye@careersystemsintl.com

www.CareerSystemsintl.com

Chapter 39

Building Your
Business Acumen®

ACUMEN LEARNING

In This Chapter

- Importance of taking on personal responsibility for building business acumen for career development.

- Seven steps an individual can take to build business understanding.

"What lies behind us and what lies before us are tiny matters compared to what lies within us."

—Ralph Waldo Emerson

When I first graduated college, I began my career in banking. I remember my enthusiasm and desire to excel in my first job, to set the organization on fire with the sheer brilliance of my performance.

Well, as it turned out, I created more smoke than fire. I quickly began to realize how little I had actually learned in school. I struggled even to keep up a stumbling pace with my associates who had spent a few years in the real world.

I remember how there was nothing more discouraging than being dressed for success and feeling like a failure—sitting in a meeting with managers and senior executives, totally in over my head, trying to follow basic concepts of the financial discussion.

I was usually at a loss to make any intelligent comments, much less any meaningful contribution. I regularly found myself hoping that no one would call on me for anything important, in case I actually had to say something and reveal that I had only faint clues as to what they were talking about.

So early in my career, the embarrassment of ignorance compelled me to make a commitment to competence.

There is no more empowering feeling in business than to be in the company of experienced leaders and to be able not only to follow the flow of their discussion, but to make intelligent contributions to it. To sit in important meetings with professional colleagues, peers, and managers and have others nod their heads in acknowledgement of your insightful comments and recommendations.

Believe me when I say, "If *I* can do it, *you* can do it!" Really! *Anyone* can build business acumen. The key will be to move forward, adopting Nike's slogan at face value. *Just do it!*

Whatever your background, schooling, or experience, there is nothing about business that is beyond your grasp. Make a commitment to building your business acumen through ongoing study and action.

Securing Your Seat at the Table

A Fortune 500 CEO says, "When I walk into a meeting, I want to see people surrounding me who are smarter than I am."

Securing your seat at the table means developing and continuing to exercise your ability to influence decisions and decision-makers within your organization. You must study business generally, your business specifically, and then make and act on sound decisions.

Your application of business acumen requires a focus on the chief concerns and goals of your boss or CEO. You'll need to develop and apply continued insights concerning market trends, competitor analysis, partner relationships, strategic choices, financial markets, consumer trends, technology, and more. You'll need to effectively communicate strategic goals if you want to contribute to your company's growth, and to your own.

As you grow in your influence at the decision table, you'll need to stretch yourself, move outside your comfort zone. It can be challenging to find the time and energy, but the rewards will be worth it. Your knowledge, contributions, and impact on your company and career will be obvious.

I challenge you to move forward with a commitment to *do it*.

In pursuing your worthy personal or business objectives, you must never omit the hard work of preparation. An admiring audience member said to the virtuoso concert pianist, "I'd give my life to play like that." The predictable response: "I have."

Seven Steps for Building Business Acumen

Following are seven practical ideas to encourage and support your ongoing development and application of sound business acumen.

1. COMMIT THE TIME TO STUDY AND RESEARCH

Set aside time for regular study and research. Your days are already full, crowded with professional and personal activities. Find opportunities to carve out the time to advance your career and your business. How much time do you spend watching television? Can you chat with co-workers less and read industry information more? Can you use your lunch time more productively? An hour of "preparation" even once a week will have a great payoff.

Whether you can spend an hour a week or a half-hour daily, set aside time for study and preparation—regularly. Then DO IT!

Devote time to learning how your company is organized and operates: its organization and internal structure, who the key officers are, your primary products and services, your present and future goals. Understand the important priorities, values, and strategies of your CEO, division head, and direct supervisor.

Do you know how your company is doing financially or what its financial goals are? Go deeper than the big picture of your company and explore the financials of each division or department if you can.

You can learn this by reading the annual report, email and other communications from your boss and company officers, company press releases, all materials on the company website, information about your company on the SEC website, quarterly Form 10-Q filings and annual 10-K filings, and other resources about your company, including interviews of your senior leadership in all media. Ask your supervisor how to access more internal operating data if it isn't publicly available.

Also, if possible, listen to your CEO's quarterly conference calls with Wall Street analysts. Or get a summary from your public communications department or company website. This quarterly call provides a current report on your company's operations, financial performance, and your CEO's priorities and future plans.

You should also know who your three to four most important competitors are and learn their basic financial data and organizational structure, strategies, products and services, and strengths and weaknesses. Read their annual reports, their websites, and information about them in the media.

Finally, learn what is happening in the external environment that might affect your company. Read or listen to financial, economic, and business news from websites, print and broadcast media, books, magazines, or *The Wall Street Journal* or the business section of any large metropolitan daily paper.

As Harold S. Geneen, once CEO of ITT and father of the international conglomerate, once said, "When you have mastered numbers, you will in fact no longer be reading numbers, any more than you read words when reading books. You will be reading meanings."

2. TALK WITH KEY COMPANY MANAGERS

Build relationships with your key company leaders and managers. Start with your boss or supervisor. Talk regularly with peers or teammates in different departments who have specific expertise. Ask questions that reveal your own research. Share your helpful insights in return.

Talk with your boss or supervisor about the big picture of your organization and how your work team or department, and you personally, can have a more significant impact.

Learn the key measures and "dashboard metrics" that your boss and division or company senior management are focused on. Discuss with your boss or supervisor how to better achieve these targets so you know how your team, and your job function, fits in.

Meet people for lunch; set brief appointments in their offices.

Let your reasons be known: you want to become more knowledgeable in order to make more effective contributions.

Build relationships!

3. BE PROACTIVE—CONTRIBUTE AND FOLLOW THROUGH

Whenever an assignment or opportunity for action results from your study, discussions, or meetings, follow through and *do it.* Report back in a timely way to the appropriate parties so others will realize you have *done it!*

When realistic or appropriate, put your comments and questions into succinct, meaningful, and timely emails or memos addressed to appropriate personnel. However, don't overwhelm people with a flood of ideas or recommendations. Be targeted in your approach.

Draw up a brief written action list. Link your actions to results that "move the needle" in areas important to your boss and senior management and that support the key measures they have identified. Identify in writing how your actions impact the business. Give a copy to your boss or supervisor and discuss it.

4. ATTEND INDUSTRY MEETINGS AND MAKE OUTSIDE CONTACTS

If your company provides any occasion for you to attend industry or major customer conferences or meetings, take the opportunity. Network with those you meet there. Read the literature available. Grow your own database of contacts. Keep in touch with them over time, as possible. Gain your own direct sources of helpful industry, economic, or business information. Stay in communication with those you meet.

5. USE A BUDDY FOR ACCOUNTABILITY AND MENTORING

Use the buddy system. Ask a co-worker—perhaps a peer or senior manager—to work with and mentor you. At least identify someone to whom you can make a commitment regarding your business acumen action plan and to whom you can be accountable. Perhaps that person would want to further his or her own knowledge, and you can help and support each other. *Being* a mentor to someone else will help you both.

Above all, accept an assignment from and be accountable to *yourself* to continue to develop your business acumen.

6. INFLUENCE MANAGEMENT

To influence senior management, you have to follow all of the above recommendations to prepare yourself to present an idea or opportunity.

Then, when asking a leader to consider seriously your views or recommendations, follow these four important suggestions—principles that have worked for thousands of employees across many industries and types of companies:

Listen to understand: Listen first. Your sole purpose in listening. To *understand* where the individual or management team is coming from, to get what's important to *them*. In every meeting, listen carefully for opportunities to ask insightful questions to learn even more. If you deeply understand *their* points of view, *their* needs and priorities, it will first influence you. Then you'll better be able to influence them.

Present their case and needs to them: Once you have deeply listened, in classic consultative form, make a "my understanding of your needs and objectives" summary before making your own proposals. Once managers know that you really do understand their perspective, they will be more open to listening to your analysis and proposals. You'll have built greater trust.

Talk their language: Once you've established mutual understanding, connect your analysis and recommendations to their strategic goals, concerns, needs, and mindset. Link your message to what's important to them, in financial language they understand. Demonstrate the impact of your proposal or analysis on those drivers important to them. Remember that every department or function has somewhat differing priorities.

Use ROI analysis: Ultimately, every business decision boils down to determining how best to use capital for maximum return on investment. Make a convincing case for a favorable ROI through your recommendation.

7. INCREASE YOUR VALUE ADDED

Your ultimate ability to become a more valuable, and valued, employee is primarily up to you. Your contribution to the success of your department, division, or company at large will add to your own career success. Helping others along the way will add dimensions of experience, knowledge, and insights that will benefit both them and you.

As you become better known for your insightful business acumen, you will become more visible as a contributor and a more valued member of your company team. Wherever you go in your future professional career, your ability to understand the keys that drive business and to exercise the acumen associated with them will lead to sustained profitable success.

Get Started Today

I encourage your continued commitment and hard work. You can begin by turning to the online tools that accompany this book and use the worksheet to consider what you need to do. Persevere. I'm confident it will pay off. The ultimate key? To *engage.* My very best wishes for your success, and my encouragement once more to stay with it!

About Acumen Learning

Acumen Learning, a leader in business acumen training, helps organizations align their learning strategies with executive initiatives. We help employees, no matter their role or experience, understand how their decisions impact the company they work for, sell to, or compete against. The results are employees who understand how to make faster and more profitable business decisions.

Founded in 2002, Acumen Learning has helped design and deliver business acumen training programs for sixteen of the Fortune 50 and hundreds of other companies that are renowned for their learning and development strategies.

Submitted by Kevin Cope, President, CEO

Acumen Learning

226 North Orem Boulevard

Orem, UT 84057

(801) 224-5444

info@acumenlearning.com

www.acumenlearning.com

Chapter 40

Resilience—Build This Essential Personal Capability

RESILIENCE ALLIANCE

In This Chapter

- Key elements and characteristics of personal resilience.
- The importance of resilience in today's changing world.
- Payoff for increased resilience.

As the pace of change in the world continues to increase, managing the many disruptions in our lives has become one of the most important tasks we face. If you work in an organization, you are almost certainly involved in a number of major transitions, such as new technology, shifts in systems and structures, and reorganizations of teams and functions. You probably have additional changes affecting you and those close to you, such as health issues, moving to a new home, or changes in relationships (such as marriage, divorce, having kids, or losing loved ones).

We are not always very good at adapting to this accelerated pace of change. Research suggests that a large number of organizational changes fail to accomplish their desired goals, and our personal changes don't do much better, even when we think they're the right thing to do—think of the number of marriages that fail, and the New Years' resolutions that are never kept.

At its core, successful change depends on whether you as an individual can adapt to new ways of thinking and operating, and whether a critical mass of individuals in an organization can adapt together. But many people lack an understanding of how change affects them and what they can do to better anticipate and adapt to changes that come their way.

Why Change Is Challenging

Although we don't always like to admit it, humans seek control. We use our past experiences to establish *expectations* about how things in our lives are likely to unfold. These expectations provide a sense of control. Change is challenging precisely because it disrupts our expectations—it creates a new reality that doesn't match the expectations we have created. This causes us to feel a loss of control. We sometimes exert a lot of effort to try to get the world to match our expectations. When that doesn't work, we try to establish expectations that match the new reality. This, however, takes energy.

Adaptation is the process we use to adjust to the positive or negative implications of a major shift in our expectations. *Adapting to* or *assimilating* change is costly because it requires personal resources to make the shift. The resources we use include mental energy (to unlearn old ways of doing things and learn new ones), emotional energy (to work with our feelings and reactions), and physical energy (to engage in new behaviors).

Everyone has capacity available for adapting to change. Some have more than others do, but no one has an unlimited amount. Think of your adaptation capacity as a "bank account" of points you can use to pay for changes that take place in your life. Each change draws on this account. When the level of demand for adaptation to change exceeds the energy available, people display a wide range of behaviors that do not contribute to their own well-being or that of their organizations, families, or others. This dysfunction can show itself in a variety of ways, including defensive behavior, stress-related illness, depression, and increased errors and accidents.

Personal Resilience

Of all the factors that contribute to adapting to change, the single most important factor is *resilience*—the capacity to absorb high levels of change and maintain high levels of performance. When resilient people face the ambiguity, anxiety, and loss of control that accompany change, they tend to grow stronger from their experiences rather than feel depleted by them.

What is resilience? Based on a great deal of research and observation of people going through change, we have identified a set of characteristics that help people use their adaptation energy more effectively. We think of these characteristics as *change muscles*. We believe that everyone has the ability to apply and develop each one. Just as certain physical muscles are stronger in some people than others, people differ in the strength of their resilience muscles. And, just as regular exercise will strengthen physical muscles, so resilience muscles can be strengthened through practice. When a change muscle is weak, it can certainly still be used, but the person must apply more effort to get the same result as a person who has developed greater strength in that area.

There are seven resilience characteristics:

1. *Positive—The World:* Resilient individuals effectively identify opportunities in turbulent environments.

2. *Positive—Yourself:* Resilient individuals have the personal confidence to believe they can succeed in the face of uncertainty.

3. *Focused:* Resilient individuals have a clear vision of what they want to achieve and use this as a guide when they become disoriented.

4. *Flexible—Thoughts:* Resilient individuals generate a wide range of ideas and approaches for responding to change.

5. *Flexible—Social:* Resilient individuals draw readily on others' resources for assistance and support during change.

6. *Organized:* Resilient individuals effectively develop and apply systems, processes, and structures when dealing with change.

7. *Proactive:* Resilient individuals initiate action in the face of uncertainty, taking calculated risks rather than seeking the comfort of the status quo.

Each of these characteristics plays a role in the effective use of energy during change.

- The two *positive* characteristics allow you to engage your energy in addressing the challenge, rather than draining energy by retreating into worry and defensiveness.

- The *focused* characteristic allows you to direct energy toward your most important goals, rather than diffusing it across too many options.

Resilience—Build This Essential Personal Capability

- The two *flexible* characteristics allow you to open up a wide range of possibilities and resources, rather than limiting yourself to the familiar.

- The *organized* characteristic allows you to generate efficient, effective approaches, rather than applying your energy unsystematically.

- The *proactive* characteristic allows you to experiment with action in the face of uncertainty, rather than holding back until everything is clear.

Each of these seven characteristics of resilience is important by itself, yet they are most effective when combined in action. This allows you to call on the specific change muscles that are most needed to address a particular challenge. As an example, you might run into a situation where the most important element is the ability to be extremely flexible and think of a wide range of possible actions. Another situation might call for you to stay deeply focused on your objective. At various points in time, all the characteristics are important. For this reason, it is impossible to say that there is a single trait called resilience. Instead, we view resilience as the ability to draw on whichever characteristic, or combination of characteristics, is called for in a particular situation.

Developing Resilience

Each of the resilience characteristics can be developed through consistent practice and development of new mental habits. For example, developing strength in the *Positive: The World* characteristic involves taking time to look for possibilities and opportunities in situations that may at first seem primarily negative, and doing this consistently enough that it becomes a regular part of your thought process. It's important to practice during the times when you are not overwhelmed with disruption, so your muscles are ready when the challenges hit. It may also be helpful to identify someone who can serve as a resource or a coach as you work to develop one or more of the characteristics.

The payoff for increased resilience is strong for both organizations and individuals. Organizations benefit from being able to implement changes more quickly and effectively, which gives them a competitive advantage compared to organizations with less-resilient people and protects them from lower levels of unproductive behavior during turbulence. Individuals benefit from being able to achieve their own goals in the midst of uncertainty with less wasted energy, leading to greater productivity and greater satisfaction.

With this in mind, while the challenges of change place significant demands on everyone, both inside and outside organizations, a focus on identifying and developing resilience can help you use your available mental, emotional, and physical energy to respond to these challenges with higher levels of performance. The activity in the online tools section for this book is one you can use in a group setting to help individuals identify next steps for strengthening their resilience.

About Resilience Alliance

Resilience Alliance helps organizations, teams, and individuals thrive in turbulence. We offer engaging, research-based tools and training materials. Our delivery model is flexible—we train and license internal and external practitioners, and we also deliver assessment, training, and consulting services directly to clients. More than seventy thousand individuals have used our *Personal Resilience Profile* in one-on-one, team, and classroom settings, generating insights to help them strengthen their change muscles and use their energy more effectively during change. An online learning game and a rich set of training modules further enhance individual and team resilience development.

Resilience Alliance also offer a range of assessments, courses, and other materials designed to help practitioners maximize the flow of productive energy during major change initiatives. Our materials are easy to use and are designed to integrate with a broad range of frameworks and methodologies.

Submitted by Linda Hoopes, Ph.D., President

Resilience Alliance

315 West Ponce de Leon Avenue, Suite 433

Decatur, GA 30030

(404) 371-1011.

info@resiliencealliance.com

www.resiliencealliance.com

RESILIENCE ALLIANCE

Chapter 41

The Promise of Peer Group Coaching to Develop High-Potential Leaders

THE EBLIN GROUP

In This Chapter

- Field-tested advice for how to start a peer group coaching program.
- Advantages of a peer coaching group.

The story is familiar. A rising corporate star with a track record of success is promoted to an executive-level role but quickly fails to deliver the results that are expected of someone in that role. The reasons are varied and usually interconnected. The confidence the person exhibited on the way up visibly fades. Under pressure, the person tries to do everything by him- or herself and micromanage his or her teams. The person is so busy running flat out that he or she fails to build the relationships needed for long-term success. Within a few months or a few years, the individual has left the organization to "pursue other opportunities," and the search is on for a replacement. A once-promising career has run off the rails. Meanwhile, the cost to the organization in terms of lost productivity and transactional expenses can easily run into the millions of dollars.

Since it's usually the best and the brightest who are promoted, this scenario begs the question: "What is everybody missing?"

Based on my work as both an executive and a leadership coach, I set out to answer this question in my book, *The Next Level: What Insiders Know About Executive Success*. What I learned in conducting the research for the book and in ongoing research and work with rising executives since its initial publication in 2006 is that most high-potential leaders share a common background.

What High-Potential Leaders Have in Common

What gets many high potentials noticed and promoted is that they have a reputation as being the go-to people. They're smart, motivated, and accomplish things. They exhibit a lot of the characteristics that senior leaders are looking for and believe they see in themselves. Being a go-to person is great until it isn't. At the executive level, the scopes of responsibility are too broad and complex for go-to people to personally ride to the rescue whenever there's a problem or exciting opportunity. They need to let go of many of the behaviors that led to the promotion and pick up a whole new set of behaviors, approaches, and perspectives that the more senior leaders in their organization often take for granted.

The challenge and the opportunity for those charged with supporting the long-term success of high-potential leaders is to create development opportunities that make the implicit assumptions and expectations that come with next level roles much more explicit. Just about everyone in an organization's pool of high-potential leaders has a common dilemma, which is how to come up with an approach to leadership that is scalable as they advance in their careers. Whether or not they can articulate how they did it, successful senior leaders have figured out how to scale. Leadership development professionals need to help their high-potential leaders learn how to scale.

A Scalable Approach to Preparing High Potentials

One way to do that is to scale the widely used intervention of executive coaching. In a typical executive coaching engagement, an individual works with a coach for a number of months to identify and improve on the behaviors he or she has to master to operate successfully at the next level. Individual coaching can be an effective approach to development, but it's usually expensive and the results are often hard to measure or clearly observe. Because of understandable norms around confidentiality, the lessons learned from individual coaching are usually not very scalable across an organization. As such, there can be a lot of time and effort spent on reinventing the wheel with each new coaching engagement.

For high-potential leaders moving to the executive level in their organizations, a peer group coaching approach is a measurably effective and much more cost-efficient solution than is individual executive coaching. Peer group coaching is not team coaching. Team coaching focuses on improving the collective performance of an intact team. Peer group coaching focuses on improving the individual performance of a group of peers who have something in common. The common focus in this case is that the high-potential peers are at a similar point in the development of their careers.

The Basics of a Peer Group Coaching Approach

Over a five-year period, my company has developed and delivered a peer group coaching program called Next Level Leadership™ dozens of times to hundreds of high-potential leaders in companies in the manufacturing, technology, research, media, and services sectors. The program is based on the model of leadership described in *The Next Level*. Let me describe how we structure the program and what we've learned about success factors in delivering a peer group coaching program. The basics of what we've learned should be applicable to any peer group coaching program that you might design for your organization.

The group coaching program brings together cross-functional cohorts of high-potential leaders in an organization for a seven-month period of behaviorally focused coaching. Based on feedback from colleagues, participants create a highly focused development plan to improve one or two high-leverage behaviors. During the course of the program, participants engage with stakeholders, each other, and their coach to follow through on their development plans in what we call "the school of real life."

Our research shows that high potentials moving to or arriving at the executive level generally have the same types of development opportunities as they make the transition upward. In particular, our 360-degree survey data shows that rising high-potential leaders struggle most with mastering the following five behaviors:

- Pacing oneself by building in regular breaks from work.
- Managing one's workload so there is time to deal with unexpected problems or issues.

- Spending less time using one's own functional skills and more time encouraging team members to use theirs.

- Regularly taking time to step back to define or redefine what needs to be done.

- Focusing less on day-to-day operations and more on identifying and taking advantage of strategic opportunities.

One of the most common responses from participants in our group coaching programs is something along the lines of "I'm so glad to know it wasn't just me." When participants understand that their peers are grappling with the same development opportunities, they begin to relax a little. The group coaching approach creates an opportunity for them to learn from each other and gain confidence from that process. As each cohort moves to the end of the program, we conduct follow-up mini assessments on each participant's developmental focal points by asking his or her primary stakeholders to assess the change in the participant's effectiveness on both an overall basis and a developmental behavioral basis. Our aggregate mini-assessment results over the past five years show that an average of 85 percent of responding stakeholders observe a positive change in the effectiveness of the group coaching participants.

With the right design and execution, any group coaching program should be able to achieve similar results. Here, then, are eight lessons we've learned about how to design and deliver a peer group coaching program for high-potential leaders. You will find this information in this book's tool section in an easy downloadable format.

Eight Guidelines About What Makes a Successful Peer Group Coaching Program

1. Choose a leadership model to organize the program around. Behaviors are more important and relevant for participants than competencies.

2. Take the time to map your process so that everyone is clear about what's expected of him or her.

3. Assemble your cohorts carefully and thoughtfully so that there is a functional and geographic mix that helps participants build their networks more quickly.

4. Go lighter on content and tools. Go heavier on coaching. The stickiest learning occurs from the coaching.

5. Choose your coaches carefully. The most successful artfully blend coaching with training skills.

Developing Talent for Organizational Results

6. Encourage transparency. Participants improve more and faster when they share what they're working on with each other and with their stakeholders.

7. Create and mix lots of touch points so that participants are regularly engaged with the program. One simple and highly effective touch point is regular peer coaching conversations (see the sidebar on peer-to-peer coaching below).

8. You can't over-communicate. People are busy and they process information at different rates and in different ways. Don't make them guess about what the program's goals are, how it works, what's next, and what they need to do next. Keep your program communications brief but frequent and consistent.

THE POWER OF PEER-TO-PEER COACHING

Establishing peer-to-peer coaching relationships that extend over the duration of the peer group coaching program is a great way to help participants learn and sustain momentum. You can ask participants to randomly pair up during lunch at the first group session. The only requirement is that they pair up with someone they don't know very well.

From there, the strong request is that participants set a regular weekly day and time for a twenty-minute coaching call. The agenda for the weekly call is simple. Each participant spends ten minutes coaching the other by asking simple, open-ended questions that help them self-observe and think about how to calibrate their actions around their development objectives.

To get things started, we give the participants a list to work from that includes the following questions:

- What behavior are you working on?
- What's coming up on your calendar this week when you'll have a chance to practice that?
- What actions steps or game plan do you have in mind to follow through?

(continued)

- Looking back at last week, what have you learned about what you want to keep doing or do differently this week?
- What impact is your behavioral focus having on your results and relationships at work?

The majority of our participants report that the weekly peer coaching conversation is one of the most meaningful and high-impact parts of the group coaching program. Many of our alumni continue with their peer coaching relationships after the formal program ends.

The Benefits of Peer Group Coaching

With some thought and planning, your organization can offer peer group coaching to your high-potential leaders. There are many benefits to doing so. You can reach more leaders more quickly at a lower cost per person than is usually possible with individual coaching engagements. The group approach allows you to target the focus of your coaching expenses. Learning is maximized because peers learn from each other. You can create a coaching mindset in and build the coaching skills of your next generation of leaders. You will support your high potentials in building the peer networks they need to succeed as next-level leaders. When the group coaching program ends with a closing mini-assessment, you can clearly measure the overall impact of the investment. Of course, the biggest benefit is in developing high-potential leaders who are better prepared for the next challenge or opportunity that awaits them.

About The Eblin Group, Inc.

The Eblin Group, Inc., is a leadership development and strategy firm that supports organizations in ensuring the success of their leaders. The Eblin Group offers executive coaching, peer group coaching, assessments, keynotes, workshops, and training programs that provide leaders and the professionals who support them with the insights and tools they need to succeed at the next level. Co-founder and president Scott Eblin is the author of *The Next Level: What Insiders Know About Executive Success*. Through his work as an executive coach, leadership strategist, speaker, and author, Scott has become known as a thought leader in identifying the behaviors that leaders need to pick up and let go as they transition into new roles and situations that require different results.

Submitted by Scott Eblin, President

The Eblin Group

13126 Pelmira Ridge Court

Herndon, VA 20171

(888) 242-4680 x702

contact@eblingroup.com

www.eblingroup.com.

Chapter 42

Maximize the Results and Multiply the Impact from 360-Degree Assessments

THE GLACEL GROUP

In This Chapter

- Definition of 360-degree feedback.
- Logistics to consider before, during, and after a 360-degree implementation.
- Relationship of 360-degree to other instruments, development, and organizational impact.

Many corporations of all sizes and in a wide variety of industries have jumped on the 360 bandwagon with varying degrees of success. In my twenty-five years of working with 360s, I have seen the best and the worst of these efforts. This chapter will suggest a plan to get the very most out of the 360 effort so that it accomplishes three things: development for the participant managers; guidance for the participants' superiors in their own roles as coaches; and aggregating the 360 feedback for an organizational needs assessment on training opportunities and organization development.

What Is 360-Degree Assessment?

A 360-degree assessment is an opportunity to provide feedback to managers from 360 degrees around them—their superiors, peers, and subordinates. Often the 360 also includes feedback from other groups, such as customers, matrix teams, or lateral superiors. The 360 can be carried out by survey or by interview. In this chapter, 360 by survey is the focus.

At its very best, 360-degree is assessment for later development. It is used in a confidential way in which the participant (the Self) is the owner of the data and solely determines how it is used and with whom it is shared. Although feedback from a survey 360 assessment is exhibited in a quantitative form and often with graphs comparing the measures to a predetermined norm group, in reality those numbers are simply a quantification of subjective data. Too often, the numbers are taken as gospel when they are merely the interpretation of a rater's subjective view. Therefore, it is not appropriate to use 360-degree assessment surveys as means for promotion, annual performance review, succession planning, or bonus allocation.

The 360 survey itself is assessment, pure and simple. It is not development. The assessment forms the basis for creating a development plan. The plan forms the basis for ongoing individual development efforts. Each builds on the other, and the 360 is only the start. To build on the feedback in the 360 assessments, participants will need guidance through several phases by a professional coach who is experienced in the use of the survey and in development planning.

The effective coach will adhere to several key principles. First and foremost, there must be good trust and chemistry between the coach and the 360 participant. There must be absolute confidentiality about the contents of discussions on the 360 and other real-time issues. While internal HR facilitators may be competent to perform this role, participants may doubt whether issues discussed are truly confidential within the organization. Unfortunately, even the best internal HR practitioners can be tarnished by examples of the few times when confidentiality is broken or 360 assessment is misused internally.

What 360-Degree Assessment Is Not

The 360-degree assessment and associated coaching are not a substitute for the services and functions of an organization's internal human resources department. The 360 is an effort that complements and supports the mission and the function of HR. Because it is assessment for development, the 360 is also not a guaranteed path to promotion. Many times, high potentials are selected to participate in the 360 assessment. While that selection may send a message, it does not guarantee a result. Only continued or improved high performance can lead to a positive action by way of promotion or other recognition.

The coaching that accompanies the 360 assessment is not intended to provide legal advice on personnel issues. While the handling of personnel issues may certainly be discussed as a part of the participants' managerial roles, the coach does not provide legal counsel. Neither does the coach become a message service between the participant, the boss, or the subordinates. The coach may advise the participant on meetings with the boss and subordinates, but as the owner of the data, the participant speaks for him- or herself without the coach as the interpreter.

The 360-degree assessment is not a one-time training workshop. Group meetings may be conducted to kick off the 360 initiative or to instruct how to read the results. Group sessions may be held to incorporate other psychometrics, such as the Myers Briggs Type Indicator® or the DiSC® survey that help the participant put the 360 results in context with personal style. However, to get the full impact of the 360 and to use the results for development planning, the intervention will take several months, not a one-time seminar.

Why Conduct a 360 Assessment?

Implementing a 360-degree assessment is a lot of work. It should not be undertaken simply because it is the latest fad or because the competition is doing it. It should only be done to meet a specific individual or organizational goal and when management is truly committed to spending the time and effort to complete the surveys, to administer the process, and to provide coaching for development.

Sometimes the impetus for a 360 project comes from annual employee opinion surveys that highlight particular deficiencies or needs of the management. A goal for conducting the 360 might be to implement a feedback culture in the organization whereby managers will regularly receive feedback and use it to make personal improvements. It could be to assist high potentials who can make significant improvements in their management practices by understanding their impact on others. A goal could be to help under-performers to understand their own development needs in order to become solid managers.

From an organizational perspective, the aggregated data can better inform the organization about training needs for managers so that the management training courses offered are the ones most needed by the participants in the 360 initiative.

Whatever the particular goal, the 360 assessment will gain more support if the participants and their raters understand why their time and effort are being requested and what the expected outcome will be—for them, for the managers, and for the organization.

Who Will Participate?

It makes sense for the line management or the HR department to define who will be the participants in the 360 process. Particularly if it is being done for the first time, a small pilot group may be selected. They should be informed of why they were selected: Are they high potentials? Are they at risk? What is the message being sent by their selection? If they are not told, they tend to fear the worst.

The 360 process will be more successful when the participants buy into it. That means being absolutely transparent with them about why they were chosen, the timeline, who will see the results, and what is expected of them. They will buy in the most when they have control—control over the data and how much they choose to share, with whom they share it, how the raters are chosen, or whether they will even participate at all. If the data will be made available to the boss or to HR, this must be obvious before the 360 process begins. The most successful 360 initiatives provide the data only to the participants and give them full control over the decision of whether and how much of it to share.

Expectations of the participants include that they will make time to participate in the 360 assessment for a development program; that they will share their insights and development plans with their bosses; and that they will hold themselves accountable to improve their management practices to benefit themselves, their teams, and the company.

When Will You Conduct the 360 Assessment?

The biggest considerations for when to conduct the 360 initiative involve what else is happening at the same time. Because the 360 is assessment for development, it should not coincide with the annual performance review or the allotment of bonus payouts. Even if it is not used in those evaluations, the coincidence of timing could lead to confusion about the confidentiality of the results.

The administration of the 360 is time-consuming—for the logistical administrator, for the participants, and for the raters. Therefore, it makes sense not to put too many people through the 360 process all at one time. If they work together, they may ask many of the same raters for feedback. That can lead to a poor response rate when the same people are called on to answer too many 360 questionnaires. Therefore, a large group should be sequenced over time to reduce the time burden on raters.

Which 360 Will You Administer?

There are a variety of off-the-shelf 360 instruments available that include competencies of good general management and leadership. Some providers will customize a standard 360, allowing an organization to choose the competencies that best match their own performance measures. Some companies hire professional firms to create a company-specific 360 survey. When working with an established and reputable provider, the surveys are professionally created, the competencies are research-based and have been determined to be valid indicators of managerial performance, and often the results can be compared to a normative group of managers by level, industry, or geography.

The Kick-Off

An open, public, transparent kick-off with the senior executive sponsor and the line managers of the participants will lay the groundwork for a successful 360 process. If the sponsor is not the line manager of the participants, then the direct line manager of each participant should attend the kick-off as well. This allows participants and managers to hear the same information, understand each of their roles, and ask any questions to clarify the process. The sponsor can add validity and importance to the 360 effort by telling about his or her own experience with assessment and coaching.

During this meeting, the participants should be told why they were selected for the 360 assessment and what is expected of them in terms of the time commitment, the visible effort, and any sharing of information or development plans. The rules and logistics for administration must be explained, particularly around the selection of raters to include the number of raters and the types of categories to fill. Raters should include people who interact often with the participant. They should include a variety of others with whom the participant works well or those who may have some conflict. A conversation between the participant and the direct boss is suggested to aid in the selection of the raters. All of these instructions are best understood if presented in a follow-on email to the participants, as shown in Exhibit 42.1.

EXHIBIT 42.1. SAMPLE INTRODUCTORY MESSAGE TO 360 PARTICIPANTS

In order to participate in the 360, please access the 360 assessment site immediately. Your final 360 is due on [date], but you must allow that same amount of time for your respondents to answer as well. You will be asked to give email addresses for:

- *Superior (optional)*—this is your boss's boss or another superior, but not your immediate boss. This person's answers will be identifiable to you.

- *Boss*—this is your immediate boss. This person's answers will be identifiable to you.

- *Peers*—you are required to have a minimum of three responses to see the results. Please ask five to seven people.

- *Subordinates*—you are required to have a minimum of three responses to see the results. Please ask five to seven people.

- *Others (optional)*—you may have one or more. I suggest you ask five to seven customers, matrix peers, or a group of your choosing.

Please compile your list of suggested respondents and consult with your boss before submitting them on the site. Please be sure to ask a sufficient number to receive at least three responses for peers and subordinates. You want a good mix of people with whom you interact often and who will give you both positive and constructive answers.

Please send a personal email to all those whom you name so they will expect to receive the email directly from the assessment site asking them to participate. If you do not let them know in advance, they may not even open the email request.

You will be able to track your own number of respondents during the two-week period that the survey is "open." I will also track the site. Feel free to send reminders to your potential respondents asking them to complete the survey by the due date.

I am happy to answer any and all questions. Please do not hesitate to email me for any reason.

I look forward to working with all of you in the next few months.

Although 360s are often seen as a rating of quality, most of the responses are actually frequency counts. The rater can only speak accurately to the participants' activities that are observed. Therefore, it makes sense to choose raters who are in a position to observe the participant in a variety of settings, to include virtually.

When the raters are chosen and submitted to the organization conducting the 360 survey, the participant should notify each rater personally and request his or her time in filling out the survey. It makes sense to explain to the raters why the survey is being done—based on what was explained by the executive sponsor. The participant may choose to speak personally with each rater or to send each one an email that might say something like the example in Exhibit 42.2.

EXHIBIT 42.2. SAMPLE PARTICIPANT MESSAGE TO SELECTED RATERS

Dear Colleague,

As part of my professional development, I am participating in a 360 assessment of my management behaviors. Following the survey, I will work with an executive coach to create a development plan and to implement some changes to be a more effective manager. I am writing to ask you to help me in this effort by answering questions about my management in an online survey. You will be receiving an email instructing you on how to respond. Please be honest about my strengths and my development needs. Your responses will be collated with those of others and will be passed on to me anonymously. The survey will take you about [fill in] minutes to complete and should be submitted no later than [date]. Many thanks in advance for your time.

[Your Signature]

Logistics

The logistics of administration can be time-consuming, but are necessary for the successful completion of the surveys. A due date should be established within two to three weeks of initiation. That gives sufficient time for raters to complete the surveys, but does not give so much time that people put off their responses. A third-party administrator should carefully track the response rate as the due date nears so that stragglers can be encouraged to complete the surveys. If the participant does not have sufficient input, the deadline should be extended while more responses are secured. At this point, the administrator may need to send out daily reminders for how many and what category of raters are insufficient for a robust report.

Some respondents may not complete the survey due to other work demands, vacation periods, and the fact that another person's 360 is not a priority for a respondent. When the boss does not complete the survey, however, the message that is conveyed is that the 360 effort is not important. Therefore, the 360 should not be scored until the boss has completed the survey.

The Role of the Superior Managers

The participants in the 360 process will get more out of the entire effort if they work in conjunction with their own superior managers. The superior managers have the opportunity to coach their direct reports and learn along with them. While the superior managers may not receive a copy of the 360, they should meet regularly with the participants to discuss the process and ask what the participants are learning and how they can provide support. If the client organization does not have a coaching culture, it may be necessary to conduct a coaching workshop for the managers. At the least, the managers should be kept informed of the process and given access to an external coach who can answer their questions and guide them in the process of coaching their subordinates.

The external coach for the 360 participants may choose to keep the superior managers informed as the process unfolds. A message, such as the one shown in Exhibit 42.3, is a good way to inform the superior managers.

Feedback

The 360 feedback results do not stand alone. The meaning of the quantitative and qualitative responses makes sense only within the context of the participant's work environment. The participant is the expert on that environment, and the coach can help interpret the feedback with a better understanding of the context. Before the

EXHIBIT 42.3. SAMPLE COACH MESSAGE TO THE PARTICIPANTS' MANAGERS TO INTRODUCE THE PROCESS

Hi Managers,

I want to keep each of you informed as I work with your subordinate managers in the upcoming 360 program. Your role will be key in coaching and supporting your subordinates throughout the feedback and development process. While my work with them will be confidential between each of them individually and me, I will encourage them to share with you what they learn and the goals they set. You might consider this to be part of your own management training and development in terms of how you can coach and develop subordinates. During and after this program, you will be asked to provide feedback on how the program worked for your subordinates and what progress you saw in their efforts to work on their development goals.

At any time during the process, please feel free to contact me with your questions and concerns.

Attached is the email I have just sent to them to outline the process. [*Include a copy of your email similar to Exhibit 42.1.*] Please note that you are asked to work with them and advise them on the people whom they choose to respond to the 360. Please do that immediately so they can submit the names and start the process to meet the deadline.

feedback is presented, the coach would be well served by getting to know the participant's background. A questionnaire, such as the one in Exhibit 42.4, is a helpful way to start a discussion between the coach and the participant to enable an introduction to the participant and the work context. A copy of this background questionnaire can be located in the online tools that support this book.

EXHIBIT 42.4. BACKGROUND QUESTIONNAIRE

Biographical Information—Confidential

Name:

Personal Information

Date of birth: _____

Single/married/divorced/committed partner: _____

Number of children/ages: _____

Education/Training

Level of education/degrees/subject area: _____

Occupational Data

Current position: _____

Number of people reporting to you: _____

What do you like about this position?

What do you do well? What do you need to improve?

Previous Positions (Please answer for each previous position.)

Company name: _____

Responsibilities: _____

Number of people reporting to you: _____

What did you like about the job?

Reason for leaving: _____

General Interests

Leisure time activities: _____

Clubs/organizations: _____

How do these contribute to your personal development?

Descriptive Data

How would your friends describe you?

How would you describe yourself?

What do you think are your strongest points?

What would you like to improve or change about yourself?

What kinds of people do you find it hard to work with?

If I were to talk with your direct reports, what would their criticisms be of you?

If I were to talk to your peers and boss, what would their criticisms be of you?

(continued)

Have you experienced any dangerous or stressful events in your life? Please describe:

What has been your biggest disappointment or sense of failure?

What has been your biggest achievement or success?

How do others see you that is different from how you see yourself?

What pressures do you feel at work or at home?

What is your goal for this coaching opportunity?

The coach is also well served by administering a personality inventory such as the Myers Briggs Type Indicator®, the FIRO-B® or the DiSC®. An understanding of personality style and preferences often supports the analysis of the 360 feedback ratings.

The coach will instruct the participants on how to read the 360 results. It is important to emphasize that the numbers alone mean very little. Raters may use only a limited amount of the available scale for rating. A halo effect or negative halo effect may skew the numbers. One person's rating of 4 may not mean the same thing as another person's rating of 4—and the same is true for any number. Typically, the 360 response report is many pages long and there is a lot of data to digest.

A typical reaction to this data is the grief response—Shock, Anger, Rejection, Acceptance. In order to work through that process, some time to wallow in the data is important. The coach may encourage the participant to suspend making decisions on what the data mean and what to do about it, and rather just to immerse him- or herself in the data. Read it several times. Take lots of notes. Write down the questions that arise from confusing or contradictory data. Live in the shock and anger phases for a time and do not go back to raters for clarification during that emotional response time. That is the time for the coach to be on call to help the participant make sense of the data and enable the participant to move on to accept what makes the most sense within the context of the work environment.

A helpful way to sort the data is to use a 2 × 2 matrix like the one in Figure 42.1 to categorize the most important data as either Good News (surprising and not surprising) or Bad News (surprising and not surprising). This matrix forms the basis for development planning and can also be used in a conversation with the boss. Many

Good News	Bad News
Surprise	Surprise
Not a Surprise	Not a Surprise

Figure 42.1 Good News/Bad News Matrix

people focus only on the bad news when analyzing the 360, but it is equally important to analyze the good news and to share the good news. If one only shares the bad news, that behavior becomes what others look for. By sharing the good news, one is saying, "This is why you hired me. I do these things well. You can count on me to continue to do these things well while I am also working on improving some other areas." You can download this matrix in the online tools that support this book.

Coaching for Development

The coach should be available to the participant throughout the process of wallowing in the data, putting context into the results, and helping to clarify contradictory feedback. If the coach cannot help with answers, the coach can help the participant frame the questions to go back to raters in a non-threatening manner to seek clarification. At the very least, the participant should thank all the raters for giving the gift of their time and their feedback on the 360.

When that is said and done, it is time to create a development plan. In creating this plan, the 360 is only one input into the goals. The goals should be based on the job requirements, previous feedback on performance, the expectations of the boss and the organization, and the issues that the participant has the energy to work on. The 360 typically does not measure technical skills, so the participants should choose two or three management behaviors as their goals. Each goal must include specific actions that will be taken that can be measured to show progress over time.

In formulating the goals, the participant conducts a cost/benefit analysis considering the advantages of achieving the goal when compared to the energy it will take to accomplish it. It is helpful to identify potential obstacles to achieving the goal. The obstacles may be the time required, immediate work deadlines, the culture of the organization, or the lack of support for the new behavior.

In the months that follow, as the participant practices new behaviors, support is a crucial element of success. Support can be provided by the coach. More importantly, support should be provided by the participant's boss and by others who are impacted by the new behaviors. That requires the participant to share the development plan as appropriate. Regular one-on-one meetings with the boss to review the progress and the obstacles to new management behaviors will measure results.

Organizational Impact

When a critical mass of participants within the same organization have completed 360 surveys, the results can be combined into a composite report to show themes and patterns of managerial strengths and development needs within the organization. This information provides a valuable basis on which the organization can develop training programs and organizational initiatives.

This data turns an individual leadership development effort into an organizational result as the organization takes action to provide training and organizational experiences to build up the management talent base.

Incorporating comprehensive 360 assessment into the overall organizational strategy for human resources and talent management pays multiple dividends. Individual managers receive real-time feedback allowing them to continuously work on improving their management skills. Superior managers increase their coaching skills by working with their subordinate managers and providing support as the subordinates practice new behaviors. The organization benefits by overall improved management practices, by creating a culture of feedback, and by monitoring organizational needs for training and development.

About The Glacel Group

The Glacel Group is a group of associated senior professionals in the United States and Europe who have significant experience working within organizations and as coaches and consultants to organizations around the world. They specialize in executive coaching, executive team and board facilitation, and organization development. They have worked with major international businesses, governments and government agencies, and non-governmental organizations on all continents.

Dr. Barbara Pate Glacel is founder and principal of The Glacel Group. She is co-author of a business bestseller on teams and many articles on leadership. With over thirty years experience in executive coaching and leadership development at all levels of organizations, she works with executives in North America, Europe, Asia-Pacific, and South Africa.

Submitted by Barbara Pate Glacel, Ph.D., Principal

The Glacel Group

12103 Richland Lane

Oak Hill, VA 20171

(703) 262-9120

bpglacel@glacel.com

www.glacel.com

Chapter 43

How to Present 360-Degree Feedback Effectively

WEST END CONSULTING

In This Chapter

- Explore why people reject feedback.
- Practical, proven techniques to make 360-degree feedback more effective for individuals and the organization.
- Various feedback approaches and delivery systems.

The 360-degree feedback process involves collecting perceptions about a person's behavior and the impact of that behavior from the person's boss or bosses, direct reports, colleagues, fellow members of project teams, internal and external customers, and suppliers. Other names for 360-degree feedback are multi-rater feedback, multi-source feedback, full-circle appraisal, and group performance review. The term "360-degree feedback" has come to be synonymous with feedback from multiple sources, even though the data may not be gathered from every possible source.

By gathering information from many different people, 360-degree feedback provides a complete portrait of behavior on the job—one that looks at people from every angle and every perspective, in their roles as direct reports, team members, managers of both internal and external relationships, and sources of knowledge and expertise. It is like having a full-length portrait, a profile, a close-up shot of the face, and a view from the back all in one.

When feedback from all these sources is presented within a framework that gives people the chance to practice key behaviors and plan for improvement, it can serve as a lever to bring about real, measurable changes in people's behavior. However, while 360-degree feedback is a powerful tool, it may give us information we did not expect and do not want to hear. That is why decisions concerning the forum for presenting and interpreting the feedback can be as important as choosing the method of data collection or the instrument.

While you may be gathering data on the right behaviors and ensuring that they are reliable, if the feedback is presented poorly and recipients are not able to make sense of it and use it to plan their development, the entire process will have been a waste of everyone's time. In the following pages, we will take a look at what you need to do to help recipients get the most out of the feedback process, including reviewing the barriers that keep people from accepting their feedback, your options for how to present the feedback, and a typical work session agenda.

Understanding Why People Reject Feedback

In many cases, participants' first reaction may be to look for ways to rationalize the information to better fit their self-perceptions or idealized views of themselves. An unwillingness or inability to challenge self-perceptions is one of the three most common reasons that people reject their feedback. The other two are a fear of having weaknesses exposed and the perception that the feedback is unbalanced. Understanding and addressing these potential barriers will enable you to design a successful work session. While you cannot control how people feel coming into the session, you can certainly relieve their anxiety once they are there by maintaining their self-esteem and providing a constructive experience.

UNWILLINGNESS TO CHALLENGE SELF-PERCEPTIONS

Most people who have experienced a degree of success in their careers will attribute that success to, among other things, their own capability and expertise. A strong belief in oneself and one's ability is frequently a characteristic of successful people in organizations. Their current styles and behaviors are what got them to where they are today. So why mess with a sure thing? Challenging this self-perception is difficult and usually not high on people's agendas.

This obstacle becomes less of an issue when people see feedback as a contributing factor to continuous learning and improvement. As one technology manager in a large pharmaceuticals company remarked, "It never feels good to find out that the people you work with believe that you're more focused on your agenda than theirs or that you're not spending enough time with your team. But the way I see it, the more I know about how others see me and what they expect from me, the more effective I can be. It's ammunition to improve my performance."

So how do you ensure that people will be open to hearing information that contradicts their sense of themselves? When their belief in their abilities is challenged, the validity of the data is often challenged as well. Positioning the feedback as a single snapshot of the individual at a specific point in time will better enable people to accept the messages others are sending them. Emphasizing that this is not the absolute and final truth about the recipient will help put the feedback into perspective.

Changing a person's self-image is a slow and difficult process. During the initial review of the feedback, you should ask only that people walk away with one or two key learnings, not that they get every message from which they might benefit. When people are allowed to hold onto what they see as the fundamental elements of their success, they are more accepting of information that challenges their images of themselves. Given the proper guidance and support, additional insights will come over time.

During a recent feedback session, a senior investment banker became quite vocal about his reactions to data he perceived as negative and attempted to disprove each data point one by one, arguing that people just did not understand the requirements of his job and the pressure he was under. Instead of trying to defend the feedback he had received, the facilitator listened in silence and then began to ask questions about what was going on in the organization that might cause people to misperceive him. He seemed surprised that the facilitator was not trying to convince him; gradually, his tone and attitude changed, and he seemed more comfortable with the idea that some of the data might be relevant. He even acknowledged that there could be reasons for people responding the way they did.

In situations like this, it is generally better to let recipients argue with and reject some of their feedback, even if the data seem perfectly plausible. By letting recipients vent, you are clearing the way for them to acknowledge and accept at least a few of the messages they received and thereby increasing the likelihood that they will act on them.

FEAR OF EXPOSING WEAKNESSES

No one wants to look ineffectual or foolish—particularly managers who are conscious of the need to appear confident and self-assured to those around them. By asking people to rate our behavior, however, we run the risk of having our weaknesses exposed—weaknesses we either compensate for or keep hidden and have never shared with anyone.

To minimize the anxiety associated with having one's weaknesses brought out into the open, make sure that people are given complete control of their feedback during the session. They should be allowed to make choices about what results they will share, and how. They should never be required to show or discuss their specific feedback with others. Any group activity should be focused on the participants' analyses and conclusions from the data, not on their specific results for any scales or items. This type of control enables people to concentrate on understanding the data rather than protecting their self-esteem. In addition, if they do elect to share what they have learned after the session, they should be given guidance on how to do so effectively. Focusing on learning and next steps, as opposed to specific numbers and ratings, is the most effective approach.

UNBALANCED FEEDBACK

Another factor that influences the acceptance of feedback is the message itself. Obviously, positive feedback is more readily accepted than negative feedback, since it tends to fit with our own self-image. Feedback should give people a sense of what behaviors they ought to continue, not just what they ought to do differently. Such an emphasis not only provides a more accurate, balanced picture of the person's overall effectiveness, but it also increases the probability that, having examined the good news, the recipient will be open to hearing the bad as well.

What does this mean for how the feedback should be presented? It means that the facilitators, through the design of the work session, must ensure that there will be as strong a focus on strengths as on weaknesses during the analysis and consolidation of the feedback. People should have an opportunity to identify—and celebrate—those behaviors and characteristics that have served them well and contributed to their success. Before they start considering how to overcome or compensate for their weaknesses, they should decide how they will leverage their strengths.

Scheduling the Feedback Session

Once a manager has agreed to participate in the 360-degree effort, the feedback session should be scheduled as soon as possible. If there is a gap between when the questionnaires or interviews are completed and when participants receive their results, people may begin to lose interest. In addition, if the organization is going through a restructuring or major change, people may no longer perceive the feedback as relevant.

Choosing the Location of the Feedback Session

As valuable and rich as the feedback may be, if people are unable to concentrate on the goals of the feedback session or remain focused on the behaviors they need to develop, it may not produce the desired results. Select a location for review and analysis of the feedback that will ensure a minimum of interruptions, enable people to focus and concentrate on the task, and provide privacy if desired.

Ideally, feedback recipients should be removed from their daily grind by holding the session in another building, such as a nearby hotel or conference center, or a conference room in another area of the building. This helps eliminate interruptions, provides an environment in which they can focus only on themselves and their personal development, and lets recipients know that the event they are taking part in is seen as important.

Methods for Delivering the Feedback

There are three primary methods for getting the results of the feedback to participants—one-on-one meetings, group presentations, and self-study, which can be conducted using workbooks or web-based tools. Your choice will depend on the level of the population you are working with, the nature of the feedback, and factors such as your budget, the availability of staff, the time frame for project completion, the location and availability of participants, the extent to which people have experience with 360-degree feedback, and the extent to which feedback is valued and accepted in the organization.

ONE-ON-ONE FEEDBACK DELIVERY

For senior-level or high-potential managers, the one-on-one delivery session in which the recipient meets individually with the facilitator or coach to review and analyze the data is commonly chosen. In a 2008 survey conducted by Lucia and Lepsinger (2009) for *The Art and Science of 360-Degree Feedback*, 60 percent of the HR professionals who reported being satisfied with their organization's multi-rater process use this method. No matter how the data were collected, higher-level people typically do not want to be part of a workshop. They want a more tailored program, and often have tough issues to deal with that cannot be discussed in a group.

GROUP FEEDBACK WORKSHOPS

In the 2008 survey cited above, 45 percent said they used group feedback sessions for delivery of multi-rater results. Many organizations bring fifteen to twenty people together for a one- or two-day workshop.

SELF-STUDY

As the name implies, the self-study approach calls for people to receive their feedback reports, review and analyze the data, and identify next steps on their own, with the help of a self-paced guide that can take the form of either a printed workbook or an electronic program. In organizations in which this method is effective, there is a history of successful implementation of 360, participants have previous experience with a user-friendly feedback report and support materials, and organizational resources are available to provide assistance upon request of the recipient. Twenty-one percent of the HR managers in the 2008 survey cited above said they use self-study as a way to deliver feedback.

Choosing the Right Approach for Your Organization

As you narrow your options for the delivery of the feedback, keep in mind the following questions:

- What is the overall purpose of the feedback initiative?
- What form does the feedback take?
- How many people will be receiving feedback?
- What is the time frame for getting the feedback to the recipients? How difficult will it be to deliver all the feedback within your time frame?
- What is the expected deliverable after people receive their feedback?
- What staff resources and budget can you dedicate to the project?
- How familiar are recipients with 360-degree feedback?

Your answers to these questions, along with the information about the delivery options summarized in the chart shown in Table 43.1, should enable you to select the method that will work best for you, the recipients, and your organization.

Making Sure Your Chosen Feedback Delivery Method Is Effective

As outlined earlier, there are three reasons why people resist feedback and three ways to overcome that resistance: by giving people control over their data, by making sure they do not lose sight of their positive feedback and concentrate wholly on the negative, and by seeing to it that they understand the extent to which the data explain and account for their overall effectiveness. Whatever delivery method you use to present

Table 43.1 A Comparison of Feedback Delivery Options

Method	Participant's Perspective	Delivery Considerations	Resource Considerations
One-on-one	Personalized Highly confidential	One-on-one coaching available Skilled facilitator required	Easy to schedule Time-intensive Costly
Group workshop	Supportive environment Less privacy	Opportunity for skill practice Less individual attention	Potential scheduling conflicts Cost-effective
Self-study	Convenient No interaction	Requires self-motivation Requires user-friendly, robust support materials Works best when recipient is 360 savvy and organizational support can be provided upon request	Low per-person cost Easy to schedule

the feedback to recipients and ensure that they receive the key messages from the data, there are four requirements for making the experience successful.

EXPLAIN THE UNDERLYING MODEL BEING USED

The previously cited 2008 survey revealed that 83 percent of line managers believe that the multi-rater survey should be well-researched. The questions you have asked about people's behavior should be based on a model that describes the behaviors that are important for effectiveness on the job and why they are effective (Yukl & Lepsinger, 1995). Whenever possible, this model should be explained to people so they can relate their feedback and the need to modify their behavior to their specific situation, objectives, and priorities. The technical report should be made available to people who are interested in learning more about how the model was developed and what research went into formulating the questions. One caution—a model that is too complex may be worse than no model at all if it confuses people rather than helps them interpret the feedback.

INVOLVE PEOPLE IN INTERPRETING THE DATA

In some systems, computer programs provide a narrative interpretation of the feedback and tell people what they must do to improve. Although this might sound like a very efficient approach, people who are responsible for making decisions about millions of dollars worth of company assets are likely to resent having a computer tell them to change their behavior. Given some assistance, most people are quite capable of evaluating their own feedback and determining its implications; they also know better than anyone else about special circumstances that have affected their results. Moreover, allowing people to interpret their feedback increases the likelihood that they will accept it and do something with it.

HAVE EACH PERSON DEVELOP AN IMPROVEMENT PLAN

Feedback is more likely to result in behavior change if the manager develops an improvement plan with specific targets and realistic strategies for achieving them. Such action planning, which focuses on both strengths and weaknesses, encourages people to take control of their lives and to decide for themselves how to become more effective. Moreover, in combination with a theory to guide the process, the action planning will help people learn how to best address their specific needs.

CHOOSE A CREDIBLE FACILITATOR TO MANAGE THE PROCESS

Whether you are using a group method or delivering the feedback one-on-one, the capability of the person selected to run the session is critical. That person sets the tone, serves as the primary resource to help people understand their feedback, and assists them in devising strategies for overcoming any obstacles to meeting their development targets. The facilitator's role will be discussed in more detail later in this chapter.

The online tools section supporting this book includes a downloadable list of Do's and Don'ts of some of the actions that will be helpful as you design a successful delivery plan.

The Group Work Session

Because it allows them to engage many people in the process quickly and cost-effectively, decision-makers often opt for the group workshop method of delivering feedback. Two approaches have proven to be practical and engaging: the first is to conduct a workshop that focuses on creating an awareness of how others perceive the feedback recipient; the second is to conduct another type of workshop, one that builds on this awareness and provides skill-development activities to help people apply new behaviors back on the job. Research has shown that individuals who receive their feedback as part of a workshop with a competent, supportive facilitator will demonstrate increased use of certain behaviors and report the feedback to be of more value than those participants who receive only a printed feedback report (Seifert & Yukl, 2007).

APPROACH I—CREATING AWARENESS

The first type of workshop includes three components: presenting the feedback, coaching group activities, and preparing for a sharing and clarifying meeting.

Presenting the Feedback

This segment of the workshop begins with a brief overview of the research and model upon which the questionnaire is based. The content of the feedback report will vary depending on what types of feedback are provided (for example, importance, frequency of use, recommendations for use, highest- and lowest-rated items, comparison to norm group). Before participants receive their individual feedback reports, they are given a few key pointers for getting the most out of their feedback. These include:

- *Pay attention to your first impression of the data*. We typically have an immediate reaction to the data we see. They either make us feel great (Hey, I didn't know I was doing that!) or terrible (I can't believe people see me that way!). There is no real reason to fight the feeling, but we do need to move through it in order to see the data for what they represent.

- *Focus on the messages, not just the measures*. Recipients must look at the data in the context of their jobs—the nature of their work, the goals they are trying to achieve, and the skill and experience of their team members. High ratings are not always good, and low ratings are not always bad. For example, low frequency ratings in "monitoring" may not be bad news for someone working with an experienced team in a reasonably stable environment. However, high frequency ratings in the same situation may raise concerns of micro-managing or lack of confidence in others' ability. Also, to go beyond the averages or the numbers per se, recipients should look at the relative highs and lows, as well as patterns that might appear either within or between the scales.

- *Appreciate the perceptions of others*. Recipients may believe that other people's perceptions of them are incorrect—that their raters neither understand their jobs nor understand the demands and constraints they must work with—and they may even be right. Unfortunately, in this case, being right is not worth much. Ratings reflect the manager's effect on others, not his or her intent. The questions recipients need to ask themselves, therefore, are: "What am I doing that causes people to see me differently than I see myself?" or "What is going on in the organization that could affect people's perceptions of me?"

As people review the feedback report, ask them to consider the following questions to guide them in their analysis and interpretation of the relative importance of the practices:

- Which practices do you and your boss agree are the most important to the effective performance of your job? On which practices do you disagree?

- What issues need to be clarified or discussed with your boss?

- Based on this information, which practices would you say are most critical for the effective performance of your job?

When recipients analyze the data on how frequently raters perceive that they are using specific practices and behaviors, they also have an opportunity to compare their own self-ratings with the ratings of their evaluators. Ideally, the report should display the data using average scores, frequency distributions, and comparisons to national or industry norms (percentile scores).

People should keep in mind the following questions as guides when analyzing how they were rated on frequency of use:

- Which people did you ask to provide you with feedback? Are they in a position to observe and evaluate your performance? To what extent do you depend on them to get work done? How important are these relationships?

- How consistent are the responses across rater groups (boss, colleagues, direct reports)? How consistent are the responses within each rater group?

- How consistent should they be? Are you trying to treat each rater the same, or have you been working with each rater differently based on his or her needs and the situation?

- What patterns emerge within each scale? Are there any patterns across the scales?

- To what extent do you agree with the opinions of those who completed the questionnaire about you?

- How do you compare with the database?

If people receive feedback on how frequently raters feel they should use each practice in order to be more effective, recipients have the opportunity to learn how many of their raters want them to use a particular practice less, more, or as often as they currently do. Coupled with the information on the importance and the frequency of use of the practice, this helps them zero in on strengths and weaknesses.

The following questions are provided as guidelines for interpretation:

- What are your strengths (high frequency of use, top quartile compared to database, the majority of raters recommending using the practice as much as you now do)?

- What areas need further development (low frequency of use, bottom quartile compared to database, the majority of raters recommending using it more or less)?

- How does this feedback fit with feedback you've received before? What surprises did you have? What was confirmed?

- What have people recommended you do more, the same, and less to improve your effectiveness?

Coaching Group Activities

After recipients have taken an initial pass at analyzing their feedback, the coaching group exercise provides an opportunity to discuss specific skills with other workshop participants. Typically, the most effective format is one that includes a structured, small group discussion and a development guide for each practice—an easy-to-read supplementary set of materials that includes additional information about the practice, suggestions for when to use it more or less, and tips and pointers for using it more effectively on the job.

Preparing for a Sharing and Clarifying Meeting

The last component of the workshop provides people with tools and techniques for finalizing development targets. These segments, although begun during the workshop, provide the foundation on which to build follow-up activities that help clarify feedback messages and ensure meaningful action back on the job. During the consolidation process, people are asked to isolate key strengths, weaknesses, and areas that must be clarified.

As noted before, it is crucial to focus on strengths as well as weaknesses during this activity. The consolidated data become the basis for the sharing and clarifying meeting. Before development targets are finalized, recipients should meet with their raters to confirm their findings, clarify messages that were confusing, and ask for suggestions for actions that would improve effectiveness. Pointers on holding effective meetings with raters should be offered during the workshop.

APPROACH II—CREATING AWARENESS AND SKILL DEVELOPMENT

The most effective approach to skill development will first ensure that people understand the fundamentals of using each skill appropriately and then let them practice using the skills in situations that gradually get closer to what they might encounter in their jobs. Therefore, because this workshop provides skill practice in addition to creating awareness, it has several additional features.

Identifying a Business Challenge

To make the feedback even more relevant, as part of the pre-program preparation, ask people to identify a business challenge that currently confronts them and the people whose commitment they need to resolve the issue. Then ask participants to distribute feedback questionnaires to the individuals they have identified as critical to their success in the situations they have identified. This provides two benefits—the feedback will be in the context of a real event and not generalized across many situations, and it is provided by the specific people they are currently trying to influence. Thus, the messages they receive are firmly anchored in the real world, which makes the learning more immediately useful.

Using Video Models

Video models are used to illustrate the effective use of the behaviors covered during the workshop. People can not only read about a given skill but also see examples of its effective use in various situations before they are asked to try using it themselves. Video models also ensure that the skills are presented in a consistent manner from group to group rather than relying solely on the capability of the instructor to demonstrate them clearly and effectively.

Using Case Studies

Once people understand the rudiments of the skill and have practiced using it in generic exercises, they should be given the opportunity to practice it in a situation closer to home. As part of the pre-program preparation, develop case studies that describe typical situations people in the workshop face day-to-day. Such case studies should involve role plays that begin the process of transferring what participants have learned back to their jobs. They are also the springboard for discussion of the unique aspects of the recipients' company and what it will take to use the skills effectively in their particular culture and organizational structure.

Rehearsing Skills

Finally, participants rehearse the skills in the context of a real job situation. Ask participants to use the business challenge they identified as part of the pre-program preparation or to select another situation in which they are currently involved. Using the other participants as resources and coaches, and following a plan they have devised with the help of guidelines provided by the facilitator, they rehearse what they would do and say in this situation. The rehearsal enables people to obtain additional feedback on their use of the skills and enhances their confidence in their ability to use them effectively in a real situation.

Choosing Facilitators and Coaches

People new to receiving 360-degree feedback often have a number of questions such as, "Why are these behaviors being measured?" "How can I use this information to enhance my performance?" "What next steps should I take?" The role of the facilitator is to help participants interpret their feedback and to answer any questions they have. If a facilitator is unable or unwilling to provide the answers to important questions, participants may become skeptical about both their own feedback and the feedback process in general.

For that reason, facilitators must be able to talk intelligently about the model on which the behavior items are based, the development of the instrument and its correlation to effectiveness on the job, the specific behavior items and how they relate to each other, the possible correlation between quantitative data and qualitative responses, as well as the relationship there might be between this and other underlying models of leadership or personal style. They must be able to help recipients put the feedback into context, identify key themes and patterns of behavior, clarify next steps to address weaknesses and leverage strengths, and answer the various questions people ask.

It is essential for facilitators to have gone through a 360-degree feedback experience themselves. They will then be much better able to put themselves in the place of the participants, feel the same feelings, and understand the importance of their role in analyzing the data.

DECIDING WHETHER TO USE INTERNAL OR EXTERNAL FACILITATORS

You have two options when you are deciding who should facilitate the group workshop or present individual feedback—you can use internal or external facilitators.

Depending on the size of your organization, the number of managers participating in the feedback program, and the expertise available within the human resource department, an internal facilitator may be the best choice to deliver the workshop or present individual feedback. The advantages to using an internal facilitator include familiarity with the organization's development objectives and the culture and environment in which its managers operate. To present the feedback effectively, facilitators need to understand how the feedback program relates to other organizational efforts and goals.

An inventory of your available internal resources may reveal a need to look outside the organization for a facilitator. If you are using an outside provider to develop, administer, collect, and process the feedback, you may want to use a facilitator from the same firm to ensure familiarity with the instrument or process. To be effective, however, an external resource must also understand the issues the feedback process is trying to address, the internal dynamics of your company and its culture, and the people with whom he or she will be working. In many cases, such understanding can be gained by briefing external facilitators on the overall development goals of the organization or allowing them to meet or speak with a cross-section of the managers who will receive feedback before the program is launched.

Managers receiving feedback often appreciate having a third party involved. An outside person can both help recipients get a feel for what people in other companies are doing and increase the sense of confidentiality among the recipients.

FACILITATOR CERTIFICATION

If an organization prefers to use internal trainers, a train-the-trainer program is often the answer. Most providers offer a two- or three-day program to train in-house resources in the use of their instrument. Usually, a certified trainer experienced in delivering 360-degree feedback begins by facilitating a program with the would-be trainers as participants to give them a sense of what it is like to look in the mirror and receive feedback on their own behaviors. The consultant then answers questions about the process and the instrument. Finally, the potential trainers practice presenting key information and analyzing sample reports, with the consultant providing coaching and offering suggestions for improvement.

The certification process generally includes having the consultants observe the newly trained facilitators when they deliver their first programs. Frequently, the provider will also provide follow-up and coaching as needed to ensure that the programs are running smoothly. They may also review program evaluations as a source of tips and ideas for improved performance.

SKILL LEVEL AND EXPERIENCE

A skilled facilitator can add a lot of value to the feedback, while an untrained or clumsy facilitator can render it virtually useless. To make the most of the feedback experience for participants, facilitators must be skilled at spotting trends in the data, pulling out key messages, and helping participants interpret their feedback. Facilitators doing one-on-one feedback are likely to be working with senior managers, sometimes only with qualitative results from a series of interviews. They will be particularly effective if they have a business orientation and can provide advice that will appear credible given the work and role of a senior leader. A workshop facilitator should have experience in a classroom setting, effective speaking and listening skills, and the knowledge and background to cite real-life examples of people using effective managerial and leadership behaviors. A well-designed feedback report will help managers work through the meaning of individual scores and comments, but a gifted facilitator can move them from understanding to action.

Conclusion

However you choose to present the feedback in your organization, everyone involved should be conscious of its potential impact. After all, these are not data about production quotas or budget parameters but evaluations of people's individual styles, skills, and effectiveness. Because of people's sensitivity to this type of feedback, the process should always be designed to maximize their willingness to act on the information they receive. Presenters should be prepared to respond not only to what recipients say but also to lessexplicit emotional reactions. By helping feedback recipients understand and work through their reactions during the presentation process, they can clear the way for the next stage: translating the feedback into action back on the job.

REFERENCES

Lepsinger, R., & Lucia, A. (2009). *The art and science of 360-degree feedback* (2nd ed.). San Francisco: Pfeiffer.

Seifert, C.F., & Yukl, G. (2007, August). The effects of repeated feedback on behavior change for managers. Paper presented at the Academy of Management annual meeting, Philadelphia.

Yukl, G., & Lepsinger, R. (1995, December). How to get the most out of 360-degree feedback. *Training*, pp. 45–50.

About West End Consulting

West End Consulting works with organizations to build skills and competencies in leaders and teams for optimal organizational and individual performance. With our help, senior leaders are better able to clarify what is required to implement their strategies, and senior teams are better able to identify and adopt the competencies and processes to work together on shared goals. As a result of working with us, senior executives improve their ability to foster partnerships, gain commitment, and develop people in order to translate strategies into action.

The ways we provide value to our clients include facilitating strategic organizational change; building effective senior management teams; helping executives improve effectiveness through one-on-one coaching; and linking human resource plans to strategic plans. Anntoinette "Toni" Lucia has authored numerous books and articles, including *The Art and Science of 360-Degree Feedback* (2nd ed.) and *The Art and Science of Competency Models*. She is an honorary member of the Instructional Systems Association (ISA) and on the advisory board of Better Communications, Inc.

Submitted by Anntoinette "Toni" Lucia, President

West End Consulting

55 East End Avenue, #12 D

New York, NY 10028

(917) 261-2151

toni@tonilucia.com

www.we-consulting.net

Composing Your Personal Credo

JAMES M. KOUZES AND BARRY Z. POSNER

OVERVIEW

Leadership is personal. It's about leaders and their relationship with others. If people don't believe in the messenger, they won't believe the message. If people don't believe in the leaders, they won't believe in what they say. This activity helps current and future leaders explore their beliefs, values, and principles to begin to create their personal credos.

OBJECTIVE

- To be able to articulate who you are, what you believe, and what you stand for, which is the first step toward being a credible leader.

AUDIENCE

Current or emerging leaders in any size group.

TIME REQUIRED

30 minutes.

Adapted from *Strengthening Credibility: A Leader's Workbook* by James M. Kouzes and Barry Z. Posner, with Jane Bozarth.

MATERIALS AND EQUIPMENT

- A Personal Credo Worksheet for each leader (a sample is provided with this activity; an electronic copy can be downloaded at the website that supports this book).

PROCESS

1. Hand out a Personal Credo Worksheet to each participant.

2. Say: "Through their extensive research, Jim Kouzes and Barry Posner have found that credibility is not based on job titles or hierarchical positions but with the human being in the leader's shoes. Above all else, they found that *leadership is personal*. It's not about the corporation, the community, or the country. It's about *you* and your *relationship* with others. If people don't believe in the *messenger,* they won't believe the message. If people don't believe in *you,* they won't believe in what *you* say. And if it's about you, then it's about your beliefs, your values, and your principles. It's also about how true you are to your values and beliefs. Your credibility journey begins with the process of self-discovery. Their research indicates that, to genuinely know the level of commitment you are willing to make, you must discover three essential aspects of yourself: your credo, your areas of competence, and your level of self-confidence."

3. Ask participants to form pairs and discuss their understanding of the phrase personal credo, then share their thoughts with the group.

4. Say: "Let's revisit your childhood, say, until you were ten years old. This is when you learned to think and act and navigate in the world. Think about parents, relatives, neighbors, friends, and teachers who influenced you. What do you remember being told about how to act and what to think? Do you remember hearing, "If you can't say anything nice, don't say anything at all"? How about, "Don't be such a tomboy" or "Boys don't cry" or "You must respect your elders"? Did you hear that work could be exciting and meaningful, or drudgery to be carried out? What were your beliefs about education? What shaped your beliefs about marriage and family? What did you learn about money and the definition of success or failure? What were the implicit messages about happiness, or making mistakes, or asserting yourself?"

5. Ask participants to fill out their Personal Credo Worksheets. Allow ample time for completion.

6. Encourage participants to pair and share their thoughts with someone.

7. End by asking participants to volunteer what they will do as a result of this activity or what their next steps might be as they shape their Personal Credos.

About the Authors

James M. Kouzes is a professional speaker, cited by *The Wall Street Journal* as one of the top twelve executive educators in the U.S., and an executive leadership fellow at the Leavey School of Business, Santa Clara University, California. **Barry Z. Posner** is professor of leadership at Santa Clara University and former dean of the Leavey School of Business. Jim and Barry are the co-authors of *The Leadership Challenge*, *The Truth About Leadership,* and *Credibility: How Leaders Gain and Lose It, Why People Demand It.*

They also developed the highly acclaimed Leadership Practices Inventory (LPI), a 360-degree assessment tool based on The Five Practices of Exemplary Leadership®. They created the LPI to enable leaders to be the best they can be and continually improve their leadership skills. Used by more than three million people worldwide, this 360-degree assessment tool is part of the pre-work that participants complete before The Leadership Challenge Workshop®—or it can be used as part of an existing leadership development program. It approaches leadership as a measurable, learnable, and teachable set of behaviors and helps individuals and organizations like yours measure leadership competencies, while guiding leaders through the process of applying The Five Practices of Exemplary Leadership® model to real-life organizational challenges.

Submitted by James M. Kouzes, Dean's Executive Fellow of Leadership, Leavey School of Business, Santa Clara University; Barry Z. Posner, Professor of Leadership, Leavey School of Business, Santa Clara University

Jim Kouzes

117 Casa Vieja Place

Orinda, CA 94563

Jim@kouzes.com

Barry Posner

15419 Banyan Lane

Monte Sereno, CA 95030

PERSONAL CREDO WORKSHEET

James M. Kouzes and Barry Z. Posner

You can't do what you say if you don't know what you believe. The first stage of your credibility journey is to clarify your values and determine the roots of your personal credo. Use this worksheet to capture what you believe as the first step in developing your personal credo.

1. Where did your beliefs about what is important in life come from?

2. Which of these ideas or principles still guide you now?

3. Which are still useful? How do they help, support, or guide you in your daily life now?

4. Which are no longer useful? Do any ever cause you conflict or uneasiness?

5. Is it time to let go of some old ways of thinking and acting?

SECTION IX

CARING CUSTOMER SERVICE AND SALES

Introduction

Satisfied customers are the most integral part of any successful business. Without customers there is no business. But having genuinely satisfied customers is never an accident. Satisfied customers are the result of combining knowledge and application: reliable knowledge of what your customers want and the persistent application of the service they expect.

Customers have more options and more information than ever before. Predicting what customers want and the best way to provide it to them is a key focus of most businesses. Your challenge is to anticipate customer needs as opposed to responding to requests. Customers meet with a barrage of new services and products daily, but they don't buy products or services. They buy good feelings and solutions to problems. Many customer needs are emotional rather than logical. The more you know your customers, the better you anticipate their needs.

Good customer service is about bringing customers back and about sending them away happy enough to market your business for you to others, who may also become repeat customers. Businesses can offer promotions and slash prices to bring in new customers, but unless some of those customers come back, your business won't be profitable for long. A good salesperson can sell anything to anyone once, but it is your customer service approach that determines whether you will sell anything to that person again. The essence of good customer service is forming a relationship with customers—a relationship that the customer wishes to pursue.

You know the statistics. A typical dissatisfied customer will tell eight to ten people and one in five will tell twenty. To make matters worse, a typical business will hear from only 4 percent of its dissatisfied customers. The other 96 percent will just quietly slip away, and most never return. On the other hand, seven out of ten complaining customers will do business with you again if you resolve their complaints in their favor. If you resolve it on the spot, 95 percent will do business with you again. One last note—a business spends six times as much to attract a new customer as it does to keep a current one.

So today's businesses must not only learn, but keep on learning, about their customers' needs—surprising them with solutions before they know they have problems! Every year at ISA's Annual Business Retreat a session is held called "The Voice of the Customer" that reviews data in the industry. It helps ISA members stay in touch with what customers want. All businesses need to pay attention to the voice of their customers to stay in sync with customers' needs, to solicit their desires, and to tap into hidden opportunities.

Today's businesses must design a customer experience that goes beyond the customer being satisfied to his or her being ecstatic, gaining not just mere loyalty but fanatic devotion. Know how to meet your customers' emotional needs as well as their product needs.

The chapters in this section take on some of these issues, ensuring that you hear the voice of your customers.

- In Chapter 44, "Twelve Building Blocks of an Uplifting Service Culture," UP! Your Service shares suggestions for implementing a service culture and advice to ensure optimum service delivery. The suggestions can help you better hear the voice of your customers.

- In Chapter 45, "Who Killed Service?" by Sigma Performance Solutions, Inc., you are introduced to a four-step process called LIST that will help you manage your customer interactions. The tips and ideas for dealing with customer problems will help you get through even the most difficult situations.

- Chapter 46, "Taming the Sales Manager Ego" by Amplify, is a sometimes tongue-in-cheek look at sales leaders, their downfalls, and their best qualities. If you work with internal sales staff, this chapter will help you with a few coaching tips. Don't miss the Ego Check Survey in the online tools section of this chapter. It is beneficial for managers of all types.

Chapter 44

Twelve Building Blocks of an Uplifting Service Culture

UP! YOUR SERVICE

In This Chapter

- Twelve suggestions with accompanying rationale for building a service culture.
- Practical advice for service leaders and service providers to ensure optimum service delivery.

Great stories about leading service organizations have been around for years: Nordstrom's, Southwest and Singapore Airlines, Disney. New leaders emerge as business models change and adapt: Zappos, Google, GoDaddy.

But these stories are anecdotes, and many in other industries find their lessons difficult to apply. How many business-to-business or government organizations want a service culture like Zappos that promises to be "a little weird"?

What's needed is more architecture than anecdotes, with a firmer set of foundational principles, leadership rules, and culture-building blocks that make sense and apply across all industries, geographies, and cultures.

In this chapter, we explore the Twelve Building Blocks of Service Culture and provide checklists for self-assessment and questions for designing new action to move from a Confused Culture to an Aligned Culture in your organization.

567

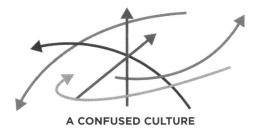

A CONFUSED CULTURE

Figure 44.1   From a Confused Culture

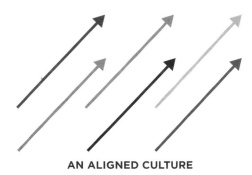

AN ALIGNED CULTURE

Figure 44.2   To an Aligned Culture

1. Common Service Language

Understood and frequently used by service providers at all levels and in all parts of the organization, a common service language enables clear communication and supports the delivery of superior internal and external service.

Every industry and most departments have a common language—think finance, production, sales. What is not as common is a service language everyone can use to describe—and appreciate—a service experience from someone else's point of view. For example, organizations may refer to a service experience as "basic," "expected," or "desired" instead of something more descriptive: "fulfilling the requirements," "following the checklist," or "hitting the KPI."

An effective common service language meets these criteria:

Checklist for Assessment

- Easy to understand
- Applies to real work
- Makes sense at all levels
- Applies to external/internal service
- Connects to culture building
- Is both emotional and rational

Questions for Service Leaders

- Have you developed a common service language everyone in your organization can use to communicate with each other about service?
- Do you use this language frequently and publicly? How can you better "talk the talk" of uplifting service?
- How can you embed your common service language into communications, recruitment, orientation, recognition programs, service improvements, and other daily processes?

Questions for Service Providers

- Do you know the common service language in your organization? If you do not yet have this, how can you help create it?
- Do you use your common service language with your colleagues every day? How can you do this more frequently or creatively to make your culture stronger?

2. Engaging Service Vision

Widely embraced and believed, an engaging service vision energizes everyone in the organization. Each person knows how the vision applies to his or her work and knows what action to take to make the vision real.

An engaging service vision is an articulation of what you want to do, deliver, or become and the experience you want others to have when being served by you. For example, "Service even other airlines talk about" at the luxurious Singapore Airlines and "We make flying fun" at the budget Southwest Airlines. Or "know how, act now, create wow!" at Nokia Siemens Networks and "proactive, value-adding service partners" at Wipro Ltd.

An engaging service vision meets these criteria:

Checklist for Assessment

- A mantra to motivate your team
- Aligned to core brand values in your organization
- Aligned to your customers' values
- Understood at all levels
- Easily translates into action
- Applies to external and internal service providers

Questions for Service Leaders

- Have you articulated an engaging service vision that stimulates and captivates the emotions of your people?
- How can you highlight and promote examples of your engaging service vision in action?

Questions for Service Providers

- Do you know your organization's service vision?
- Can you describe ways in which your daily actions make this vision come alive?

3. Service Recruitment

Effective recruitment strategies and tactics attract people who support your organization's vision and screen out those who may be technically qualified but not aligned with the service spirit and purpose of the organization. For example, one strategy might be to ask candidates to provide real examples of personal actions in alignment with your vision and your values.

Highly effective service recruitment meets these criteria:

Checklist for Assessment

- Your vision is communicated in advance of any interview
- Candidates self-select based on clarity of your recruitment advertisements

- Best customers and staff members are involved in recruitment
- Multiple interviews for new candidates with current staff members
- Use psychometrics for job fit and cultural fit
- Provide the opportunity to leave with dignity after a short trial period

Questions for Service Leaders

- Is your service recruitment process attracting and selecting new staff members who make your culture better and stronger?
- How are you improving your recruitment process right now?

Questions for Service Providers

- How can you help attract and recruit new people to join your organization?
- How can you participate in your company's recruitment process?

4. Service Orientation

Your service orientation for new staff members must be motivating, encouraging, and effective. New team members feel welcome and inspired to contribute to help your service culture even stronger.

Orientation is not the same as induction. Induction is about who sits where and reports to whom, passwords, places to eat, benefits. Orientation answers who we are, who are our customers, how are we doing vs the competition, how are we changing to improve, and how can you—a new team member—help us to succeed?

Highly effective service orientation meets these criteria:

Checklist for Assessment

- Provides new hires with vital content and vibrant cultural context
- Utilizes best practice buddies and management mentors
- Provides cross-functional exposure and real customer/partner contact
- New hires are given early opportunities to contribute to the culture
- Reality check is a fundamental part of the process

Questions for Service Leaders

- Is your service orientation uplifting, engaging, and real?
- Do new hires feel motivated to contribute to your culture?
- What else can you do to make your orientation program stronger?

Questions for Service Providers

- What can you do to make new staff members feel more appreciated and welcome?
- How can you teach and share what you know works well to someone new on your team?

5. Service Communications

Service communications inform, educate, and motivate the entire organization. Creative communication channels surround everyone with relevant service information, timely customer feedback, uplifting success stories, and current challenges and objectives. For example, right now, what is on your walls, website, intranet, chat room, newsletter, video, meeting agenda, email signature file, next presentation, announcement, or speech? Is it the kind of service message you want to communicate?

Effective service communications meet these criteria:

Checklist for Assessment

- Engaging and everywhere
- Leveraged at every opportunity
- Are directed both internally to employees and externally to customers
- Involve new rituals and old traditions
- Include two-way communication
- Frequently quote examples of uplifting service

Questions for Service Leaders

- Do you participate personally in a variety of service communications?
- Do you participate frequently in service communications with employees, customers, and partners?
- Are you supporting innovation in service communication? What's new? What's next?

Questions for Service Providers

- How many channels of service communication can you find at work?

- What can you do to keep these communications fresh and vibrant?

- Where and how can you share these ideas, and contribute your own questions and suggestions?

6. Service Recognition and Rewards

Recognition and rewards motivate your team to stretch for service improvement and celebrate service success. Incentives, acknowledgement, prizes, promotions, and praise all focus attention and encourage greater service results. Examples of topics for service recognition include most service compliments, best service recovery, greatest service improvement, most appreciated service innovation, most collaborative improvement of service between departments, and many more.

Effective service recognition and rewards programs meet these criteria:

Checklist for Assessment

- Recognize service improvement efforts and results

- Praise improvement of external and internal service

- Recognize the achievement of individuals and teams

- Acknowledge great service by employees, managers, and partners

- Build consistency, diversity, and frequency into your programs

- Build service performance into your formal appraisals and promotions

Questions for Leaders

- Are you personally involved in recognizing and rewarding your team for uplifting service?

- Do you have an engaging, fresh, and robust set of service recognition programs?

- Are your team members inspired and motivated by the recognition you provide?

Questions for Service Providers

- Do you participate fully in the service recognition programs where you work?

- How can you praise and appreciate the colleagues who give you uplifting service?

7. Voice of the Customer

The voice of the customer is subjective, qualitative, and emotional. These are the actual words, tones, and gestures that tell you what customers and colleagues think and feel about your service. Voice-of-the-customer feedback systems capture solicited and unsolicited comments, compliments, and complaints through many possible channels and listening posts, including feedback forms, hotlines, interviews, surveys, and others unique to your organization. Frequent voice-of-the-customer input should be anticipated and appreciated by every service provider in your organization.

Effective voice-of-the-customer efforts meet these criteria:

Checklist for Assessment

- Actively seek emotional, subjective, qualitative comments
- Utilize multiple "listening posts" for complaints and compliments
- Channel voice of the customer to service providers throughout the organization
- Use voice of the customer to focus service improvement efforts and investments

Questions for Leaders

- Are you personally involved in your voice-of-the-customer programs?
- How do your drive voice of the customer to all members of your organization?
- What latest investments or improvements have you made based on voice-of-the-customer complaints, compliments, and suggestions?

Questions for Service Providers

- How can you more actively participate in voice-of-the-customer programs?
- What have you learned from recent voice-of-the-customer comments, inputs, and ideas?
- What changes have you made—or can you make—to improve based on the voice of the customer that you hear?

8. Service Measures and Metrics

Measuring what matters focuses attention and leads to positive results in many areas: market share, profitability, reputation, customer loyalty and satisfaction, employee engagement, and performance improvement. Measures and metrics identify problems with concrete data to help you see what must be fixed right away. Measures and metrics can also be used to incentivize service performance, set targets and goals, and clearly measure their achievement.

Effective service measures and metrics meet these criteria:

Checklist for Assessment

- Create value for customers; not just collection of data
- Lead to new service improvements and actions
- Results are widely communicated and understood

Questions for Leaders

- Are your service measures useful in driving service improvements?
- Is your measurement system appreciated by your customers?
- Do your team members understand and act upon the data you now collect?

Questions for Service Providers

- Do you understand what is being measured, and why?
- Do you see how your service affects the metrics your organization collects?
- Can you identify new actions to improve the scores and measures?

9. Service Improvement Process

Continuous service improvement can become everyone's ongoing project and passion. The key is to create a process that continuously brings service issues and opportunities to the forefront for review, reflection, creative consideration, and collaborative problem solving.

Effective service improvement processes meet these criteria:

Checklist for Assessment

- Frequent service improvement workshops
- Contests focused on internal and external service improvement
- Front-line suggestion schemes attracting new ideas
- Creation of cross-functional teams to solve service problems

Questions for Leaders

- Is everyone on your team engaged in a service improvement process?
- Do your team members feel motivated and empowered by the improvement processes you use?
- Do you personally support service improvement workshops, initiatives, contests, and suggestion programs?

Questions for Service Providers

- How can you participate fully in your organization's service improvement process?
- What issues do you think should be addressed in a service improvement process?

10. Service Recovery and Guarantees

When things go wrong, you can bounce back! Effective service recovery and guarantees turn upset customers into loyal advocates and team members into true believers. Great recovery programs send the right signal to customers, and to staff members, focusing on setting things right, and then fixing the source of what went wrong.

Effective service recovery and guarantees efforts meet these criteria:

Checklist for Assessment

- Fast discovery of problems
- Fast recovery for customers
- Front-line empowerment to take action quickly
- Investment in recovery is investment in reputation and lifetime value
- Guarantees are easy to understand and to invoke
- Guarantees provide valuable compensation and lead to meaningful changes

Questions for Leaders

- Do you see and seek out problems as opportunities to bounce back?
- Do your staff members bring up problems to you eagerly, or hide them quickly?

- How can you demonstrate to your team it is okay to make a mistake (and learn from it)?
- When was the last time you shared with everyone a mistake you made and what you learned?

Questions for Service Providers

- Are you familiar with your company's service recovery policies and procedures?
- What can you do to quickly set things right the next time service goes wrong?
- When something goes wrong, you can learn something new. What have you learned lately?

11. Service Benchmarking

Discover and apply best practices of leading organizations inside and outside your industry. Service benchmarking reveals what others do to improve their service and points to new ways you can upgrade yours.

Effective service benchmarking programs meet these criteria:

Checklist for Assessment

- Benchmark leaders inside and outside your industry
- Benchmark across departments inside your organization
- Involve staff from all levels in your benchmarking visits
- Share insights from benchmarking throughout the organization

Questions for Leaders

- Who are you benchmarking right now? What do you hope to learn?
- Who have you invited to benchmark your organization?
- What are the latest lessons you have learned from benchmarking, and how widely are these known inside your organization? What actions have you taken from these insights?

Questions for Service Providers

- What can you learn by studying the service performance and culture in other organizations?

- Who delivers great service inside your organization?
- What can you learn by visiting and observing others in service?

12. Service Role Modeling

Everyone is watching. Everyone is a service role model. Leaders, managers, and front-line staff consistently provide superior service to customers and to each other. Service role modeling is listed last for two reasons: (1) if you act in all the other building blocks and not in this one, the whole culture-building effort will be weakened, and (2) if you are an excellent role model, people will support your efforts, even if it takes time to get the other building blocks into shape.

Effective service role modeling meets these criteria:

Checklist for Assessment

- Talk the talk by using the common service language
- Walk the walk by providing uplifting service to external customers and clients, and internal colleagues and partners
- Empower and enable your staff. Don't just delegate, educate!
- Be predictable in service support, spontaneous with positive service surprises.

Questions for Leaders

- When was the last time you did something that caused your employees to say, "Wow! our manager really *believes* in uplifting service!"?
- What else can you do to be seen and heard uplifting service for colleagues and customers?
- How can you and your peers work better together as leadership role models of service?

Questions for Service Providers

- What can you do today to set the tone and the pace for uplifting service?
- How can you and your colleagues take the lead as service role models in your organization?

Figure 44.3 shows the twelve building blocks of an uplifting service culture.

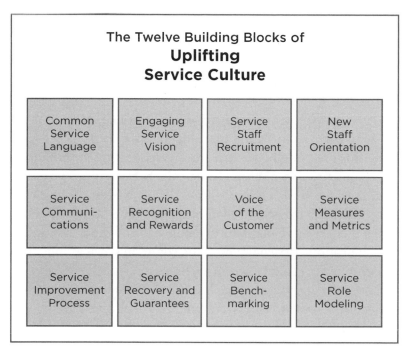

The Twelve Building Blocks of
Uplifting
Service Culture

Common Service Language	Engaging Service Vision	Service Staff Recruitment	New Staff Orientation
Service Communications	Service Recognition and Rewards	Voice of the Customer	Service Measures and Metrics
Service Improvement Process	Service Recovery and Guarantees	Service Benchmarking	Service Role Modeling

Figure 44.3 The Twelve Building Blocks
© Ron Kaufman, Up Your Service.com

A Final Note: Where and How to Begin

While all of the Twelve Building Blocks of an Uplifting Service Culture are valuable, action in some areas will be easier and faster to achieve than others. Depending on your situation and self-assessment try some of these:

1. *Find and act on the low-hanging fruit.* There are some actions you can take quickly and at low cost that will yield speedy and early results. Do those now!

2. *Stop those things that send contrary messages.* You may find legacy programs and procedures that are inconsistent with your service vision, ineffective and inefficient, or simply out of date. Stop those now!

3. *Plan for improvements that take more time and money.* Some improvements are worth making but require resources and planning to organize and execute well. Identify those opportunities and then prioritize them for implementation over time.

About UP! Your Service

UP! Your Service helps organizations achieve business results, solve critical problems, and gain a sustainable competitive advantage. Founded by Ron Kaufman, it is the world's leading educator and motivator for uplifting customer service and building service cultures.

UP! Your Service applies a proven methodology distilled from Ron's extensive experience working with organizations globally, and his obsession with results and practical action. This methodology uses a proven architecture for building a service culture that integrates top-down service leadership, bottom-up service education, and The Twelve Building Blocks of Service Culture. UP! Your Service helps clients apply this methodology through a customized implementation roadmap to achieve fast, systematic deployment to large numbers of employees and quick realization of results.

Our service education curriculum creates a common service language and practical action steps employees can take on a daily basis. This is achieved through learning and applying fundamental service principles. The UP! Your Service curriculum has been proven effective across industries, cultures, and at all levels and in all departments of an organization.

Submitted by Ron Kaufman, Founder, Chairman

UP! Your Service Worldwide

Enquiry@Up.YourService.com

www.UpYourService.com

Chapter 45

Who Killed Service?

SIGMA PERFORMANCE SOLUTIONS, INC.

In This Chapter

- A four-step process for managing customer interaction.
- Description of the four levels of customer service and response.
- Tips and clarification for successfully dealing with customer problems.

Imagine a recent customer conversation: What do you do when the customers make impossible demands, or they're asking for something but you don't think it's what they really need? Do they keep repeating themselves, over and over, long after you understand? Have you ever finished a conversation, only to find out later that it was a waste of time, and now you have to start over? Unfortunately, we all have—whether our customers were patients, employees, co-workers, or family members. When we miss the mark, we damage our relationships, wind up frustrated, lose someone's trust, or worse. Picture if you could use a simple four-step process that will help your conversations be more enjoyable, productive, and fulfilling. That process is called LIST®.

In this chapter we describe the LIST® process and why it will be of benefit to you and your organization. The accompanying online tools include a conversation calibrator (self-assessment) and several different quick reference guides related to different aspects of a LIST® conversation. We encourage you to use these tools for your own professional development or with your team—at a staff meeting, brown-bag lunch, a mini-training session, or off-site retreat. But first, let's explore the who, what, why, where, and when of LIST®.

Who Are Customers?

Our customers are typically technical professionals. But don't stop reading just yet—technical is not a synonym for technology. We have a long history of working with computer professionals, but also front-line service professionals such as doctors, nurses, accountants, financial planners, HVAC mechanics, call center reps/CSRs, dispatchers, and engineers. Our clients represent the elite in high-tech, financial services, and healthcare providers worldwide, as well as government agencies, insurance companies, airlines, telecommunications, and management consultants, in entire organizations or just one department.

Your customers may be revenue-generating customers who pay the bills, your employees, internal customers, co-workers, or others who look to you to provide advice. A customer can go by many names—customer, client, patient, subscriber, consumer, patron, or end-user. You may have other names for them, but let's stay positive! For ease of reading, we'll focus on customers in a work situation, but LIST® can also be used with family members, spouses, partners, your mother-in-law, and teenagers! Yes, we knew we were onto something when we discovered that LIST® even works with "that" age group. Imagine bridging the generation gap, without having to know the difference between Gen X, Gen Y, Boomers, and other labels that may not help much. Using LIST® with a person (regardless of age, gender, education, or other attributes) will help you interact in a positive and productive way.

What Is LIST®?

LIST® is a four-step process for managing customer interactions:

Step 1: Learn the person's perspective.

Step 2: Indicate your understanding of the person's needs and perspective.

Step 3: Solve to satisfy the needs and address possible concerns.

Step 4: Tell the person what to expect and recap next steps.

Use this flexible process when you want to work with anyone more effectively. LIST® is like a road map—it is not step-by-step instructions or specific scripted words you need to memorize. Use LIST® as a structured approach to lead the way and provide guidance in your conversations with customers.

The LIST® process is presented in graph form to show how much time we usually spend on each step as we progress from the beginning, sequentially, without skipping any steps, through to the end of a professional interaction. By studying Figure 45.1

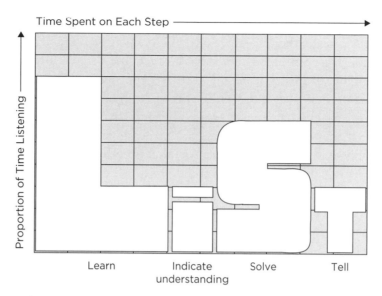

Figure 45.1 The LIST Process

you can see the relative amount of time you can expect to spend on each step and the proportion of that time you should be listening, learning, and observing rather than talking. Note the following:

- The width of each letter suggests the relative amount of time usually spent on that step.
- The height of each letter suggests how much of the time you can expect to be listening rather than talking during that step.

What do the letters mean? The purpose of the L-step is to gain an understanding of the customer's perspective. This is required to develop successful solutions. You will do more listening and less talking! Learning the customer's perspective is hard work, but necessary. With time, listening for the facts and the customer's perspective will be easier and more comfortable. You'll be listening at a higher, more productive level. The time you invest in learning at the beginning of an interaction pays off later. Get it right the first time and build trust with the customer. As we listen, we may also uncover additional needs that translate to new service or sales opportunities.

The purpose of the I-step is to show that you understand not just the customer's needs, but especially his or her perspective and concerns. Done properly, the I-step is the power step or green light to move forward in the LIST® process. This is the point at which we visibly take charge of an interaction. It earns our customers' confidence that we will take care of their needs because they see that we understand. Customers will be inclined to reciprocate the respect we gave them when we listened attentively and accurately demonstrate our understanding is correct. The I-step is also helpful to move the conversation forward when a person starts recycling and repeating the same things.

The purpose of the S-step is to seek the best solution. This is the point during the process when we gather whatever facts and other information we need to determine the best course of action. We demonstrate our professional competence by asking for information and solving the problem in a way that is both logical and comfortable for the customer. "This is the step we know and do best," we are told by many professionals. You, too, are probably very good at obtaining the factual information you need to address the customer's immediate problem. However, sometimes we are so eager to obtain these specific facts that we respond to a customer's *first mention* of a need and leap immediately to the S-step, without getting a complete picture.

In the T-step, tell the customer what he or she should know about what to expect going forward. Verify his or her understanding *and* acceptance. Explain what the customer should know about the plan of action. Verify that the customer understands and accepts the plan. If not, you repeat the LIST® process to gain clarity. Do not add any additional details in the T-Step.

The size of the letter has nothing to do with the importance of that LIST® step. Remember, the I-step, which is the shortest and smallest letter on the graph, is actually the power step or the "green light" to move forward to a solution. Early in the LIST® process, listen rather than talk about two-thirds of the time (or more!). The I-step is a concise statement, articulated by you, to summarize the needs of the customer.

As we work with technical professionals, we discover that most people have used each of the LIST® steps, but perhaps not in order or not consistently. LIST® is a repeatable, predictable process. By intentionally adding the L-step and I-step in front of the solution phase, professionals find "dealing with the customer" is easier.

Providing technical expertise in the SOLVE phase is usually the most comfortable piece of the LIST® process for many people, since you may be most proficient in this phase. However, we should say that, despite your expertise you may not always be able to provide a solution that is the "final answer." While it's nice to close the ticket or complete that task, this is not always possible.

Several years ago, I worked at a large metropolitan hospital as an organization development consultant. The hospital has won many awards, and the nurses had the best and most current training and certifications possible. I was working the night shift on the critical care unit (CCU) As I was walking down the hall, I heard the phone ringing and ringing and ringing, and ringing and ringing. Obviously, everyone, myself included, thought someone else would answer the phone. I had no idea how to use the multi-line switchboard, but it was that or listen to that ringing.

You may not be the right person to "fix it" if the wrong replacement part was ordered or, like me, you may not have a clue on how to transfer a call to the appropriate nurses' station. In these situations, your best solve might only leave a customer with the assurance that you have a plan to solve the problem. I probably violated a few HIPPA privacy laws that night, but I don't think the family members, desperate to hear an update about a loved one, cared. Organizations spend much time and effort making sure that service providers are trained on the how-to, compliance, safety, and technical aspects of their jobs, but all too often, not enough time on the service side, like answering the phones! You may have lots of certificates and certifications, and perhaps a string of letters after your name, but when is the last time you focused on your customer service skills? By now you're probably thinking, "I don't have more time to spend with my customers. How long will this take?"

We know that technical professionals are often pressed for time If you are concerned that you don't have time to use LIST®, there is good news. You will find that as you master the LIST® process, it ultimately saves you time.

You do need to use the steps sequentially, and you cannot skip any steps, but having a systematic process will serve you well. We equate the process to an accordion—the total time can expand and contract depending on the specifics. You can have an entire LIST® conversation in forty-five seconds or, if you're dealing with more than one person and/or a complex situation, it might take an hour to reach closure, or several meetings where you repeat the LIST® steps (not the same conversation) as you move through different aspects of a more complicated project. You will find tips for using LIST® in this chapter's online tool section.

LIST® requires more of your time up-front, at the beginning of the interaction, in the L-step. However, with practice and mastery of the process, you will discover that the extra time you invest in listening and improving your understanding will reduce the total overall time for that interaction. With LIST® you can get it right the first time, reduce repeat calls, and strengthen customer relationships.

Specifically, people who use LIST® report that they consistently save time in two ways:

- The customer doesn't continue talking about, or repeating, the uniqueness and importance of his or her need, because you indicate your understanding.

- By listening up-front, the service pro is less likely to misinterpret the problem and waste time pursuing the wrong line of questions (or worse, the wrong course of action).

While most clients tell us that using LIST® reduces the average "talk time" for service professionals, the primary goal is to get it right the first time, not necessarily a faster conversation.

Why Do We Use LIST®?

We use LIST® for two main reasons:

- To gain the control we need, but not dominate, to make the conversation more productive and mutually satisfactory.
- To help us clarify the other person's perspective and concerns about the situation or opportunity.

I mention "control" first because it is important that we, as service professionals, lead the way. The ability to lead and guide is especially critical when we work with customers who have complex or unclear requests. It also helps in our encounters with demanding customers.

At the same time, LIST® provides clarity about our customers' needs by giving technical professionals a step-by-step needs clarification process. Because people want us to focus on their needs, they willingly follow the LIST® steps with us (and accept our leadership in the process). The better we are at clarifying and fulfilling a customer's needs, the more success we both experience.

Our clients measure success in many ways, but frequently report that LIST® helps them establish more productive relationships with their customers—relationships that last and make working together more efficient in the future. People frequently equate customer service with handling problems, and LIST® turns that focus into more positive thinking; there will be opportunities, issues, and even problems, but fewer crisis/panic moments. True service will proactively satisfy customer needs—before the needs become problems. Problems are usually needs that have not been addressed, and therefore have escalated in urgency, along with a new mindset toward the issue. During the LIST® process, we may sometimes discover that a customer has a requirement for additional products or services that our company can provide. That's how LIST® can help us identify sales and other opportunities as a natural extension of our service role.

When Can You Use LIST®?

You can use LIST® whenever you deal with people who need your advice, help, or technical expertise. In fact, the next time a person—any person—starts telling you about a problem or opportunity, try using LIST®. LIST® will serve as your guide to build better relationships.

LIST® is useful in just about any conversation (face-to-face, email, or "chat") you may have. In some cases, customers may have the solutions, but simply want to share their thoughts and ideas about doing something differently, and want reassurance or advice.

You can use LIST® to take your customer service to new levels. Figure 45.2 displays four levels of service conversations. You may want to move your skills from reactive to consultative.

The *reactive level* is focused on problems; the provider only responds when asked. This typically creates frustration on both sides. Almost every interaction is urgent or high-priority, just-in-time or too late. Frequent calls, unplanned interruptions, and

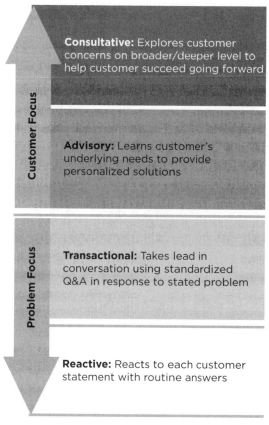

Figure 45.2 Levels of Service Conversations

surprises create stress for clients and customers. The *transactional level* is focused on the task. At the transactional level, focus moves beyond the immediate problem. More complex issues require some planning, although a narrow focus still means there are missed opportunities for real long-term results, frequent rework, and perhaps a panic call, maybe directly to the boss. The *advisory level* is focused on the customer. With advisory conversations, customers begin to expect you will be there when they need you and that they can ask your advice in decision making and sometimes the planning phase. You and the customer are usually in sync and work together well, even in difficult times. *Consultative* conversations are focused on the relationship and are frequently seen as strong partnerships by others. Customers wouldn't dream of moving ahead without your expertise and opinions—even if they may not like what you have to say. Customers may ask you for guidance, even in areas that are not in your field of expertise. You are a valuable team member; outsiders may not know that you are not an employee because the connection is so strong.

When Not to Use LIST®

LIST® is not intended for handling clear, routine requests in which the person asks for something simple and we can provide that something. These are straightforward transactions, and it would be foolish to waste either our time or the person's time going through a needs clarification process.

Also, when people are angry or upset, we must help them calm down before having a conversation. An angry person has diminished ability or willingness to be rational. People who are complaining, angry, manipulative, or demanding feel more intensely about their needs. Once you address their sentiments, LIST® works well, but not before. You must "defuse" a person before you use LIST®.

Measuring the Success of LIST®

Research from the Gallup Organization suggests that "In spite of the latest in technology tools, processes, and systems . . . the customer experience still depends largely on the [individual]." In their case study, Fleming and Asplund discovered that the best 10 percent . . . produce six positive interactions for every negative one, leaving the customer feeling alienated. Meanwhile, the bottom 10 percent only delighted three out of seven customers (2007, p. 46). With odds like this, doing nothing is not an option!

Our clients use many indicators to measure success. Some of these may be important to you, or you may have other metrics to add to these:

- First contact resolution
- Customer or patient satisfaction
- Maintenance renewals
- Referrals to other customer
- Sales through front-line personnel (not the sales department)
- Employee retention or turnover
- "Transfer to supervisor" requests

Why LIST® Works

Envision your technical expertise is like riding a unicycle. One wheel. It gives you power, but it's not always enough. So let's add a front wheel to that skill set—your conversation/customer relations expertise. The back wheel of the bicycle moves you forward and the front wheel helps you steer in the right direction, avoid potholes, or navigate rough patches when needed. Using the bicycle analogy helps us remember that both wheels are important, but working together is even better. (See Figure 45.3.)

In the beginning, we started by sending technical professionals to "charm school." We asked them to be nice and polite. Adding the front wheel gives the technical expert the skills they need to genuinely engage with the customer, without having to make it up.

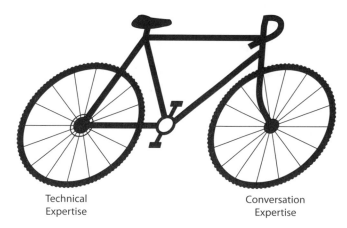

Technical
Expertise

Conversation
Expertise

Figure 45.3 Balancing Technical and Conversation/Professional Expertise

LIST® may require that you spend more time listening to the customer at the beginning of an interaction, but it can save time overall and improve relationships. LIST® is about implementing a clear sequential process that leverages your technical expertise and acknowledges the customer needs. LIST® does not replace your technical expertise, or put words in your mouth. Riding a bicycle is easier than riding a unicycle! Enjoy the process.

In addition to the online tools provided with this chapter, feel free to visit our website for additional resources. There you will find other assessments and tools that may be helpful in your endeavor to provide better service. You can also preview Who Killed Service? on our YouTube channel.

REFERENCE

Fleming, J.H., & Asplund, J. (2007). *Human sigma: Managing the employee-customer encounter.* New York: Gallup Press.

About Sigma Performance Solutions, Inc.

Sigma Performance Solutions addresses the human side of customer service. Our name comes from the lower case Greek sigma—measuring the distribution of performance levels along a bell curve . . . striving for higher levels of performance. Sigma's programs and processes produce measurable performance improvements. Our products and services include needs assessments, instructor led workshops, webinars, online reinforcement modules, games, facilitator certification (train-the-trainer), and LIST® certification for service professionals. Our products include:

- LIST®—our flagship product provides technical professionals a flexible, four-step process for leading consultative conversations.

- DEFUSE—how to deal with a difficult person or calm an angry person.

- RELATE—understand personality styles to leverage your relationships.

- SEIZE THE OPPORTUNITY— leverage LIST® for front-line personnel to identify and generate sales

- WHO KILLED SERVICE?®—Humphrey Bogart meets customer service . . . watch as our private eye interrogates six suspects! Winner of the Telly for Outstanding Video.

- YOU BE THE JUDGE™—Using customized scenarios your team can hand out verdicts, recommend rehabilitation plans, and debate a wide variety of issues. Honored as a "Top 20 Training Tool" by *Human Resources Executive* magazine.

Submitted by Karen A. Travis, CPLP, SPHR, President, CEO

Sigma Performance Solutions, Inc.

28 Sugar Tree Place

Hunt Valley, MD 21030

(410) 667-9055 or (800) 658-8893

karen@sigmatraining.com

www.sigmatraining.com

Who Killed Service?

Chapter 46

Taming the Sales Manager Ego

AMPLIFY

In This Chapter

- Red flags that signify dysfunctional sales leadership.
- Eight qualities of great sales leaders.
- Coaching tips to improve sales leaders' skills.

Many leaders hear the term "sales manager" and have an instant reaction—often not a very good one.

We've all experienced it in one way or another. Whether you were buying a car, eating at a restaurant, or working with a consultant, the sales manager came into the picture as the person whose job it is to be the bearer of bad news, the calmer of angry customers, or the bad cop in closing deals.

If you've been a customer negotiating a price, complaining about a product or service, or just trying to understand an agreement, perhaps you heard the sales person say, "Let me get my sales manager." They might as well say, "Let me bring in the big guns."

If you've been in a sales role, you may have thought of your sales manager as the nag, always asking you about forecast data, number of phone calls per day, and whether you've entered your notes in the CRM (customer relationship management) system. They were so busy managing internal politics that they didn't stand up for you when you needed them, and it seemed they felt that no idea was legitimate unless it came from them.

As a peer or colleague of the sales manager, you may have found that sales managers were one of two extremes: never around when you needed them or challenging everything that came up. They either showed up to be the meeting contrarian or they didn't show up at all.

It's almost inevitable that the role has become viewed in these ways. To be a successful sales manager, you have to have tough skin, be a chameleon, produce results, convey your reports with conviction, be in ten places at once, and balance advocating the front line with managing the bottom line. The role often comes with a high level of influence in the organization and, with it, a blurring of the lines between confidence, competence, and arrogance.

As a result, sales managers have built up quite a reputation for themselves over the years. You may have some vivid images and descriptors of sales managers of your own in mind. Egomaniacs. Schmoozers. Embellishers. Short-sighted bulldozers who level everything in their paths. With all that baggage, it's no wonder so many CEOs view the sales manager role as a necessary evil.

Ironically, the sales manager position came about because most CEOs are willing to do just about anything to avoid having salespeople reporting to them. (If they could avoid having a sales staff altogether, even better!) Even for those CEOs who like to go on sales calls and close business, the idea of actually managing a salesperson or team probably sounds about as pleasant as an airport security screening or a proctology exam.

At the same time, many CEOs have learned the hard way that some sales leaders can come with a hefty price tag—one that's beyond their compensation. These negative experiences make them wary of turning over the reins and potentially making expensive mistakes.

But whether they want to do it or not, *no* CEO should be running the sales department. Just like other functional area leaders, sales leaders serve a specific, important function and are vital to the company. If you're not getting the full value from your sales manager—or if you're thinking you can just "get by" without one—you're putting the organization's financial future and overall business health at risk. Stop avoiding the issue. It's time to tame the ego monster and move forward!

Red Flags

Breaking free from the dysfunctional sales leader trap starts with understanding what the problem traits are. Whether you made the mistake of assuming your top-performing salesperson could move seamlessly into a sales manager role or whether you've hired an experienced sales leader from the outside, what follows are some red flags to watch out for. See whether you recognize any of these people:

- *The Smooth Operator:* Unflappable, tightly scripted and using lyrical, radio-ready voices, Smooth Operators all sound the same. They have an answer for everything, and what they say always sounds good—too good. Every response seems perfect on the surface but is empty underneath. They're so slick that you walk away feeling like you need a shower.

- *The Time Drainer:* Chronically late and never quick to respond, Time Drainers don't care about anyone's time but their own. They saunter in to meetings when it suits them, take forever to respond to voicemail and emails (if at all), and rarely bring decisions to closure. Your time is spent trying to track them down and tie up loose ends.

- *The Conversation Dominator:* The art of listening is truly lost on Conversation Dominators. They don't let you finish a sentence without interjecting an opinion or idea. Details, subtleties, and nuances are irrelevant because they have a knee-jerk response ready and aren't interested in going any deeper. Conversation Dominators like to talk at people rather than with them, and they love the sound of their own voices. You may think you're having a conversation, but in reality, it's always a one-way street with a Conversation Dominator.

- *The Name Dropper:* They always want you to be aware of whom they know, met with, or had an email exchange with—even if it was only for a few minutes. By dropping the names of people with (real or perceived) high credibility, they're hoping some of that credibility aura will extend to them, too. If the person likes to talk about book authors as if they were close personal friends or reference high-profile projects or marquis companies as if they were the key to their success, you're probably dealing with a Name Dropper.

- *The CEO's Best Buddy:* Best Buddies will do anything to suck up to the CEO. They agree with everything the CEO says, pal around during and after work hours, take trips together, and sometimes even copy the way the CEO dresses.

- *The Stat Spouter:* Numbers are critical in sales, but Stat Spouters are always throwing out suspicious-sounding statistics to support an opinion. They primarily focus narrowly on the numbers and don't balance their thinking with the activity that is happening behind the numbers. Often, it's a short-sighted system that serves only them, not the business.

- *The Schmoozer:* That old sales stereotype can manifest itself in new and potentially less obvious ways when a Schmoozer is a sales leader. Schmoozers are always working a deal or angle, and when it comes to justifying behaviors, issues, or motives, the Schmoozer is most likely working a deal on you.

- *The Memory Keeper:* Ah, the glory days. Memory Keepers can't stop talking about the good old days when they were the top-producing sales person or worked for that famous brand-name company. They can't make a point without referring back to their big "win" or the extra special secrets they know from having managed "hundreds" of salespeople back in the day. You're left wondering, "But what have you done lately?"

- *The Report Junkie:* Report Junkies live in sales funnels and sales activity reports. There's a human side to effective sales? They didn't get that memo. If it's not on paper or in the report, they don't see the value.

- *The Indiscriminate Entertainer:* Indiscriminate Entertainers are terrific company. Always the life of the party and quick with a joke, they're great at keeping things light. But where's the line between a fun little break and an entire day wasted? Indiscriminate Entertainers have no idea. They're going to keep on entertaining.

So we know what we *don't* want.

But what about the ideal sales manager? There are great sales leaders out there, both those you can hire and those you can develop. You just have to know what to look for. The checklist below will help you narrow the search. As you consider your recruitment and development priorities, keep in mind that each of these qualities overlaps with the others and adds to their cumulative impact. Finding everything you're looking for requires work. Most people don't arrive fully formed, but that doesn't mean you should give up. Targeted training and development, practical coaching, thoughtful mentoring, and expert recruiting strategies will be necessary if you're serious about getting what you want from a sales leader.

Qualities of Great Sales Leaders

- ❏ *Collaborators:* They work individually and collectively with people and teams in the company for the greater good. Sometimes that means having to say "no" to a salesperson, and sometimes it means going to bat for the salesperson.

- ❏ *Architects:* They build sales processes and systems that connect to marketing and operations. They develop the plans and tools the sales team will need to drive sales.

- ❏ *Barrier Eliminators:* Great sales leaders know that the salesperson's time is best spent engaged with prospects and customers, not fighting internal battles. They take the drama off the salesperson's plate. As the voice of the customer on the leadership team, they also help break down operational barriers that can destroy customer relationships, retention, and, ultimately, sales.

❑ *Diplomats:* As the official representative of the business to customers, great sales leaders take the responsibility for initiating tough conversations around price increases or policy changes. But what separates the great from the ordinary is the ability to have honest, sometimes difficult conversations in a way that doesn't do damage to the relationship.

❑ *Bridge Builders:* Great sales leaders understand that both increasing sales and delivering on the company's promises require partnerships among all the departments. They build plans in conjunction with marketing and other functions rather than working in a vacuum or throwing up roadblocks between the groups.

❑ *Engagers:* They are active participants in everything that is going on in the sales organization. You won't find them rolling their eyes or checked out when they're in meetings with salespeople; you'll find them dynamically engaged in each team member's issues and sales conversations.

❑ *Inspirers:* Great sales leaders go beyond motivating performance through traditional incentives. They have the charisma to ignite a fire that prompts performance.

❑ *Balancers:* They encourage work/life balance *and* model the practice with how they manage their own work and personal lives. Most importantly, they respect their direct reports' personal lives by not demanding calls after hours. As generational shifts and expectations change the workplace, this will be an increasingly important quality for great sales leaders.

Tips to Improve Sales Leaders' Skills

So what happens if you have a sales leader who is fairly proficient but has some of the red-flag traits we have talked about? A few red flags aren't the end of the world, but they have to be addressed. It comes down to the ego-quotient of the sales leader:

- Does he or she have enough humility to accept and apply coaching?
- Or is the person like some superstar athletes who believe they know more than their coaches?

If he or she knows it all and won't accept or apply coaching, then you don't have a leader—you have an individual contributor in a leadership role and you have to make a change. Remove the person from the position quickly and don't hesitate. If you notice it, it's a guarantee his or her direct reports notice it, too. You need to show strong and decisive leadership; otherwise you will lose the respect and morale of the entire sales team.

If, on the other hand, the person is coachable, then you may want to engage an external coach for your sales leader. In the meantime, here are a few coaching tips you can try:

1. Ask your sales leader to map the sales process for the business. Your goal is to find out how familiar he or she is with how leads flow into the business, how those leads are nurtured, and how they are managed through to close and post-sales support.

   - If he or she tells you the sales process begins with an RFP, fire him or her.

   - If he or she tells you that marketing doesn't give the salespeople enough leads, get ready to fire him or her.

2. Ask your sales leader for a concrete business plan. Besides the math, what is he or she specifically going to do to make the goal? Anyone can distribute quota across salespeople; that's not a plan, and it's not being a leader. While not an exhaustive checklist, the sales leader's plan should include the following:

   - Strategies to further penetrate key markets through people and process

   - Specific steps to be taken in collaboration with marketing and operations

   - Development and mentoring of sales representatives

   - Performance management that addresses hiring, on-boarding, and termination

   - Territory/portfolio compaction and distribution

3. Observe your sales leader in a one-on-one conversation with a salesperson. The point is for the salesperson to share what is going on with his or her account portfolio. That means the conversation should be collaborative, and the salesperson should be talking 70 percent of the time. Here is a sampling of the kinds of questions you should hear your sales leader asking the sales representative:

   - What are the barriers to being able to advance opportunities with a particular prospect or the overall pipeline?

- What are the specific actions the salesperson is taking to close the opportunities that are projected to close in the next thirty days?
- What are the objections the prospect is raising (or that the salesperson anticipates will be raised) and how does he or she plan on overcoming the objections?

4. Have your sales leader explain how he or she reviews sales reports and interprets the data received in pipeline/forecast reports. Be on the lookout for the following:

- Does your sales leader know specifics (the business issues that are being addressed, the decision-making process, etc.) about high-potential accounts?
- Does your sales leader have a clear understanding about the forecast probabilities that the salesperson is using? Do each of the salespeople use the same interpretation of the probabilities? How accurate is the sales leader's forecast?
- If your sales leader blames the sales people for inaccurate forecasts, fire him or her.

5. Where does your sales leader spend time? Ask yourself:

- Does he spend a lot of time on the Internet or "networking"?
- What percentage of her time is spent in the field with salespeople?
- How much presence does he have with your customers?
- Is she busy creating internal reports and sitting in internal meetings? If the answer is "yes," is that a broader organizational issue that needs to be addressed?

Sales managers should be the heartbeat of an organization. They have enormous influence on driving sales results, building culture, bringing new product concepts forward, establishing infrastructure for growth, and taking care of customers. Like any thoroughbred or high performer, the minute they cross the line from confidence and competence to arrogance and self-importance, their—and your—organization's success will be at risk. Tame the sales leader's ego and your business will leap forward.

Ready for an Ego Check?

Whether you want to check your own ego or someone else's, the Ego Check Survey is a great tool for highlighting potential red flags and providing an opportunity for reflection and correction. You will find this self-assessment in the online tools that accompany this book.

About Amplify

You're ready to grow your business. Are you ready to cut to the chase? At Amplify we don't waste time on hot air and doubletalk. We give it to you straight and back it up with experience—real-world, in-the-trenches, roll-up-your-sleeves experience—in sales, marketing, service, and learning performance. No theoretical concepts. No nonsense. Just time-tested, proven tools, processes, training, and strategic thinking that put positive momentum on your side.

Amplify is an organization of experts and practitioners who ignite business growth and people performance in sales, marketing, operations, and learning. No matter where they are in their current stage of growth, our clients receive the practical guidance and hands-on support to make smart moves today so they can reach new heights tomorrow.

Submitted by Joe Trueblood; Lisa Fagan, President

Amplify

11818 Marblehead Drive

Tampa, FL 33626

(813) 704-5028

Info@AmplifyGrowth.com

www.amplifygrowth.com

Recommended Additional Reading

Chapter 1

- *Peer Power: Transforming Workplace Relationships* by Cynthia Clay & Ray Olitt. Punchy Publishing, 2011.

- *Reversing the Ostrich Approach to Diversity: Pulling Your Head Out of the Sand* by Amy Tolbert. Nasus Publishing, 2002.

Section I Bonus Activity 1

- *Instant-Answer Guide to Business Writing* by Deborah Dumaine & the BC Team. Writers Club Press, 2003.

- *Write to the Top: Writing for Corporate Success* by Deborah Dumaine. Random House, 2004.

Section I Bonus Activity 2

- *Crucial Conversations* by Kerry Patterson, Joseph Grenny, Ron McMillan, & Al Switzler. McGraw-Hill, 2002.

- *Put the Moose on the Table* by Randall Tobias & Todd Tobias. Indiana University Press, 2003.

- *Speed of Trust* by Stephen M.R. Covey & Rebecca R. Merrill. The Free Press, 2006.

Chapter 9

- *A Whole New Mind: Why Right-Brainers Will Rule the Future* by Daniel H. Pink. Riverhead Books, 2005, 2006.

- *Financial Intelligence: A Manager's Guide to Knowing What the Numbers Really Mean* by Karen Berman, Joe Knight, & John Case. Harvard Business School Publishing, 2006.

Section II Bonus Activity

- *Driving Fear Out of the Workplace: Creating the High-Trust, High-Performance Organization* (2nd ed.) by Kathleen D. Ryan & Daniel K. Oestreich. Jossey-Bass, 1998.

- *Organizing Genius: The Secrets of Creative Collaboration* by Warren Bennis & Patricia Ward Biederman. Basic Books, 1998.

- *Radical Collaboration: Five Essential Skills to Overcome Defensiveness and Build Successful Relationships* by James Tamm & Ronald Luyet. Harper Paperbacks, 2005.

Chapter 12

- *A Leader's Legacy* by Jim Kouzes & Barry Posner. Jossey-Bass, 2006.

- *Authentic Leadership: Rediscovering the Secrets to Creating Lasting Value* by Bill George. Jossey-Bass, 2003.

- *Be Your Own Brand* by David McNally & Karl Speak. Berrett-Koehler, 2003.

- *Credibility: How Leaders Gain and Lose It, Why People Demand It* by James M. Kouzes & Barry Z. Posner. Jossey-Bass, 1993.

- *Even Eagles Need a Push* by David McNally. Delacorte Press, 1990.

- *True North* by Bill George & Peter Sims. Jossey-Bass, 2007.

- *Ethics4Everyone* by Eric Harvey & Scott Airitam. Walk The Talk Company, 2006.

- *Walk The Talk . . . And Get the Results You Want* by Eric Harvey & Alexander Lucia. Walk The Talk Company, 2003.

Chapter 13

- *Talk Your Way to the Top* by Kevin Daley & Laura Daley-Caravella. McGraw-Hill, 2003.

Chapter 17

- *Awaken, Align, Accelerate: A Guide to Great Leadership* by MDA Leadership Consulting. Beaver's Pond Press, 2010.

- *Linkage Inc.'s Best Practices in Leadership Development* by David Giber, Samuel Lam, & Marshall Goldsmith. Pfeiffer, 2009.

- *The Center for Creative Leadership Handbook of Leadership Development* by Cindy McCauley & Ellen Van Velsor (Eds.). Jossey-Bass, 2003.
- *The Leadership Pipeline: How to Build the Leadership Powered Company* by Ram Charan, Stephen Drotter, & James Noel. Jossey-Bass, 2011.

Section IV Bonus Activity

- *Churchill on Leadership: Executive Success in the Face of Adversity* by Steven Hayward. Three Rivers Press, 1998.
- *Into the Unknown: Leadership Lessons from Lewis and Clark's Daring Expedition* by Jack Uldrich. AMACOM, 2004.
- *Leadership the Eleanor Roosevelt Way* by Robin Gerber. Portfolio Trade, 2003.
- *Lincoln on Leadership: Executive Strategies for Tough Times* by Donald Phillips. Warner Books, 1993.
- *The Leadership Moment: Nine True Stories of Triumph and Disaster and Their Lessons for Us All* by Michael Useem. Crown Business, 1999.

Chapter 19

- *Firms of Endearment: How World-Class Companies Profit from Passion and Purpose* by Raj Sisodia, Jag Sheth, & David B. Wolfe. Wharton School Publishing, 2008.
- *Helping People Win at Work: A Business Philosophy Called "Don't Mark My Paper, Help Me Get an A"* by Ken Blanchard & Garry Ridge. FT Press, 2009.
- *Illusions: The Adventure of a Reluctant Messia* by Richard Bach. Dell Publishing, 1977. Creative Enterprises, Inc., reprinted by arrangement with Delacorte Press/Eleanor Friede, 1989.
- *The Corporate Shaman A Business Fable* by Richard Whiteley. HarperCollins, 2002.
- *The Four-Fold Way: Walking the Paths of the Warrior, Teacher, Healer and Visionary* by Angeles Arrien. HarperCollins, 1993.

Chapter 22

- *Maslow on Management* by Abraham H. Maslow. John Wiley & Sons, 1998.
- *The Diamond Cutter* by Geshe Michael Roach. Doubleday, 2000.

Chapter 25

- *Beyond Change Management: How to Achieve Breakthrough Results Through Conscious Change Leadership* by Dean Anderson & Linda Ackerman Anderson. Pfeiffer, 2010.

- *The Change Leader's Roadmap: How to Navigate Your Organization's Transformation* by Dean Anderson & Linda Ackerman Anderson. Pfeiffer, 2010.

Section V Bonus Activity

- *The Art of Engagement: Bridging the Gaps Between People and Possibilities* by Jim Haudan. McGraw-Hill, 2008.

Chapter 26

- *Getting More from Your Investment in Training: The 5As Framework* by Sean P. Murray & Stephen J. Gill. RealTime Performance, Inc., 2010.

Chapter 27

- *Implementing the Four Levels* by Don Kirkpatrick & Robert Brinkerhoff. Berrett-Koehler, 2007.

- *Kirkpatrick Then and Now* by Jim Kirkpatrick & Wendy Kirkpatrick. Kirkpatrick Publishing, 2009.

- *The Success Case Method* by Robert Brinkerhoff. Berrett-Koehler, 2003.

- *Training on Trial* by Jim Kirkpatrick & Wendy Kirkpatrick. AMACOM, 2010.

Chapter 28

- Getting More from Your Training Programs by Aaron DeSmet, Monica McGurk, & Elizabeth Schwartz. *McKinsey Quarterly*, October 2010.

- *Getting Your Money's Worth from Training and Development: A Guide to Breakthrough Learning* by Andrew Jefferson, Roy Pollock, & Calhoun Wick. Pfeiffer, 2009.

- *Improving Learning Transfer: A Guide to Getting More Out of What You Put into Training* by C. Kirwan. Surrey, UK: Gower, 2009.

- *Learning Paths: Increase Profits by Reducing the Time It Takes Employees to Get Up to Speed* by Jim Williams & Steve Rosenbaum. Pfeiffer, 2004.

- *The Checklist Manifesto: How to Get things Right* by Atul Gwande. Picador, 2009.
- *The Six Disciplines of Breakthrough Learning: How to Turn Learning and Development into Business Results* by Calhoun W. Wick, Roy Pollock, Andrew McK. Jefferson, & Richard Flanagan. Pfeiffer, 2010.

Chapter 29

- Blended Learning: Best Practices (white paper). EPIC The Attention Project, Linda Stone. http://lindastone.net/
- *The Blended Learning Book* by Josh Bersin. Pfeiffer, 2004.
- *The Creative Brain Book* by Ned Herrmann. Brain Books, 1989.
- *The Whole Brain® Business Book* by Ned Herrmann. McGraw-Hill, 1996.

Chapter 33

- *Facilitator's Guide to Participatory Decision Making* by Sam Kaner, Michael Doyle, Lenny Lind, & Catherine Toldi. Jossey-Bass, 2007.
- *Facilitating with Ease!* by Ingrid Bens. Jossey-Bass, 2005.
- *The Secrets of Facilitation: The SMART Guide to Getting Results with Groups* by Michael Wilkinson. Jossey-Bass, 2004.
- *The Skilled Facilitator: Practical Wisdom for Developing Effective Groups* by R. Schwarz. Jossey-Bass, 2002.

Chapter 34

- *Teach What You Know* by Steve Trautman. Prentice Hall, 2006.

Chapter 37

- *Handbook for Developing Competency-Based Training Programs* by William Blank. Prentice Hall, 1992.
- *The Competent Manager: A Model for Effective Performance* by Richard Boyatzis. John Wiley & Sons, 1982.
- *The Extraordinary Leader* (2nd ed.) by John Zenger & Joe Folkman. McGraw-Hill, 2009.
- *The Value-Added Employee: Competencies to Make Yourself Irresistible to Any Company* (2nd ed.) by Edward J. Cripe & Richard S. Mansfield. Butterworth-Heinemann, 2001.

Chapter 38

- *Agile Career Development: Lessons and Approaches from IBM* by Marry Ann Bopp, Diana A. Bing, & Sheila Forte-Trammell. IBM Press, 2010.
- *Career Contentment: Don't Settle for Anything Less!* by Jeffrey Garton. ASTD Press, 2008.
- *Linchpin: Are You Indispensable?* by Seth Godin. Penguin Group, 2010.
- *Mass Career Customization: Aligning the Workplace with Today's Nontraditional Workforce* by Cathleen Benko & Anne Weisberg. Harvard Business School Press, 2007.
- *The Corporate Lattice: Achieving High Performance in the Changing World of Work* by Cathleen Benko & Molly Anderson. Harvard Business School Press, 2010.

Chapter 39

- *What the CEO Wants You to Know* by Ram Charan. Crown Business, 2001.

Chapter 40

- *Managing Change with Personal Resilience: 21 Keys for Bouncing Back & Staying on Top in Turbulent Organizations* by Linda Hoopes & Mark Kelly. Mark Kelly Books, 2003.
- Resilience Alliance Blog. www.resiliencealliance.com/index.php/blog.

Chapter 41

- *Coaching for Performance: GROWing Human Potential and Purpose: The Principles and Practice of Coaching and Leadership* by John Whitmore. Nicholas Brealey Publishing, 2009.
- *Managing Transitions* by William Bridges & Susan Bridges. Perseus Books, 1991.
- *The Leadership Pipeline: How to Build the Leadership Powered Company* by Ram Charan, Stephen Drotter, & James Noel. Jossey-Bass, 2000.
- *The Next Level: What Insiders Know About Executive Success* (2nd ed.) by Scott Eblin. Nicolas Brealey Publishing, 2010.
- *The Power of Full Engagement: Managing Energy, Not Time, Is the Key to High Performance and Personal Renewal* by Jim Loehr & Tony Schwartz. The Free Press, 2004.

Chapter 42

- "Coaching the Super Stars—Learning the Lessons of Hardship" by Barbara Pate Glacel. *2003 Pfeiffer Annual.* Pfeiffer, 2003.
- "How to Evolve from Boss to Coach for Increased Performance" by Barbara Pate Glacel. *McGraw-Hill Annual.* McGraw-Hill, 2001.
- "The Role of the Executive Coach" by Barbara Pate Glacel. *2002 Pfeiffer Annual.* Pfeiffer, 2002.
- "Why Executive Coaching? Significant Lessons Learned" by Barbara Pate Glacel. *2006 Pfeiffer Annual.* Pfeiffer, 2006.

Chapter 43

- *The Art and Science of 360-Degree Feedback* (2nd ed.) by Richard Lepsinger & Anntoinette Lucia. Pfeiffer, 2009.
- *The Art and Science of Competency Models* by Anntoinette Lucia & Richard Lepsinger. Pfeiffer, 1999.

Chapter 46

- *Egonomics: What Makes Ego Our Greatest Asset (or Most Expensive Liability)* by David Marcum & Steven Smith. Fireside, 2008.
- "Level 4 Leaders." *Good to Great* by Jim Collins. HarperBusiness, 2001.
- *The Little Book on Big Ego: A Guide to Manage and Control the Egomaniacs in Your Life* by Joel Epstein. Alnola Productions, 2006.

Website e-Tools

The contributors to this book provided tools to assist you with implementing the concepts they present in their chapters. The tools can be downloaded at a companion website: www.pfeiffer.com/go/isa. (Username: training; password: biech) As long as you maintain the copyright information and the "used with permission" designation on the tool, you will be able to use it with your organizations and clients.

Section I

TOOL 1.1. STORIES I COULD TELL AS A LEADER IN A BUSINESS SETTING

The Ariel Group

A tool to help you identify stories that you can tell in various business settings to make a point.

TOOL 2.1. ABOUT YOU QUESTIONNAIRE

NetSpeed Learning Solutions

A self-assessment that helps you understand your personal communication beliefs that are the basis for your communication philosophy.

TOOL 3.1. PERSONAL CANDOR CHECKLIST

Ridge Training

A self-assessment to help you focus on how candid you are and to help you become more aware of your communication patterns.

TOOL 3.2. CANDOR CHECKLIST FOR TEAMS

Ridge Training

An assessment that can be used individually or with a team to explore the team's collective candor.

TOOL 4.1. COMMUNICATION AND BEHAVIORAL STRATEGIES FOR EFFECTIVE GLOBAL INTERACTIONS

ECCO International

A quick reference guide to help you improve global communication and interaction.

BONUS ACTIVITY I.1: TURNING E-MAIL DRAINS INTO PRODUCTIVITY GAINS: PRE-WORK AND EXAMPLES

Better Communications

Downloadable before and after e-mails for the bonus activity.

BONUS ACTIVITY I.2: BUILD OR REPAIR EXERCISE WORKSHEET

Global Novations

Worksheet that accompanies the bonus activity to explore building or repairing a relationship in a group setting.

Section II

TOOL 5.1. WORK BREAKDOWN STRUCTURE TEMPLATE

Sytemation

A template used in project management to identify and organize the work in each phase of the project.

TOOL 6.1. LEVELS OF INVOLVEMENT IN DECISION MAKING

Interaction Associates, Inc.

A discussion tool or situational assessment tool used to determine how much involvement is required in making a decision based on the level of ownership required.

TOOL 7.1. THE SIX SOURCES OF INFLUENCE

VitalSmarts

A matrix leaders can use to increase their level of influence in various situations by tapping into six different sources of motivation.

TOOL 8.1. NINE TIPS FOR SUCCESS AT THE C-LEVEL

PowerSpeaking, Inc.

Nine reminders of how to increase chances of success when presenting to the C level.

TOOL 9.1. SENIOR LEADER SURVEY: ASSESSING THE NEED FOR BUSINESS ACUMEN DEVELOPMENT

Paradigm Learning, Inc.

Survey that can be used online or in person to build a business case for establishing business acumen as a key leadership competency.

TOOL 10.1. THE PHASES OF THE US VS. THEM CYCLE

Learning as Leadership

Complete overview of the three phases (downward spiral, emotional investment, reversing the spiral) that lead to, maintain, and can change the Us vs. Them mentality.

Section III

TOOL 11.1. SIX WAYS TO MANAGE BRIEF INTERACTIONS

Zenger Folkman

Short self-assessment that measures a leader's ability to manage brief interactions.

TOOL 12.1. LEADING WITH INTEGRITY: A TOOL TO HELP LEADERS WALK THEIR TALK

Strategic Leadership Collaborative

An extensive exercise to help leaders get to the core of their leadership values.

TOOL 13.1. HOW TO TELL A STORY

Kevin Daley Communications

Techniques to make a story for any presentation memorable.

TOOL 14.1. HOW EFFECTIVE ARE YOU AS A LEADER?

Impression Management Professionals

Hard-hitting leader self-evaluation that measures effectiveness.

TOOL 15.1. FIERCE'S BEACH BALL MODEL

Fierce, Inc.

Open and inclusive process for preparing and conducting a Beach Ball meeting to solve problems in a group setting.

Section IV

TOOL 16.1. ORGANIZATIONAL LEADERSHIP READINESS AUDIT

ebb associates inc

A tool to measure an organization's readiness to implement or improve its leadership development efforts.

TOOL 17.1 AWAKEN, ALIGN, ACCELERATE®

MDA Leadership Consulting

A worksheet for leaders to establish a plan for their development.

TOOL 18.1. TEN STEPS TO DESIGNING GREAT LEADERSHIP DEVELOPMENT WORKSHOPS

Bluepoint Leadership Development

List of design elements to incorporate into any leadership development workshop.

BONUS ACTIVITY IV.1: HISTORICAL ORIENTEERING: LEADERSHIP LESSONS FROM HISTORY

Sonoma Leadership Systems

Includes sample handout and card to accompany the bonus activity.

Section V

TOOL 19.1. USING CULTURAL MOMENTS OF TRUTH TO CREATE A HIGH-PASSION/ HIGH-PERFORMANCE WORK ENVIRONMENT

The Whiteley Group

Individual exercise designed for any leader to explore and practice cultural moments of truth to create a high-passion/high-performance work environment.

TOOL 20.1. EMPLOYEE WORK PASSION FACTORS

The Ken Blanchard Companies

List of twelve factors in three categories—organizational, job, and moderating—that create employee work passion.

TOOL 21.1. HOW TO IDENTIFY OWNERS

Center for Creative Leadership

A checklist of ideas for how to identify and develop owners in organizations.

TOOL 22.1. APPLYING ALIGNED ENGAGEMENT IN YOUR OWN COMPANY

Performance Connections International

A checklist to identify areas where an organization can focus to increase engagement.

TOOL 22.2. HOW ENGAGEMENT AFFECTS BUSINESS FUNCTIONS

Performance Connections International, Inc.

A tool to identify how aligned engagement, or the lack of, may be affecting organizational functions.

TOOL 23.1. RATE YOUR HIGH-PERFORMANCE MANAGEMENT COMPETENCY I.Q.

The Emmerich Group

Self-assessment to determine a leader's ability to lead a culture shift.

TOOL 24.1. POLICY AND PROCEDURE TOOL

Crisis Prevention Institute, Inc.

An outline to create an organizational policy and procedure tool to prevent an organizational crisis.

TOOL 25.1. ASSESSING YOUR NEED FOR AN ENTERPRISE CHANGE AGENDA

Being First, Inc.

Tool to assess an organization's need for a corporate change agenda.

TOOL 25.2. ASSESSING THE EFFECTIVENESS OF YOUR CHANGE MODEL(S)

Being First, Inc.

Tool to assess the effectiveness of the various change models an organization is using.

TOOL 25.3. VALUE PROPOSITION FOR A CHANGE CENTER OF EXCELLENCE

Being First, Inc.

Assessment to determine an organization's need to centralize change activities.

BONUS ACTIVITY V.1: THE CANYON

Root Learning, Inc.

Downloadable illustration that can be used with the bonus activity.

Section VI

TOOL 26.1. 5A'S FRAMEWORK AUDIT

RealTime Performance

Organizational audit to measure the effectiveness of an organization's learning interventions based on the 5A's.

TOOL 27.1. METHODS TO INCREASE LEARNER CONFIDENCE AND COMMITMENT

Kirkpatrick Partners

Techniques to ensure learners have confidence in their own abilities and are committed to making the necessary change.

TOOL 27.2. "TRAINING FIRST" VERSUS "BUSINESS RESULTS FIRST"

Kirkpatrick Partners

Chart that compares past and current training approaches.

TOOL 28.1. CHECKLIST FOR THE COMPLETE EXPERIENCE

Fort Hill Company

Checklist to ensure a complete learning experience has been developed.

TOOL 29.1. MATCHING E-LEARNING ACTIVITIES TO LEARNING STYLES

Herrmann International

Diagram that maps specific e-learning activities to learning preferences.

TOOL 30.1. SUSTAINMENT ACTIVITIES TOOL

Forum

Table that illustrates four categories of sustainment activities and examples for implementation.

TOOL 30.2. STRATEGIES FOR MEASURING IMPACT

Forum

Guidance for measuring the impact of training to an organization.

TOOL 31.1. PREPARE FOR YOUR REINFORCEMENT DISCUSSION

MOHR Access

Pre-meeting tool to prepare to coach and reinforce an employee who has recently experienced training.

TOOL 32.1. SELF-ASSESSMENT TOOL: MEASUREMENT AS A CORE STRATEGY

Beyond ROI, Inc.

A tool to assess and map an organization's progress with measuring training results.

Section VII

TOOL 33.1. THE FACILITATOR'S METHODOLOGY™

Leadership Strategies

A diagram that explains the facilitation cycle.

TOOL 33.2. ARE YOU A GOOD OR A GREAT FACILITATOR?

Leadership Strategies

Self-assessment to determine a facilitator's abilities based on seven actions.

TOOL 34.1. WISDOM QUESTIONS
The Steve Trautman Company

Tool that provides twenty question stems used to identify the most critical aspects of any job and to assist in knowledge transfer.

TOOL 35.1. A CHECKLIST FOR DESIGNING MORE IMPACTFUL SIMULATION-BASED LEARNING EXPERIENCES
Insight Experience

Checklist to increase the impact of simulation learning experiences.

TOOL 36.1. CHECKLIST FOR PLANNING EFFECTIVE VIRTUAL CLASSROOM EXPERIENCES
DDI

Checklist for planning effective virtual classroom experiences based on seven categories.

TOOL 37.1. REFLECTING ON MY HIGH-PERFORMING PRINCIPLES
VisionPoint®

A personal reflection activity that assesses a leader's competency in five high-performing principles.

Section VIII
TOOL 38.1. QUESTIONS TO STIMULATE CAREER CONVERSATIONS
Career Systems International

Questions and tips for a more productive and pleasant career development discussion.

TOOL 39.1. STEPS TO BUILD YOUR BUSINESS ACUMEN
Acumen Learning

Personal development plan to increase business acumen.

TOOL 40.1. RESILIENCE REFLECTION AND DEVELOPMENT PLANNING EXERCISE

Resilience Alliance

Exercise intended to be used in a group to help participants to take ownership of developing their resilience.

TOOL 41.1. EIGHT GUIDELINES ABOUT WHAT MAKES A SUCCESSFUL PEER GROUP COACHING PROGRAM

The Eblin Group

Guidelines and tips to create a peer coaching group.

TOOL 42.1. BACKGROUND QUESTIONNAIRE

The Glacel Group

Tool used by coaches to gather information about an individual to understand the context of the feedback that will be delivered.

TOOL 42.2. GOOD NEWS/BAD NEWS MATRIX

The Glacel Group

Tool to sort data from a 360-degree instrument that balances the feedback.

TOOL 43.1. DO'S AND DON'TS FOR PRESENTING 360-DEGREE FEEDBACK EFFECTIVELY

West End Consulting

Guidelines for preparing to deliver feedback.

BONUS ACTIVITY VIII.1: PERSONAL CREDO WORKSHEET

James Kouzes and Barry Posner

Worksheet that accompanies the bonus activity to develop a leader's personal credo.

Section IX

TOOL 45.1. SELF-ASSESSMENT: CONVERSATION CALIBRATOR

Sigma Performance Solutions

Self-assessment that measures the level of customer conversations.

TOOL 45.2. ATTRIBUTES OF A CONSULTATIVE CONVERSATION USING LIST®

Sigma Performance Solutions

Tips for effectively managing a difficult customer conversation—or any difficult conversation.

TOOL 45.3. QUICK REFERENCE FOR USING LIST®

Sigma Performance Solutions

Reference guide for remembering the LIST process for dealing with customers.

TOOL 45.4. LIST® POCKET GUIDE

Sigma Performance Solutions

Brief reference guide for learning and remembering the LIST process for dealing with customers.

TOOL 46.1. EGO CHECK SURVEY

Amplify

Manager's self-assessment for identifying potential red flags and tendencies toward being egotistical.

About the Editor

Elaine Biech is president and managing principal of ebb associates Inc, an organization and leadership development firm that helps organizations work through large-scale change. She has been in the training and consulting field for thirty years, working with private industry, government, and non-profit organizations.

Elaine specializes in helping people work as teams to maximize their effectiveness. Customizing all of her work for individual clients, she conducts strategic planning sessions and implements corporate-wide systems such as quality improvement, change management, reengineering of business processes, and mentoring programs. She facilitates topics such as coaching today's employees, fostering creativity, customer service, creating leadership development programs, time management, speaking skills, coaching, consulting skills, training competence, conducting productive meetings, managing corporate-wide change, handling the difficult employee, organizational communication, conflict resolution, and effective listening. She is particularly adept at turning dysfunctional teams into productive teams.

She has developed media presentations and training materials and has presented at dozens of national and international conferences. Known as the trainer's trainer, she custom designs training programs for managers, leaders, trainers, and consultants. Elaine has been featured in dozens of publications, including *The Wall Street Journal, Harvard Management Update, Washington Post, Investors Business Daily, and Fortune* magazine.

As a management and executive consultant, trainer and designer, she has provided services to Outback Steakhouse, FAA, Land O' Lakes, McDonald's, Lands' End, General Casualty Insurance, Chrysler, Johnson Wax, PricewaterhouseCoopers, American Family Insurance, Marathon Oil, Hershey Chocolate, Federal Reserve Bank, the U.S. Navy, NASA, Newport News Shipbuilding, Kohler Company, ASTD, American Red Cross, Association of Independent Certified Public Accountants, the University of Wisconsin, The College of William and Mary, ODU, and hundreds of other public and private sector organizations to prepare them for the challenges of the new millennium.

She is the author or editor of more than fifty books, including *The Book of Road Tested Activities, 2011; A Coach's Guide to Exemplary Leaders, 2010; ASTD Leadership*

Handbook, 2010 [*Choice Magazine's* Outstanding Academic Title Winner]; *The Leadership Challenge Activities Book*, 2010; *ASTD's Ultimate Train the Trainer*, 2009; *10 Steps to Successful Training*, 2009; *The Consultant's Quick Start Guide* (2nd ed.), 2009; *ASTD Handbook for Workplace Learning Professionals*, 2008; *Trainer's Warehouse Book of Games*, 2008; *The Business of Consulting* (2nd ed.). 2007; *Thriving Through Change: A Leader's Practical Guide to Change Mastery*, 2007; *Successful Team-Building Tools* (2nd ed.), 2007; *90 World-Class Activities by 90 World-Class Trainers*, 2007 [a Training Review Best Training Product of 2007]; a nine volume set of *ASTD's Certification Study Guides*, 2006; *12 Habits of Successful Trainers, ASTD Info-line*, 2005; *The ASTD Info-line Dictionary of Basic Trainer Terms*, 2005; *Training for Dummies*, 2005; *Marketing Your Consulting Services*, 2003; *The Consultant's Legal Guide*, 2000; *Interpersonal Skills: Understanding Your Impact on Others*, 1996; *Building High Performance*, 1998; *The Pfeiffer Annual for Consultants and The Pfeiffer Annual for Trainers* (1998–2013); *The ASTD Sourcebook: Creativity and Innovation: Widen Your Spectrum*; 1996; and *The HR Handbook*, 1996. Her books have been translated into Chinese, German, and Dutch.

Elaine has her bachelor's degree from the University of Wisconsin–Superior in business and education consulting, and her master's in human resource development. She is active at the national level of ASTD, is a lifetime member, served on the 1990 National Conference Design Committee, was a member of the National ASTD Board of Directors and the Society's Secretary from 1991 to 1994, initiated and chaired Consultant's Day for seven years, and was the international conference design chair in 2000. In addition to her work with ASTD, she has served on the Independent Consultants Association's (ICA) Advisory Committee and on the Instructional Systems Association (ISA) Board of Directors.

Elaine is the recipient of the 1992 National ASTD Torch Award, the 2004 ASTD Volunteer-Staff Partnership Award, and the 2006 ASTD Gordon M. Bliss Memorial Award. She was selected for the 1995 Wisconsin Women Entrepreneur's Mentor Award. In 2001 she received ISA's highest award, the ISA Spirit Award. She has been the consulting editor for the prestigious Pfeiffer training and consulting *Annuals* for the past fourteen years.

Index

Page references followed by *fig* indicate an illustrated figure; followed by *t* indicate a table; followed by *e* indicate an exhibit.

engagement by, 201–207; engagement promoted by, 301; Inclusion + Engagement = Execution Muscle formula for, 202. *See also* Executives

Chambers, J., 254, 258–259

Change Anything Training program (VitalSmarts), 125

Change capacity: definition of, 332; leverage of building, 332–333*fig*; strategies for building, 335–346

The Change Leader's Roadmap, 338, 339*fig*

The Change Leader's Roadmap: How to Navigate Your Organization's Transformation (Ackerman Anderson & Anderson), 338, 347

Change management: definition of, 92, 101; engagement eroded by poor, 303–304; High-Performing Workforce Model on competency related to, 479*t*, 488*t*, 492*t*; key leadership competencies for, 334–335; manager roles for, 92–93*fig*, 94*t*; training and development of leadership in, 333–334; as vital project discipline, 88. *See also* Management

Change managers: activities of, 92–93*fig*; assignment scenarios for, 94*t*; project building role of, 99–100; specifying project role of, 99–100

Change strategies: change infrastructures, 338–340; common change process methodology, 337–338; creating strategic change center of excellence, 341; enterprise change agenda, 336–337; SCO (Strategic Change Office), 344–346; Value Proposition for a Change Center of Excellence, 342–343

Charan, R., 31

Chinese multinational subsidiary communication, 53–54

Choctaw Indians oral tradition, 3–4

Chubb Group of Insurance Companies, 380

Ciampa, D., 130

Cisco Systems, 254

Clay, C., 30

Clear communication practices, 195–196

Clinton, B., 255

CLO magazine, 128

Coaching: based on 360-degree assessments, 542; group feedback workshop, 557; by leaders before a new assignment, 215; peer, 232–233; peer group, 498, 521–526; strategic leaders capable of, 195

Cohen, H., 306

Cohen, S. L., 183, 184

Collaboration: benefits of learning, 163; as employee work passion factor, 267, 271*t*; 3D Perception Sharing exercise for, 164–167

Colleague connectedness, 268, 271*t*

Collins, J., 31

Communication: appreciating the importance of, 1–2; based on false assumptions, 297; brief interactions form of, 172–175; clarity of, 195, 196; congruent, 195; engagement eroded by failure of, 303; engagement impacted by lack of active and strategic, 297; global, 48–56*t*; practicing personal candor in your, 36–38; redirecting the

development dialogue with employees, 498, 499–505; service, 572–573; sustained behavior change and training, 411. *See also* Language; Listening

Communication tools: Build or Repair, 69–83; e-mail, 59–68. *See also* Storytelling

Communispond, 191

Compaq, 128

Compensation-engagement relationship, 301–302

Competencies: High-Performing Workforce Model on critical, 478–495; for leading organizations, 479*t*, 491*t*–492*t*; for leading teams, 479*t*, 488*t*–491*t*; for managing others, 479*t*, 482*t*–487*t*; for managing self, 479*t*–482*t*

Complete experience for learning: checklist for the, 382–384; description of the, 378; four phases of learning for, 378–382

"Composing Your Personal Credo" (Kouzes and Posner), 498

Conference Board, 307

Congruent communication, 195

Connectedness to colleagues, 268, 271*t*

Connectedness to leaders, 268, 271*t*

Consequences-accountability relationship, 170, 194, 197–198

Cope, K., 513

The Cornere Office (Bryant), 132

Corporate Leadership Council, 209

The Corporate Shaman (Whiteley), 258

Covey, M. R., 70

CPI (Crisis Prevention Institute, Inc.): about, 329; on improving workplace culture, 246, 317–329; *Nonviolent Crisis Intervention* program of, 329

Credibility: How Leaders Gain and Lose It, Why People Demand It (Kouzes and Posner), 563

Cripe, E. J., 476

Crisis: Johnson & Johnson's Tylenol, 252; perceived as opportunity, 319

Critical mass drag, 298

Criticism vs. disclosure, 37

Cultural continuums: business applications of, 53*t*; five different, 50*fig*

Cultural differences: High-Performing Workforce Model on competency related to, 479*t*, 490*t*–491*t*; how global communication is impacted by, 48–49; language vs. understanding, 49–50; time and, 49; Whole Brain Model consideration of, 395

Cultural moments of truth, 252–253

Culture: C-level power culture form of, 128–130; The Canyon exercise for exploring, 349–352; definition of, 50; of employee work passion, 265–277; failure to teach executives how to master, 310–311; how behavior is determined by values of, 50–51; learning, 354, 357–363, 395; service, 566, 567–579; stereotypes vs. generalizations of, 51*t*–52; strategies for improving, 246, 317–329. *See also* Engaging environment; Organizations

Culture improvement strategies: crisis as opportunity, 319; employee interactions with other employees and customers for, 319; Policy and Procedure Development Tool for, 319–329; respect, service, and safety guiding, 318, 320–321

The curfew story, 188–189

Customers: building a service culture for your, 566, 567–579; building service culture by incorporating the voice of the, 574; culture for employee interactions with, 319; High-Performing Workforce Model on competency related to, 479*t*, 486*t*–487*t*, 491*t*; impact of engagement on care of, 294*fig*–295; LIST process to improve service to, 566, 581–590; performance connections strategy alignment ladder on, 296*fig*; why executives care about engagement impact on, 298–299*fig*

D

Daley, K., 188

De Pree, M., 257, 261

De Vries, M. K., 233

Deci, E. L., 121

Decision making: Bon Secours ConnectCare system used for, 104; Interaction Associates' Facilitative Leadership model for, 105–108; levels of involvement in, 106*fig*–107

Dede Henley Group: about, 167–168; 3D Perception Sharing exercise from, 164–167

DeNisi, A., 222, 223

DeSmet, A., 378

Development Dimensions International, Inc. (DDI): about, 473; creating compelling virtual learning experience focus of, 432, 467–473

Diehl, J., 278

Digh, P., 50

DiSC survey, 531, 540

Disclosure, criticism versus, 37

Discretionary effort: employee work passion and, 268, 271–272; engagement eroded by lack of compensation for, 301

Disengaged employees: actively looking for alternative employment, 308; executive behavior to blame for, 308–311; Gallup study (2006) on number of, 307; how employees are to blame for, 314–315; management breakdown causing, 311; Rate Your High-Performance Management Competency I.Q. to turnaround, 312–313. *See also* Engagement

Distributive justice, 267, 271*t*

Domain experts: assignment scenarios for, 94*t*; planning role of, 96; product developer activities by, 92*fig*; roles of, 92

Drive (Pink), 382

Drolet, R., 134, 136

Dumaine, D., 62

Dunlap, A. "Chainsaw," 259

DWYSYWD (doing what you say you will do), 181

Dyer, W., 259

Dysfunctional dynamics: developing personal self-awareness to transform, 160–161; importance of dealing with, 149; "unconscious demonization" as, 150–160

E

E-mail communication: "before and after" e-mail examples, 63–68; group session to improve, 61; importance of writing good, 59; insider tips for effective, 61; pre-work required for effective, 60–61; strategies for avoiding mistakes in, 59–60

ebb associates inc.: about, 217–218; leadership development focus of, 210, 211–217

Eblin Group: about, 526–527; peer group coaching program focus of, 498, 521–526

Eblin, S., 526, 527

EECO International: about, 57; global communication focus of, 47–54; Quick Reference Guide for effective global interactions by, 54*t*–56*t*

The Effective Facilitator (Wilkinson), 443

Ego Check Survey, 566, 599

Eichinger, R., 380

Eli Lilly, 281

Ellison, L., 131

Elop, S., 201, 202

The Emmerich Group, Inc.: about, 315–316; on converting disengaged employees, 307–315; manager self-assessment tool of, 246, 312–313

Emmerich, R., 315–316

Emotional learning issues, 394–395. *See also* Motivation

Emotional quotient/intelligence (EQ), 256

Emotionally contagious, 173

Employee endorsement, 268, 273–274

Employee work passion: appraisal process used to create, 269–270; autonomy and, 267, 271*t*, 274; comparing engagement and, 268–269; correlation analysis between workplace intentions and factors of, 271*t*; definition of, 270; discretionary effort and, 268, 271–272; distributive justice and, 267, 271*t*; employee endorsement and, 268, 273–274; examining the power of, 265–267; factors of, 267–268; intent to perform, 268, 273; intent to remain and, 268, 274–275; organizational citizenship behaviors and, 268, 275–276; procedural justice and, 267, 271*t*, 272–273, 274; understanding how factors influence intent and behavior, 270–271*t*

Employee work passion model, 270*fig*

Employees: building high-performance teams out of disengaged, 307–315; change-readiness by, 288; culture for interactions between, 319; feedback for managing, 282; hiring "owners" and not "renters," 246, 279–282; Proximity Effect on, 295; redirecting the development dialogue with, 498, 499–505; safety expectations/responsibilities of, 327; service expectations/responsibilities of, 324–325; training triage applied to individual, 493–494; transferring wisdom of aging, 446–453; work passion by, 265–274. *See also* Engagement; Talent management

Empowerment: of building your business acumen, 508; engagement eroded by lack of, 302; as great facilitation attribute, 434*fig*, 437–438

Engadget, 201

Engagement: aligned, 288*fig*–289*fig*; beach ball meetings for, 204–207; a business-driven view of, 286–291; business-results training focusing on relevance and, 372–373; commercial impact of, 246, 285–304; comparing employee work passion and, 268–269; defining, 287*fig*; as emotional issue, 203; executive effectiveness in orchestrating, 300*fig*; factors that erode, 301–304; as great facilitation attribute, 441, 442*t*; how business functions are impacted by, 291*t*–292*t*; impact on customer care by, 294*fig*–295; Inclusion + Engagement = Execution Muscle formula for, 202; leadership development workshop use of, 230; service vision, 569–570; strategy alignment and, 295–297; virtual classroom, 469; why executives care about, 298–299*fig*. *See also* Disengaged employees; Employees

Engaging environment: commercial impact of, 246, 285–304; company turnaround through, 250–251; the final word on importance of, 262–263; leadership creation of engaging, 251–263; "twelfth man" phenomenon and, 249–250, 261–262. *See also* Culture

Engaging environment building: be a healer, 258–260; be present, 255–256; "cultural moments of truth" for, 252–253; lead yourself, 260–261; tell stories, 257; tell the truth...hear the truth, 254–255

Engren, J., 293

Epiphany, 133

Erez, A., 222

Ernst, C., 280

Evaluation: the complete experience of learning component of, 384; 5As Framework Audit for training, 363; The Kirkpatrick Model of, 366–368, 375, 424; leading with integrity and role of, 181; learning environment assessment (LEA), 407; New World Kirkpatrick Model for, 368–369*fig*; policies on issue notification and process for, 323; of results of leadership development, 215; self-assessment for, 199. *See also* 360-degree assessments

Everett, L. T., 73

Execution (Bossidy and Charan), 31

Executives: C-level, 128–138; disengaged employees due to behavior of, 308–311; effectiveness in orchestrating engagement, 300*fig*; engagement influence by, 298–301; examining the essentials for, 169–170; failure to teach them how to master culture, 310–311; Inclusion + Engagement = Execution Muscle engagement formula for, 202; leading with integrity, 178–183; why they care about engagement, 298–299*fig*. *See also* CEOs (chief executive officers); Leaders

F

Facilitation: The Facilitator's Methodology process for training, 433–434*fig*; group feedback workshop, 557; presenting attributes of great, 432, 433–444; seven separators between good and great, 434*fig*–443; virtual classrooms, 470–471

Facilitative Leadership model: on the decision-making process, 105–107; deploying the, 107–108; on levels of involvement in decision making, 106*fig*–107

Facilitators: group feedback workshop, 557; group feedback workshop certification of, 558–559; group feedback workshop skill level and experience of, 559; internal vs. external group feedback workshop, 558

Fagan, L., 600

Fast Company magazine, 131

Feedback: Awaken, Align, Accelerate model use of, 222–223; as employee work passion factor, 267, 271*t*; leading with integrity and role of, 181; managing talent and role of, 282; providing to employees, 281–282; unbalanced, 548; understanding why people reject, 546–548. *See also* 360-degree assessments

Feedback-rich environment, 231

Fern, B., 306

A Few Good Men? (film), 32

Field Theory, 33

Fierce Conversations: Achieving Success at Work and in Life, One Conversation at a Time (Scott), 207

Fierce, Inc.: about, 207; employee engagement focus of, 170, 207; principles and methods used by, 207

Fierce Leadership: A Bold Alternative to the Worst "Best" Practices of Business Today (Scott), 207

Financial Times, 283

The Financial Times, 504

FIRO-B, 540

Five forms of evidence, 186

The Five Practices of Exemplary Leaders model, 237, 563

5As Framework Audit, 363

Flander, S., 293

Folkman, Z., 170

Fort Hill Company: about, 385–386; ensuring transfer of learning to improve performance, 354, 377–385; *ResultsEngine* online learning transfer management system, 385; *The Six Disciplines of Breakthrough Learning* by, 377, 385

Fortune magazine, 250

The Forum Corporation: about, 413; co-founded by Richard Whiteley, 263; pioneering organizational climate work practiced at, 251; sharing a process for sustained learning, 355, 405–412

Forum Folklore: Unique Stories of Innovation and Inspiration, 257

The Four-Fold Way (Arrien), 259

Freud, S., 113

Future Point Systems, 131

L

Lahey, L., 158

Lang, A., 473

Language: using a common service, 568–569; understanding vs., 49–50. *See also* Communication

Lankford, M. G., 118

Latham, G. P., 224

Leaders: born vs. made, 193–194; connectedness to, 268, 271*t*; high-potential, 522–524; "Historical Orienteering" activity to learn best practices of, 210; providing feedback to, 281–282; setting the right example as, 280–282; shortage of effective, 209; taking action to become a great, 199; taking responsibility for developing future, 211–217, 217; three-step system for building strategic, 194–199; walking the talk, 179–181; who are healers, 258–260. *See also* Executives

Leaders Make the Future (Johansen), 280

Leadership: creating an engaging environment through, 251263; engagement eroded by negative, 302; High-Performing Workforce Model on competences for, 479*t*, 488*t*–492*t*; "Ten Traits of Leadership" (Ridge), 256, 260

Leadership brand, 180

Leadership building system: step 1: practice top ten traits of strategic leaders, 194–197; step 2: build accountability with consequences, 197–198; step 3: build strategic leaders on your team, 198–199

The Leadership Challenge (Kouzes and Posner), 563

The Leadership Challenge Workshop, 563

Leadership development: actions for successful, 212–214; Awaken, Align, Accelerate model for, 210, 219–227; designing workshops for, 229–234; improving C-level presentations, 127, 132–138; Leadership Reminder List for, 214; for leading with integrity, 177–183; learning how to transform dysfunctional dynamics, 149–161; Situational Leadership II system for, 278

Leadership development actions: accepting full responsibility for developing leaders, 214; listed, 212; prioritizing quality of bench strength, 213; strategic and future focus on leadership development, 213; taking a long-term systemic approach to, 216–217; taking responsibility for, 211–217, 217

Leadership development workshop design: accountability for learning component of, 233–234; appreciation component of, 231–232; engagement component of, 230; feedback-rich environment included in, 231; intense experiences included in, 232; peer coaching component of, 232–233; performance breakthroughs as part of, 233; research-based content included in, 230; self-awareness development included in, 233; storytelling part of, 230–231

Leadership Practices Inventory (LPI), 563

The Leadership-Profit Chain model, 265

Leadership Reminder List, 214

Leadership story, 180

Leadership Strategies: about, 443–444; facilitation-related training courses offered by, 443; presenting attributes of great facilitators, 432, 433–443

Leading by example, 181

Leading yourself, 260–261

Learners: assisting them to determine their values, 498; engagement by increasing relevance to, 372–373; methods to increase confidence and commitment, 371–372; need for confidence and commitment by, 371; providing a complete experience to, 354, 377–385; Whole Brain Model consideration of, 392–395. *See also* Motivation

Learning: the complete experience to ensure transfer of, 354, 377–385; efficient and tactical formal, 370; information overload and, 387–390; leadership development workshop accountability for, 233–234; process for sustained, 355, 405–412; training to support on-the-job, 368–370*fig*; Whole Brain Model for, 354–355, 387–402. *See also* Training

Learning as Leadership (LaL): about, 161; transforming dysfunctional dynamics focus of, 149–161

Learning culture: before, during, and after learning interventions, 361–362; creating a, 354; examples of employee training for creating, 359–360; 5As Framework Audit to assess, 363; missed opportunities for creating, 358–359; organizational benefits of, 362–363; organizational factors in creating, 359, 360–361; training to create a, 354, 357–363; Whole Brain Model consideration of, 395

Learning design: face-to-face/workshop, 396–397*fig*; offline individual learning methods and resources, 397–398; online technology methods and resources, 398*fig*–400

Learning environment: engaging, 246, 249–263, 285–304; sustained behavior change and role of the, 407–408; Whole Brain Model consideration of, 400

Learning environment assessment (LEA), 407

Learning Map module experience, 349–352

Learning objectives: selecting simulation that best fits, 456–457; types of, 457*t*–458*t*

Learning organizations, 216

Learning path, 378

Learning styles, 392–393

LeFave, S., 250, 251, 252

Lepsinger, R., 549, 551, 560

Lewin, K., 33

LIST process: four-steps in the, 582; graph presentation of, 582–583*fig*; levels of service conversations, 587*fig*–588; measuring the success of, 588–589; overview of the, 583–586; reasons for using, 586; service improvement through, 581; when not to use, 588; when to use, 586–588; why it works, 589*fig*–590

Listening: Build or Repair tool practice of active, 72; disciplined, curious, and skillful, 38; as forgotten skill of